# THE BULLET AND THE BALLOT BOX

# THE BULLET
# AND THE
# BALLOT BOX

The Story of Nepal's Maoist Revolution

Aditya Adhikari

**VERSO**
London • New York

First published by Verso 2014
© Aditya Adhikari 2014

1 3 5 7 9 10 8 6 4 2

**Verso**
UK: 6 Meard Street, London W1F 0EG
US: 20 Jay Street, Suite 1010, Brooklyn, NY 11201
www.versobooks.com

Verso is the imprint of New Left Books

ISBN-13: 978-1-78168-564-8
eISBN-13: 978-1-78168-565-5 (US)
eISBN-13: 978-1-78168-681-2 (UK)

**British Library Cataloguing in Publication Data**
A catalogue record for this book is available from the British Library.

**Library of Congress Cataloging-in-Publication Data**

Adhikari, Aditya.
The bullet and the ballot box : the story of Nepal's
Maoist revolution / Aditya Adhikari.
    pages cm
 Summary: "In 1996, when Nepal's Maoists launched
their armed rebellion, their ideology was widely
considered obsolete and they had limited public
support. By 2008 they had gained access to state
power and their ambitious plan of social
transformation dominated the national agenda. How
did this become possible? The Bullet and the Ballot
Box offers a rich and sweeping account of a decade
of revolutionary upheaval. Adhikari draws on a broad
range of sources, including novels, letters and diaries,
to illuminate both the history and human drama of
the Maoist rebellion. An indispensible guide to Nepal's
recent history, the book also offers a fascinating case
study of how communist ideology has been
reinterpreted and translated into political action in the
twenty-first century" – Provided by publisher.
 Includes bibliographical references and index.
 ISBN 978-1-78168-564-8 (hardback)
1. Nepal – History – Civil War, 1996–2006. 2. Nepal
– Politics and government – 1990–3. Communism –
Nepal – History. 4. Social change – Nepal – History.
5. Elections – Nepal – History. 6. Political
participation – Nepal – History. I. Title.
 DS495.6.A332 2014
 954.96 – dc23

2014019101

Typeset in Minion Pro by MJ & N Gavan, Truro, Cornwall
Printed in the US by Maple Press

For my parents,
Neelam and Ramesh Adhikari

# Contents

# Preface

You can tear down Lenin's statue
Rip Marxist doctrine to shreds
Bury the history of revolution
Why just the statue?
You might as well chop Lenin's corpse into pieces
And feed crows and vultures ...
It won't make a difference
O prosperous beings of the world
O capitalists
You who are driven by revenge and rejoice in bloodshed
We are countries. Give us autonomy.
We are nations. Give us liberation.
We are the people. Give us revolution.

– Ahuti[1]

In 1992, when these lines were published, Bishwa Bhakta Dulal, commonly known as 'Ahuti', was a member of the Unity Centre. This was a small communist party that would later split into two factions, one of which became the Communist Party of Nepal (Maoist). Ahuti's poem declared undying allegiance to an ideology that was widely thought to have been defeated. It was as though the poet were trying to smother his anxieties by sheer force of conviction. Ahuti eventually joined the faction that did not support armed struggle. But, four years after his poem came out, the rage and anguish felt by his comrades in the other faction erupted in an armed rebellion that altered the course of Nepali history.

Most leaders of the Maoist rebellion had come of age during the 1970s, when Nepal was ruled by an absolute monarch. King Mahendra Shah believed Nepal was not ready for democracy: he had seized power through a coup in 1960, banned all political parties and established what was called the Panchayat system. In Mahendra's view, this was the only system that could protect and strengthen the nation's independence and lead the country towards modernization. But the Panchayat regime allowed no room for political dissent, and its modernization programme reinforced rather than eliminated traditional social hierarchies. In such circumstances, it was natural that large numbers of young men and women who sought social and political change became drawn to communism.

In 1990, a popular movement led by a number of banned parties succeeded in bringing down the Panchayat regime. The Maoists, then scattered among various marginal factions, were ambivalent about this political gain. Many others, however, believed that Nepal had finally gained a system that matched both its citizens' aspirations and the globally hegemonic paradigm of liberal democracy. The Nepali Congress, Nepal's largest party, despite its sometime profession of socialism, had in practice always been committed to liberalism. The country's two largest communist parties, duly chastened by the widespread liberal triumphalism, united to form the Communist Party of Nepal (Unified Marxist–Leninist) (CPN–UML), and pledged allegiance to the new parliamentary order.

With their firm commitment to revolution, the Maoists were thus swimming against a powerful tide. They not only rejected the parliamentary system, but also denounced – despite Nepal's heavy dependence on foreign countries – 'imperialist' and 'expansionist' powers such as the United States and India. It was generally thought that no Nepalese government could survive without Indian support. A political group that was openly hostile towards India was not expected to go far. Both Nepali and foreign observers saw the Maoists as an irrelevant and faction-ridden groupuscule obsessed with an obsolete ideology.

But the Maoists remained undeterred. In February 1996 they declared their People's War by attacking several police posts in remote parts of the country. The government led by the Nepali Congress mobilized the police in response. Despite police reppression, the rebellion spread across the country over the next few years. The government declared a state of emergency and deployed the national army. In 2002, the king stepped forward to reclaim his power over the polity. All foreign powers with influence in Nepal – India, China, the US and the UK – backed the state against the Maoists, with the US alone providing over 20 million dollars in military aid.

In contrast, the Maoists had no external support. They initially relied on rudimentary weapons, and operated out of far-flung villages. Most of their cadre came from poor, rural backgrounds, and a significant section belonged to marginalized ethnic and caste groups. And yet, by 2005, the Maoists had gained control over most of Nepal's countryside, and their rebellion had changed the face of the nation.

After a decade-long armed struggle, the Maoists finally signed a peace agreement with the mainstream parties that were opposed to the king's usurpation of power. Together they led a historic uprising that brought down the monarchy and paved the path for elections to a Constituent Assembly, one of the rebels' key demands. The Maoists won around 40 per cent of seats in the Constituent Assembly. Other parties trailed far behind. The Maoists joined the government, and their political agenda came to dominate Nepal's public debate.

However, when the Maoists launched the rebellion their ambition had been much grander: total state control. Now inside mainstream politics, they found themselves mired in a dysfunctional multiparty system, and were forced to compromise. Nonetheless, their growth as a political force had been extraordinary. Despite all the odds stacked against them, they became the only rebel group in the post–Cold War era to gain state power through Mao's strategy of a protracted People's War. How was this possible?

This question is central to the history of the Maoist rebellion offered in this book. Many observers say it was poverty that made large sections of the population receptive to a radical ideology. Others attribute the Maoists' rise to the weakness of the state. Indeed, no account that aims to provide a comprehensive picture of the movement can ignore these points. However, this book is primarily concerned with what the Marxists call the 'subjective factor' – the personal journeys of Maoists who participated in the rebellion, their beliefs and aspirations, their experiences in forests, villages and prison cells, their relationships with one another and with local communities, the tensions between individual Maoist leaders, their conflicting aims and strategies.

Who were the Maoist leaders and what were their motivations? How did they relate to and direct their cadre? How did their ideological and personal differences shape the dynamics of the movement?

Tens of thousands of young men and women from Nepal's villages took part in the rebellion. They were inducted into a tightly knit body of cadres with a fierce sense of mission and commitment. What drove them to join the Maoist cause despite the great risks involved? A large proportion of Maoists were women, many of whom joined the rebels in the hope of breaking the shackles of patriarchy. How did they experience the war? Was it fear or sympathy that led civilians in Maoist-controlled villages to acquiesce to Maoist demands? How did the ill-equipped, loosely organized bands of fighters grow into the formidable People's Liberation Army? In order to illustrate the gradual expansion of the Maoists' military power, this book will pay close attention to a few of the decisive battles that took place between 1996 and 2005.

A large proportion of the Maoist rank and file belonged to historically marginalized castes and ethnic groups. What led many members of these groups to support a movement led primarily by high-caste men? How did the Maoist leaders seek to resolve the tension between class struggle and ethnic assertion? Did they mobilize caste and ethnic groups for purely instrumental reasons, as some critics claim?

This book tries to answer such questions by drawing on the vast corpus of Maoist writings from Nepal. These include ideological and strategic documents, statements and circulars issued by the leadership, battle plans drafted by Maoist military commanders, and the memoirs, novels, diaries and letters that reveal the inner lives of those who fought the war. The present narrative is largely based on the evidence found in these sources, the bulk of which have not been translated into English or otherwise used by scholars. Interviews with militants at various levels of the party hierarchy supplement this material. I have also made use of the large body of scholarly and journalistic literature that explores various aspects of the Maoist movement. By weaving personal stories into an account of the broader social and political process, the book tries to depict Nepal's Maoist rebellion as a human event made up of individual choices and destinies – something more than the ineluctable march of history.

*Aditya Adhikari*
*25 April 2013*

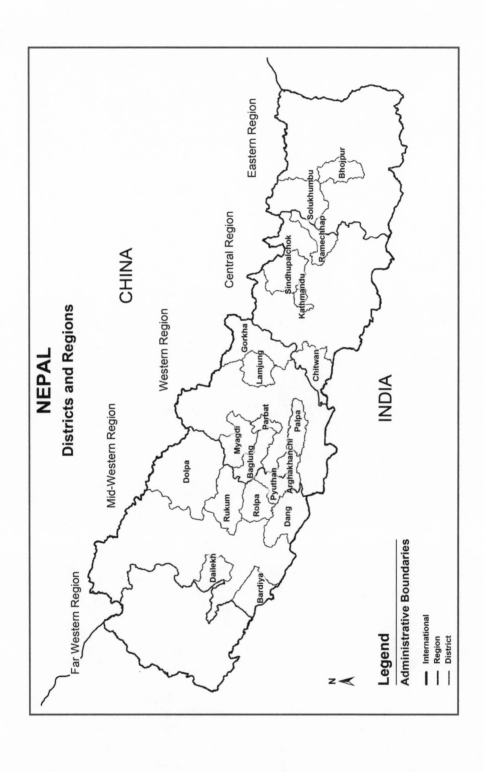

CHAPTER 1

# The Sun in the Hearts of the People: Origins

## China's Cultural Revolution in Nepal

The Nepali monarch and the Chinese leaders of the 1960s were poles apart in their worldview. While King Mahendra Shah was the scion of a dynasty that had reigned over Nepal for two centuries, the communist leaders in Mao's China had risen by struggling against the feudal and aristocratic remnants in their society. And yet the king and the Chinese leaders maintained friendly relations. The Chinese media often referred to Mahendra as a 'progressive king'.[1] In 1966, China granted 16.8 per cent of its total foreign aid commitment to Nepal. But things began to change a year later when the frenzy generated by the Cultural Revolution spilled over into Nepal, disrupting diplomatic ties. The official Chinese attitude towards the Nepali king became hostile. In a speech to the Shanghai Revolutionary Committee in 1968, Yao Wenyuan, who was later imprisoned for twenty years as part of the Gang of Four, described Mahendra as an 'insignificant reactionary'.[2]

China had been sending teams to build roads in the hills of northeast Nepal since 1963. In 1967, the activities of the Chinese technicians working at the road-building sites began to alarm the Nepali government. The press reported that they were distributing Chinese revolutionary literature and Mao badges to the construction labourers. They were also showing films promoting Chinese socialism. These 'gullible' Nepali workers, it was claimed, were forced to salute Mao's portrait and chant slogans praising him before they received their wages. When

King Mahendra and China's acting minister of foreign trade inaugurated a stretch of the road on 26 May, *Peking Review* reported that the crowd shouted, 'The great leader Chairman Mao is the red sun which shines most brightly in the hearts of the people of the world!' A few days later, the *Nepali Times* dryly responded, 'Nobody heard the Nepalis present on the occasion praising Mao as the red sun.'[3]

On 17 June, the Chinese ambassador to Nepal and around 300 workers gathered at Kathmandu's international airport to welcome nine Chinese diplomats expelled from India on espionage charges. The welcoming party displayed portraits of Mao and shouted slogans praising 'Mao's warriors' as they waited. The plane from Delhi arrived, but the expelled diplomats were not on it. The Chinese assembled at the airport flew into a rage, shouting slogans against Indian 'reactionaries' and 'revisionists', and trying to attack journalists who wanted to take their pictures. When the diplomats did finally arrive on 24 June, they were given a hero's welcome in a ceremony attended by, among others, the Chinese and Pakistani ambassadors.

The episode naturally offended the Indian government. The Indian ambassador in Kathmandu, Sriman Narayan, sent two notes to the Nepali foreign ministry expressing surprise that anti-Indian activity had been permitted in Nepal, and urging the Nepal government to distance itself publicly. Soon after that the US embassy, too, raised an objection with the Nepal government: it turned out that the Chinese stall at an expo organized for King Mahendra's birthday had included displays of anti-American propaganda.[4]

This put the Nepali government in a difficult situation. As a landlocked country sandwiched between the giant nations of India and China, Nepal had long been forced to maintain a delicate diplomatic balance between its two neighbours. The Indian influence far exceeded the Chinese, and various Nepali leaders had dreamed – and continue to dream today – of using Chinese support as a counterweight to Indian attempts at domination. But their efforts were rarely successful. The tenor of Nepal's foreign policy has been marked by great caution, and its primary concern is to avoid offending either neighbour.

The Chinese provocation and the complaints from the Indians and the Americans did, however, require a response. Eventually the foreign ministry issued a circular that blandly requested all foreign missions to refrain from disseminating propaganda against one another.[5]

But a retaliation of sorts occurred soon after. On 1 July, over the Chinese stall at the aforementioned expo, a portrait of Mao was displayed in a more prominent position than that of King Mahendra. A large red star had been placed above the Nepali flag hung on the wall. A group of young men – mere onlookers, according to news reports, although quite possibly organized supporters of the regime – grew restive at this affront to Nepali pride, and demanded that Mahendra's portrait be placed parallel to Mao's and that the red star be moved away from the Nepali flag. When the Chinese officials responded rudely, the young men threw stones at them and ransacked the stall.

The disturbance escalated. A procession formed and marched around the city centre, chanting slogans in praise of the king and the political system he led. Demonstrators attacked a jeep belonging to the Chinese embassy, pelted stones at the office of the Nepal–China Friendship Association in New Road, and ransacked bookstores selling communist literature in Bhotahity and at least two other places in the Kathmandu valley.[6]

Seven years before these events took place, in 1960, the ambitious King Mahendra had declared an end to a short experiment in parliamentary democracy: elected leaders were imprisoned with the help of the army, and political parties banned. Most affected was the Nepali Congress Party, the champion of liberal democracy, which had formed a government after winning 74 of the 109 seats in the 1959 general election.[7] Mahendra then introduced what he called Panchayat democracy, a partyless system in which the monarch, as the embodiment of sovereignty, stood at the helm of a bureaucracy whose purported aim was the rapid modernization of Nepal. He hoped to accomplish this by appealing to his traditional legitimacy and without greatly upsetting the social order.

As part of his strategy to isolate and weaken the Congress, Mahendra sought to woo the Communist Party of Nepal, which had won a meagre four seats in the elections and was substantially weaker than the Congress. Attracted by the perks of power, a number of prominent communists – most notably, Keshar Jung Rayamajhi – claimed that a state led by the king would be more progressive than one led by the bourgeois Nepali Congress, and came over to the regime's side. Pushpa Lal Shrestha and his supporters, however, maintained that parliamentary democracy was preferable to direct rule by the king, and remained opposed to the Panchayat.[8] In 1967, when the Cultural Revolution hit Kathmandu, most of the leaders of the latter faction were living in India.[9]

With their leaders in exile, the radical communists who remained in Nepal did not pose any real threat to King Mahendra. But the ruler no doubt recognized that the socio-economic conditions in the country could give rise to a strong communist movement. Nepal was a predominantly agrarian society, with highly unequal and exploitative land relations and a discriminatory and exploitative caste system. Meanwhile, with the spread of modern education, the Nepali population was becoming increasingly aware of the country's peripheral position in the world. Although the Nepali masses did not rise up in 1967 (the year the trouble broke out around the Chinese exhibition stall), stirrings of discontent with the Panchayat system and sympathies for Maoist ideology were already becoming apparent. The young men who rampaged through Kathmandu attacking symbols of revolutionary China on 1 July were in several places resisted by Maoist sympathizers.

These resisters did not include the leaders of the Maoist armed rebellion that shook the foundations of the Nepali state three decades later. It is clear, however, that along with other young people across the world, a generation of Nepalis in their teens and twenties, many of whom were to become Maoist leaders in the 1990s, became radicalized around that time. The Naxalite movement in India was a source of inspiration. The encounter with the Chinese and their ideology, too, inflamed the imagination of many future Maoist activists. Agni Sapkota, then growing up in Sindhupalchok, a district on the Nepal–Tibet border, remembers being moved by the patriotic songs and dances the Chinese cultural groups performed for the workers at the road construction sites.[10] Indra Mohan Sigdel, also a child at the time, was impressed to discover that the Chinese were so egalitarian that the supervisors, technicians and workers all wore the same clothes and stayed in the same accommodation, regardless of their status.[11]

Thanks to its effective propaganda, the impact of the Cultural Revolution reverberated through the country's hills and plains. Pushpa Kamal Dahal, the future 'Prachanda', foremost leader of the Communist Party of Nepal (Maoist), remembers that when he was a teenager a friend showed him a portrait of Mao, and said: 'This is the supreme leader of

China, where there is no disparity between the rich and the poor, or the weak and the powerful. There, everyone is equal.'[12]

B orn in 1954 in Kaski, a district in Nepal's central hills, Pushpa Kamal Dahal came from a peasant family that was impoverished despite belonging to the privileged Brahmin caste. Like him, most of the top leaders of the future CPN (Maoist) were born in the 1950s in Nepal's hill region. Their families were mostly upper-caste (and predominantly Brahmin), but lacking access to state power, engaged in small-scale agriculture or traditional Brahminical occupations such as ritual per-formance or astrology. When Dahal was eight, his family migrated to Chitwan, a Tarai district southeast of Kaski, in search of more fertile land.[13] But hardships persisted. Pushpa Kamal Dahal would later readily recount how a moneylender had insulted and kicked his father. This, he claimed, 'was a political lesson I would never forget'.[14] The families of many other senior Maoist leaders likewise relocated to Nepal's south-ern plains in the 1960s, to till land that had recently been opened up for cultivation, and had similar experiences of injustice that made them receptive to a radical political ideology.

In the late 1950s, Dahal's father Muktiram went to find work in Guwahati, in the Indian state of Assam. He collected and sold firewood for a year, and later worked at a company that sold Italian-made Fiat cars, before returning home in 1961.[15] Other future Maoists or their relatives also temporarily migrated to India in search of opportunity. Some – such as the future Maoist leader Ram Bahadur Thapa's father – found stable and relatively well-paid employment in the Indian Army.[16] Others – such as Post Bahadur Bogati or Krishna Bahadur Mahara's father – had to work menial jobs in 'hotels' (in reality, ramshackle eateries) or as security guards before returning to Nepal.[17] These early experiences of India – the neighbour that casts such a large shadow over the Nepali psyche – are often remembered as episodes of shame and humiliation. Shame and humiliation at having to leave one's family behind to scrabble for a living in an unfamiliar land; shame and humiliation at being treated as second-class citizens by the host community; and shame and humili-ation at belonging to a country that could not even provide its citizens with a basic standard of living.

After completing primary and secondary education in Chitwan, Pushpa Kamal Dahal moved to Kathmandu in 1971 and studied at the

Patan Multiple Campus for two years. He then moved back to Chitwan, where he received a bachelor's degree in agriculture at the Institute of Agriculture and Animal Sciences in Rampur. Like Dahal, many other future Maoist leaders moved to Kathmandu or other larger towns to pursue advanced studies in the late 1960s or '70s. They were often the first in their families to receive formal higher education. The colleges they attended had only recently been established by the state as part of its modernization drive (the Rana oligarchy that ruled Nepal for a century until 1950 had actively discouraged the spread of education, knowing that an aware population could threaten its hold on power). The young men who came to Kathmandu to study may have experienced material deprivation, but in the context of Nepali society they were relatively privileged. They were upper-caste men whose mother tongue was Nepali, the language of the state elite and administration.[18] They belonged to the lower echelons of the class that the Panchayat elite sought to groom, which it did by employing them in the rapidly expanding bureaucracy and enlisting them in the modernization mission.

During their school and college years, the future Maoist leaders almost invariably came into contact with individuals involved in Nepal's clandestine communist movement. They gained access not just to the works of Marx, Engels, Lenin and Mao but also to translations of Russian and Chinese revolutionary novels such as Maxim Gorky's *The Mother*, Ostrovsky's *How the Steel was Tempered* and Yang Mo's *The Song of Youth*. At the time, such books were provided by the Soviet and Chinese cultural centres in heavily subsidized mass editions.[19]

After completing their degrees, some briefly took low-level jobs in the government bureaucracy. Others, including Pushpa Kamal Dahal, failing to find such jobs went on to become village schoolteachers. Meanwhile, their affiliations to particular communist parties deepened. At one point in the late 1970s, the core leaders of the future CPN (Maoist) were all members of a party called the Fourth Convention and deeply influenced by one of its leaders Mohan Bikram Singh, an older communist born in 1935.

These activists gradually gave up full-time employment (Dahal worked as a schoolteacher till 1979) and devoted more and more time to the party. They would secretly instruct students, peasants and workers in communist doctrine, explaining to them the oppressive nature of the Nepali state and organizing them into local cells. They were harassed, arrested and beaten up by the police. The severely restricted political space of the Panchayat era limited their activities. But opportunities did arise on a number of occasions. For example, in 1979–80, the communists joined the Nepali Congress in a massive student-led movement that forced the palace to stage a referendum, offering the Nepali people a choice between continuing the Panchayat system and adopting multiparty democracy. Although the referendum of 1980 was won in favour of the Panchayat (many believe through fraud), it did usher in a period of marginally greater political freedom. For the political parties, including the radical communists, the student movement was a resounding lesson in political mobilization.

During the 1980s, many communists in Nepal as elsewhere began losing faith in orthodox communism. Dahal and his comrades, however, became more committed to the notion that Nepal could only be liberated through a violent capture of the state by a communist party. The hardline faction, Masal, which espoused this radical aim under the leadership of Mohan Bikram Singh, split from the The Fourth Convention in 1983. But many of Mohan Bikram's younger followers soon became discontented with his authoritarian style of leadership, and began doubting his commitment to armed rebellion.[20] They left him in 1985 to form a new faction, which they called Mashal – a name that differed from that of Mohan Bikram's faction by the sound of a single syllable.

Mashal was led by Mohan Baidya, alias 'Kiran', who would become one of the Maoists' three most important leaders. It was among the smaller communist parties in Nepal in the late 1980s; its members were less concerned with expanding their organization than in the idea of instigating a war against the state. Much of their time was spent studying texts on ideology and military strategy, acquired through Mashal's membership of the Revolutionary Internationalist Movement (RIM) – a forum consisting of radical Maoist groups from various countries. Of all the RIM members, Peru's Shining Path was the most successful in waging guerrilla war at the time, and thus a major source of inspiration.

On 28 April 1986, Mashal activists launched attacks on nine police posts across the Kathmandu valley. The authorities retorted with a crackdown on the would-be revolutionaries, who fled to safe houses. The party's top leaders acknowledged their tactical mistake, but many cadres insisted that this action was not enough. In October 1989, Mohan Baidya stepped down as the faction's top leader and nominated Pushpa Kamal

Dahal as his replacement. Despite this change, the group remained committed to armed struggle. The major lesson it drew from the failed attack on the police posts seems to have been that, given the state's power in urban areas, it was necessary to begin the armed struggle from the villages. The following year Dahal and C. P. Gajurel travelled to Bihar, where the Indian Maoist Communist Centre (MCC) trained them in guerrilla warfare. Around that time another Mashal leader, Dev Gurung, managed to acquire two rifles used by Tibetan Khampa rebels during their attempt at armed struggle against the Chinese in the 1970s. In 1989, Dahal trained thirteen core Mashal activists in the fundamentals of guerrilla warfare in a remote part of the Gorkha district.[21]

## An End to Autocracy

By the late 1980s the Panchayat had lost whatever reforming zeal it once possessed. Confronted by various challenges to its authority, most notably the student movement and the referendum of 1980, the regime had grown primarily anxious to perpetuate itself and the privileges of its elites. It maintained a secret police and deployed groups of violent youth – popularly called *mandales* – to identify and crush subversive activity. But the system was inefficient and had lost legitimacy, leaving plenty of space for banned political parties to spread their networks among the urban population.

The democratic uprisings that swept across the globe after the fall of the Berlin Wall strongly influenced political leaders in Nepal. Around this time India had imposed a trade blockade on Nepal, causing much resentment among the Nepali population. Taking advantage of the public mood, the banned political parties came together to instigate a mass uprising against monarchical autocracy. The movement was led by the Nepali Congress, the party that had been struggling for parliamentary democracy for over four decades. Some of the more influential communist parties joined the movement, forming an alliance called the United Left Front (ULF).[22]

The most important party in the ULF – the Communist Party of Nepal (Marxist–Leninist) – had Maoist roots. It had attempted an armed insurrection in Jhapa (a district in the south-eastern corner of Nepal) in the early 1970s, an action that killed a number of landowners before being suppressed by the government. Several of the party's most important leaders were imprisoned. Weakened and disheartened by the setback, these communists decided that armed revolution against the state was not feasible under current political circumstances.[23] In subsequent years, events in other parts of the world– notably the ascendance of Deng Xiaoping after Mao's death, and the advent of glasnost and perestroika in the Soviet Union – convinced the ULF parties that traditional communism had failed.[24] It was this belief that led them to ally with the Nepali Congress in the 1990 movement that demanded the dissolution of the Panchayat system, and the establishment of a parliamentary democracy under a constitutional monarch.

At the other end of the communist spectrum was the United National People's Movement (UNPM), an alliance of radical Maoist parties including Mashal. The UNPM was an unwanted interloper in the movement, and the Nepali Congress and the members of the ULF did their best to ignore it. Compensating for what they lacked in popular support by voluble rhetoric and violent street action, this alliance had made clear from the outset that they were not merely demanding a parliamentary democracy – a system they continued to define, in keeping with the traditional Marxist view, as the dictatorship of the bourgeoisie. They attempted to buttress the crumbling bastion of Marxism-Leninism-Maoism against the current of the times, rejecting the idea that the movements of popular resistance in Eastern Europe represented a moral victory of liberal democracy over communism. Rather, claimed Pushpa Kamal Dahal, the movements in Eastern Europe were against regimes that had abandoned crucial communist principles such as belief in class struggle and the necessity of the dictatorship of the proletariat. They had thus become 'fascist, capitalist dictatorships'. In his view, rather than marking the death of communism, the popular movements would in fact foster the growth of genuine Marxist movements.[25]

Baburam Bhattarai was the coordinator and the most visible face of the UNPM. He was born in the Gorkha hills in 1954 to a Brahmin agricultural family, and received his early education at a local school. On reaching young adulthood, however, his life took a different trajectory to that of his later colleagues in the Maoist movement. While most of the other Maoist leaders attended government-run schools, Bhattarai had the opportunity to study at a school run by Christian missionaries. The education the school provided was of superior quality to that of government schools. A diligent student, Bhattarai excelled through school and went on to score the highest marks in the nationally held School Leaving Certificate (SLC) exams.[26] Having topped the SLC 'board' – the top ten SLC candidates – Bhattarai achieved national celebrity status at the age of sixteen.[27]

His academic merit was duly rewarded with scholarships for higher education. After completing his intermediate level studies in Kathmandu, he went to Chandigarh, India, to complete a bachelor's degree in architecture (later claiming that he chose architecture without knowing anything about it except that all who did well in the SLC exams went in for it).

While in Nepal, Bhattarai, unlike his future colleagues, was not drawn into the illicit and intoxicating camaraderie of the underground communist networks. Early on, his political views were limited to general antipathy towards the institution of monarchy – an attitude instilled in him during childhood by a relative who was a member of the Nepali Congress. This antipathy deepened after he came to Kathmandu at sixteen and witnessed, over the next two years, student protests and the arrest of a prominent proponent of republicanism, Ram Raja Prasad Singh. During this time Bhattarai did come into contact with young communists, but he also met other party activists of various stripes and was particularly sympathetic towards the Nepali Congress. In contrast, his future colleagues in the Maoist movement had been taught to think of the Congress as the party representing the bourgeoisie and hence a 'class enemy'.

While Pushpa Kamal Dahal and the other budding Maoists learnt their doctrine through clandestinely distributed literature and training sessions in underground party cells, Bhattarai deepened his knowledge of Marxism during the long hours he spent reading history and politics in the university library while pursuing his architecture degree. In the late 1970s, when he was in Delhi studying for a master's in town and country planning, he formed the Independent Indian Nepali Students' Organization, which included Nepali students of all political hues and served as a cross-party forum for anti-Panchayat forces in India. Through this organization he came into contact with the eminent opposition leaders of the time – B. P. Koirala and Ganesh Man Singh of the Nepali Congress, and Tulsilal Amatya, Nirmal Lama and Mohan Bikram Singh among the communists.

In the early 1980s, Bhattarai was at Delhi's Jawaharlal Nehru University working on his PhD dissertation, which was later published under the title *The Nature of Underdevelopment and Regional Structure of Nepal: A Marxist Analysis.* By then he had grown disillusioned with the Nepali Congress's recent attempt to seek some accommodation with the king (called the policy of 'national reconciliation'), and gravitated towards the communists, becoming a member of Mohan Bikram Singh's Masal. He started working full-time with the party after he moved back to Nepal in 1986. He stayed with Singh even as Dahal and other future Maoist leaders left the party to form their own faction. It was only in 1991, following the anti-monarchy uprising, that Bhattarai, along with a few others in Singh's faction, came over to join those in Mashal.

Bhattarai's Marxism, acquired as much through solitary study in universities as through activism, was of greater scope and flexibility than the doctrinaire variety propagated and debated in the underground communist circles of Nepal. His sympathies also extended to certain non-communist political forces struggling against the monarchy. Having been exposed to the intellectual and political circles of Chandigarh and Delhi, he was not, like other Mashal leaders, unremittingly hostile towards India. Moreover, by the time he entered the tight-knit world of the underground Mashal party, its other leaders had already forged intense bonds through over a decade of working together. Although he went on to become one of the most important Maoist leaders, and certainly the movement's public face during the years of the armed rebellion, these differences in experience and outlook between Bhattarai and his colleagues would often give rise to sharp antagonisms, with major implications for the Maoist party and the direction it would take.[28]

During the 1990 uprising, the UNPM, along with the Nepali Congress and the ULF, demanded the immediate abrogation of the Panchayat constitution and the dissolution of the regime structure, from the national legislature to the village councils. Unlike the Congress and the ULF, however, the UNPM also had additional demands: the formation of an interim government through a convention of all the parties, prominent individuals and other organizations participating in the movement against the monarchy; and nationwide elections to a Constituent Assembly tasked with drafting a new constitution for Nepal.[29]

In making these demands, the Maoist parties in the UNPM hearkened back to a particular strand in the Nepali communist movement. The First All-Party Congress of the Communist Party of Nepal, held in 1954, stated that one of the party's chief goals was to replace the monarchy by a republican system through an elected Constituent Assembly.[30] At the time, this appeared to be a feasible goal: after all, only two years before King Tribhuvan, Mahendra's father, had declared that an assembly of elected representatives would draft a constitution.[31] But in 1958, following Tribhuvan's death and a long period of political turmoil, Mahendra, who had ascended to the throne, cancelled the elections to the Constituent Assembly and promulgated a constitution that, while providing for a parliamentary system, ensured that sovereignty was invested in the monarchy. This was the constitution that provided the framework for the general elections of 1959.[32]

By cancelling elections to a Constituent Assembly, the king was clearly trying to prevent the formation of a body that would diminish his authority and power. The communists recognized the significance of Mahendra's act. Some of them were outraged, but compelled to acquiesce given their limited support base and other political constraints of the time.

Baburam Bhattarai and some of the younger followers of Mohan Bikram Singh would perceive this event not just as a betrayal on the part of the king, but as yet another example of the communist leaders' ineffectuality and their tendency to succumb before obstacles placed in their way by the feudal state elite. The idea of a Constituent Assembly persisted. It evolved into the dream of creating a political body that represented all sections of society, particularly the poor and toiling masses, who would come together to draft the law of the land on their own terms. And since it was assumed that a truly representative body would want to cast off the yoke of the monarchy, the vision of a Constituent Assembly became intertwined with the idea of a republic.[33]

In February and March 1990, thousands of people representing diverse classes and interests took to the streets of Kathmandu. On 9 April, King Birendra offered to lift the ban on the political parties and remove the word 'partyless' from the definition of the Panchayat system in the constitution. The Nepali Congress and the UML decided to accept these terms. Indeed, by early April the Congress itself was keen to halt the uprising, as it was becoming violent and slipping from the party's control. In response to further popular pressure, the entire Panchayat system was dissolved a few days later and an interim government under the leadership of Krishna Prasad Bhattarai of the Nepali Congress was formed. The following month a Constitutional Recommendations Commission was established. Its members, nominated by the interim prime minister, represented the Congress, the ULF and the palace. The Commission spent a protracted period of time negotiating over the specifics of the constitution.[34]

Ignored by the other political parties and excluded from the Commission, the UNPM grouping condemned the Congress and the ULF for their compromise with the king. The UNPM continued to demand elections to a Constituent Assembly and the Congress continually rejected the idea, not wishing to antagonize the king with whom it now sought to cooperate.

On 8 November 1990, King Birendra promulgated the new constitution that established a parliamentary democracy, with regular elections, political freedoms, a bicameral legislature and the separation of powers. Executive authority was jointly vested in the king and the elected council of ministers, but the former could exercise authority only on the recommendation of the latter.[35]

The radical Maoist parties in the UNPM (including Dahal's Mashal and Mohan Bikram Singh's Masal), along with one of the communist parties in the ULF (Nirmal Lama's Fourth Convention), held that the Congress and its allies on the left had once again betrayed the Nepali people by conniving with the monarchy to thwart the Constituent Assembly. These Maoists refused to recognize the legitimacy of the constitution. But given their limited power at the time, their stance was of little consequence.

CHAPTER 2

# Democracy and Its Discontents

## A Fresh Start

The political parties began preparing for general elections soon after the constitution was drafted. Two major parties in the United Left Front – the CPN (Marxist) and the CPN (Marxist–Leninist) united to form the Communist Party of Nepal (Unified Marxist–Leninist) or CPN–UML. A number of radical Maoist parties, including Mashal, the Fourth Convention and a section of Masal led by Baburam Bhattarai, united to form a party called the Communist Party of Nepal (Unity Centre). Its leader was Pushpa Kamal Dahal, alias 'Prachanda'. Still committed to armed rebellion but aware that this was not immediately practicable, the members of the Unity Centre decided that the bulk of the party would remain underground. Meanwhile, they would float a front organization called the Samyukta Jana Morcha (SJM), which would participate in parliamentary elections and use the bourgeois democratic system to serve their own radical ends. Baburam Bhattarai headed the SJM.

The Nepali Congress won a majority in the May 1991 elections, taking 110 of the 205 seats in parliament. The CPN–UML won sixty-nine seats, and the SJM got nine.[1]

Amid newfound political freedoms, Nepal's polity underwent profound transformation in the 1990s. There was a proliferation of private newspapers, magazines and radio stations that vied with one another in being outspoken. Interest groups of all kinds emerged, campaigned for support and demonstrated on the streets against the government. The country's public sphere, dominated by paeans to the monarchy during the Panchayat era, now turned vibrant and raucous. With the adoption of a liberal economic and social regime, Nepali citizens became more aware of the wider world. The government solicited foreign investment and aid.[2] The distribution of passports, tightly controlled under the Panchayat, was liberalized. Thousands of people left the country for study and employment. Those who could afford it went to the United States or Europe; many others sought jobs in the Gulf states.

And there was the inevitable disappointment, as economic growth failed to match the expectations aroused by the arrival of democracy. Those on the left criticized the government for adopting neoliberal policies and cutting subsidies to the poor.[3] Although the political culture of Kathmandu and other cities changed dramatically, there was no immediate improvement in the lives of the people in the countryside. The media became preoccupied with the country's new leaders, who seemed just as corrupt and venal as the old ones.

To the communists in the Unity Centre, those early years of democracy confirmed that parliamentary democracy was a sham: they believed it could never bring about the necessary transformation of Nepali society, making it necessary to wage war against the state and seize state power.

## The Persistence of Rural Oppression

What aspects of Nepali society did the Maoists have in mind when they claimed that Nepal remained a semi-feudal country? In his 1999 novel *The Music of Fireflies (Junkiriko Sangeet)*,[4] the leftist writer Khagendra Sangroula provided a vivid illustration of the exploitative social relations that many on the Nepali left condemned. Sangroula has influenced and enjoys close links with communist leaders across generations. Although never a member of any party and despite his often ambivalent relationship to them, he has, in his own words, 'walked the shores of Nepal's communist movement' for much of his life.[5] *The Music of Fireflies*, which spans the period from the decline of the Panchayat in the late 1980s to its replacement by an elected parliamentary system in the 1990s, explores the evolving relations between a community of Dalits, the lowest-ranking group in the Hindu caste hierarchy, and their upper-caste neighbours in a village in the hills of western Nepal. The novel is based on the author's experience in a Dalit settlement in Parbat district, where he spent several months observing the social and cultural dynamics of the local Dalit community and the efforts of social activists to work with them.[6]

Simring, the village in which the novel is set, lies on a barren hillside. There is a forest on top of the hill, above the arid land inhabited by impoverished Dalits. The soil becomes gradually more fertile and yielding as one descends from the Dalit settlement towards a cluster of upper-caste homes. At the foot of the hill, green fields spread out as far as the eye can see. Owned by the upper-caste families, they are tilled by the Dalits in return for meagre wages that constitute their chief source of income.

At the start of the novel we meet Gopilal Upadhayay, the *pradhan pancha* (village chief), whose sick buffalo has died. The custom is for the Dalits to receive the carcass of dead animals; as they cannot afford to buy meat, the Dalits of Simring only get to eat it when an animal dies a natural death. In return they provide labour on the fields of the animal's owner. This time, however, the *pradhan pancha* has buried the buffalo. When the *katuwal* (village crier) asks him why, the *pradhan pancha* says he does not want to give the carcass to the Damais (the sub-caste to which these Dalits belong) because once they eat it they will promptly forget their promise to tend his fields. Sensing an opportunity for profit, the *katuwal* promises Gopilal that he will make sure the Dalits pay for the carcass with their labour.

At the *katuwal*'s suggestion, several Damai men unearth the carcass, cut it up and share it out. Harkay, who has received a basketful, goes home excited: it has been a while since he ate meat. His wife Jiri feels misgiving when she sees what he has brought. Although she has eaten rotting meat many times before, on this occasion it looks excessively slippery and mushy and gives off an extremely rancid smell. But when she mentions this to her husband, he scolds her and tells her to hurry up and prepare dinner. She cooks the meat, and Harkay, Jiri and their son Aaite eat their fill before going to bed.

The family, Harkay in particular, spends the night in torment. After hours of uncontrollable diarrhoea and vomiting, in the morning he dies. Four other Dalits who had partaken of the meat from the carcass also suffer the same fate as Harkay and the community performs funeral rites for the five victims.

Harkay's death exacerbates Jiri's hardships. Her older son, who has gone to work in Bombay, has lost contact with the family, and her younger son is still a child. One day she goes to Gopilal Upadhayay's house to ask for some grain. To her shock and dismay, Gopilal insists she sign a promissory note confirming that she owes him 2,500 rupees for Harkay's funeral. Only then does Jiri realize that her husband's funeral expenses were borne by Gopilal, and not by her neighbours who had taken charge of the final arrangements while she was delirious with grief. Poor, illiterate and helpless, Jiri is in no position to challenge the village chief. She puts her thumbprints on the loan paper before asking Gopilal for the grain she so desperately needs. Obviously Jiri cannot repay the loan, and eventually Gopilal confiscates her small patch of land in lieu of payment.

Khagendra Sangroula's depiction of the relations between Dalits and upper castes in a village in western Nepal would have been instantly recognizable to his audience. Gopilal is an archetypal village chief: an upper-caste landowner who also plays the role of local moneylender. Most village chiefs of the Panchayat era derived their power and authority from their caste status. As local representatives of the supreme state authority, they had access to the state's legal and security apparatus, and this allowed them to dominate and exploit the lower castes.

The social and economic relations represented in Sangroula's novel and their impact on the broader Nepali economy were analysed by Baburam Bhattarai in his PhD dissertation.[7] This text, which attempts to develop a comprehensive theory of Nepal's continuing underdevelopment, formed the basis of Bhattarai's later article, 'The Politico-Economic Rationale of People's War in Nepal'.[8] The article denounces the highly unequal land distribution and the precarious living conditions of the poor in the Nepali countryside: 'Statistics suggest that about 70 per cent of poor peasants own about 2 per cent of the land, 25 per cent of middle peasants own around 45 per cent, and about 5 per cent of rich peasants and semi-feudals own 30 per cent.'[9] Poor and landless peasants are forced to work as sharecroppers on the fields of landowners. Yet they find it hard even to make ends meet. 'The rights of tenants are not secure, the rate of rent is high and the tenants are often "bonded" to the landlord through high interest rates charged on loans and other labour-service conditions.'[10]

Baburam Bhattarai admits that at the time of writing his article, which was published in 1998, the majority of Nepal's agricultural population, especially in the hills, owned at least some of the land they farmed. By and large he accepts the validity of a report that claimed that 65 per cent of Nepali farmers owned the land they cultivated, which amounted to 49 per cent of total landholdings. But he also points out that most owner-cultivators were marginal farmers who could barely produce enough to meet their subsistence needs and were subjected to various kinds of exploitation. For instance, most peasants depended on loans from 'feudal usurers' like Gopilal Upadhayay who provided credit 'at high interest rates and under oppressive conditions', thus 'entrapping them in a vicious cycle of indebtedness.'[11]

In Bhattarai's view – shared by the Maoists in general – the unequal land relations and the resulting exploitation were not only condemnable on moral grounds, they also imposed severe constraints on Nepal's economic growth. By forcing the majority to accept the cycle of low productivity and subsistence livelihoods, these relations impeded Nepal's transition from feudalism to capitalism (hence condemning Nepal to its semi-feudal state). Radical measures, including far-reaching land reform, were required to ensure a more equitable distribution of land, increased productivity and the emergence of fully-fledged capitalist relations of production.

In fact, the necessity of land reform had been clear to King Mahendra when he took over power in 1960 and established the Panchayat system. He understood that land reform was required to modernize Nepal, as well as to assuage demands for political and social reform. Under his aegis Nepal's first land reform legislation was passed in 1963. But the Panchayat's support base comprised the very class of people (those who were models for the character of Gopilal Upadhayay) who would be disadvantaged by redistribution. Some land reform did occur, especially in the Kathmandu valley. However as there was little political will to implement the effort, many landlords succeeded in evading redistribution and the process was largely a failure.[12]

Would parliamentary democracy be able to do what the Panchayat could not to improve the conditions of the peasantry? What impact did the transition of 1990 have on the countryside? *The Music of Fireflies* attempts an answer.

The tremors of the momentous 1990 uprising are barely felt among the Dalits of Simring. The effects are somewhat greater among the upper castes. When Gopilal, some time after forcing Jiri to sign the promissory note, announces that she still owes him for the buffalo meat that killed her husband, she is unable to control her anger and lashes out at him. Gopilal bristles and blames her uncharacteristic outburst on the 'mad democracy' gripping the country. 'How will the *sanatan dharma*[13] be preserved,' he wonders, 'when wives stop obeying their husbands, servants stop obeying their masters and the lower castes stop obeying the upper castes?'[14]

In elections held soon after the toppling of the Panchayat, Gopilal stands for the Rastriya Prajatantra Party (RPP), comprised mostly of loyalists of the old monarchical regime. But the national mood is in favour of the Nepali Congress and the UML. The former *pradhan pancha*, who had repeatedly won local elections under the Panchayat through bribery and coercion, loses badly this time, receiving a mere fifty votes. Shocked to find that the RPP has been reduced to a marginal party, Gopilal joins the Nepali Congress.

The episode captures the trend that swept across Nepal following the 1990 uprising when thousands of Panchayat loyalists joined the Nepali Congress. The Congress was eager to welcome leaders of the old regime into its ranks, as their influence over local populations could be used for electoral benefit.

Khagendra Sangroula had previously condemned this political manoeuvring in a slim volume of essays titled *Fragments of the People's Movement* (*Jana Andolanka Chharraharu*), published barely three months after the 1990 upheaval. In one essay Sangroula bitterly denounced the leaders of the movement for allowing Parshu Narayan Chaudhary – a politician who had long ago left the Nepali Congress to join the Panchayat, and who headed the retaliation committee formed to suppress the uprising – to rejoin the Nepali Congress:

There was one voice and one demand of all Nepalis reverberating in the Nepali sky: Brother, punish the murderers! Punish the murderers! But a strange thing happened. The Nepali Congress paid obeisance to the murderers, honoured them with garlands and escorted them home. It was a grand reunion between the leaders of the people and the killers of the people. The Nepali Congress put the murderers on a pedestal and trampled upon people's aspirations in that moment of disgrace.[15]

Among the main characters in *The Music of Fireflies* are two social activists, Sheshkanta and Kapil, who have been trying to educate the Dalits of Simring and rouse them from their fatalistic acceptance of their social position. They have an antagonistic relationship with Gopilal Upadhyay, who thinks they are stirring up the lower castes and tries to set the police against them. When Sheshkanta returns to Simring after a period of absence, he is astonished to see Gopilal in the attire of a Nepali Congress activist, sporting a pin badge on his lapel with the image of the legendary Nepali Congress leader, B. P. Koirala. Sheshkanta cannot resist teasing Gopilal about his shift in allegiance. The former *pradhan pancha* is not amused, and he struggles to reconcile his new party identity with his private interests:

> Look here, sir, you and I have now come closer. We were allies during the people's movement. Together we achieved this multi-party democracy ... My party is not against the work you are doing in the village up there. But we should first sit and talk to each other, come to an agreement, and then slowly bring development. Let us not destroy our *sanatan dharma* right away. We two brothers worked together for the people's movement; we should work together for development as well ... Sir, our path, too, leads to socialism.[16]

Sangroula's readers on the left would have enjoyed the irony in this exchange. They would have read in Gopilal's seeming effort to adjust to the new political order the accommodation of the new regime with the old, the perpetuation of entrenched privilege and inequality, and the difficulty of undertaking the necessary social reforms under these conditions.

An elected government led by the UML did establish a land reform commission in 1994, which in 1995 recommended abolishing tenancy and lowering the ceiling on landholdings. But due to the alliance of the landowning classes with the dominant political parties, and the rapid turnover of governments hampering stability and policy implementation, these recommendations were not immediately taken up. Some began to be implemented six years later, in 2001. A modicum of progress was made in ensuring better conditions for tenant farmers. But the delay had given landowners ample time to manoeuvre so as to evade redistribution.[17] Land obtained through land reform efforts amounted to a total of 29,124 hectares, a mere 0.85 per cent of cultivated land. Of this, only about half was redistributed; the rest remained in the hands of the original proprietors.[18]

Meanwhile, the National Population Census of 2001 found that 58.97 per cent of Nepal's total households owned less than 0.5 hectares of land each, making them 'functionally landless in terms of agriculture'.[19] Additionally, 75 per cent of rural households owned less than a hectare of land, the size necessary to provide basic subsistence and provide a tiny surplus to meet other needs.[20]

So what was to be done? In his novel, Sangroula is sceptical of the ability and intentions of the parliamentary political parties, but nonetheless values the open political environment provided by the new dispensation. Through the characters of social activists Kapil and Sheshkanta, he implies that the new freedoms can be utilized to inform the oppressed about the structural causes behind their socio-economic position, and to organize collective action that challenges traditional class and caste relations.

The Maoists were inevitably scornful of this view. In an extended criticism of Sangroula's novel, the senior Maoist leader Mohan Baidya, also the party's chief literary theorist, claimed: 'It is clear that the writer has chosen NGOs over the revolutionary communist party, NGOism or decadent capitalism over Marxism, and capitalist-imperialist thought over New Democracy and socialism.'[21] From the Maoist perspective, the early years of the 1990s confirmed that the parliamentary regime amounted to a combined dictatorship of the feudal class and the bourgeoisie, which would do nothing to transform Nepal's social and economic relations. The efforts of NGOs to bring development to the countryside were merely a ploy to pacify the poor, defuse class struggle and ultimately preserve existing social relations. Violent class struggle, led by a revolutionary communist party, was necessary to uproot the feudal class from the countryside and to eventually abolish the monarchy, its ultimate protector and guardian.

## Is Nepal Sovereign?

The boundaries of Nepal contain many of the highest Himalayan peaks, the source of the rivers that rush down to the plains. Generations of Nepalis have been taught that, in the absence of any other significant natural resource, it is the waters of these rivers that will make the nation rich. They could be harnessed, so it is claimed, to produce enough electricity not just for domestic consumption, but also for sale to the energy-hungry markets of India.

In reality, however, the process of establishing power generation plants on the rivers has been protracted and painful. Even at the beginning of the twenty-first century, Nepal could barely produce half of the electricity required by its own population, particularly during winter when rains are sparse and the rivers reduced to a trickle. The causes of the dysfunction in the energy-generation sector are largely political. Nepal, lacking capital and technical capacity of its own, needs investment and support from other countries, primarily India, to develop power generation projects. But given Nepal's complicated relationship to the Indian state, economic cooperation has rarely been easy. In fact, Nepal's long history of attempted cooperation with India in the hydropower sector provides the clearest illustration of why the Maoists continued to view Nepal as a semi-colony.

In the late 1980s, India constructed the Tanakpur barrage and powerhouse on the Mahakali, a river lying on the western Nepal–India border. Initially, India had claimed that the barrage was being constructed on its own soil and was of no concern to Nepal. However as the construction neared completion in 1988, it became clear that it would need to be anchored to land on the Nepali side of the border. The Indian government had to request Nepal for the use of 2.9 hectares of Nepali land for this purpose.[22]

The Tanakpur project then became an important part of India's agenda in its dealings with Nepal, but it was unable to secure an agreement with the Panchayat regime. Almost as soon as the Panchayat was toppled, however, the Indian government began to pressure the interim government to negotiate an agreement.

The prime minister of the first elected government of the post-1990 era, Girija Prasad Koirala of the Nepali Congress, visited Delhi soon after assuming office in December 1991. His entourage was not prepared to undertake any negotiations on Tanakpur, and there had been a decision to avoid that topic altogether. At a final press conference the Indian prime minister, Narasimha Rao, stated that no agreements regarding water-related matters had been reached. However, the joint communiqué released at the end of the visit indicated that, on the contrary, a deal on Tanakpur had been made. The details of the agreement, published in the official *Nepal Gazette* on 24 December, revealed that India had been allowed to use the land on Nepali territory to affix the Tanakpur barrage, and in return Nepal was to receive 10 million units of electricity as well as 150 cusecs of water for irrigation. Further, work on attachment had been set to begin by 15 December. This meant the Nepali public only learned about the details of the agreement nine days after the construction was scheduled to begin.[23]

The impression was that Koirala had secretly signed a deal compromising Nepal's interests. The communist parties – including the UML and the Unity Centre – were the most strident in their opposition. They demanded that as the Tanakpur barrage stood on a border river, all benefits from it should be equally shared between the two countries. The Tanakpur agreement was a treaty that would have 'pervasive, long-term and serious' ramifications, they claimed, and according to the constitution, such cases required ratification by a two-thirds majority of both houses of parliament.[24] The Koirala government maintained, on the other hand, that the agreement was a mere 'understanding' and did not require parliamentary ratification. In response the communists wreaked havoc, marching though the streets and uprooting the railings on sidewalks. They disrupted parliamentary proceedings by surrounding the speaker and chanting slogans against the government. When the Indian prime minister came to Kathmandu to offer Nepal increased benefits from the Tanakpur project, the communists were not placated; they waved black flags as his convoy drove by.[25]

The Supreme Court ruled in December 1992 that the Tanakpur agreement was indeed a treaty, and needed ratification by parliament. It did not specify, however, whether the treaty was so important as to require a two-thirds majority of both houses for ratification. The Nepali Congress government held that its ratification required only a simple majority; the communists disagreed. Parliamentary committees were formed to resolve the dispute. Two years had elapsed since the agreement was signed, and by then the conflict had become so intense and animosities between political leaders so deep that an amicable resolution appeared impossible.[26]

The Koirala government collapsed in 1994, partly due to antagonisms engendered by the Tanakpur dispute. Fresh elections were held. Though lacking a majority, the UML emerged as the most powerful party, and with 88 of the 205 seats they went on to form a minority government.[27]

The Unity Centre and the other small communist groupings had agitated on the streets alongside the UML against the Tanakpur agreement for the first few years of the democratic era. It was clear, however, that the UML was different from the other communist parties. For one, it was substantially more powerful; no other communist party (except for the Nepal Workers' and Peasants' Party, which won three seats) had won even a single seat in the 1994 elections.[28] Also, while the UML had declared its full commitment to the parliamentary system, most of the other communist parties joined the system with the stated objective of undermining it from within. The smaller communist parties thus had little stake in the system and mattered little to the government, even as they vehemently agitated on the streets. By contrast the UML mattered a great deal to the ruling party, the military and business elite of Kathmandu, and foreign interests. Thus the UML, hitherto driven by communist concerns such as organizing workers for militant action and resisting perceived encroachment by India on Nepal's autonomy, came under the influence of traditionally powerful social forces in the early 1990s. And once it gained the opportunity to lead in government, it felt even more obliged to adopt a position of engagement and negotiation.

The UML therefore had to engage with the Indian government on the Tanakpur agreement, which remained to be ratified by Nepal's parliament. The two sides reached a preliminary agreement in April 1995 to replace the Tanakpur accord with a 'package deal' on Mahakali. India was to increase the amount of electricity and water that Nepal would receive from the Tanakpur project. In return, Nepal had to agree to the development of a number of other projects on the Mahakali River, including a massive storage dam at Pancheshwar, some distance upstream from Tanakpur.[29]

The UML government claimed that the Mahakali package would rectify the inequities of the Tanakpur accord, and that Nepal's interest would not be compromised by Pancheshwar and other projects. The other large political parties – the Nepali Congress and the RPP – received the news of the proposed agreement with euphoria. In the immediate aftermath of the 1990 movement, Nepal's newly elected leaders had aggressively sought to open up to the outside world and attract as much foreign investment and aid as possible. The dominant ethos held that this process would constitute the most promising avenue for the country's development, and so the Mahakali package – a mega-project that the country would undertake jointly with its colossal neighbour – came to be seen as an important step in this process. The radical communists and some on the nationalist right, however, were sceptical. In their opinion, the Mahakali package, if acceded to by Nepal, would be the latest in a series of agreements in which the Nepali ruling class had surrendered the country's resources to India.

The UML government collapsed after nine months in power. It was replaced by a coalition headed by the Nepali Congress, but the Mahakali agenda remained on the table. In January 1996, the foreign ministers of the two countries signed the Mahakali Treaty[30] during a visit by Indian Foreign Minister Pranab Mukherjee to Kathmandu. Apparently the challenges involved in the Tanakpur agreement had taught India that it was not enough to sign an agreement with representatives of the Nepali government; it was also necessary to secure the support of other important political actors in Nepal's turbulent democracy. Therefore, two representatives each from the major political parties – the Nepali Congress, the UML and the RPP – were asked to sign a document titled 'National Consensus on the Use of the Waters of the Mahakali River' in the presence of the Indian foreign minister. Some within the UML had voiced dissent against this proposal. It was reported that the Indian foreign minister had extended his stay in Nepal by a day to ensure that these voices were subdued. The following month, the prime ministers of the two countries – Nepal's Sher Bahadur Deuba and India's Narasimha Rao – jointly signed the treaty in New Delhi.[31]

However the Mahakali Treaty, given its 'pervasive, long-term and serious' nature, still required ratification by a two-thirds majority in the legislature. By this time the details of the treaty had become public. The radical left had developed a substantial critique of the treaty, and remained implacably opposed to it, with their most serious charge that it did not provide for an equitable distribution of the waters of the Mahakali. It had also come to light that the Indian army had been occupying an area on Nepali soil – Kalapani in Darchula district – along the bank of the Mahakali since before the Sino-Indian war of 1962, which gave the fringe communists further cause for agitation and the heaping of abuse upon the UML.

Vexed by the party's supposed capitulation to Indian designs, a section within the UML began to lobby against voting for the treaty.[32] The two factions were unable to reach a compromise, so on the morning of 20 September 1996, the day that the treaty was to be voted in parliament, the central committee of the UML met to decide whether the party should accept it as it stood or demand its modification. Seventeen members of the central committee voted in the treaty's favour; sixteen voted against. The circumstances surrounding the votation appeared suspicious. The party chairman, Manmohan Adhikary, who had previously publicly opposed the treaty, abstained from the vote on grounds of ill health. The party's General Secretary Madhav Kumar Nepal, who was in favour of the treaty, had nominated another person to vote in the chairman's place, and this person voted for ratification. There were rumours that he had been taken to the Indian embassy where Madhav Nepal and the Indian ambassador cajoled and coerced him into voting for the treaty. Not least were the claims from the Kathmandu press in the weeks preceding the UML central committee meeting that the Indian embassy had distributed millions of rupees and promises of political favours to UML leaders in an attempt to buy support.[33]

Madhav Nepal publicly disputed these accusations. But for those on the radical left and across large segments of Nepali public opinion, the rumours had already acquired the status of fact, for they were consonant with the view of India that dominated the Nepali imagination. The Indian embassy, located in a place called Lainchaur, was popularly known as the Lainchaur Darbar (the court at Lainchaur). The term, a play on the phrase 'Narayanhiti Darbar' (the royal palace), recognized the embassy as a centre of intrigue where shadowy and powerful envoys beckoned Nepali political figures in order to manipulate them.

The faction of the UML opposed to the treaty thus claimed that the majority attained in its favour in the central committee meeting was counterfeit. Students affiliated to the party ransacked the UML parliamentary party office in protest. A number of small parties tried to encircle and barricade the parliament, but were dispersed by police. On the night of 20 September 1996, 220 of the 265 total members of the combined upper and lower houses of the Nepali parliament voted to ratify the Mahakali treaty.[34]

The monthly magazine *Mulyankan*, a preeminent forum for analysis and discussion among the Nepali left throughout the 1990s, asked: 'Who was responsible for accepting the "Mahakali Package", which revived the notorious Tanakpur agreement in a roundabout way … even after widespread popular opposition?' The reason the political parties had ratified the treaty, the editorial stated, was because they still thought power could only be attained with India's blessing, rather than through domestic popular support. In the past, *Mulyankan* claimed, this attitude prevailed only among leaders of the Panchayat and the Nepali Congress. But now, even the leaders of the largest party on the left had capitulated to the desires of the Indian ruling class.[35]

In the Maoist view, the Mahakali Treaty was just another in a long list of agreements, beginning with the 1816 Sugauli Treaty, which had reduced Nepal to an Indian semi-colony. They held that while the democratic transition of 1990 had weakened the monarchy and the feudal system to some extent, it had also led to an increase of Indian dominance. Nepal's communists had long considered the Nepali Congress to be an instrument of Indian foreign policy. Their reasons were, firstly, that the Nepali bourgeoisie represented by the Congress was primarily 'comprador' in nature and beholden to Indian capitalists. Secondly, Congress leaders had spent many years in the political wilderness in India and had cultivated close relationships with members of the Indian ruling class. Thirdly, the preferred political system of the party was closely modelled on the Indian parliamentary system. These affinities, it was believed, made the Congress very susceptible to Indian influence.

The Maoists also believed that, despite the arbitrary nature of the monarchical Panchayat regime, its political centre was at least unified and capable of protecting the national interest. The establishment of the multi-party polity set a trend of intense rivalry between political parties, great factionalism within them, shifting parliamentary coalitions and the formation and collapse of short-lived governments. This enabled the Indian government, through its embassy in Kathmandu, to extend its influence to political parties and to play off individual leaders and parties against each other. As Bhattarai noted some time later, parliamentary democracy entails 'endless adjustment of the balance of power and the buying and selling of parliamentarians.'[36]

For the Maoists, the events surrounding the signing of the Mahakali treaty provided further confirmation that unreserved participation in open and competitive politics would spell disaster for a communist party. 'The CPN–UML … has degenerated into an openly reactionary [party] since it vowed to serve and strengthen the existing constitutional multiparty system,' said Baburam Bhattarai. He added that by prostrating itself before 'Indian expansionism', the UML had proved the validity of 'the charges we have levelled against [it].'[37]

Attempts to implement the Mahakali treaty were no less convoluted than the process leading up to its ratification. As popular opinion remained strongly opposed to the treaty and it became increasingly clear that the treaty did not provide for an equitable division of waters, all parties sought to distance themselves from it. A Nepali Congress leader remarked in 2000 that the treaty was unlikely to be implemented until the dispute over the Indian military occupation at Kalapani was resolved.[38] The projects mentioned in the treaty have not materialized to this day.

## The Stirrings of Rebellion

I f there is a single person whose career could be said to represent Nepal's experiment with democracy in the 1990s, it is Girija Prasad Koirala. Having become politically active in 1947, at the age of twenty-two, he toiled for decades as a foot soldier and organization builder under the direction of his brother Bishweswar Prasad – the reflective and charismatic chief of the Nepali Congress who died in 1982. By 1990 Girija Prasad had become, along with Krishna Prasad Bhattarai and Ganesh Man Singh, one of the three most prominent leaders of the party. G. P. Koirala had imbibed a belief in the superiority of multi-party democracy from his brother. Over time he came to see himself as a champion of its principles. But he was not a man of great learning, and his certainties were largely a hardened and simplified version of the convictions of his more cerebral brother.

Nonetheless, Girija Prasad managed to become prime minister following the 1991 elections. Thrust into the midst of innumerable negotiations by virtue of his position, he emerged as what his late and now mythologized brother never became: a master tactician skilled at adapting and manipulating political exigencies to his own ends. Thus by the early 2000s, the political power of his main rivals within his party, Bhattarai and Singh, had been effectively anulled. Despite his belief in democracy, Koirala possessed an authoritarian streak. He was also ardently anticommunist. When the civil service union affiliated to the communists –

chiefly the UML – agitated for increased pay and benefits soon after he became prime minister, Koirala summarily sacked 400 civil servants and transferred or demoted many more.

The Unity Centre–SJM, to which Prachanda and Bhattarai belonged, played only a minor role in the struggles unfolding in Kathmandu. But in Rolpa and Rukum, two remote hill districts, the tussle between the party's cadre and Nepali Congress supporters constituted the principal political conflict. In April 1992 Koirala travelled to Libang, the district capital of Rolpa, for a local election campaign. A large group of SJM supporters had gathered at the venue where he was to deliver a speech. They chanted slogans against the prime minister and his party, waved black flags and forced him to abandon his speech almost as soon as it had begun.[39]

Shyam Kumar Budha Magar was one of the organizers of this disruption. Having been informed about Koirala's visit to Libang the day before, he had gone to the nearby Village Development Committee (VDC[40]) of Gajul, where he collected 150 people and brought them to Libang the next day for the protest. His friends had similarly fetched hundreds of other people from various parts of Rolpa. Bands of Nepali Congress supporters attacked them on the way. After Koirala returned to Kathmandu, violent brawls continued in Rolpa, leaving scores of activists severely injured.[41]

Rolpa and Rukum districts lie in the mid-western region, one of the most neglected areas of Nepal. In the mid-1990s, it took two full days of travel by road to get to Rolpa's capital Libang from Kathmandu, and many other villages of Rolpa were over a day's trek away from Libang. As for Rukum, not a single road had been built in the district until 2003. Much of the area in both districts is heavily forested. Although the vast majority of people rely on agriculture, only 10 per cent of the land is arable. Most families tend small plots; the grain and potatoes they grow is hardly enough to feed them for six months. Many migrate to India and work as seasonal labourers to supplement their income. Traditional livelihoods include sheep rearing and hashish cultivation, though the latter has declined in importance since the 1980s.[42]

The majority of the people in this region are Kham Magar – a particularly isolated segment of the Magar group, one of the largest ethnic groups of Nepal. The terms used to classify the Magars have varied over the years. When the Indic Hindu state elite in Kathmandu sought to assimilate all of Nepal's communities into a formalized caste hierarchy in 1854, the Magars were classified as 'non-enslaveable alcohol drinkers' (a category that nineteenth-century law deemed inferior to the *tagadhari*[43] upper castes but still superior to the 'enslaveable alcohol drinkers', the 'impure but touchable castes' and the 'untouchable castes').[44] During the 1990s, as a result of activism by groups seeking redress for centuries of oppression by the Hindu ruling castes, the Magars were classified by the state as one among fifty-nine of the country's 'indigenous nationalities' (Adivasi Janajati or simply Janajati in Nepali).

One of the incidents stamped on the historical memory of the Rolpa district dates back to 1956, when the communist leader Mohan Bikram Singh and three of his comrades, after a period of imprisonment in a nearby district, stopped by the village of Thabang, on their way home to Pyuthan district. During this visit Singh apparently helped resolve a feud between two community leaders, spoke of Marx and Lenin and communist doctrine to the locals, and encouraged them to form a commune. Before they left, they set up a peasant organization that was to work as a front for the banned communist party.[45]

A primary school was established in Thabang in 1959, and Barman Budha, one of the two local leaders in the conflict that Mohan Bikram had resolved, invited a communist from Pyuthan to teach there. Over the years, it became something of a tradition for communists of the Mohan Bikram faction to come and teach children at Rolpa. Thus, while the central government in Kathmandu embarked on a nationwide expansion of formal education, teaching the diverse Nepali people about the grand attainment of their nationhood through the efforts of the glorious Shah royal family, small sections of the population, introduced to another kind of modern education, were simultaneously learning that the state elite was guilty of feudal oppression and had to be overthrown. By the early 1980s the teachers of the region were organized into a communist-affiliated union. They encouraged their students, many of whom were barely in their teens, to form cells of the communist student union at their schools. When the Mashal party broke away from Singh's Masal in 1985, most of the communist teachers in the area chose to go with the former; as a result, their students too became loyal to the radical communist party that was later to become the CPN (Maoist).[46]

Shyam Kumar Budha Magar, one of the organizers of the 1992 protest against G. P. Koirala, came under the influence of communist teachers at an early age. Having completed primary school in Rolpa's Gam VDC in 1986, he prepared to move to Libang, the district capital, for further schooling. He was not yet twelve years old. Before he left, one of his teachers informed him about the clandestine political activity he would encounter in Libang and urged him to seek out and join the underground All-Nepal National Free Students' Union. For it was, he was told, the responsibility of all educated people to fight against the Panchayat autocracy. According to his memoirs, Shyam Kumar felt he had found his guiding light when his teacher assured him that the communists would put an end to caste and ethnic discrimination.[47]

Shyam Kumar's political activity escalated radically four years later, after the uprising of 1990. Still residing in Libang, he witnessed political parties proliferating like 'mushrooms in the monsoon'.[48] The inhabitants of Rolpa soon aligned themselves with one or another of the three parties with the strongest presence in the district – the Nepali Congress, the Rastriya Prajatantra Party (RPP), and the front of the Unity Centre, the Samyukta Jana Morcha, to which Shyam Kumar was loyal.

The general elections of 1991 approached. The old guard from the Panchayat, now organized into the RPP, sought to appeal to voters by displaying the might they had accrued through their years in power. Recognizing that this might not be sufficient, they also sent out old loyalists to drum up votes, through coercion and bribery if necessary. The Nepali Congress candidates could plausibly claim to be the champions of liberal democracy and highlight their party's role as the chief protagonist of the recent political transformation. But lacking deep roots in the area, they relied – in Rolpa and Rukum, as in some other places – on former Panchas[49] who had recently joined the party to get out the votes. Ultimately, then, the electoral efforts of the Congress came to resemble those of the RPP.

In Magar's view, voters fell into three distinct categories: the older generation supported the RPP; the schemers and opportunists who wished to benefit from proximity to power supported the Congress; and the young, energetic people up-to-date with the ways of the world joined the leftist parties, particularly the Unity Centre and its front the Samyukta Jana Morcha.[50]

As part of its election campaign, the SJM organized mass meetings in VDCs across the district and formed local committees, and its cultural troupes performed songs and dances that conveyed revolutionary messages using local folk idiom. Shyam Kumar recalled years later that these performances expressed the 'sorrows of the people', and that the audience invariably broke down in tears. While the other political party candidates travelled with large entourages to flaunt their power, the SJM candidates tried to come across as humble and in touch with the people. One of them, Krishna Bahadur Mahara, a schoolteacher in Libang, was known for his inspirational pedagogy and austere lifestyle. The other, Barman Budha, sixty-one years old at the time, later told the anthropologist Anne de Sales that as part of his campaign effort he had walked from village to village, staying in people's houses regardless of their caste or political affiliation and sharing in tasks such as childcare, winnowing and ploughing.[51]

SJM supporters also included groups of aggressive young men, Shyam Kumar among them, who set out across the district 'punishing' members and supporters of rival parties who had allegedly siphoned off state resources in connivance with local authorities. They smeared their faces with soot, garlanded them with shoes and made them do *uth-bas*, a common corporal punishment in which the wrongdoer is made to hold his ears while doing repeated squats. During the 1992 local elections, SJM supporters in Iribang VDC prevented candidates from other parties from registering their candidacies. This campaign to intimidate and humiliate political rivals was in accordance with the directives of the party leadership to intensify the 'class struggle'.[52] For cadres trained to view themselves as the liberators of the *sarvahara* (a term by which Nepali Marxists specifically refer to 'the proletariat', though it has a more diffuse meaning, closer to 'the dispossessed'), it was easy to lump together all political rivals into the category of 'class enemy'.

The SJM won both constituencies in Rolpa district in the general election of 1991. Krishna Bahadur Mahara and Barman Budha became parliamentarians. The following year, the party gained a majority of local government positions in the district. But the Nepali Congress was all-powerful at the centre, and through the early 1990s it infiltrated the entire bureaucracy and police force with its supporters. In Rolpa, too, the local administration appointed from Kathmandu became the Nepali Congress's chief source of power. As the conflict between the Congress and the SJM intensified (according to Shyam Kumar, the two parties clashed at every public event following Koirala's visit to Libang), the administration detained SJM supporters at the behest of Congress activists. Many of the detained were elected local representatives; they were mostly arrested on cooked-up charges that included murder and theft. Policemen along with Congress activists ransacked entire settlements, harassed women, and confiscated goats and chickens. SJM supporters in custody were often severely beaten, and forced to dip their hands in the blood of a slaugh-tered goat and pledge allegiance to the Nepali Congress. Violent clashes between the political parties continued. In some incidents, individuals from the Nepali Congress as well as Maoists were beaten to death.[53]

Soon after the local elections, Shyam Kumar went to check on friends being held at the prison in Libang. One managed to tell him through a window about the physical abuse they were receiving at the hands of the police. At this, Shyam Kumar went to the police station with some companions and shouted at the officers, protesting against the inhumane treatment. A group of policemen took the aggressive and defiant Shyam Kumar inside for interrogation and he was beaten to the point of uncon-sciousness, as a result of which he permanently lost hearing in one ear. Shyam Kumar and his comrades were locked up in a room so cramped they had to sleep sitting up. The police brought them out at regular inter-vals and beat them. The detainees (among whom was Barsha Man Pun, alias 'Ananta', a SJM cadre who would later rise high in the Maoist party) resolved in the course of long, searching conversations to employ all their strength to bring down the oppressive state authority, which meant to urge – and to drag, if necessary – the party leadership towards armed rebellion. It was then, Shyam Kumar recalls, that 'dreams of guerrilla war began to dance in my mind.' He was released after thirty-three days.[54]

In 1991, the Unity Centre reconfirmed its decision to 'follow the path of People's War with the strategy of encircling the city from the country-side', a strategy 'developed by Comrade Mao.'[55] In subsequent years, while the party's conflict with the Congress and the state authorities was spiral-ling in Rolpa and Rukum, its chiefs were engaged in a vehement dispute over ideology and strategy. A section including Prachanda, Mohan Baidya, Bhattarai and others from the former Mashal wanted to with-draw from legal politics, go underground and launch an armed struggle against the state. Another faction, led by Nirmal Lama and supported by his colleagues from the former Fourth Convention, did not believe that the 'objective conditions' for such a revolt existed yet, and that substantial gains for the *sarvahara* could still be made through participation in open politics. The Unity Centre split in 1994, as did its political front the SJM.

The radical section of the SJM led by Baburam Bhattarai was denied recognition by the Election Commission, and the party decided to boycott the November 1994 mid-term elections. These had been announced by King Birendra following the dissolution of parliament in July of that year, at the behest of Girija Prasad Koirala, whose government had collapsed when it failed to gain majority endorsement in a vote of confidence. Antagonism towards Koirala ran deep that year for several reasons: his stance on Tanakpur, his contemptuous dismissal of the communists and his attempts to undermine rivals within his own party. Prachanda, sensing an opportunity to fuel discord, claimed in an article that the decision to abruptly dissolve parliament and call for fresh elections was a conspiracy by Koirala and the king to perpetuate their 'fascist rule'. Repression had caused such great polarization, he wrote, that the Nepali political sphere was now divided into two camps: 'fascist reactionaries' and 'armed revolutionaries'. Members of Nepal's political class, Prachanda affirmed, had no option but to choose between the two sides.[56]

It is clear that the escalating violence in Rolpa and Rukum played a part in emboldening the party's leaders and pushing them towards a long-term armed struggle against the state. In 1995, the faction of the Unity Centre intent on a protracted People's War decided to rename their party the Communist Party of Nepal (Maoist) and to begin preparations for the revolution. The political report of the meeting that took this decision states:

> The class struggle launched by [politically] conscious peasants in the western hill districts, particularly in Rolpa and Rukum, represents a high level of anti-feudal and anti-imperialist revolutionary struggle. Despite severe reactionary repression and terror, the movement has not only managed to survive, but, in taking a retaliatory form, has made a qualitative advance. This struggle has given birth to a new element in the Nepali communist movement and inspired us to become increasingly serious about undertaking armed struggle.[57]

Preparation for armed struggle obviously required the training of guerrillas and the procurement of arms, but of equal importance was political training for the cadre and rallying the support of the broader population among whom the party was most active. Thus began the Si-Ja campaign, named after the first syllables of the names of two mountains in Rukum and Rolpa: Sisne and Jaljala. Party cadres from all over the country came to learn from the activities in those districts and emulate them when they went back to their own areas. They travelled to villages across Rolpa, Rukum and also the district of Jajarkot, to build roads, toilets and water taps side by side with the locals. Mass meetings were held where party leaders explained that it was necessary to violently confront the 'reactionary' state power, and cultural troupes filled these political messages with emotive force through songs and dances.[58]

The other parties were increasingly perturbed by the Maoists' newly dynamic political activity and by the violence they deployed against their rivals. On 8 October 1995, on the occasion of a local religious festival, the Maoists staged a session of revolutionary song and dance in Rolpa's Gam VDC. This was followed by a violent clash in which over 160 people were injured,[59] most of whom were supporters of the Nepali Congress. According to Shyam Kumar who was present, the Maoists assaulted the Congress supporters after the latter harassed the girls from the Maoist-affiliated Jaljala cultural troupe while they were dancing on stage.[60] Since a large number of Nepali Congress supporters were beaten, and many of the Maoists were outsiders to the district (presumably party cadres who had been brought in for the political campaign), the authorities interpreted the clash as an unprovoked attack for which the Maoists were solely to blame.

At the command of Home Minister Khum Bahadur Khadka from the Nepali Congress, 2,200 policemen descended on Rolpa and Rukum to suppress what the minister called 'anti-monarchy and anti-democracy activities'.[61] They ransacked houses and arrested, according to the police's own estimate, over 300 people ranging in age from twelve to seventy-five. Women were sexually assaulted; many were raped. Men were tortured. Over 6,000 people from Rolpa and Rukum fled to other districts or went into hiding. State brutality was not a new phenomenon for people in these districts, but the scale of Operation Romeo – the government's term for this police action – was unprecedented.[62]

The escalating conflict between the Nepali Congress and the Maoist SJM had penetrated society and was drawing increasing numbers of people into its orbit. In a land dispute, for instance, one party might ingratiate himself with local Nepali Congress leaders to obtain the backing of the local administration. The other, feeling unjustly dispossessed, would then urge SJM cadres to seek redress on his behalf. The Maoists would declare the person who had the Congress's support a 'class enemy' and physically attack him, sometimes even killing him. Even personal conflicts thus grew politicized over a period of time.[63]

Faced with intensified state repression and the brutality of a police force that consisted largely of outsiders, many in the Kham Magar regions of Rolpa and Rukum began to feel that the state (and its Nepali Congress affiliate) was intent on waging war against the resident Magars and Dalits of these districts. Many among the thousands who fled during Operation Romeo joined the Maoists when they returned to their villages. According to a Maoist activist, at a mass meeting in Libang in the aftermath of Operation Romeo the party announced, to an approving audience of 10,000–15,000 people, that it would soon launch a People's War against the state.[64]

On 4 February 1996, Baburam Bhattarai, along with his colleague Pampha Bhusal, visited Prime Minister Sher Bahadur Deuba at his office in Singha Durbar and submitted a letter containing a list of forty demands. From the government's perspective these demands were impossible to fulfil (except perhaps for a few, such as an end to the 'state-sponsored terror' inflicted upon Maoist activists). The Maoists, however, did not expect a compliant response. They had already decided on armed rebellion, and the forty-point list was more of a manifesto outlining their reasons for doing so. Demands included the drafting of a new constitution 'by elected representatives for the establishment of a people's democratic system'; an end to all privileges enjoyed by the royal family; and confiscation of land from 'feudal' landowners and its redistribution to the landless. The nine demands pertaining to 'nationality' were mainly concerned with curtailing Indian dominance over Nepal, via the abrogation of 'all discriminatory treaties' and repeal of the Mahakali Treaty, 'as it is designed to conceal the disastrous Tanakpur Treaty and allows Indian imperialist monopoly over Nepal's water resources.'

'We would like to inform you,' the letter stated in conclusion, 'that if the government gives no positive indications towards this by 17 February 1996, we will be forced to adopt the path of armed struggle against the existing state power.' There would be no 'positive indications' forthcoming from the government. It regarded the Maoists as a fanatical and inconsequential communist group that posed little threat.

# CHAPTER 3

# Blinding the Elephant

## 'When the Enemy Advances, Withdraw'

On 12 February 1996, a group of thirty-six Maoist activists crept up a forested hill near Holeri in Rolpa district. They spent the night and the entire next day in a dilapidated shelter at the summit, trying to avoid the notice of shepherds who came to graze their sheep in the forest. As darkness fell, they gathered their weapons: an assortment of primitive homemade guns and grenades, as well as the only functioning rifle in the Maoists' possession. This rusty .303 was one of the original two rifles that the party had acquired in the late 1980s from Tibetan Khampa rebels.[1] Though by no standards sophisticated, it was considered so indispensable that it was nicknamed 'whole-timer', the term used for the few activists who had committed their lives to the party's cause.[2] The night was pitch-dark, and as the group stealthily descended though thick forest towards the police post, they lost their way. The attack, scheduled to begin at 8 pm, was delayed by two hours.[3]

There were eight policemen stationed in the two-storey building of Holeri police post. The Maoist plan was to catch them unawares as they were having dinner. One group of fighters, led by the raid's main commander Barsha Man Pun 'Ananta', would quietly creep up to the top floor where the policemen slept, and lock the door, trapping whoever had finished their meal and were preparing to go to bed. The others would attack those who were still eating on the ground floor. One of the policemen at the station had shot at the Maoists at a recent local festival. The Maoists would make sure to beat this policeman, before seizing the rifles at the post.

Due to the delay, however, by the time the Maoists got there all the policemen had already gone upstairs to sleep. The rebels surrounded the police post and opened fire. Nanda Kishore Pun 'Pasang', the raid's deputy commander, loudly announced that the *sarvahara* of Nepal had now launched their armed revolt, and urged the policemen to surrender. There was pandemonium in the upper storey of the police station. But instead of surrendering, the policemen fired back from their quarters, and the Maoists were unable to take the building. The firefight lasted for a few hours, until the Maoists, having captured some gelatin and logistical equipment from the ground floor, retreated back to the jungle.

The specific goals of the raid – to punish the policeman and seize the rifles – had thus not been met. Nonetheless, the Maoists claimed the action as a success. They had launched other attacks in different parts of the country on the same day and, collectively, Prachanda announced, these attacks had brought the party closer to its goal to 'establish the politics of armed revolution and initiate the process of making … armed action the principal form of struggle'.[4]

This was not simply an attempt by the party leadership to put a positive gloss on a failed action. The Maoists were well aware of their military weakness; they knew they could not immediately achieve decisive victory over the state's security forces. Their selection of targets for 13 February 1996, the day they launched their rebellion, was hence guided by symbolic considerations.

Besides the attack in Rolpa, the Maoists had also attacked police posts in Rukum and Sindhuli districts. In Sindhuli, they had captured the police position but left the personnel unharmed, as per the instructions of their leaders.[5] In his review of the first year of the People's War, Prachanda wrote that through this humane act the Maoists had shown that they were not 'worshippers of terror', but rather 'creators of a new society where everyone is equal and prosperous'.[6] In Kavre district, Maoist cadres had stormed the house of a landlord-moneylender and burnt the loan documents they found there. This was meant to demonstrate the party's commitment to liberating peasants from feudal oppression. They launched a similar attack in Gorkha district, burning loan documents held at the branch of the Agricultural Development Bank – an act that symbolized an assault on 'the bureaucratic capitalist class, the bastard child of imperialism and feudalism'.[7] In Kathmandu they threw an explosive at the Pepsi factory, representing the class of 'broker capitalists'[8] who, in the Maoist worldview, colluded with foreign capitalists to flood the market with imported goods at the expense of the domestic economy.

According to Mao Zedong's strategy of protracted People's War, the revolutionary party had to first expel the forces of the state from the countryside by the use of violence before establishing their dominance over the population. Between February 1996 and July 2001 the Nepali Maoists developed seven plans in which they outlined their strategies for converting parts of the countryside into base areas. They selected districts where they already had a significant presence, primarily in mid-western Nepal, as well as some areas further to the east.[9] The plan was to gradually expand their presence across the countryside until they encircled the cities and finally took them over by military force.

To this end the rebels needed to create a military force capable of increasingly audacious attacks. In the initial months, small, loosely organized fighting groups (*ladaku dals*), consisting of seven to nine Maoists each, raided police stations, banks and government offices, and confiscated the property of local landowners and politicians from the Nepali Congress and other parliamentary parties. Over time the party planned to form larger platoons and companies capable of handling the logistical and military demands of large-scale attacks, while operating under a centralized chain of command. Meanwhile, the rebels worked to convince the population of the necessity of armed struggle. They printed and distributed posters and pamphlets, painted slogans on walls, and, in areas where the Maoists were strong, assembled the villagers and instructed them in their ideology.[10]

The Maoists had studied guerrilla warfare, primarily the strategies and tactics adopted by the Chinese communists, and they had experienced police repression. Therefore they understood perfectly well that escalating attacks on the state security forces right away would be suicidal. The party leadership explained to its activists that they were in the phase of 'strategic defence' – Mao's term for a situation in which the state security forces are far stronger than the revolutionary party. It was in the state's interest to provoke the party into blind and frenzied encounters with the police. The Maoists would instead lie low, lure police personnel into traps, frustrate and tire them out, and attack only in favourable situations.[11] When chased by the police, they would disperse, taking refuge in remote hamlets, and often too in jungles and caves. As Mao had said,

'When the enemy advances, withdraw; when he stops, harass; when he tires, strike; when he retreats, pursue.' Concerned for their own safety, the top political leadership including Prachanda and Bhattarai, after some months of travel in Nepal's western hills, went to live incognito in North Indian towns close to the border. For much of the next decade they would direct the rebellion in Nepal from Indian soil.

During the early phase of armed rebellion, the Maoists lacked the capacity to launch guerrilla attacks on permanent police positions, and most of the assaults against the state fell under the category of 'defensive actions'. These included sabotaging state-owned buildings and facilities and ambushing police patrols. However, given the Maoist fighters' lack of experience and weapons, even these were difficult to bring off. Most of the ambushes during this stage, launched mostly in Rolpa, Rukum, Jajarkot and Salyan districts, failed entirely.[12] In January 1997, when the rebels attacked a police position in Ramechhap district in the eastern region and managed to capture a paltry four rifles, the party hailed it as a major success.[13]

In fact, it was not until February 1998 that the Maoists of Rolpa were able to capture arms from the police. On that occasion, all of the combatants in the district were mobilized at a place called Nimri. The group waited for three days for the regular police patrol to show up. When the 'signal group' indicated that the police had arrived at the 'killing ground' by raising a white flag, the combatants attacked with mines and homemade guns. They killed two policemen, wounded some others and confiscated two rifles from the patrol.[14]

## Terror against Terror

The government deployed large numbers of police to the epicenter of Maoist activism: Rolpa, Rukum and other mid-western districts, as well as to other districts further east like Sindhuli, where the rebels had a concentrated presence. The police detained hundreds of people on the charge of participating in the rebellion. Reports published by human rights organizations in the late 1990s amply document the kind of treatment they received in custody. Detainees were beaten with bamboo sticks, iron rods and PVC pipes until they lost consciousness, or suffered severe muscle damage or renal failure. Women were assaulted and raped.

Expressing concern over the 'lack of adherence to legislative procedures', Amnesty International reported that none of the ex-detainees it interviewed had received 'warrants at the time of arrest or were presented before a judicial authority within twenty-four hours, as required under the constitution of Nepal'.[15]

Many individuals suspected of being Maoists were taken to a nearby forest or other secluded area and summarily shot. The police claimed that the deaths had occurred in armed clashes, but eyewitness reports indicated that the victims were typically already in police custody and thus defenceless. Often the corpses were not returned to families for cremation, doubtless because they bore the marks of extrajudicial execution.

Officials at the highest levels of the administration casually condoned the methods used to suppress the Maoists. The chief district officer (CDO) of Gorkha district, interviewed in March 1996, opined that since the Maoists 'do not abide by the present constitution, ... the present government is not compelled to [respect] their human rights'.[16] It seems there was a widespread assumption that the Maoist revolt could only be contained by unlawful means. As the CDO of Sindhuli district stated, 'Merely appealing to the law and human rights is not enough to control Maoist activities and provide relief to the people'.[17] And in the words of a deputy inspector general of police in charge of the entire mid-western region: 'Terror must be created to control terrorism'.[18]

These police actions were hardly out of character. Police brutality has long been a fact of life across South Asia. People in the region are often inclined to believe that anyone reportedly killed in an 'encounter' was actually killed when unarmed or in police custody.

The Nepali police force is known to have been modelled after the colonial Indian Police Service, whose purpose was to protect and perpetuate British colonial rule and suppress 'political agitation or agrarian disorder', rather than to protect civilians.[19] To this day the excesses and brutalities of the Indian police are often ascribed to the structures inherited from colonialism. Although Nepal was never directly colonized, this legacy is perhaps even more pronounced in Nepal than in India.

During most of the Panchayat era, at a time when India was trying to consolidate and expand its democracy, a prime concern of the Nepali state elite was to establish the absolutist monarchy and its bureaucratic apparatus as the sole legitimate authority. In districts across the country, the CDO and the police devoted all their energies to stifling any political activity that posed a threat to the regime. In keeping with the Panchayat's centralizing ambitions, the CDO and senior police officers for each district were selected and dispatched from Kathmandu. District officials were ignorant of the local context and had little sympathy for the local inhabitants, particularly in areas with high concentrations of indigenous groups or lower castes. In any case, they were only accountable to their superiors in Kathmandu; how the local population perceived them was of little consequence. The police force also lacked training. In the absence of effective investigative mechanisms, they used torture as a means of extracting confessions that could be used as evidence against the accused in courts.[20] Even after the dawn of multi-party democracy in 1990 laid a new stress on human rights and freedom, the administrative structures of the Panchayat remained more or less intact. Perhaps the only substantial change was that the police and the bureaucracy transferred their loyalties from the monarchy to the newly elected political parties.

'It is characteristic of the reactionary class to harbour the illusion that it can stop the revolution by murdering the people,' Prachanda wrote in 1997. 'But history has proved that [repression] instead fertilizes the revolution and helps it to grow.'[21] However, there were grounds enough for believing that brute suppression might contain and even eradicate the Maoist movement. The Kilo Sierra II operation, for instance, where the government deployed tens of thousands of armed police to twenty districts to crush the revolt after May 1998, caused major losses to the Maoists. At least 200 people, mostly party cadres, were killed during the first two months of the operation.[22] 'At the time we fled like rats scurrying into their holes,' recounted Surul Pun Magar, a Maoist guerrilla from Rolpa.[23] For six months, he said, Maoist activists dispersed to other districts hiding wherever they could, and lost all contact with the party. Over time, however, it became clear that government repression actually increased people's sympathy towards the Maoists, helping to turn the fledgling armed revolt into a raging insurgency. Almost all traveller accounts to the mid-western districts during the conflict describe how mothers, fathers, daughters and sons joined the movement to take vengeance on the police for the murder or enforced disappearance of relatives who had previously joined.

The Maoists worked to channel this hunger for revenge. They probably understood that hatred of the state security forces would not necessarily engender sympathy for the Maoists: this hatred might well extend to the rebel group that had propelled their family members into violent confrontation with the state. The Maoists therefore declared almost every person killed by the police a 'martyr of the revolution', regardless of their relation to the party. By according dignity to suffering families, they hoped to draw them into the orbit of the struggle against the state. Maoist activists also provided support that was more than symbolic. 'Though I have no sons any more,' said a woman from Rukum whose two sons were killed by the police in October 1998, 'the party comrades are cultivating our fields and helping to build a house. Now the party is my son...'[24]

But the Maoists' treatment of the general population was not uniformly benign. They constantly strove to convince the non-aligned that armed revolt was the only cure for the ills of Nepali society, but murder and coercion were equally central to their strategy. Human rights reports from the later part of the 1990s describe numerous incidents in which Maoist activists hacked civilians to death with *khukuris* and hammers, killed captured policemen and inflicted humiliating and degrading punishments.

These killings were intended, in the first instance, to eliminate political rivals from areas where the Maoists had a strong presence. Most of the political activists killed by the Maoists in the early years of the conflict were affiliated to the Nepali Congress. In districts such as Rolpa and Rukum, Congress workers were threatened with death if they did not transfer their allegiance to the Maoists; such warnings were communicated via letters or notices posted on the walls of public buildings. Anyone suspected of having tipped off authorities about the rebels' identities or location was specifically targeted for assassination. In July 1996, for example, Deuchan Basnet, a Nepali Congress member and VDC chairperson in Rukum district, was murdered after he allegedly informed the police about the hideout of several Maoists, leading to their arrest.[25] A few months into their armed movement, the rebels began a campaign called 'Blind the Elephant', in which the huge and lumbering beast was the symbol of the state.[26] The Maoists taught their cadres that although the 'elephant' was still too powerful to be overwhelmed, its 'eyes', or the state's informants at the local level, could be eliminated with relative ease. The police who would come hunting for Maoists would then be as though blind and unable to track them down.

In contrast to the police, the Maoists were aware that indiscriminate murder, torture and abduction would only serve to alienate the population from the party. The various plans circulated by the party leadership to cadres across the country caution against the use of excessive force. During the early stage of the People's War, the party was instructed to 'physically annihilate' only spies and notorious oppressors. The second plan of June 1996 states: 'If we want to attack a bloodsucking feudal at the local level, we must try to win over, or neutralize, others of his own class who harbour enmity towards him and expose his atrocities among the people.'[27] In other words, rivals of the targeted individual should feel safe, at least for the time being, and could afford to take satisfaction in the fall of their rival. Meanwhile, the rest of the population should be convinced of the justice of the Maoists' action.

But with increasing levels of violence, such subtle directives were often disregarded. The cycle of murder and counter-murder took on a life of its own, driven by the intoxicating urge to take revenge and consolidate power. By September 1999 the leadership was warning party members that they were beginning to display an excessively intolerant and anarchic attitude that was 'helping the enemies to become more united rather than increasing the contradictions among them.'[28]

Nonetheless, the combination of propaganda, targeted killings and other forms of punishment inflicted on political rivals did gradually fortify Maoist power. Moreover, by seizing and distributing land and destroying loan records, they won the support of sections of the poorer peasantry. In areas like Rolpa, where the local leaders of all parties mostly belonged to the same ethnic group, the Maoists focused on the difference between themselves and the cadres of the mainstream parties. While the rebels were fighting for the people, they claimed, the rest were working on behalf of the exploitative and repressive state.

As a party that adhered to the dictum that 'political power flows from the barrel of a gun', the Maoists well understood the value of calibrated terror in gaining a population's cooperation. A tea shop owner in a village in Rolpa, for example, told a journalist how the Maoists handcuffed, blindfolded and beat him repeatedly over a period of six months for serving tea to policemen.[29] A man who had only applied for a job in the police force was severely tortured; he fled his village, and, when interviewed by a human rights activist a few weeks later, he still had no sensation in his fingers and right arm.[30] Now that activists of the Nepali

Congress and other political parties were retreating from the villages of Rolpa and Rukum to district capitals and other areas where they would be safe, those who remained learned to support the rebels, or at least to offer them the degree of support required for survival. As the Maoists' grip over the population in these areas became stronger, they became increasingly recognized as a legitimate political authority. And there grew a kind of acceptance – though often grudging – of their political logic and ideology.

## The War in the City

'**P**rioritize work in the villages, but do not abandon work in the cities,' went an early formulation of the Maoists' strategy.

> Prioritize extra-legal struggle, but do not abandon legal struggle. Prioritize war work, but do not abandon open [political] activism. Prioritize military organization, but do not abandon the work of mass organization. Rely on our own organization and force as far as possible, but do not abandon the effort to forge tactical unity [with sympathetic political forces] and win over international public opinion.[31]

And so, while Maoist activists in the mid-west and other rural areas were tasked with building up a military force and progressively gaining control over territory, activists in Kathmandu were responsible for disseminating propaganda and cultivating public opinion.

The party organization in Kathmandu, which had always been weak, became more so after the formal declaration of war against the state. Ganga Bahadur Lama, a member of one of the three Maoist committees responsible for the three districts of the Kathmandu valley, recalls how scores of his friends were rounded up and imprisoned throughout 1996. After his house was repeatedly raided by the police, Lama, along with his party colleagues, had to rent accomodation in scattered locations across the city. The shortage of party funds forced them to find jobs. These efforts at survival consumed most of their energies during the early months of the People's War, and restricted their political work to distributing pamphlets and pasting propaganda posters on walls across the city.[32]

As police repression escalated in the countryside, the Maoists' organization in Kathmandu became increasingly important. It was inevitable that the state would violently retaliate against the Maoist attacks on the police and other authorities. During such periods of retaliation, the Maoists would suspend their armed activities and focus on a 'political assault', in the form of public denunciation of state excesses and attempts to mobilize public opinion. With the government thus put on the defensive, military action would once again be resumed. 'Repeating this dialectical process will gradually expand our influence among the people and weaken the enemy's power', Prachanda observed.[33]

Meanwhile, with the restoration of democracy in 1990, hundreds of political and civil society groups had emerged in Kathmandu, each making extensive demands of the government. Human rights organizations and the media became increasingly active, not least in exposing the brutality with which the government was trying to suppress the Maoists. Kathmandu's fractious democracy thus provided the Maoists with opportunities that would have been inconceivable during the days of absolute monarchy.

In response to the Maoist assault, a coalition government of the RPP and CPN–UML attempted to pass into law the 'Anti-Terrorist and Destructive Crime (Control and Punishment) Act' in 1997.[34] According to the provisions of the draft bill, the police would be given blanket powers to arrest without a warrant, and anyone suspected of acting or planning to bring harm to the country's 'security, law and order, or system of governance' could be detained for up to ninety days. Those suspected of aiding or sheltering 'terrorists' would also be treated as terrorists. Other provisions granted the police the right to 'kill anyone who appears to be fleeing or seeking to flee or is in a situation that prevents arrest'.[35] Successive governments attempted to pass laws with similar provisions in 1998 and 1999.

These draconian provisions echoed the laws used by the Panchayat regime to stifle political dissent in the 1980s. This attempt to resuscitate what were popularly known as the 'black laws' was immediately opposed by a wide range of civil society activists and political parties. A prominent oppositional coalition formed at this time was the Movement to Save Democratic Rights (MSDR).[36] Founded in August 1997, it was led by Padma Ratna Tuladhar, a member of parliament and a long-standing leftist activist. Daman Nath Dhungana, a former speaker of parliament from the Nepali Congress was also a participant, as were many other prominent human rights activists, writers and intellectuals. To pressure the government into rescinding the anti-terrorist legislation, members of the MSDR met with ministers and other leaders of the parliamentary parties, held seminars and protested on the streets. 'This proposed legislation,' stated a declaration by the coalition, 'should be seen as an effort to push Nepali society away from pluralist democracy towards an autocratic police state.'[37]

Having found allies in their 'political assault' on the state, the Maoists sought to penetrate and influence the coalitions' campaign against the 'black laws'. At least one member of the MSDR – Khimlal Devkota – was later to become a full-time Maoist activist. Maoist penetration was deepest, however, in a coalition of nine communist parties that launched its protest around the same time as the MSDR, demanding the rescission of the proposed 'black laws', a moratorium on police action, the investigation of police excesses and the prosecution of those found guilty of murder. Most of these small communist parties believed, like the Maoists, that Nepal's societal ills could only be ameliorated through the establishment of a Maoist New Democratic regime. Unlike the Maoists, however, they felt that the conditions for an armed assault against the state were still not ripe, and therefore they continued to participate in open politics in Kathmandu. One of the nine communist factions in the coalition – the Rastriya Janaandolan Samyojan Samiti (National Mass Movement Coordination Committee), led by Bhakta Bahadur Shrestha and Shakti Lamsal – was, in fact, a Maoist front. Despite their long history of factional infighting and splintering, Nepal's communist parties came from the same milieu and shared extensive links. For this reason, the Maoists had no difficulty entering into the communist coalition that was agitating on the streets.[38]

The police and the parliamentary parties were, of course, suspicious of Bhakta Bahadur Shrestha and his organization, but he publicly disavowed his identity as a Maoist activist and was to some extent protected by his affiliation with other communist parties that operated firmly within the legal system. When he organized a public meeting urging a boycott of the local elections in 1997, the police detained him and many of his colleagues for eighteen days. But some of his friends filed a writ at the Supreme Court, and he was released when the police failed to produce adequate evidence that he was a Maoist.[39]

By this stage the Maoist movement had spread across the hills of Nepal even more rapidly than its leaders had expected, further embold-ening the Maoist activists in Kathmandu. The *banda* (general strike) they organized prior to Shrestha's arrest was just one example. Maoist cadres had been instructed to throw petrol bombs at vehicles plying the streets the evening before the strike, so as to intimidate people into staying at home the next day. Ganga Bahadur Lama waited on the stretch of the Ring Road between Jorpati and Chabahil and threw a homemade bomb at a passing bus. The bus stopped, and several teenage students came out and started chasing him. He fled the scene, jumping over walls and muddy fields, and losing his shoes along the way. After he finally got back to his room, he rested for a while before heading out to a local teashop to eavesdrop on people's reactions to the attack on the bus. The customers were excitedly discussing the incident. One of them said that the Maoist who had hurled the bomb looked frightening. Another exclaimed that he vanished into thin air after the attack. Ganga Bahadur Lama was thrilled to have made such an impact on people's minds.[40]

The anonymity afforded by the city of Kathmandu, with its many recent migrants from other parts of the country, enabled Lama to evade arrest by the police. And it allowed the Shrestha-led Maoist front to participate in legal protests as part of the coalition of the nine communist parties.

In late July 1998, following extensive agitation on the streets, the government invited the nine-party coalition for talks. Bhakta Bahadur Shrestha was appointed leader of the negotiation team. The Koirala gov-ernment eventually agreed to cease pushing the proposed anti-terrorist legislation through parliament, and acknowledged that the government may have been responsible for the use of excessive force that sometimes resulted in the murder of innocents. It also promised to release political detainees – excluding those charged with serious crimes such as murder and arson.[41] Prachanda released a statement asserting that the agreement represented a 'betrayal of the people', as it did not include any provisions to recall the 'government's murder-force' from the villages or to take action against those policemen guilty of breaches of the law.[42] Privately, however, the Maoists considered their activity in Kathmandu to have been successful. A document issued by the Maoist central committee in September 1998 claimed that the party organization in the valley 'has played an important role through both independent action and by forging tactical unity in the struggle against the enemy's repression.'[43]

## The Police Withdraw

On the evening of 18 February 2000, around 250 Maoist activists led by Pasang took shelter at a settlement a few hours' walk from Ghartigaun village in Rolpa district. The following night they were to gather up their weapons and walk to Ghartigaun to attack one of the more strongly fortified police positions in Rolpa. This three-storey building housed sixty-one police constables, their leader Inspector Shriram Acharya and the assistant CDO. The force was responsible for operations throughout western Rolpa, and its environs were considered to be a stronghold of the Nepali Congress.[44]

The police at Ghartigaun had recently killed eleven Maoist activists at their military training camp. According to Pasang, the forthcoming attack was meant to avenge those killings. It was also thought necessary because the Maoists had not carried out a successful raid on a police position since 2 May 1999. This, the rebels believed, had sown 'pessimism among the people and confusion among the cadre.'[45] And yet the attack showed that the guerrillas' capabilities had grown tremendously over the past three years. Only a few years before, they would not have had the confidence to raid such a formidable police outpost.

The guerrilla force that was to attack Ghartigaun included a number of individuals who had participated in the 1996 attack in Holeri. The commander of that first raid, Ananta, was the political commissar on this occasion, and the then vice-commander, Pasang, was now the commander. But this time their force was eight times larger and far better organized than the one at Holeri. It was comprised of eighteen assault groups of four combatants each, assigned to surround the police position; two groups of eight assigned to surround another police position an hour away from Ghartigaun (to prevent the arrival of reinforcements); three groups of six to serve as backup units; and one group of ten to provide medical treatment to the wounded.

Back in 1996 the rebels had spent the night before the attack in a forest, taking pains to hide not just from the security forces but also from the locals. Now, they felt secure enough to spend the night in village homes only a few hours' walk from the target. The rebels had also mustered a significant number of people from across the district, around 250 in Pasang's estimate, to accompany the Maoist force during its raid. Some of these locals may have freely volunteered, others may have been persuaded, and yet others were undoubtedly coerced. The Maoist plan was to capture and destroy the police position, and then to loot a state-owned granary in Ghartigaun. The locals were to take rice sacks from the granary for distribution in the villages.[46]

At 6 pm on the evening of 19 February, the Maoist fighting force stood in formation at the place where they had taken shelter the previous night. After taking a roll call, Pasang the commander and Ananta the commissar delivered their final speeches. The force then set off towards Ghartigaun. They paused after an hour and a half, waiting for a scout who had gone ahead to reconnoitre. The scout returned at 11:30 with news that everything was going as planned, and there was no sign that the police were prepared for the assault. The force advanced after midnight. There was a full moon and the combatants had to move stealthily, crouching and crawling all the way.

Having surrounded the police position, the Maoists opened fire at around 1 am. Groups of Maoist sympathizers had gathered on the slopes around Ghartigaun, waiting for the raid to begin. As soon as the firing started they raised their flaming torches, shouting slogans and playing traditional horn instruments. The police fired back. Amid the chaos, some guerrillas approached the police office and set off a mine on its roof. The explosion made a hole through which the locals who had come to plunder the granary hurled blazing dry grass and maize stalks into the building.[47] When the roof collapsed and the Maoists began throwing grenades, the policemen, having fought for two hours, surrendered.

At least fifteen policemen, including Inspector Sriram Acharya, were killed in the attack; twenty-eight were wounded. The Maoists captured the station's .303 rifles, pistols, revolvers, ammunition, logistical equipment and communication sets. The granary was ransacked and the locals made off with sacks of rice as planned. One Maoist fighter was shot dead in the confrontation, and another was injured. It was dawn by the time the Maoists retreated northwards. At a confluence of two rivers, where party activists were waiting to receive them, they wrapped the body of their dead comrade in the party's flag and performed his last rites. After eating, the group distributed the seized weapons and dispersed to various areas of Rolpa and Rukum.

A few days later, on 22 February, thirty policemen arrived in Khara, in Rukum, where they believed the guerrillas that had attacked Ghartigaun were hiding. They burned down houses and killed over fifteen people,

including a number of Nepali Congress supporters.[48] But this act of vengeance did not ultimately serve much purpose. By then the police force in
the villages of the mid-western hills was thoroughly demoralized, and had
already begun vacating many of its stations. The attack on Ghartigaun
had revealed that even relatively well-fortified positions were vulnerable,
and so police offices were shut in Rolpa, Rukum, Salyan and Jajarkot districts. By mid-2000, only eight of the thirty-nine original police stations
in Rolpa remained, and in Rukum, the numbers came down from twenty-
three to six. As one newspaper reported, 'Earlier the police ruled by day
and the Maoists by night. No longer so. Now Maoists roam through
villages in broad daylight.'[49] The CDO of Rukum told the reporter that
police personnel only went into the villages when locals had specifically
requested their help. Even then, 'they go by helicopter and come back as
soon as their work is over.'[50] The withdrawal of the police left local government employees and members of parties such as the Nepali Congress
even more vulnerable, forcing most of them to leave their villages.

## Parliamentary Disarray

Although protests by civil society groups and the coalition of
communist parties prevented the passage of anti-terrorist legislation, they were unsuccessful in ending the violent suppression of the
Maoists in the countryside. The G. P. Koirala government largely ignored
the agreement it had reached with the nine parties, and continued its
extensive anti-Maoist operation – Kilo Sierra II – for over eight months.
(There was a decline in the number of killings by the police the following year, from 328 in 1999 to 180 in 2000.[51] This, however, probably
responded more to the weakening and demoralization of the police force
in Maoist-affected areas than to a shift in government policy.) The communist coalition took to the streets again, demanding implementation of
the agreement, but their protests were ineffectual. In any case, the government at the time was embattled with demands from other more powerful
oppositional groups, primarily the UML, which though nominally communist was not part of the coalition of the minor communist factions.

The animosity between parliamentary parties had intensified after
the 1994 elections, in which the UML won the highest number of seats
but was unable to gain a majority. The UML led a minority government

for nine months, after which it was voted out by a majority in parliament and replaced by a government that included the Congress and the RPP. Thus began the era of coalition politics. From then on, the chief task of the parliamentary opposition was to undermine and replace the government. To that end the opposition would vehemently denounce all the actions of the government, try to dissuade coalition partners from supporting it and cultivate powerful interest groups, including the monarchy and the Indian establishment. When out of power, the UML treated the Maoist problem as one among many issues that could be used to castigate the government. In its November 1998 protests against the Congress-led government, for instance, the UML demanded a halt to 'state terror' against the Maoists, corruption, price hikes and the politicization of the bureaucracy.[52] In the five-year period between the 1994 and 1999 elections, no less than seven coalitions came into and were ejected from power.

As the efforts of all the parliamentary parties were focused on breaking alliances and forming new ones, it was natural that governance suffered, as did the attempt to contain and neutralize the Maoists. As the human rights organization INSEC pointed out in a report, the lack of cooperation between the political parties in government and in opposition was a major reason behind the failure to contain the armed movement. While in opposition, the parties 'claim that the Maoists present a political problem and try to protect [the rebels].' Once in power, however, 'they accuse the Maoists of violent and criminal activity and seek to crush them with force.'[53] The state was paralysed by the friction among parliamentary parties. And this, more than the Maoists' attempts to 'politically attack' the government, was what had boosted the power of the insurgents.

## Exploiting Contradictions

In September 2000, 566 Maoist guerrillas, once again commanded by Pasang, trekked for days across perilous mountain passes from Maikot in Rukum towards Dunai, the capital of Dolpa, a remote mountainous district that borders Tibet. Army personnel at the barracks in Dunai noticed their movement and, suspecting an attack, the chief district officer of Dolpa, Parsuram Aryal, requested reinforcements from Kathmandu. A forty-eight-strong police contingent was flown into

Dunai on 23 September.[54] Local spies informed the Maoists that they had been spotted. This made the Maoists hesitate, but they decided they had invested too much in the preparations to back off now. On 24 September, in the small hours of the morning, they launched a ferocious attack on the political and administrative centre of Dolpa.

Fourteen policemen were killed and forty-one wounded during the six-hour battle. The Maoists managed to take over the police positions, the local government offices and the jail. They forced the manager of the Nepal Bank branch to open its vaults, and removed Rs 50 million in cash and gold and silver deposits.[55] According to Pasang's account, they retreated at around 6 am, carrying their sick and wounded comrades. Two died on the way. They arrived at their camp at 5 pm, hungry and exhausted, and then counted the seized weapons, ammunition and cash. They left the gold and silver with the Dolpa district committee of the party, to be distributed to the local population for repayment of their loans. The next day the contingent dispersed, making their way back to the adjacent Jajarkot and Rukum districts.[56]

All Maoist attacks prior to this had occurred in villages some distance from the district capitals. Dunai, however, was itself a district capital: one of the seventy-five administrative nerve centres of Nepal. Therefore the news of its defeat and temporary occupation was received with shock in Kathmandu. The recriminations were intense, with the opposition UML and Sher Bahadur Deuba, Girija Prasad Koirala's arch-rival in the Nepali Congress, deriding the government for incompetence and demanding its immediate resignation. The government, on the other hand, directed its ire against the army. Home Minister Govinda Raj Joshi, among other Congress leaders, accused the Royal Nepal Army (RNA) of refusing to come to help the police, even though the government had purportedly appealed for its assistance after hearing an attack was imminent; and this despite the fact that an RNA company (130–150 personnel) was stationed at a barracks an easy forty-minute walk from Dunai bazaar.[57] A few days later Joshi was forced to resign, along with Inspector General of Police Achyut Krishna Kharel and the top bureaucrat at the home ministry, Padma Prasad Pokharel.

In a diary entry dated 26 September, the military secretary at the palace, Vivek Shah, who was responsible for communication between the king and the army, noted that Prime Minister Girija Prasad Koirala had decided to demand the resignation of these three individuals for their failure to provide adequate security at Dunai. Shah adds that the army, stung by their criticism, had been lobbying for their dismissal.[58] In any case, it was widely believed that the home minister, home secretary and police chief were forced to resign less for their failure at Dunai than for causing displeasure to the palace and the army. The belligerent statement Joshi issued on 29 September, the day of his resignation, strengthened this perception. In it he once again condemned the RNA for simply standing by while the Maoists massacred the policemen. He also recalled that although the government had given funds to the army for training the police and providing them with sophisticated weapons, the RNA had refused the task.[59]

In their defence, army officials claimed that the home ministry had not 'formally' called for help, and besides the army company was unable to come to the police's rescue as the Maoists had destroyed a bridge on the route from the barracks to Dunai bazaar. There is some evidence from the Maoist side to buttress this claim: Pasang states that the Maoists had planned to prevent the army from joining the battle.[60] This was in line with the strategy the Maoists had been scrupulously following: to strike the weaker enemy while taking care not to provoke the stronger. In 2000, for instance, even as they were inflicting immense damage on the police, the Maoists had allowed the military to build a road in their heartland of Salyan and Rukum, thus enabling it to earn points with the local population.[61]

According to Pasang, during the raid on Dunai, a guerrilla contingent was indeed deployed on the banks of the Bheri River to destroy the bridge that led to the army barracks. The army fired at the rebels, but stopped after the Maoists fired back and cautioned them against a confrontation. Other sources, however, such as the former army brigadier-general Keshar Bhandari, claim that no such skirmish took place; that the army, lacking orders from military headquarters to undertake any action, simply stood by as the Maoists devastated Dunai.[62] Even if Pasang's account is true, it indicates that the army had no intention of coming to the rescue of the police; any weapon fire was purely in self-defence, and the soldiers remained quiescent throughout the six-hour-long attack on the police positions. The account also suggests that despite having prior knowledge of the Maoist assault, the army made no effort to defend the bridge that was just a few minutes away and which constituted its only link to the nearest town.[63]

More significantly, the debacle at Dunai marked the beginning of a period in which the historical tensions between the elected government on one side, and the palace and the army on the other, would erupt into open conflict. These tensions, which dated back to the 1950s, had been only partially and half-heartedly overcome in the 1990 political settlement.

The RNA traced its ancestry to the fighting force organized by King Prithvi Narayan Shah, a direct ancestor of Birendra, in the mid-eighteenth century. Under Prithvi Narayan's leadership, the force captured numerous small principalities and consolidated them into the territory that is modern-day Nepal. Over the next two centuries, the army came to form the backbone of the state. Its upper ranks were drawn almost entirely from the few courtier families of the Thakuri caste – to which the monarch also belonged – that constituted Nepal's aristocracy. In 1960 King Mahendra used the army to arrest B. P. Koirala and other elected political leaders of the Nepali Congress before instituting the partyless Panchayat regime. Over subsequent years, Mahendra cultivated the army as a crucial tool of power, according it privileges and trying to modernize it while making sure that it did not emerge as an independent political force.[64]

Even after the popular uprising of 1990 demonstrated that absolute monarchy no longer enjoyed widespread legitimacy, the military remained staunchly loyal to that institution. Top army generals tried hard to ensure that the balance of power reflected in the 1990 constitution tipped in favour of the palace. They pressed the Constitution Recommendation Committee to advise that both the army and the police remain under the direct control of the monarch.[65] However, amid the democratic fervour sweeping the country, this was not a sustainable position. The police was brought under the control of elected governments, but the provisions for the army were more ambiguous. Article 118 of the 1990 constitution provided that the king could operate and mobilize the army 'on the recommendation of the National Security Council' (NSC), a three-member body comprising the prime minister, the defence minister and the army chief.[66] The next clause states: 'His Majesty is the Supreme Commander of the Royal Nepal Army.'[67]

These provisions could be interpreted to mean that the elected government had total control over the army, in keeping with the precedents set by European constitutional monarchies. Two of the three members of the NSC were, after all, elected to office. The king's position as 'Supreme Commander' could be construed as being purely titular and his decisions as mere rubber stamps, based on the Council's recommendations. But the time-honoured relations between the palace and the army were still intact in the 1990s. The king continued to control top-level appointments and promotions in accordance with the Army Act of 1959.[68] Similarly, army chiefs continued to be more loyal to the monarch than to the government. To justify this, they invoked another law from 1969 that states: 'The Commander-in-Chief is responsible to His Majesty rather than to the government.'[69] Throughout the era of constitutional monarchy, political commentators described the defence ministry as a 'post office', responsible only for transmitting messages between the army headquarters and the military secretariat at the palace. The army's traditional hostility towards the parliamentary parties continued. As late as 2001, the RNA still had not accepted the legitimacy of the historic struggle for democracy led by the Nepali Congress; according to an RNA publication from that year, the Nepali Congress's aborted attempt at armed struggle following the royal coup of 1960 was the work of 'anti-national elements'.[70]

Girija Prasad Koirala had run into problems with the RNA even before the attack on Dunai, when he had started exploring the possibility of deploying it to fight the rebels. The army leadership, backed by the palace, had informed him that the government must fulfil a number of preconditions for that to happen. First, any decision to deploy must be taken through the three-member NSC and ratified by the king, 'in accordance with constitutional provisions'; second, all political parties in both the government and the opposition must reach unanimous agreement on deployment; and third, the Maoists must be declared a terrorist force, all their sister organizations banned, an anti-terrorist act promulgated and a state of emergency imposed in the Maoist-affected districts where mobilization was to take place.[71]

These stipulations reflected the army's mistrust of the political parties – a feeling that increased through the 1990s as it witnessed the instability caused by the constant inter-party wrangling. In their struggles for power, army officials maintained, Nepal's politicians showed a total lack of concern for the larger national interest. By insisting that the NSC, which included the army chief, take the decisions regarding the security sector, the RNA sought to establish greater authority over political decisions affecting the institution. They wanted unanimity on deployment so as to ensure that the army did not get implicated in the political games between the government and the opposition.[72]

But the army's stipulations were difficult for the government to follow. The fractious political climate made it virtually impossible to reach all-party consensus on deployment and to impose a state of emergency. G. P. Koirala and others in the Congress also believed that taking the decision through the NSC would allow the army, and through it the palace, to wield inordinate influence on government policy. The provision for the NSC had in fact been inserted into the constitution as a result of a compromise between the parliamentary parties and the palace.[73] The parliamentary parties had never become entirely reconciled to this provision, believing that in a democratic system, elected representatives in the Council of Ministers should have sole authority over the military.[74]

In 1968, after eight years' imprisonment in an army camp, the Congress leader B. P. Koirala had written: 'The palace guard [and by implication the entire RNA] is the greatest reactionary force in the country. It has only served authoritarianism by oppressing the people.'[75] He warned that the Congress government had blundered in not attempting to bring the army under civilian control, and that 'due to this mistake all our efforts and successes [were] rendered useless'.[76] B. P.'s remark more or less encapsulated the Nepali Congress's unofficial position on the army.

But Girija Prasad Koirala, once he became prime minister, failed to heed his late brother's warning. Either because he was consumed by other political conflicts, or because he was worried about the repercussions of trying to wrest control of the army, G. P. Koirala did not devote much attention to this matter. Rather, he focused on consolidating control over the bureaucracy and the police, filling these bodies with loyalists. Koirala responded to the growth of the Maoist movement by allocating tremendous resources to the police: between 1990 and 2000, the police budget was increased by 800 per cent.[77] Meanwhile, he continued to believe, as many in the Congress do to this day, that the palace and the army had at least tacitly encouraged the spread of the Maoist rebellion, in hopes that it would damage the parliamentary order and enable a reassertion of royalist power.[78]

Once the fiasco in Dunai had made it clear that the police force could not contain the insurgency, G. P. Koirala embarked on fresh efforts to involve the army. Resistance continued, however, with the army chief

Prajwal Shamsher Rana holding fast to the preconditions he had previously set for the government. Rana stated that he would rather deploy the army as part of its own Internal Security and Development Plan (ISDP) than as a fighting force to take on the Maoists. According to the plan, the army would provide security to implement a Rs 400 million scheme to build roads and carry out other development activities in Maoist-affected districts. On 11 April 2000 a meeting was held at the palace to discuss this possibility; participants included the prime minister and a number of his cabinet colleagues, the king, the army chief, and the heads of other security agencies. It was decided that the ISDP would be immediately implemented in Gorkha and later in Rukum, Rolpa, Jajarkot and Pyuthan.[79] 'It was hoped,' wrote the palace military secretary Vivek Shah, 'that this would somewhat improve the relations between the government and the army.'[80]

But it was not to be. A week after the meeting at the palace, on 20 April, Army Chief Prajwal Shamsher made a speech that implicitly blamed the political parties for the 'deterioration of human values and institutions.'[81] The RNA, he stated, would deploy as part of the ISDP only if all parties were firmly and unanimously committed to the plan. The prime minister was, of course, dismayed by the army's public defiance of the government. He was also put on the spot by the army chief's new stipulation, as the UML, which was in opposition, had opposed the ISDP. According to the diaries of Vivek Shah, Prime Minister Koirala summoned the army chief for consultations on 15 May. Prajwal Shamsher instead sent a deputy with orders not to make any commitments to the prime minister, merely informing him that the ISDP had been initiated in Gorkha but not in other districts and demanding that the NSC ratify its mandate.[82]

It was in this context of a bitter struggle between the government and the army, and increasing demoralization of the police, that the Maoists launched their second attack on Holeri. Since the first, failed attack in 1996, the police had substantially increased their presence in that location while withdrawing from other areas across Rolpa. But on 11 July 2001, an 800-strong Maoist force completely overran the Holeri police position. Taken by surprise, the police put up feeble resistance before surrendering. The guerrillas, again led by the Maoist commander Pasang, held around seventy officers hostage and took them to nearby Nuwagaun, where they spent the night.

An already embattled G. P. Koirala recognized that the debacle at Holeri could further undermine the government. Soon after news of the incident reached Kathmandu, on 12 July, he met the army chief and instructed him to organize a rescue mission. On 13 July, the RNA flew three helicopters to Nuwagaun. The Maoists reportedly fired at the helicopters as they took off after depositing a contingent of soldiers who were apparently startled to discover that they had landed in the midst of hundreds of Maoist guerrillas. Nevertheless, news came back that despite difficulties and bad weather, the soldiers had surrounded the Maoist force. In the following days, broadcasts on the state-run Radio Nepal claimed the military had sent in reinforcements and tightened its encirclement of the rebels. The army, reports said, though quite capable of inflicting great damage on the rebels, was under 'tremendous pressure to exercise restraint'. It was working to secure the release of the policemen and disarm the Maoists while ensuring that casualties were kept to a minimum.[83]

This was the version given out by the army and disseminated through the media. The Maoists' statements declared precisely the opposite: it was the rebels who had surrounded the army contingent. 'Since journalists have not been allowed in,' concluded a news report, 'most Nepalis must choose between the official account of a disciplined army trying to avoid casualties and the Maoists' account that the army is at their mercy and has been advised to desert.'[84] The media in Kathmandu, unfamiliar with the rebels and accustomed to regarding them with suspicion, chose the former.

In reality, the army was facing major problems. In his diary entry dated 15 July, the palace military secretary Vivek Shah noted that all three helicopters had been grounded at the barracks in Dang district after the Maoists fired at them. The contingent that had managed to land in Nuwagaun was surrounded and under attack by the rebels. The soldiers, far from rescuing the policemen, were themselves in need of rescue. For this purpose the RNA had deployed a fresh company from nearby Salyan district, which, however, seems to have never arrived at Nuwagaon. The diary entry of the following day records that Shah explained the situation to the new Gyanendra, king who had ascended to the throne only the previous month, telling him that the action had failed because of poor and hasty planning and a lack of communication between the local military commander and headquarters. The army had decided to abandon the operation, and Shah advised the king that the utmost secrecy would have to be maintained while recalling the contingent, as they risked severe criticism from the parties and the public if it came to light.[85]

Shah's diaries thus suggest that Pasang's account, despite its potential omissions and embellishments, contains more than a grain of truth. Pasang claims the guerrillas were astonished when they saw three military helicopters hovering in the sky above Nuwagaun. They couldn't conceive that the army would come after them. After shooting at the helicopters, Pasang says, the guerrillas surrounded the army contingent and sent in a messenger with a note that read, 'We do not currently have a policy to attack you [the army]. Why are you here? If you have come to fight, we will be forced to fight back. We have completely encircled you. There is no chance of escape.'[86] Ananta, the Maoist political commissar for the battle, claims that the soldiers demanded the release of the police as a precondition for negotiation, but when this was refused, they agreed to send two unarmed personnel to negotiate with two of the rebels.[87] This detail is not mentioned by Pasang, but his description of the negotiations is consonant with Ananta's. The RNA spokesmen apparently told the rebels that they did not intend to fight them, and requested leave to depart. The rebels then pulled back, and 'they went their way, and we went ours.'[88]

At all events, when a group of human rights activists from Kathmandu arrived at Nuwagaun a few days later to help negotiate the 'stand-off' between the army and the guerrillas, they were surprised to discover that both the army contingent and the Maoist force that had raided the police station at Holeri had vanished; only a few dozen members of the Maoist militia were still about.[89]

It seems that Girija Prasad Koirala was not informed of the details of the military operation. He interpreted the failure of the army to engage the Maoists and rescue the policemen as a clear sign of insubordination by the RNA leadership. The seventy-eight-year-old prime minister tendered his resignation on 20 July 2001. Dunai had been repeated, he claimed: the army had refused to follow his orders once again.

The army bridled at this accusation. It blamed the elected government for thrusting it too abruptly into the conflict, making it impossible to formulate and implement an adequate strategy. The prime minister's order to intervene at Holeri had besides been unconstitutional, the army claimed, for it was not issued through a decision of the National Security Council or ratified by the king. For years afterward, the army nursed a grievance against the Nepali Congress, which it held responsible for its having been 'defamed on account of the Holeri incident.'[90]

During the early phase of the conflict, the Maoist leadership had instructed its cadre: 'We have to ... exploit the contradictions between the enemies in a conscious manner, assaulting only one enemy at a time, trying in the meantime to immobilize another.'[91] By assaulting only the police and avoiding engagement with the army, the Maoists indicated that their principal enemy at that time was the Nepali Congress and the parliamentary system, not the monarchy. The top rebel leadership had also established covert links with the palace. As Prachanda disclosed many years later, 'Birendra's youngest brother Dhirendra was in touch with us and we were to start direct talks with [the king].'[92]

The Maoists had even initiated preliminary talks with Dhirendra regarding future power-sharing arrangements. The palace was pleased that the Maoists were undermining the political parties and confident that the army would swiftly be able to bring the rebels under control if required.[93] The Maoists' tactic of avoiding confrontation with the army lulled the palace into complacency, and raised suspicions in the Nepali Congress that the palace was abetting the rebels. Violent attacks on the police continued, deepening the resentment between civil and military authorities. The fundamental contradictions papered over in the 1990 constitution were gradually being exposed. By 2001, it was evident that the rebels had succeeded in exploiting these rifts to their advantage.

CHAPTER 4

# The State at War

## A New King in Charge

A few weeks before the debacle at Holeri, the state faced another major crisis. On 1 June 2001, King Birendra and his entire immediate family, as well as five other royal relatives, were murdered during a dinner party at Narayanhiti Palace. Gyanendra, Birendra's sole surviving brother, ascended the throne, and at his behest a probe commission conducted an investigation into the massacre. The investigation report identified Crown Prince Dipendra as the perpetrator. He had for some time been angry with his parents for not letting him marry the woman of his choice. At the gathering of the royal family on 1 June, he had got drunk on whisky and was taken to his room by his sister and brother. He then smoked a cigarette filled with marijuana and an 'unknown black substance', and talked to his girlfriend on the phone. Around 9 pm he changed into battle fatigues, picked up two rifles and a revolver which he apparently always kept at his bedside, and walked into the hall where his family was having dinner. He shot both his parents, his two siblings, and eight other relatives, only three of whom survived. Dipendra then shot himself, and went into a coma for four days before he died.[1]

Both in temperament and public perception, the new king Gyanendra was very different from his deceased brother. Birendra had been groomed for the crown from childhood, and attended Eton and Harvard. In contrast, Gyanendra's education had not taken him far afield: he had completed secondary school in the Indian hill town of Darjeeling, and taken a degree at Kathmandu's Tribhuvan University. During the 1990 uprising, Birendra was popularly viewed as a king of liberal disposition, with a degree of sympathy for the demands of the protestors. Gyanendra was thought to be a member of the palace's hard-line 'underground clique' (*bhumigat giroha*) that opposed all democratic reform. Where Birendra was relaxed and convivial around his subjects, Gyanendra was stiff and unsmiling.

Though enjoying relative popularity when he was alive, Birendra's image further improved after his death: he was often recalled as a wise and benevolent monarch who supported the new democratic structures and accepted his own diminished role. This was partly due to the widespread sympathy aroused by the horrific circumstances of the massacre, as well as the public disillusionment with the poor performance of Nepal's elected leaders. In reality, Birendra was weak and enabled those within the palace who wanted to use the situation with the Maoists as part of a campaign to derail the fledgling democratic system. Nonetheless, he was generally seen as standing above the fray.

In contrast, Gyanendra and his family were widely disliked. In August 2000, Gyanendra's son Paras, notorious for his dissolute lifestyle, had run over and killed a popular musician while driving home late at night, presumably after a session of heavy drinking. The incident received wide media coverage and provoked a wave of public revulsion. Later, there was suspicion when he acceded to the throne under such dramatic circumstances. In the initial days following the massacre of the royal family, the authorities seemed somewhat tight-lipped, providing only hazy details of the incident. The investigation was hastily conducted and failed to answer important questions. How credible was it that the inebriated prince, who could barely walk to his room, could find the strength to carry those heavy guns and accurately kill so many people? Why was Gyanendra absent from the gathering? Why had his wife and son been spared, when all of Birendra's family had been mowed down? The shoddiness of the investigation fuelled all kinds of rumours. A large swathe of the public rejected the official version of events, and thought that Gyanendra had conspired to murder his brother's family in order to usurp the throne.[2]

Gyanendra thus became king in circumstances that were far from propitious. And yet he soon made it clear that he sought a much greater role in state affairs than his brother. As noted by an article from September 2001, 'The king [has been releasing] assertive press statements, making himself and Queen Komal more visible in the public eye, and subtly rebuilding the image of a battered monarchy.' King Gyanendra had reportedly told a journalist: 'Unlike my brother, I cannot just sit and watch the country and the people slide into [such a terrible] situation.'[3]

Narayanhiti Palace was notoriously secretive. To get a sense of what was going on there, journalists often had to rely on gossip, speculation and the enigmatic statements issued by its officials. Therefore, although it was evident that King Gyanendra was much more hands-on than his brother, the nature of his influence over elected political leaders and his ultimate intentions were not so clear. Much of what happened at the palace in the immediate aftermath of the royal massacre remains shrouded in mystery. However, in 2010, ten years after that fateful incident, the chief military secretary at the palace, Vivek Shah, published his diaries.[4]

Shah's diaries shed important light on the mood inside Narayanhiti and the king's political goals between April 2000 and November 2003. They reveal that the palace viewed the political party leaders as venal, corrupt men whose power struggles had wrecked the state's institutions and undermined national sovereignty. As early as 2000, the palace firmly believed that the parties were incapable of achieving unity of purpose or the will to tackle the growing Maoist threat. In its view, the police had been hopelessly undermined by political interference, and only two institutions – the monarchy and the army – had avoided being manipulated and preserved their integrity. The palace interpreted the public disillusionment with the parliamentary parties as a call for the king to assume a directly political role. On 27 July 2000, when Birendra was still king, Shah wrote in his diary: 'There is discussion in the palace about the monarchy's role in a situation where the parties have been unable to establish good governance ... There should be public discussions on how the palace can act in the people's interest without coming into direct conflict with the political parties.'[5] Even amid such pressure, Birendra was hesitant to take on a directly political role.

By contrast, Gyanendra seemed intent on assuming greater powers almost as soon as he became king. This required stealth and cunning; otherwise it would be clear that the king was trying to grasp executive power and undermine the constitution. 'An elephant shows its tusks but hides its chewing teeth,' Gyanendra told Shah, referring to a well-known

Nepali proverb. 'Likewise, the palace must project itself as a highly democratic institution while secretly carrying out its strategy.'[6]

The chosen instrument of Gyanendra's strategy was Sher Bahadur Deuba, Koirala's chief rival within the Nepali Congress. Throughout 2000 and 2001, Deuba had tried to establish himself – in opposition to Girija Prasad, who had tried to suppress the rebels by force – as a leader who could solve the Maoist problem through negotiations. While Koirala was still prime minister, Deuba had established contact with Maoist leaders. But these preliminary overtures did not lead to any tangible outcome. Deuba believed that Girija Prasad had sabotaged his efforts. Driven by resentment of Koirala, Deuba then apparently turned to the king. As Shah observed at the time, 'As far as I understand, the king thinks he can easily influence Sher Bahadur.'[7]

After Koirala resigned, the king instructed the heads of all security agencies to use every means at their disposal to help Deuba become prime minister. As soon as success was in sight, Gyanendra had the same agencies monitor his actions closely. The king wanted to assess Deuba's views on the monarchy before giving him his clinching support.[8]

Deuba's pledge to achieve a settlement with the Maoists earned him the backing of the palace as well as of a substantial section of his own party. Even the opposition UML favoured his approach. As soon as he came into power in July, he declared a ceasefire. The Maoists too suspended hostilities, and some of their leaders arrived in Kathmandu for talks. But there was little common ground between the two sides, and during the negotiation period it became increasingly clear that no solution was forthcoming. On 21 November, Prachanda issued a statement: 'Our bid to establish peace has been rendered unsuccessful by reactionary and fascist forces.'[9] Two days later, the Maoists launched a series of attacks, most notably on a military position in Ghorahi, Dang, where they killed fourteen military personnel and seven policemen. And on 25 November, the guerrillas attacked Salleri, the headquarters of Solukhumbu district in eastern Nepal, where thirty-four people, including eleven soldiers, were killed.[10]

The increasing number and audacity of Maoist attacks, the dismantling of governmental structures in the countryside and the rebels' expanding reach and power had given rise to a siege mentality among Kathmandu's bourgeoisie. On top of that the royal massacre had plunged the country into a state of national calamity. Now, even the short reprieve offered by the ceasefire and peace negotiations was over. Through their attack on the barracks in Dang, the ragtag bunch of guerrillas had challenged the ultimate bastion of national security, the Royal Nepal Army.

Finally the Deuba government decided to take some drastic steps: deploy the army against the Maoists, declare a state of emergency, and pass anti-terrorist legislation, officially branding the Maoists terrorists. Needless to say, these measures severely curtailed the constitutional freedoms that the parliamentary parties had struggled so long to win. But the recent events had alarmed the politicians and opinion makers of Kathmandu to such an extent they saw no alternative. An editorial in the *Nepali Times* stated, 'Let us be perfectly clear about this: the Maoists brought this on themselves. While there may have been a few other options, it is clear why the elected government decided to declare a state of national emergency.'[11]

A majority in parliament hence ratified the state of emergency and passed the Terrorist and Disruptive Activities (Control and Punishment) Bill in April. But as the months passed, it became clear that the Royal Nepal Army, so reputed for their valour and discipline, was nowhere close to containing the rebellion. This gave rise to another wave of discontent and divergent opinions. The state of emergency would lapse in six months, and its extension would need endorsement by parliament in May 2002. At the direction of the army and the palace, Sher Bahadur Deuba made it his mission to secure the cooperation of both his party and the opposition in extending the emergency, but this time they were in no mood to comply. Chafing under the restrictions, the UML claimed that a state of emergency was not necessary to mobilize the army. Girija Prasad Koirala accused Deuba of aiding a palace conspiracy to undermine democratic institutions. He decided that their party would not endorse the emergency extension, and began a campaign to unseat Deuba.

Meanwhile, unbeknownst to the public, the king was preparing to exploit the divisions between the government and the parties. Vivek Shah's diaries mention that in late February, Gyanendra told the army chief to offer Deuba clear-cut advice on how to resolve the political stalemate: dissolve parliament and announce fresh elections. The army chief was also to assure the prime minister that the army would do all it could to ensure his electoral victory.[12]

On the night of 22 May 2002, an embattled Sher Bahadur Deuba went to the palace. Due to Koirala's relentless campaign against him, he had failed to secure the parliament's approval for extending the state of emergency, and after a long conversation with the king, he decided to immediately dissolve parliament. Palace officials including Vivek Shah drafted the letter that Deuba submitted to Gyanendra, recommending that the king, in his capacity as head of state, announce the dissolution of parliament. Deuba's council of ministers was not informed of the decision. The royal astrologer was summoned to advise on the most auspicious hour to make the announcement and at 11 pm the king declared that parliament had been dissolved and that fresh elections would be held in November.[13] Two days later the prime minister issued an ordinance extending the state of emergency. Girija Prasad Koirala, who was still president of the Nepali Congress, then expelled Deuba from the party; Deuba gathered his loyalists and announced the formation of another party, the Nepali Congress (Democratic).

In August, the five-year tenure of elected local governments came to an end. Again at the king's instigation, Deuba decided not to renew their terms. Fresh elections to these bodies were of course impossible in such a political environment. The dissolution of parliament and local governments had left no avenue for citizen participation in the political process: the prime minister and his government became accountable solely to the palace.

Wholly alienated from his original party, Deuba understood that his political credibility could only be salvaged by ensuring timely elections. But two months before the set date, the Maoists staged two major attacks. The first took place in the capital of Arghakhanchi district, where seventy-four security personnel were killed. The other was on a police post in Sindhuli. The surprising scale of the attacks forced Deuba to reconsider his decision to hold elections and in early October he advised the king to postpone them until the following year.

On 4 October, King Gyanendra made another proclamation. Since Sher Bahadur Deuba proved 'incapable' of holding elections, the king had decided to relieve him of his post as prime minister and dissolve the council of ministers. Indefinitely postponing the scheduled elections, he had resolved to take over the executive power himself. He announced that he had to do so in order 'to save nationalism, national unity and sovereignty [and] to establish peace and security in the country', citing Article 127 of the 1990 constitution as the source of legitimacy for this action. The vaguely worded Article appeared to ascribe some emergency powers to the king.[14] The following week he appointed Lokendra Bahadur Chand, a Panchayat-era politician who was eager to ingratiate himself with the monarch, to the vacant position of prime minister. The institutions of democracy had been dismantled. It had taken the new king only seventeen months from the time he ascended the throne to wield ultimate power.

The state of emergency provided a rationale for curtailing the basic rights and freedoms of citizens. The freedoms of speech, peaceful assembly, movement and residence, as well as the right to information and privacy, were suspended.[15] The army and the other security agencies were granted substantial powers to search, detain and use 'necessary force' against those suspected of 'terrorist' activity. The Terrorist and Disruptive Activities Act granted blanket immunity to the security forces, even for grave human rights violations. 'Any act or work performed or attempted to be performed … in good faith' would be exempt from legal action.[16] In some districts, the army and police were ordered to shoot on sight anyone breaking a curfew. In such a situation, even the most excessive or arbitrary act might be said to be performed in 'good faith.' Amnesty International wrote to the prime minister, expressing its concern: 'This appears to give official sanction to the security forces to commit extrajudicial executions.'[17]

Over the following years the Royal Nepal Army occupied a prominent role in national life. For over a decade the army had seethed at its neglect by elected leaders, whom it saw as a bunch of feckless politicians. Those leaders had finally been replaced by a council of ministers who lacked a popular base and were wholly subservient to the king. The RNA felt it could now launch a sweeping campaign against the rebels without having to deal with the nuisance of political parties, the media and human rights defenders. The defence budget increased from Rs 3.8 billion in 2000 to 8 billion by 2004. Recruitment into the RNA began on a massive scale: the numbers of personnel rose from 47,000 in 2001 to around 96,000 in 2005.[18]

'Militarization is not merely the increased presence of armed forces in the public sphere,' wrote the political analyst Hari Roka. 'It is the comprehensive reorientation of national energies and resources to the prosecution of war.'[19] Not only were funds meant for development or social services channelled to the security forces, but the entire nation, including political and civil-society leaders and the media, was expected to act in total compliance with the army and assist it whole-heartedly in its counterinsurgency operations. The army demanded absolute loyalty. Army Chief Prajwal Shamsher Rana openly fulminated against the political parties that he said were playing 'a selfish game of factionalism' rather than supporting the army for the sake of 'national security'.[20]

The political parties were thus expected to remain mute spectators while King Gyanendra brushed them aside and brought down demo-cratic institutions. The media was expected to only cover news in support of the army's campaign against the Maoists. Editors were asked not to publish any Maoist statements, or report on military excesses and set-backs faced by the army in their fight against the rebels. They were also required to 'fact-check' their reports, pictures and commentary with the army before publication.[21] Soon after the emergency was declared, the army started to harass and detain journalists. 'In a situation where sol-diers of the Royal Nepalese Army are putting their lives on the line in the service of the nation,' said the army chief, 'it is natural to expect you [journalists] to bring out the facts and help raise the morale of the army.' He also warned that false and misleading reports, no matter how trivial, could damage the 'trust and confidence that we have earned from the Nepali people.'[22]

Army mobilization coincided with the aftermath of the September 11 attack on the Twin Towers, providing an opportune moment to request the United States for military hardware and training for Nepal's own 'war on terror'. Although the threat to the Nepali state was Maoism, not political Islam, the army tried to draw an analogy between the two movements: both adhered to obsolete ideologies, it argued, indiscrimi-nately terrorized the population, and sought to destroy the foundation of civilized governance.

This campaign was skilfully carried out and reaped substantial div-idends. When the US secretary of state Colin Powell visited Nepal in January 2002, he was fêted at military headquarters, and came away impressed. 'You have a Maoist insurgency that's trying to overthrow the government,' he told Nepali journalists, 'and this really is the kind of thing that we are fighting against throughout the world.'[23] Over the fol-lowing years the US sent materiel such as M-16 rifles and night vision equipment, as well as military advisors to Nepal. Between early 2002 and early 2005, the US provided military assistance worth Rs 1,716 million (US$22 million).[24] US ambassadors to Nepal – Michael Malinowski till 2004, followed by James Moriarty – consorted openly with army generals and frequently visited barracks, thus contributing to the undermining of civilian government. The American administration held the view that only a joint effort by the palace and the army could crush the Maoist rebellion, and it urged the political parties to support them. Other countries with influence in Nepal, chiefly India and the UK, seemed somewhat ambivalent about a regime that had become increasingly undemocratic, but faced with the threat of a raging communist rebellion, they too provided the RNA with arms and ammunition, vehicles and money to buy helicopters and spotter planes.

In this manner, while King Gyanendra gradually consolidated his power, the Royal Nepal Army pursued its goals through systematic subjugation of the entire Nepali polity. The state of emergency lapsed in August 2002, but the dominance of the army continued. Not content with the powers granted by the anti-terrorist legislation, the RNA proposed a Unified Military Command, whereby all the security agencies including the police would be brought under its direct command. This would allow for a more coherent war plan, according to the RNA. In November 2003, the prime minister announced the establishment of the Unified Command structure, which encompassed all state organs concerned with political, economic, informational and diplomatic affairs.[25] 'The Unified Command,' wrote Hari Roka, 'is just a more dignified name for military rule.'[26]

The army and palace claimed that once the Maoists had been dealt a decisive blow and forced to come to the negotiating table and join peaceful politics, elections would be held and state power would be handed back to the political parties. But there were signs that the army regarded its heightened power, not simply as a means to defeat the rebels, but as an end in itself. In August 2004, for instance, the RNA wrested permission from the government to independently invest its funds in business ventures both inside and outside the country. This directly counteracted a previous government's decision to bar the RNA from establishing a bank and business enterprises in 2001.[27] A return to civilian rule would entail curbs on the army, and it appeared doubtful that the RNA would willingly cede total power to civilian authorities, even if the Maoist rebellion were brought under control.

Military officials frequently claimed that they were entirely committed to the principles of democracy, and that the goal of their campaign was to defend those principles. But any such claim was belied by their constant vilification of the democratic parties and by the occasional public utterance of the top army brass. A month before Gyanendra sacked Sher Bahadur Deuba, General Rookmangud Katawal, using the pseudonym Ajay P. Nath, had published an article in the state-owned daily, *Rising Nepal*. 'In many Third World countries,' he claimed, 'a political concept is being developed which feels [*sic*] that an enlightened despotism is preferable to chaotic democracy: the masses require protection from themselves.'[28]

It was clear as day that the army had a political mission which it considered far more important than the defence of democracy: the preservation and elevation of the institution of the monarchy. Addressing a batch of graduate officer cadets at the May 2004 convocation ceremony, Chief of Army Pyar Jung Thapa said:

> The Crown is the symbol of our identity, and the kingship is the progenitor and guardian of the Royal Nepal Army [as well as] the unalterable symbol of Nepali nationalism and national unity. The faith, devotion and the trust of the people towards the Crown have remained the essence of Nepali nationalism since time immemorial. All Nepalis should therefore be united to work towards preserving the symbol of our identity along with the fundamentals of our national interest.[29]

The army's ultimate goal, then, was to consolidate power through the campaign against the Maoists and restore the monarchy's supreme position in Nepali society and politics. It was hoped that under the tutelage of an all-powerful monarchy, the army would once again enjoy a highly privileged position.

## War and Negotiation

In February 2001, the Maoists held their Second National Convention in the town of Bhatinda, in the Indian state of Punjab. According to their assessment, they had entered a phase of 'strategic equilibrium' vis-à-vis the state, where neither side could score a decisive victory over the other.

While emphasizing the need to expand their military force, the Maoists also recognized the limits of what could be accomplished through military force alone. Given the concentration of political, economic and military power in Kathmandu, it would be impossible to launch a 'decisive military strike' on the capital, even if the entire countryside were brought under Maoist control. It was hence necessary to 'fuse the strategies of armed insurrection into the protracted People's War.'[30] In practice, this meant that if they were to overthrow the regime, the Maoists had to instigate a mass uprising in the cities similar to the people's movement of 1990.

The Maoists knew the masses would not rise simply to help them seize state power and so decided to also put forward a broader political agenda. They proposed a conference that would bring together all national forces, including the Maoists, subsequent to which elections would be held and a new constitution crafted under the leadership of the elected government.[31]

Although initially shocked by the royal massacre, Maoist leaders soon realized that they could exploit the crisis to their advantage. The target of their attacks shifted from the parliamentary parties to the monarchy. Less than a week after the massacre, the Maoist leader Baburam Bhattarai published an article in Nepal's largest-selling daily, *Kantipur*. He wrote that on the instigation of the Indian intelligence agency, the Research and Analysis Wing (RAW), the new king had plotted the murder of his brother Birendra as part of a broader Indian scheme to annex Nepal. Gyanendra should be denied popular legitimacy, and the army should 'join hands with patriotic Nepalis born in small huts across the country [the Maoists] instead of joining hands with the puppet in the palace controlled by expansionist forces.'[32] Bhattarai's article received widespread public notoriety, but failed to provoke a popular reaction against the new monarch.

The Maoists refined their rhetoric against the monarchy as Gyanendra consolidated his power over the state. Bhattarai claimed that nothing in the constitution allowed the monarch to take a decision unless recommended by the council of ministers, and therefore the king's decision to dismiss Sher Bahadur Deuba and assume executive powers in October 2002 was unconstitutional. 'There should be no illusion that this is not a royal coup,' Bhattarai asserted.[33] The event had also exposed the flaws of the 1990 constitution, in which sovereignty (*sarvabhaumsatta*) was vested in the people but 'state authority' (*rajakiya satta*) rested in the person of the monarch.[34] The monarchy was thus technically above the constitution. It was this loophole that had allowed Gyanendra to exercise extra-constitutional powers and dismiss the prime minister.[35]

The time had now come, said Bhattarai, for the parliamentary parties to unite with the Maoists against the monarchy. Together they could uproot that bastion of feudalism with all its privileges, once and for all. Bhattarai, along with other Maoist leaders, fleshed out the proposal for an interim government and a new constitution. He argued that the hollow nature of the 1990s democracy had been exposed because even after the advent of the multi-party system, the privileged castes maintained their control over the state and the historically oppressed classes and nationalities (the Maoists' favoured term for caste and ethnic groups) were severely underrepresented. A new political contract to govern Nepali society was overdue.[36]

The Maoist leaders secretly met Nepali Congress and UML leaders in Indian towns near the border. Prachanda and Bhattarai urged them to accept a proposal for a round-table conference that would include all of Nepal's political parties and 'democratic, patriotic and leftist forces'[37] in order to draft an interim constitution. An interim government would then be formed and elections held for a Constituent Assembly, encompassing all political forces as well as representatives of 'various classes, nationalities, regions, genders and communities'[38]. The new constitution drafted by such an elected body would establish a deeper democracy than that which had existed through the 1990s. The country would also become a republic. The Maoist leaders did their best to allay the fears of the parliamentary parties regarding the ultimate Maoist goal: they explained that the new regime would guarantee all the rights and freedoms that exist in a liberal democracy, and all parties would be free to organize and compete, the Maoists being just one among them.

Thus the Maoists revived the old dream of a Constituent Assembly, a dream that had arisen in the 1950s and briefly flickered during the 1990 uprising as a demand of some obscure communist factions. Within the Maoist party, this meant that the minority view regarding Nepal's history and the Maoists' role in it – the view held by Baburam Bhattarai and his supporters – had prevailed as the official doctrine of the party. If the Maoists were to take this strategy seriously, not as a short-term ruse to deceive other political forces, they had to accept the fight against feudalism as the fundamental political struggle in Nepal. Meanwhile, their own revolt would be a successful culmination of all the partially successful anti-monarchy and pro-democracy movements of the past half-century, starting with the struggle led by the Nepali Congress in the 1940s.

For Bhattarai, the Maoists' acceptance of multi-party competition was a political necessity. The experience of twentieth-century communist regimes had shown how one-party states could turn into oppressive dictatorships. He believed, therefore, that Marxists of the twenty-first century had to incorporate certain aspects of liberal democracy into their model of state.

The more orthodox Maoist leaders harboured misgivings about the new strategy, even as their colleagues sought to convince other parties of its relevance. Officially, the party maintained that the monarchy and the parliamentary groups were equally harmful to Nepali society. The former was the guardian of the oppressive feudal order; the latter, as demonstrated in the 1990s, had allowed Indian 'expansionists' to increase their political and economic control over Nepal. It was of course necessary to form the occasional tactical alliance with one against the other. But the strategy of the Constituent Assembly seemed to permanently privilege the parliamentary parties over the monarchy, so that the Maoists' energies would be directed entirely against feudalism at the expense of their struggle for national autonomy.[39] In addition, leaders such as Mohan Baidya, C. P. Gajurel and Ram Bahadur Thapa 'Badal' treated the 'nationalism question' as the greater priority, and as such were keener to join forces with the monarch to bring down the parliamentary parties. In July 2001, at a Maoist politburo meeting in Sonipat, a town in the Indian state of Haryana, Baidya and Gajurel attacked Bhattarai for publishing his article in *Kantipur* without giving them prior notice. They insisted that it was not yet time to redirect their energies against the monarchy.[40]

However, the Maoists did not have a better strategy for political negotiation. According to their party's official doctrine, 'true communist policy ... should tactically concentrate the struggle against the force that has seized state power and has been directly exploiting and suppressing the people.'[41] As Bhattarai and Prachanda argued, the initial phase of the war had been directed against the Nepali Congress and the other parliamentary parties that were in power. Now that the king had taken control, the struggle had to be turned against him. Leaders such as Baidya and

Gajurel were not happy with the shift, but they could not prevent it. In any case, they believed it was only a temporary phase. They thought that once the monarch had been suitably dealt with, the party would resume its struggle against the political parties until the Maoists seized state power. As an internal party document from 2003 put it: 'We can never have ideological and political relations with either monarchical or parliamentary groups except to manage contradictions in a particular situation.'[42]

The first time the Maoists conferred with the government on their new agenda was during the 2001 truce, when Sher Bahadur Deuba was prime minister. But the negotiations had floundered and were followed by a year of bloody fighting between the rebels and the RNA. Soon after Gyanendra sacked Deuba and appointed Lokendra Bahadur Chand as prime minister, the king made overtures to the Maoist leadership through emissaries, most notably Narayan Singh Pun, a former army colonel and minister in the Chand government. The rebels agreed to a ceasefire and negotiations in late January 2003 and in return, the government lifted the terrorist label from them.

By March the two sides had agreed on a code of conduct for ceasefire. The rebels committed to desist from all forms of violence and coercion; the government promised to release political detainees and allow the Maoists free movement.[43] The rebels subsequently announced the composition of their negotiating team, which included senior Maoists such as Baburam Bhattarai, Ram Bahadur Thapa and Krishna Bahadur Mahara.

Ever since the war began, the people of Kathmandu had known these rebel leaders only from their public statements and old pictures. Now all at once they were at the centre of the public eye. Baburam Bhattarai could be heard on radio and seen in newspapers and on television, looking like an archetypal Leninist revolutionary with his beard and glasses. He and his colleagues addressed mass rallies in major towns across the country. In the capital, they participated in smaller events along with civil society members. Bhattarai reached out to diplomatic representatives from influential countries and met all those who were willing to entertain him. He visited the drawing rooms of many parliamentary politicians, regardless of their place on the political spectrum. Everywhere he conveyed the same message: 'The Maoists are genuinely committed to finding a peaceful resolution to the conflict.' However, the only peace terms they could accept were a round-table conference, the formation of an interim government and elections to a Constituent Assembly. At times he said that the Maoist rebels should lead the interim government. In other conversations, he reassured the parliamentary leaders that a Constituent Assembly would do them no harm; it would merely abolish the monarchy and bring the army under civilian control.[44]

Most of the leaders of the parliamentary parties were suspicious of the Maoists' new proposal. After all, for over half a decade their cadre had been targets of Maoist attacks, killings and evictions. In their view, the Maoists had undermined democratic institutions and created the conditions for the monarchical resurgence. Further, the Maoists had come to negotiate with a government that was controlled by the palace. The ceasefire had been brokered secretly between palace representatives and the rebels, leaving the parliamentary parties in the dark. Nepali Congress and UML leaders suspected that the king and the Maoists had made a secret power-sharing deal that would permanently sideline the mainstream parties. 'At a time when the king seems to be trying to consolidate his position,' said a member of the Nepali Congress, 'we suspect a Constituent Assembly could just be a trap to do away with the 1990 constitution.'[45] The 1990 constitution embodied the gains made by the Nepali Congress and the UML during their long struggle against the monarchy. These parties regarded the document as a political contract that legitimized their position in the political order. By taking over executive power, the king had already once undermined the contract. Now the Maoists, too, seemed intent on destroying the basis of parliamentary legitimacy by proposing a new constitution.

Therefore, what Nepali Congress President Girija Prasad Koirala demanded instead was the restoration of the last parliament, which had been elected in 1999 but dissolved by King Gyanendra in 2001. Caught between the palace and the Maoists, five major parliamentary parties including the Congress and the UML managed for once to forge an alliance. They brought their student wings and other sister organizations out into the streets of Kathmandu and other towns to hold noisy protests, claiming that the government had no purview to negotiate with the rebels. No negotiations could be carried out, they argued, until the major parliamentary parties were allowed to lead the government and the dissolved parliament reinstated. There was no need for a Constituent Assembly. Gyanendra had only to hand power back to the parties to be assured a permanent place as constitutional monarch. However, some of the Maoists' goals, such as bringing the army under complete civilian control, could be considered in the future.

Just as the parliamentary parties could not accept the Maoist demand for a Constituent Assembly, so the Maoists could not accept the parties' demand for reinstatement of parliament. 'The 1990 constitution and the parliamentary system it put in place are dead,' Baburam Bhattarai proclaimed. 'It is now impossible to revive them.'[46] The truth was that the rift between the palace and the parties benefited the rebels. The firmer the king's grip on power and the more he antagonized the parliamentary parties, the greater the Maoists' chances of rallying support for their agenda. So when Narayan Singh Pun, the king's emissary, floated the idea of replacing the Chand government with one that included the major parliamentary parties, the Maoists strongly objected and threatened to go back to war if that happened.[47] They well understood that such an arrangement would bring the monarch and the parties closer at the expense of the Maoists.

Meanwhile, King Gyanendra, ensconced on his throne and acting only through emissaries, stood opposed to the demands of both the Maoists and the parliamentary parties. Two days after the declaration of the ceasefire, he told Vivek Shah that any dialogue with the Maoists should be focused only on the 'humanitarian' aspects of the conflict, and the role and constraints of each side during the ceasefire. The political issues related to the Maoists' core demands should be addressed only at the end.[48]

In a dispatch to Washington, US Ambassador Malinowski wrote: 'The government reasons that prolonging the ceasefire will build up an internal momentum and popular expectations of peace that will make it exceedingly difficult for the Maoists to mobilize their rank and file for a return to violence.'[49] In drawing out negotiations for as long as possible, the king hoped to keep the Maoists engaged while undermining their strength in the countryside by reestablishing governance, restoring infrastructure, and cajoling Maoist activists away from the party with incentives such as food-for-work programmes.[50] The army was dispatched to the Maoist heartland in the mid-western hills to set up health camps for the local population. Baburam Bhattarai sternly protested that this was a violation of the ceasefire code of conduct. How would the government react, he asked, if armed Maoist guerrillas in combat uniform came to Kathmandu to set up health camps in front of Singha Durbar and Khula Manch?[51]

While these negotiations dragged on, the king was also making efforts to shore up his power by appealing to leaders of the parliamentary parties. Prime Minister Lokendra Bahadur Chand met the leaders and tried to persuade them to join his government. The parties rejected his overtures. They feared that joining such a government would simply legitimize the regime without giving them influence over its decisions. They said they would not stop their protests or join government unless Chand was replaced as prime minster by UML leader Madhav Kumar Nepal.

For the king, that would mean relinquishing the power he had accumulated over the past two years and he had no intention of allowing that. It was only to secure broader support for his regime that he had been reaching out to the parties. As Shah's diaries indicate, the palace realized that for all their faults, the parliamentary party organizations had deep roots in society. This was not the case for RPP, the party of the royalist old guard to which Prime Minister Lokendra Bahadur Chand belonged. To secure legitimacy for his regime, the monarch thus desired some support from the Nepali Congress and the UML.

Having failed to convince the top leadership of these parties, the palace hoped to persuade at least some of the middle-ranking leaders to support the king. Following a technique already honed by his father Mahendra during the Panchayat regime, Gyanendra instructed Shah to 'penetrate the parties and weaken them from within.'[52] Palace representatives met several Nepali Congress and UML leaders who were considered susceptible enough to quit their parties and support the monarchy in exchange for monetary and other incentives. 'We could effectively create an alternative power base,' wrote Shah in a diary entry dated 16 April 2003, 'if we could bring together leaders with a popular base and nationalist beliefs, such as Bamdev Gautam and Radhakrishna Mainali [of the UML], and Bijay Kumar Gacchhedar and Shailaja Acharya [of the Nepali Congress].'[53]

The Maoists found the negotiations with the government to be frustratingly slow. During the first round of talks held at Hotel Shankar on 27 April, the rebels presented their political proposals to the negotiating team led by Narayan Singh Pun. But, according to the king's wishes, the government refused to address the rebels' core demands. A few days later

Bhattarai complained at a public rally: 'The old establishment should stop playing tricks from behind the curtains ... The king should attend the talks.'[54] Krishna Bahadur Mahara and Ram Bahadur Thapa, the two Maoist leaders assigned to hold private parleys with Gyanendra's emissaries, repeatedly requested Narayan Singh Pun to arrange a meeting with Gyanendra. On 30 April, Vivek Shah met the two Maoists to get a sense of what they wanted to say to the king. Ram Bahadur Thapa sounded conciliatory compared to Bhattarai: while he still demanded elections to a Constituent Assembly, he concealed the Maoist ambition to abolish the monarchy. He told Shah that the Maoists wanted the king to remain as guardian of the political order, even after the elections.[55]

Gyanendra remained behind the scenes to cast himself as a neutral arbiter and protector of the best interests of the country. The Maoists wanted to make him a direct party to the talks so that he would be forced to make his position clear. 'We will not meet the Maoists,' he told Vivek Shah, 'unless they openly commit to accepting the constitutional monarchy and multi-party democracy.'[56] There were indications that Gyanendra had become ambivalent about the ceasefire and the negotiations. He was perturbed by reports of talks between the Maoists and the parliamentary party leaders and knew that the rebels had been appealing for public support and railing against the monarchy in mass meetings.

Thus, each of the three actors was suspicious of an alliance that did not include them. While the Nepali Congress and the UML feared the links between the rebels and the palace emissaries, the Maoists tried to prevent reconciliation between the king and the parliamentary parties. The king, for his part, was alarmed by the potential alliance between the rebels and the parliamentary parties.

The turning point in the palace's attitude towards the negotiations appears to have come in early May. Following the second round of negotiations at the Hotel Shankar, Krishna Bahadur Mahara announced – at a press conference attended by government emissaries – that the two sides had agreed to restrict the movement of the Royal Nepal Army to a radius of five kilometres from their barracks. The army promptly complained that the Chand government and the Pun-led Maoist negotiating team had agreed to this stipulation without their knowledge, adding that they would not accept such restriction on their movement.

Lokendra Bahadur Chand soon resigned, presumably under pressure from the king, who faulted the government for failing to secure wider support for his regime and the negotiating team for failing to control the Maoists' aggressive appeal to public opinion. There were fleeting rumours that the king would appoint the UML's Madhav Nepal as prime minister. Instead, he appointed Surya Bahadur Thapa, another old stalwart from the Panchayat era. He also dissolved the negotiating team led by Narayan Singh Pun and formed a new one that included Prakash Chandra Lohani and Kamal Thapa. According to a 'diplomatic observer' interviewed by the International Crisis Group, 'the new negotiators saw the confidence-building measures established under Prime Minister Chand as "one-sided" concessions where the Maoists got away with murder.'[57] The new team was geared to take a much harder line against the Maoists.

The negotiations made no headway, and it appeared that the Maoists were getting ready to go back to war. But the new government reiterated its commitment to the ceasefire and persuaded Maoist leaders to sit down for a third round of negotiations, which began on 17 August in Nepalgunj, a town close to the Maoist heartland in the mid-western region. For the first time the government's negotiating team offered a detailed response to the Maoists' political proposal. It sought to address some of the Maoist concerns, such as greater representation of marginalized groups in the state structure. But the idea of a Constituent Assembly was rejected. Instead the government proposed to organize a round-table conference of all parties, including the Maoists, and to hold elections to a House of Representatives. Select amendments could then be made to the 1990 constitution.

The government's proposal paid lip service to the principles of multi-party democracy. It stated that the government would be led by the political parties, and the king would exist solely as a constitutional monarch. But the war settlement process it laid out implied that the king would retain substantial authority. For one, the proposed conference of all parties would be convened under his aegis. If the Maoists and the parliamentary parties agreed to the proposal, the king and his government would receive the credit for ending the civil war. Gyanendra's official position in the new political order would be the same as, if not higher than, the one granted by the 1990 constitution. The government's negotiators had made it clear that the position of the monarchy was non-negotiable, no matter what amendments were made to the constitution.[58] In addition, the government demanded that the Maoists hand over the arms and ammunition in their possession 'in order to create an environ-ment for implementing the outcomes of the negotiations'.[59] The position of the Royal Nepal Army in the new state structure was left unaddressed. It would presumably continue to remain completely beholden to the monarch.

The Maoists rejected these terms. The members of their negotiating team went back into hiding in India. On 27 August, Prachanda issued a statement:

> The way the establishment presented its concept paper not only ignored existing, fundamental problems, but also appeared to hatch a conspiracy to strengthen the feudalistic retrogression of October 4 [2002] with sweet toffees of reform. The concept paper ... virtually finished the relevance of the talks by asking us to politically surrender by laying down our arms. ... Our Party wants to make it clear that the relevance of the cease-fire, the code of conduct, and the peace process with the old regime has ended.

Thus, after protracted and futile negotiations, the country seemed poised to return to civil war. In Kathmandu, there was much handwringing in the wake of the breakdown of negotiations. The international commu-nity largely blamed the Maoists. The American ambassador, in a cable to Washington, described their behaviour during the negotiation process as so inflexible as to 'border on the farcical'.[60] Even the International Crisis Group, which had a more nuanced understanding of the negotiation dynamics, criticized Baburam Bhattarai for lacking an understanding of compromise.[61]

What was not recognized was that there was little incentive for the Maoists to accept the terms on offer. A resolution adopted by the party's central committee in June 2003 warned against 'left adventurism', the intransigent tendency among some in the party to place too great an emphasis on military methods and view the 'ceasefire and negotiation as unnecessary and irrelevant'.[62] For the rebels, agreeing to hold negotia-tions at all was already a sign of flexibility. The same document warned against the 'right capitulationalist deviation' that viewed 'negotiations as a process of reaching a compromise at all costs instead of ... as another front on which to fight the enemy.'[63] While preparing for negotiations, the Maoists had decided that they could accept nothing less than elections to a Constituent Assembly. They could agree to a negotiated settlement only if it boosted their power and caused significant damage to the position of the monarchy.

In any case, the Maoists did make some gains during the seven-month ceasefire. Largely left alone by the army, they expanded and strengthened their military organization. And their relentless efforts to reach out to the public earned them wide recognition – both in Nepal and internationally – as a formidable rebel force with noteworthy political demands.

## The Prosecution of War

The Maoists might have continued the talks a little longer, had the Royal Nepal Army not launched a sudden operation in blatant violation of the ceasefire agreement and international humanitarian law. On 17 August 2003, a group of unarmed Maoists gathered at a schoolteacher's house in Doramba village in Ramechhap district. They were there to hold a meeting of the local area committee, and also to celebrate the wedding of two of their comrades. The next morning, a group of around eighty army personnel, presumably acting on a tip-off, arrived in Doramba on foot, made their way to the schoolteacher's house and surrounded it on three sides. Some of the Maoist cadres tried to flee, but the soldiers fired on them, killing one. Army personnel then entered the house, took the seventeen Maoists and two civilians – the owner of the house and his son – outside and tied their hands behind their backs. The detainees were made to walk for three hours until they reached a relatively isolated spot. The soldiers then lined them up, shot them dead, and dumped their bodies over a cliff.[64]

Prachanda took this incident as a deliberate provocation and ten days later announced the Maoists' withdrawal from the negotiation process. 'The massacre of nineteen people carried out by the Royal Army in Doramba', he said, was 'a virtual declaration that the peace talks had broken up.'

As shocking as the violence was at Doramba, the army's behaviour was by no means unprecedented. Human rights organizations had earlier come out with detailed reports of army excesses such as the extrajudicial executions of Maoist suspects in custody (allegedly killed in armed 'encounters'). An investigation carried out by the National Human Rights Commission brought the details of the Doramba massacre to light. The report caused a stir in Kathmandu, and led to a shift in the attitude of the international community. For once, it was recognized that the state's prosecution of war was grievously flawed. It was also widely assumed, despite the RNA's denial, that the army had carried out the attack in a deliberate and premeditated attempt to sabotage peace negotiations. 'Although the RNA has attributed exclusive responsibility to the major in command,' wrote the International Crisis Group, 'it is clear his actions were sanctioned by superiors: if he had really been a rogue operative sabotaging a sincere effort at talks his punishment would have been swift and harsh.'[65]

When the Royal Nepal Army was deployed against the Maoists in late 2001, it spread across the country, establishing outposts in the capitals of all seventy-five districts, securing urban and easily accessible terrain. Troops from the barracks regularly patrolled peripheral areas, seeking to weed out Maoists and destroy their organization.

This is typically how state forces everywhere have dealt with guerrillas, whose weak military power forces them to hide in remote villages and jungles and wait for a chance to catch their enemy off guard before they strike. Like most troops trained in conventional warfare, the Royal Nepal Army faced myriad problems when forced to fight irregular war – the absence of clear front lines, the difficulty of distinguishing rebels from civilians, inadequate government presence in the countryside, and a tough and tricky terrain with which the rebels were more familiar.

Faced with these challenges, the Royal Nepal Army made mistakes that are common in counter-insurgency. Nervous troops patrolling unknown territory often opened fire at the slightest suspicion, elicited by any movement or activity. Soon after the government declared a state of emergency in 2001, a large contingent of soldiers entered Nakhar village in Rukum district, looking for Maoists.[66] On the way they came across four young girls of the Kami (blacksmith) caste who took fright and ran away. The soldiers shot at them, thinking only Maoists would flee from the army. One of them, seventeen-year-old Pharki Kamini, was wounded and fell to the ground. One of the soldiers then shot her dead, apparently to put her out of her misery. Human rights defenders and anthropologists have provided many other instances of accidental killings by the army. In a village in the central hills, a deaf-mute man was shot dead while running away from soldiers, and a woman was killed while cutting grass for her buffalo in a forest.[67] In February 2004, a group of youngsters were collecting donations from travelers on the Muglin-Naryanghat highway when soldiers shot at them without warning, killing three.[68]

Some Maoist combatants from Rolpa claim that in certain respects the army was easier to evade than the police.[69] Before the Maoists ejected them from the countryside, police units functioned as part of the local government and were more integrated in the local context than the army. Police personnel were almost as familiar with the local topography and community as were the rebels. Unencumbered by the rules and strategic doctrine governing the army, they often used the same tactics as the guerrillas, of deceit and camouflage, and could pursue Maoist suspects deep into villages. What ultimately let them down was their lack of modern weaponry. As a Maoist combatant pointed out, the batons and single-loading rifles used by the police were not much more effective than the locally made guns used by the rebels.[70]

On the other hand, the Royal Nepal Army, which possessed far more sophisticated weaponry, had far less knowledge of the areas they patrolled. By the time the army was deployed in the countryside, the rebels had displaced most of the state institutions that might have provided military intelligence. According to a Maoist commander, army patrols in the remoter areas fumbled along 'as though blind.'[71] When the army did manage to apprehend rebels, they punished them brutally, resorting to severe torture if not summary execution. But the Maoists often received information about army patrols and fled villages before troops could get there, leaving the locals to bear the brunt of the army's ire.

An incident in early 2002 illustrates the pattern of violence endured by civilians during the war.[72] In a village in the hills of central Nepal, some Maoists killed an army officer. When troops came to the village in search of the culprits, they rounded up people of all ages and beat them with their rifles. A few days later, the army received information that the rebels responsible for the assassination were hiding in a house in a nearby village. But when the army reached the house, the Maoists had already left. The soldiers then shot and killed the family's newly-wed daughter and her husband, who worked in Saudi Arabia and was home on holiday.

Trained in conventional war theory, the RNA thought that their task was to gradually expand control over territory and erode their enemy's will to fight by inflicting maximum damage.[73] Many accounts suggest that the army often measured its success by the number of enemy casualties. This was no doubt a primary reason why it repeatedly failed to distinguish between Maoists and civilians who offered the rebels shelter and support, either out of genuine sympathy or out of fear. Tasked with collecting as many enemy scalps as possible, the army would detain rebel suspects on the flimsiest evidence, often acquired through the torture of unaffiliated villagers.

In some cases, the state security forces targeted particular communities for their supposed ties with the Maoists. These were usually the most marginalized sections of the population. In Bardiya district, for instance, army personnel would go to villages, enter homes and take individuals thought to be Maoists away with them. Hundreds of people were detained in this manner, often in army barracks. Two hundred of them remained unaccounted for until the end of the war. The UN Office for the High Commissioner for Human Rights (OHCHR) investigated many of these cases and published their findings in a report that documents the army's operational style in that district.[74]

According to the 2001 census, 52 per cent of Bardiya's population consists of Tharus, a group classified as one of Nepal's 'marginalized indigenous nationalities'. They originally inhabited the malarial forests in the western plains, a fact that gave rise to the idea that Tharus were immune to malaria. In the 1950s, the government launched a malaria eradication program, destroyed these forests and encouraged people from other regions to settle there. The settlers, predominantly upper caste people from the hills, gradually established ownership over most of the land in the region, resulting in the dispossession of large numbers of Tharus. Excluded from the structures and mechanisms of the Nepali state, Tharus not only lost their land, but also fell victim to fraudulent money-lending practices and were forced to become bonded labourers for upper-caste settler families.[75]

Following the opening of democratic space in 1990, Tharu activists mounted efforts to organize their communities and campaign for land rights and an end to bonded labour. The Maoists quickly recognized them as a community where the message of radical social transformation would resonate and, soon after the launch of their rebellion in 1996, made special efforts to organize Tharus. Maoist activists in the region would intimidate landowners into abandoning their property, and in some cases kill them. They would then settle landless peasants, including many Tharus, on the land. The landowning castes feared the growing Tharu assertion and they feared the Maoists. These two fears gradually merged into one, blurring the line between a Tharu and a Maoist. This attitude was shared by local government authorities and security personnel, most of whom belonged to the upper castes. By the time the army was deployed in 2001, the local authorities seem to have believed that all Tharus, and all organizations fighting for their rights, had links with the Maoists.[76]

Tharus were thus singled out for harassment and arrest. Based on the testimonies of former detainees, the 2009 OHCHR report provided a detailed picture of some of the wartime abuses committed at the Chisapani barracks, which operated as a detention centre in Bardiya. A majority of detainees at Chisapani were of Tharu origin. They were kept blindfolded with their hands tied behind their backs. They could not move except for meals and trips to the toilet. Many were severely tortured during interrogation, often in the presence of the company commander. A number of them were kept in muddy trenches around the barracks and forced to eat, excrete and sleep there; their bodies swelled up as a result of being constantly submerged.[77]

The detainees at Chisapani barracks lived in constant fear that they might be killed. Soldiers told them stories of others who had been killed in custody. Many were threatened with imminent death. Some of them were taken into the forest and made to lie down on the ground with a gun pointed at them or a barrel thrust into their mouths while soldiers demanded information about the rebels.[78] Two former detainees related how they had been forced to witness other prisoners lined up in a row, blindfolded and handcuffed, and shot dead at close range by soldiers. Others remember detainees awoken in the middle of the night and taken away in army vehicles into the surrounding woods. Sometimes, gunshots were heard ringing out in the dark soon after, and the vehicles returned without those who had been taken away.[79]

Most of the detainees were eventually released. Some were released because army personnel were satisfied with the accounts they provided; others went free after the local authorities intervened on behalf of the victims' relatives. Army officials often demanded cash in exchange for this favour. The historically marginalized Tharus had no influence with the local authorities, and neither funds nor information on how to make inquiries about their kin. As a result Tharus faced the toughest hurdles in their efforts to find out about their detained family members, and in securing their release. In one incident, eight individuals had been arrested and brought to the barracks: one was a member of a higher caste; the rest were Tharus. The mother of the non-Tharu man succeeded in getting her son released after a conversation with a senior army officer. She was later reported as saying: '[My son] was released because I was clever, and I got to talk to the commander, unlike those Tharu women, just hanging around and begging at the gate.'[80]

OHCHR investigated 156 cases of people who could no longer be located after they were arrested in Bardiya; they were presumably killed in custody. One hundred and thirty-five, or 85 per cent, were of Tharu origin.[81] Only twenty-three were directly affiliated to the Maoists. The rest were mostly civilians: some were Maoist sympathizers, some had at one point or another provided rebels with food or lodging or attended their mass meetings, while yet others had been arrested solely on the basis of false information, 'including that obtained through torture, and false accusations motivated by personal vendettas'.[82] A number of the disappeared were Tharu activists who had their own organizations and had refused to cooperate with the Maoists. It would seem that their efforts to urge the government to improve the lot of the Tharu people, raise awareness within their community and promote their language were taken as evidence of complicity with the insurgents.

The purpose of the mass arrests and torture in Bardiya was presumably to eliminate the Maoist presence in the district. As noted earlier, the RNA resorted to every means at their disposal to extract information about the rebel presence among the local population. Army officials surely must have realized that information acquired thus was unreliable, but given the challenge of distinguishing between rebels and local people, they decided their only option was to act on the basis of flawed information. Like military forces fighting internal insurgencies elsewhere, they must also have reasoned that a degree of indiscriminate violence could be useful: it might deter some who were attracted to the Maoist ideology from joining or abetting the rebels.

But state violence can deter collaboration with rebels only if that violence is selective. In other words, people need to feel confident that they will not be targeted as long as they stay away from the rebels.[83] This was clearly not the case in Bardiya, where Tharus felt they aroused suspicion and were targeted simply because they belonged to a particular community. Moreover, even as the army went on the rampage trying to flush out Maoists, they could not establish control over the territory. As soon as the troops had gone, the rebels would come back to the villages, seeking shelter in people's houses, imparting their political lessons and warning their hosts against cooperating with the government. Thus, despite resorting to threats and violence, the RNA could not create the conditions that would enable the locals to stay away from the Maoists.

While it was true that the Maoists were also often brutal, their violence was much more selective. They generally targeted only those who were perceived to be collaborating with state security forces. Their relationship with the Tharus and other marginalized groups was, too, based on something much deeper than plain intimidation or coercion. The rebels offered a dream of radical social transformation: their movement would ensure that Tharus owned the land they tilled and gained control of local government. Many Tharus, facing nothing but harassment and mistreatment at the hands of local authorities and security forces, saw a glimmer of hope in the Maoist promise.[84]

Caught between an army that was indiscriminately brutal, and rebels who punished non-cooperation but also offered benefits in return for collaboration, many locals tended to gravitate towards the latter. Over the years of the conflict, Tharu participation in the Maoist movement swelled and this community came to form a core support base of the Maoists.[85] The Royal Nepal Army, firmly moulded by the culture of the state elite, regarded the Tharus as a docile and cowardly people unfit for fighting. But as many accounts by both Maoists and independent researchers indicate, and as army officers themselves would eventually acknowledge, a considerable number of Maoist combatants who carried out attacks on military positions were of Tharu origin.[86]

Of course, the security forces were not universally brutal and not every marginalized group supported the Maoists. However, broadly speaking villagers tended to be more comfortable with the rebels. This was true even in villages where people were terrified of them and sought to maintain neutrality between the two sides. In an ethnographic account of a relatively prosperous village in the hills of central Nepal, the authors note how the inhabitants perceived the security forces as aloof and unpredictable. 'It is impossible to speak to them,' said one villager, 'they only ask questions and give orders.'[87] Hardly surprising, then, that local civilians were often reluctant to act as informers for the army. As a shopkeeper from Dolakha district said in 2004, 'Nobody here will reveal anything about Maoist activities to the army. But there are a few who will reveal army activities to the Maoists.'[88]

The army recognized the fact that they lacked actionable intelligence. However, this problem was often attributed to the defects of the National Intelligence Department (NID). According to army officials, the NID was a highly capable institution during the Panchayat regime; its capacity had eroded only after the parliamentary parties came to power and, using the institution for partisan ends, appointed cronies instead of competent individuals to its ranks.[89] That the army had alienated large sections of the population, and that this was one reason why it faced such difficulty in obtaining information about the rebels, seems not to have figured much in the army's strategic calculations, even though it was recognized by those who were entirely sympathetic to the army's counter-insurgency campaign. As an official at the American embassy noted, '[RNA] officers tend ... to be aloof from lower-caste ... ethnic minorities who predominate in Maoist-affected areas, making it difficult for them to gain popular support or to exploit local intelligence assets.'[90]

As it emerged that the army was guilty of major human rights violations, their international backers – the US and UK governments in particular – pressured them to respect international human rights standards and helped train soldiers on how to handle Maoist suspects. In July 2002, the army established a human rights cell to investigate reported violations. American diplomats in Kathmandu thought this was a positive sign. One of them observed in September 2002, 'The RNA's top leadership is well aware of the negative effect human rights violations would have ... on their own forces' good order and discipline.'[91] Two years later, the ambassador wrote: 'Since the establishment of the RNA's human rights cell ... we can identify a slowly evolving awareness of the need to investigate, prosecute and even convict abusers.'[92]

However, the army's 'slowly evolving awareness' was not reflected in their actions. True, they undertook joint operations with the police as part of the Unified Command mechanism, in hopes that they could benefit from information in the police's possession. They also made intermittent efforts to take action against human rights violators and improve relations with the population, as during the 2003 ceasefire when the army took health camps to villages. But on the whole their strategy and behaviour remained fundamentally unchanged. Their short-lived attempts to gain the population's goodwill did not really change public perception. In any case, poor relations with the population were rarely considered a major drawback. Instead the army leadership emphasized the shortage of personnel, weapons and other military equipment as their main weaknesses. And it was on such matters that they expended most of their thought and energy.

The army continued to regard human rights activists with suspicion and resentment. From the army's perspective, they were overly sympathetic toward the rebels. They undermined the fight against the Maoists by trying to bring those detained by the army under judicial oversight. Thus, even in the face of mounting criticism, the army continued to carry out arbitrary arrests, secret detentions and torture of suspects.[93] An OHCHR report documented such cases that occurred at a military barracks in Kathmandu, in an elite residential area within walking distance from the royal palace and important diplomatic missions. On one occasion in 2004, even officers of the National Human Rights Commission (NHRC) were denied access to the barracks. Later that year, when NHRC officials, along with representatives from the International Committee of the Red Cross, gained access to the barracks, the RNA managed to hide detainees from them.[94]

The fact was that the pressures on the Royal Nepal Army were ambiguous, even contradictory. On the one hand, foreign countries, human rights activists and parliamentary parties pressured them to demonstrate their commitment to human rights and a strengthened parliamentary democracy. On the other, the army was entirely beholden to the monarchy, and believed it was necessary to tame the political parties, human rights organizations and the media as well as to weaken the Maoists.[95] With an officer class largely drawn from the aristocratic Thakuri-Chhetri castes, the entire institution was steeped in an old royalist-feudal ethos that was reflected in their attitude of entitled superiority and lack of understanding of the political grievances festering in Nepali society. This, along with their wrong-headed military strategy, was a crucial factor underlying their callous and inhumane treatment of marginalized groups like the Tharus.[96] People in war-torn villages across Nepal thus increasingly saw the RNA as the king's instrument, whose purpose was to suppress political effervescence, reverse history and push the nation back to the era of absolute monarchy.

CHAPTER 5

# Among the Believers

## Two Regimes

The international media flocked to Nepal to cover the royal massacre in 2001 and discovered a raging insurgency. From then on, a steady flow of journalists came to explore what they perceived to be an exotic, anachronistic rebellion. By late 2004, reports in both the domestic and foreign press often stated that around 70 per cent of Nepal's countryside was under insurgent control. This was perfectly adequate shorthand: the Maoists were present and possessed influence in almost every part of the country. But the degree of their control varied considerably across districts. Their power was not absolute even in their strongholds, namely the hills and mountains of the mid- and far-western regions. Even within districts that were almost entirely controlled by the rebels, the state maintained a presence in the capitals. The Maoists did wield power in other areas, such as the hills in the eastern region, but their ability to exercise control over the population was more limited, given the frequent incursions of state security forces into those areas.

Nonetheless, the Maoists had successfully established a formidable parallel regime, and both sides strove to make territories under their sway impermeable to their enemy. The army barricaded sensitive installations and imposed curfews at dusk. In Musikot, the headquarters of Rukum, for instance, government offices and schools were surrounded with barbed wire and mines.[1] Visitors from Maoist-controlled villages were treated with suspicion and often harshly interrogated. Officials in Bajura district's capital taunted villagers who came to collect government-provided rations: 'You join Maoist marches and then presume we will give you rice?'[2] Travelling beyond the district capitals was also difficult, as people had to pass through multiple checkpoints where they had to explain the reasons for their travel. A trader in Baglung complained that his business had almost collapsed: 'We need to get special permission from the local administration to supply dry food, batteries and other goods [to the villages.]'[3]

Meanwhile, Maoists posted sentries in their base areas to guard against incursions by the army. Outsiders who wished to enter these areas required prior permission from the rebels. Local residents, on the other hand, were discouraged from leaving their villages as they could leak sensitive information to the state security forces. And if too many people left the villages, who were the Maoists to indoctrinate or depend on for their needs? Villagers were hence required to obtain travel documents from the rebels if they wished to travel to the cities. If they wished to travel to India or the Gulf states for employment, they had to acquire a travel document *and* pay a tax. In some cases, travel was forbidden altogether. These measures were not always effective. Large numbers of people evaded the rebels and fled Nepal's villages during the years of the conflict, to seek work and shelter in the cities or in India. On occasion, therefore, the Maoists took more drastic measures to deter movement. In Kalikot district, for instance, they destroyed a bridge over the Karnali River, thus cutting off fifteen VDCs from the outside world.[4]

## Among the Believers

Some joined the Maoists out of compulsion or desperation, as when security forces killed their family members and they had nowhere else to turn for protection. Some were coerced into joining the party; while some of them came to believe in the rebels' worldview, others fled at the first opportunity.[5] Then, among the thousands of young people who joined the party during the war, there were also those who saw the movement as an escape from their circumscribed social lives and opportunities. The Maoists offered them an avenue for personal advancement and a medium for expressing their rage against society.

Devi Prasad Dhakal of Sindhupalchok exemplified the latter category. Born into straitened circumstances, he was sent to Kathmandu to work as a domestic servant at the age of seven. It was only two years later, when he went back to his village, that he began primary school. Later education posed its own challenges. The secondary school in which he enrolled was over an hour's walk from his house. He was always late for school, as he could leave home only after collecting fodder for the cattle and worshipping the family gods. This bred in him resentment towards his father and a hatred of religious rituals. He took to stealing grain from home and selling it for pocket money. In the absence of a supportive, encouraging environment, he failed his SLC examination. This foreclosed opportunities for going elsewhere, and he remained in his village, helping his brothers till their small plot of land.[6]

But Dhakal wanted more from life than his peasant ancestors. He grew increasingly bitter towards his family and their ways and thirsty for adventure and independence. In late 1998, he ran away to Pokhara, the second-largest city in Nepal's hill region. After a period of sleeping on the streets, he found a job as a busboy and dishwasher at a restaurant in the city's bustling tourist area. There he came under the influence of a college student who secretly supported the Maoists. Dhakal was a willing protégé; he felt he had finally found a way to enlarge his narrow existence. Politics had always attracted him. As a schoolboy he had heard that the communists stood up for the poor, and this had led him to become involved in the UML's student wing despite his family's disapproval. More recently, he had experienced the brutality of power first-hand. During one of his first nights in Pokhara, when he was sleeping on the street with some child beggars, a group of policemen had accosted them, beaten them up and taken all their money. Later, the son of a prominent Nepali Congress politician had shown up with a group of friends at the restaurant where Devi Prasad worked. They were rude and noisy, and Dhakal muttered that the politician's son looked like an animal fit for a zoo. Someone in the group overheard him, and they called the police. Dhakal was again beaten and locked up for the night. He thus became a convert to the idea of violence against authority.

Dhakal was initially tasked with distributing pamphlets, putting up posters at night and taking food and other items to rebels in jail. Gradually his responsibilities increased, and on 31 July 2000, he quit his restaurant job and went underground as a full-time Maoist activist.

Thus Devi Prasad Dhakal became one among many who left their families and homes to join a secretive, hierarchical and tightly knit group whose members were constantly on the move. They had to flee from villages when they heard that state security forces were approaching. Those assigned to the Maoist military had to trek through difficult terrain in the hills and mountains, often under cover of darkness, to reach the site of planned attacks. Those assigned political duties had to travel from village to village taking the party's ideology to the population. They had to walk long distances to deliver messages for their leaders, meet their counterparts from across the country and establish party committees in new areas.

The hardships were severe. They often had to go hungry and sleep in the open. Then there was the ever-present fear of injury, torture or death at the hands of the security forces. Many who joined the rebels in an initial surge of enthusiasm soon fled back home, despite the possibility of reprisals.[7] But for many others, it was the first time they had become part of a collectivity with a fixed goal, and this offered a kind of fulfilment and liberation. The party satisfied their desire for power and tamed their discontent and restlessness, and it was easy to find camaraderie and companionship among fellow rebels who often came from similar backgrounds.

They were taught to see themselves as exemplars of a new *janabadi* culture in the making, a culture that would encompass the entire nation when the party took power and established a Maoist New Democracy (*Naya Janabad*). *Janabad* is the term for democracy commonly used by Nepal's communists, and as such emphasizes socio-economic rather than political equality. (In contrast, the words *prajatantra*, and later, *loktantra*, have been used to describe political systems that prioritize the values of liberal democracy.) The adjective *janabadi* is usually translated as 'democratic', although 'proletarian' better conveys its meaning.

The Maoists defined their *janabadi* culture in opposition to the dominant culture of the countryside, which they viewed as being caste-ridden and superstitious. Their activists were encouraged to deliberately transgress traditional norms. They often ate beef, for example, breaking the powerful Hindu taboo. The *janabadi* culture also opposed the 'bourgeois' culture of Nepal's urban middle class, where individualism reigned and Hindi films and images of Western consumerism shaped desires. Maoist activists were taught to embrace fierce collectivism and reject inwardness. As the Maoist leader Jayapuri Gharti wrote in a letter to a junior activist, 'You have been fulfilling your role but I feel that is not enough ... You seem rather introverted. You should open up and partici- pate more actively in debates and discussions. You should break out of the world's social formalities and expand your relationships.'[8]

These activists mostly came from rural backgrounds, and during the war they travelled extensively through villages across the country. Meanwhile the state security forces maintained a strong presence in urban areas, whose large populations were mostly unsympathetic to the Maoist cause. Whenever rebels from rural areas visited the cities, they would find themselves lost and isolated. An activist assigned to Kathmandu wrote to a fellow comrade in another region during a particularly trying moment: 'I hope you have been informed about the situation in the valley. The army has captured all of our responsible comrades. Only a few of us remain. We are not in touch with any of the responsible senior comrades. What should we do? What shouldn't we do? We are in great confusion.'[9] This was after the collapse of the second cease-fire when the army had virtually decimated the Maoist organization in the city.

In such moments of strain and hardship, the young Maoist activists would have found ideological succour in what their leaders had taught them and the books they had read. To instil *janabadi* values in their cadres, the leadership encouraged them to read the revolutionary fiction that had inspired them in their own youth. The Nepali translation of the slim Chinese novel *Bright Red Star* was especially popular among the younger Maoist activists.[10] Those who found themselves alienated in the city might have identified with Tung-Tzu, the protagonist of *Bright Red Star*.

The story begins in the 1930s. Tung-Tzu's father goes to join the Chinese revolutionaries, and then a local landowner kills his mother. He spends part of his childhood among communist guerrillas (who are depicted as universally trustworthy, brave and willing to sacrifice their lives for the cause of their country's liberation). But for reasons of safety, he is later sent to work at a rice shop in the city. Tung-Tzu has to conceal his identity, loses touch with the party comrades, and is treated harshly by his employer.

The rice shop owner is an avaricious, unscrupulous man who sells rice mixed with stones. Even when the whole city is starving, he hoards grain, hoping to sell it at a more lucrative time. Tung-Tzu witnesses how the shopkeeper bribes the police, and soon learns that the shopkeeper is also on good terms with the landowner who killed his mother and was complicit with Japanese imperialists. 'I began to understand clearly,' Tung-Tzu says, 'that the oppressive local landowner, the profiteering shopkeeper of the city, the police captain, the forces of the White Army and the Japanese imperialists all belonged to the same group.'[11]

These words must have resonated with the Nepali Maoist activist who had landed in the city. Like Tung-Tzu, he would have seen all the hostile aspects of society as branches of a single oppressive power. He would have likened himself to the young Chinese revolutionary in the novel, and gained a stronger faith in the Maoist cause. Seeing how Tung-Tzu eventually returns to the guerrillas, avenges his mother's murder, and participates in the Communist capture of Beijing, he might have thought, as his superiors insisted, that a Maoist victory was historically inevitable.

An article by the activist Khil Bahadur Bhandari echoes Tung-Tzu's feelings about the city/country divide. While spending two nights in the town of Hetauda amid fears of being captured by the army, he wrote:

> People in the city live an extremely confined life. They are status-quoists and opportunists. They lack empathy; they don't care whether other people live or die. They are only concerned with their own happiness … But people in the villages are not status-quoists and opportunists. One person's suffering draws everyone's empathy. A new ideology and new power have taken the villages by storm, and they are far ahead of the cities in the [political] movement.[12]

The Nepali Maoists, too, wrote novels glorifying their rebellion. *The Path of Struggle* (*Sangharshako Goreto*) by Manju Bam, who joined the Maoist student wing at the age of eighteen in 2001, more or less typifies the genre.[13] Yet the novel is also unique in being written by a woman, and providing an idealized account of a woman's trajectory within the Maoist movement. According to Hisila Yami, one of the two highest-ranking women in the party and the wife of Baburam Bhattarai, women comprised 30 to 50 per cent of the Maoist army, and there were hundreds of others serving in political roles.[14] The Maoist leadership encouraged journalists to report on the large numbers of women who had fled oppressive circumstances and found new lives in the party. Still, the vast bulk of Maoist literature was produced by men and rarely included a female perspective.

Alina, the protagonist of *The Path of Struggle*, is deeply discontented with her social world. After completing her SLC exam, she enrols in a college near her village in the country's south-western plains. But like many other Nepali parents, her parents want their daughter to become a docile and obedient housewife. As insurance against future deprivation, they decide to marry her to a man who holds a stable job in Delhi. The thought of leaving college to marry a man she has never met fills Alina with dread. She has a lover, Yogesh, who is studying in Kathmandu. She remembers how one of her aunts, who also had a lover, committed suicide after being forced to marry someone else. Yet Alina does not dare tell her parents about Yogesh.

Despite his conservative social beliefs, Alina's father is a Maoist sympathizer. Two Maoist activists – Comrade Manoj and Comrade Basu – regularly come to her house for shelter. One day Alina has a long conversation with them in which they explain why they are engaged in armed struggle against the state, and convince her of the futility of formal education. 'Now you should be ready to read the books without a text,' they say. 'You have to study the villages and huts of the poor.'[15] For Alina, it is like receiving a revelation.

Alina feels more and more helpless as the threat of marriage looms closer. One day she meets Comrade Manoj in the marketplace and shares her dilemma. Manoj advises her to summon up her courage and tell her parents about Yogesh. If a woman is to take charge of her destiny, he says, she should be able to decide whom she will marry and when.

To the shock and dismay of her parents, Alina soon leaves home to join the rebels and becomes absorbed in the Maoists' collectivist culture and the tasks they assign her. Yogesh learns of her whereabouts and comes to meet her. He wants them to return to Kathmandu together and get married. Alina refuses; instead she asks him to join the cause she is fighting for: 'If we have longed for each other for so many years, then why can't we tread the same path? True love is when two people invest their ideas and emotions in following the same journey to reach the same destination.'[16] Yogesh tells her he needs time to think, and leaves. But as he is desperately in love with Alina, he eventually comes back and becomes a full-time activist of the Maoist party.

Alina and Yogesh are tasked with organizing a mass meeting during the ceasefire of 2003. They help set up a large stage festooned with red flags and banners and arrange vehicles to transport people from the villages to the site of the meeting. A large crowd gathers, and a senior Maoist takes the stage. 'It is not our desire to fight a war,' he declares, 'it is our compulsion.'[17] This leader is clearly well versed in the writings of Mao, who said that communists fought wars because of their 'desire to eliminate all wars'[18] and the Nepali rebel leader echoes this sentiment when he claims that 'communists are the most peace-loving people in the world'. If the war is to end, he explains, the government has to accept the Maoist demands for a round-table conference, the formation of an interim government and elections to a Constituent Assembly. 'We have taken up arms for peace,' he says, 'and as soon as this government guarantees food, shelter and clothing for the people we will be ready to immediately throw our weapons into the sea.'[19]

These words were no doubt reproduced from a speech Manju Bam herself heard at a mass meeting held during the second ceasefire. The suggestion that the Maoists were actually pacifists and that fulfilment of their political demands would guarantee 'food, shelter and clothing for the people' must have confused at least some in the audience. The novel, however, gives no such indication – the spectators clap and cheer in unison as though all doubt and scepticism had vanished in the fervour of the moment. Next, Comrade Basu, one of the two Maoist activists who used to visit Alina's house, takes the stage and announces the marriage of a 'red couple':

> Dear audience, a new *janabadi* culture is taking root in our society, dismantling the old, superstitious customs and traditions. Respected people, comrades Alina and Yogesh ... have ended the trend of squandering one's last *paisa* on a wedding and then toiling on the streets of India to pay off one's loans. Their marriage is founded on revolutionary thought, on cooperation, on class-consciousness and on trust.[20]

Comrade Basu then reads out the letter in which the couple asked for the party's permission to marry and the letter of approval from the party's district committee. Alina and Yogesh, who are now on stage, smear vermilion powder on each other's faces, put garlands around each other's necks and exchange a firm handshake. The cultural troupe performs a song amid cheers and applause. It is now time for the newly-weds to pledge their lifelong commitment to the revolution. 'As soon as one of us deviates from the party,' the couple recite in one voice, 'our relationship will come to an end. Otherwise, we will have the same goals and destination. We will always follow the party and revolution like the star on the horizon.'[21]

Thousands of young Maoist activists met and fell in love with their fellow comrades during the war. Their weddings were rarely as politically charged as that of Alina and Yogesh, nor did they take place in front of such a large audience. But the details in the novel – the announcement of the wedding by a leader, the reading aloud of letters of request and approval, the oath of undying allegiance to the party – accurately depict the ritual of a Maoist wedding, particularly during the later years of the war.

As Comrade Basu claims, this approach signified a rejection of marriages that demanded wasteful expenditure and shackled women to a life of domestic servitude. In the Maoist conception, a *janabadi* wedding allowed two people to enter into a union in complete freedom and become equal partners for life. In contrast to traditional marriages where the idea of divorce carries a stigma, forcing women to remain trapped in loveless and oppressive relationships, *janabadi* marriages could be terminated with relative ease. The Maoists also encouraged inter-caste and inter-ethnic marriage as a measure to relieve caste discrimination, and they encouraged widows to remarry in opposition to the traditional Hindu custom that requires a widow to live the remainder of her life in seclusion and austerity.[22]

But the party was far from allowing complete freedom in matters of love and marriage. The minimum age requirement for marriage was twenty-two for male cadres and twenty for women. Those below the age limit were deemed too immature to assume marital responsibilities. The Maoist leaders encouraged marriages between cadres because they believed this would increase their commitment and energy for the revolution. Many young people had joined the movement out of a desire for adventure, rather than ideological commitment. The leaders felt that allowing too much romantic or sexual liberty could lead to dissipation and anarchy in the ranks. As Hisila Yami observed, 'History demonstrates that many brave warriors who couldn't be brought down by the gun were brought down by lust.'[23]

Maoist activists were therefore instructed to stay away from titillating literature and movies. They were not to remain idle for long periods of time. They were not to spend time alone with a member of the opposite sex unless circumstances left them no choice. They were not to engage in premarital sex. While in groups, they were to discuss 'serious matters to increase knowledge' rather than wasting time with jokes and small talk.[24] They were to keep their immediate superiors informed about all aspects of their lives, including their romantic affairs. The cadres were thus expected to live a life of sacrifice and austerity, and above all subordinate their private desires to the needs of the party.

Out-of-wedlock sexual liaisons were considered particularly damaging to the party. Euphemistically referred to as 'cultural deviations' (*sanskritik bichalan*), such transgressions were subject to harsh punishment, and even high-ranking leaders were not exempt. The most notorious case was that of Yan Prasad Gautam, alias 'Alok'. A member of the central committee since the earliest days of the rebellion, Alok was at one time very close to the party's chairman, Prachanda. In 2000, he was charged with having an illicit affair with a Maoist district committee secretary and treating his wife like a 'slave', among a long list of other 'deviations'. It turned out that the money he had been extorting from the population went not towards meeting the party's expenditures, but to fulfil his appetite for luxury. He dominated and abused lower-ranking cadres. His lust for violence had led him to murder a civilian without permission from the high command. Instead of heeding the criticisms of party leaders, he had resorted to conspiracy and blackmail to save his skin.

Alok was duly stripped of his party positions and sent to a labour camp run by the Maoists in Rolpa. He was later killed, apparently in an army operation. But his notoriety lived on. The 'Alok tendency' was defined as 'rightist opportunism cloaked in leftism', and served as a warning to the entire rank and file.[25]

The restrictions imposed by the Maoists led to a somewhat paradoxical situation. On the one hand, the party leaders desired marital unions between cadres. On the other, they discouraged them from engaging in the leisurely courtship necessary for establishing deep bonds. Leaders would pressure their juniors to marry at the first indication of budding romance. The age requirements were often overlooked. Maoist leaders complained that cadres lied about their age to get married, but they rarely took the trouble to check. More often they deliberately ignored the age factor, believing that marriages between activists would further bind them to the party.

Relatively senior activists who were divorced or whose spouses had been killed in the conflict were also pressured to remarry. Lekhnath Neupane, alias 'Nirmal', the head of the Maoists' student organization, received this letter soon after his wife Urmila Adhikari, alias 'Samikshya', was killed by the RNA:

> We are communists, and all our joys and sorrows belong to the people. Our marriage is not for individual happiness but for the benefit of the entire party and the revolution. Nirmal *dai* [brother], remember, you had said, 'Samikshya's responsibility has now fallen on my shoulders.' But after seeing you in such torment, I feel you are having trouble fulfilling even your own responsibility, let alone Samikshya's. Therefore, for the sake of the party and the revolution, you must find a comrade who can take Samikshya-ji's place and fulfil her responsibility, someone who can alleviate your physical and mental suffering and restore your vitality and enthusiasm. Every person needs a companion sooner or later, and I hope you will not push the party and the revolution backward by waiting too long to fill the vacuum left by Comrade Samikshya. Samikshya-ji's soul will find peace only when you are happy and someone fulfills her unfinished duty for the party.[26]

Neupane's marriage to Samikshya too had been encouraged and facilitated by other party leaders. He had barely met her, and had been courting her for about two weeks when they got married. In the six months of their marriage before she was killed by state security forces, the couple had barely spent two months together.[27] This was a common pattern: marriages were conducted in haste, before the partners got to know each other well, and they could be assigned to separate areas across the country even after they married. Communication between them was often limited to letters, passed from hand to hand through the underground network and taking weeks, if not months, to reach their destination.

The Maoist ideal of a marriage founded on free choice and full awareness was thus often violated in practice. One might say that the *janabadi* marriage simply replaced the pressures and obligations of the traditional marriage with the pressures and obligations of the party. The Maoists, however, would be likely to dispute this criticism on the grounds that it is premised on bourgeois individualism, which views with suspicion all systems where individuals are asked to subordinate their personal interests to a larger cause. Asked what desires she had beyond serving the party, a newly married activist said: 'We have no desires beyond the fulfilment of our basic human needs. We are communists, brother.'[28]

The marriage of Alina and Yogesh in *The Path of Struggle* is far from blissful. Alina remains entirely committed to the party and its ideology, and steadily rises up the ranks. Yogesh, meanwhile, is unable to maintain such faith. He complains that he will find it difficult to live without her when he is posted to a remote area in the mountains. Later, when they have a child, he wants to stay at home with his family. He tells Alina they are wasting their lives in the Maoist movement. Alina thinks Yogesh is guided more by his emotions than by ideology, and rebukes him for his weakness. 'Don't speak like the rich bourgeois,' she says. 'They are the ones who desire only luxury and relaxation and call that life.'[29]

Unhappy with his conditions in a remote mountain outpost, Yogesh starts drinking heavily and takes a lover. Eventually he steals money from the party and runs away with her. Alina finds out about her husband's betrayal from her region's party chief. Her initial reaction is one of intense rage: she vows to take revenge on Yogesh, and her leader has to tell her to calm down. Later, she thinks about other men in the party who have abused or abandoned their wives, and her anger hardens into a belief that men, driven by desire and lust, are inherently unreliable. In contrast, she thinks, women are far more capable of sacrifice and commitment to the revolution.

In these sections of the novel, Manju Bam obliquely expresses her frustration with the male dominance that persisted within the party. Yet the novel also contains an element of fantasy, of wish fulfilment, as it allows the female protagonist to outdo her husband and rise higher in the party hierarchy. In the end, it is the man who is disgraced.

Taking part in the Maoist rebellion undoubtedly gave many women a sense of purpose and confidence. Those who possessed some education and skills in writing, speaking or singing were given substantial responsibilities. Manju Bam herself, starting as a district committee member of the Maoist student organization, soon came to lead a cultural group and went on to become a member of the Seti-Mahakali regional bureau. And in 2006, when the Maoists abandoned armed rebellion to join multiparty politics, Bam, aged twenty-four at the time, was nominated to the country's interim parliament.

But the movement did not exist in a vacuum, and party members could not entirely escape the prejudices prevalent in the broader society. When they visited people's homes and families to engage with local populations, female Maoists often faced difficulties. Satya Shrestha-Schipper, who studied women's participation in the Maoist movement in Jumla district, discovered that men who temporarily returned home had no problems reintegrating into social life. Women, on the other hand, tended to avoid contact with their old friends, preferring instead to stay home or mix only with their comrades. Many of these women had joined the party at a young age under coercive conditions, and lacked experience of the wider world. They remained with the Maoists not out of a deep commitment to the cause, but due to fear of what lay outside.[30]

Despite the Maoists' efforts to establish a *janabadi* culture, it was not easy to root out ingrained prejudices among their cadre. Shyam Kumar Budha Magar recounts that when he was in Nuwagaon, Rolpa, in 2000, a local woman approached him and his comrade, the Maoist in charge of the area.[31] The woman was a Badi, a Dalit caste whose women have traditionally engaged in prostitution to earn their living. She asked the Maoists to help her recoup the money owed her by a man who had repeatedly used her services without paying. The young rebels were shocked by the request, and scolded her, but since their standing in the village would suffer if they did not try to resolve the dispute, they summoned the man to hear his side of the story.

The man admitted, in the presence of the Maoists and a number of villagers, that the Badi woman's allegation was true. This placed the Maoists in a dilemma. They recognized that the woman would have to be compensated if justice was to be served, but they also felt that forcing the man to pay up would encourage prostitution, which they viewed as a major social ill. They tried to force the man to marry the Badi woman, apparently without taking her feelings into consideration. He vehemently refused. Eventually they settled the matter by making him pay the amount due. If he repeated such a 'mistake' in the future, the Maoists would punish him – the precise terms of the punishment were left unspecified. The woman, for her part, was ordered to take the money and leave the village for good. If she ever came back, she was told, the Maoists would take 'physical action' (*bhautik karbahi*) – a euphemism for punishments ranging from severe beating to execution – against her.

## The Battle of Beni

The Maoists periodically reorganized their military force as its size increased. In September 2001, during the reprieve offered by the first ceasefire, they organized a battalion-level formation. A fighting force of loosely organized guerrilla bands was thus consolidated into a centralized military force, under the name of People's Liberation Army (PLA).[32] In June 2003, during the second ceasefire, they established two division-level formations. Nanda Kishore Pun 'Pasang' and Barsha Man Pun 'Ananta', the two comrades from Rolpa who had together participated in numerous and increasingly significant attacks since the one on the Holeri police post in 1996, were appointed commanders of the Western Division and Eastern Division respectively.[33]

In mid 2003, while Baburam Bhattarai and his team negotiated with the government in Kathmandu, the Maoists were also preparing their army for the period when the talks would fail and war would resume. Since 2001 they had claimed that, as they had defeated the police and were fighting the RNA on equal terms, they had attained the position of 'strategic balance' with the state. Their slogan during the second ceasefire was: 'Let us concentrate all our forces and effectively exploit the contradictions to take the planning of the offensive to new heights.'[34] This would eventually lead to the 'strategic offensive', the final phase of Maoist guerrilla war, where the rebels would be in the ascendant and the state on the defensive. The task would undeniably be a daunting one. As their slogan stated, *all* their forces would be deployed simply to *prepare* for the offensive.

Once the 2003 ceasefire ended, the Maoists decided, in line with their new strategy, to stage 'decentralized attacks' (small-scale guerrilla actions such as ambushes and assassinations), as well as 'relatively-centralized' and 'centralized' ones (assaults on fixed positions by large numbers of the PLA).[35] In October 2003, they carried out centralized attacks on Armed Police Force (APF) positions in Banke and Dang. But both these actions were unsuccessful.[36] This was also a period when the RNA managed to inflict tremendous damage on the Maoists. The rebels hence decided to focus on small-scale attacks for the time being, while preparing for a major assault.[37]

By early 2004, the Maoists were begininng to fret about their inability to undertake large-scale military attacks and progress to the strategic offensive. It had already been a year since they last attacked a district capital. Some important Maoist military commanders had surrendered to the state security forces. Pasang pointed out the multiple challenges that confronted the party during this time. The 'reactionary forces of the world, including the imperialists', he said, were trying to separate the people from the Maoist movement by claiming that the RNA had almost totally destroyed the rebel army. Many, both in Nepal and internationally, were wondering whether the Maoists had in fact been pushed back into a defensive posture.[38]

'At this juncture', Pasang told rebels under his command, 'we must launch an attack on the district headquarters of the reactionary state or a battalion of the Royal Army in order to prove to the world that the Maoists have become even more powerful, that the PLA is not finished and that no force in the world can defeat it.'[39]

As part of this objective, the PLA's Eastern Division was to attack the headquarters of Bhojpur district. On 2 March 2004, rebel troops led by Ananta attacked the telephone tower, the district police office and the bank in Bhojpur, killing twenty police and twelve army personnel.[40] The Western Division, which was far more powerful than the Eastern Division, planned to attack Beni, the capital of Myagdi district, fifty kilometres west of Pokhara. The RNA's Shri Kali Prasad Battalion was stationed in this town of around 5,000 inhabitants. The Maoists, who had hitherto targeted only company-level formations, had raised the stakes by deciding to attack a battalion.[41] According to Pasang, the rebels planned to capture all the government offices in Beni and penetrate and destroy the RNA position before retreating.[42]

Despite its unprecedented scale, the Beni attack was not vastly different from previous attacks in its immediate objective. The Maoists knew that they would not be able to capture Beni and bring it permanently under their control. Rather, they sought to demoralize state security forces and help create the conditions necessary for launching a strategic offensive. In other words the attack on Beni was to serve as an exercise through which the rebels hoped to attain a higher degree of military prowess.

According to Mao's military strategy, rebels fighting a protracted People's War start from a position of guerrilla warfare, forming small, irregular groups to ambush enemy patrols, and then gradually move on to mobile warfare, during which phase they possess a large, regular army. Mobile warfare, unlike standard conventional warfare, involves a 'high degree of mobility on extensive battlefields, swift advances and withdrawals, [and] swift concentrations and dispersals.'[43] Mobile warfare is eventually meant to progress to positional warfare, which entails 'defense works with deep trenches ... and successive rows of defensive positions.'[44] The Nepali Maoists believed they had already become adept at mobile war. The battle of Beni would be an instance of mobile warfare that incorporated some of the tactics of positional warfare.

In addition, the transition to the strategic offensive required increased public support. In February 2004, the Maoists launched a 'Special People's Military Campaign' (*vishesh jana sainya abhiyan*). Its objective was to 'militarize the entire population and create a mentality of resistance' that would drive them to participate in a 'popular armed uprising' (*am sashastra vidroha*) against the state.[45] Between February and June, Maoist activists travelled across western Nepal, trying to convince civilians to join them. There was also much coercion and in some cases, they abducted large groups of students from schools for indoctrination.[46]

The attack on Beni was part of the Special People's Military Campaign. While preparing for it, Pasang told his troops: 'At this moment the vacillating middle class is vigilantly watching us.'[47] In the Maoist worldview, the 'vacillating middle class' would support whichever side appeared to be winning. Pasang thus felt that a successful onslaught on Beni would help the rebels win the support of a constituency that had so far remained neutral.

In early March, combatants from the PLA's Western Division trekked to Lukum, a village in Rukum district, a Maoist stronghold. There were around 1,200 armed combatants from the Mangalsen First Brigade (based in the Maoist 'Special Region' covering Rolpa, Rukum and nine other districts); 1,000 from the Satbariya Second Brigade (based in the Bheri-Karnali region); 1,070 from the Lisne-Gam Third Brigade (based in the Seti-Mahakali region); and 300 combatants from the Basu-Smriti Fourth Brigade (based in the Gandaki region). They had with them 81-mm and 2-inch mortar guns, rocket launchers, general purpose machine guns, long machine guns and short machine guns captured from the state security forces; a small number of AK-47s bought from across the border; and handmade grenades, small guns and mines. In addition, there were around 1,700 'volunteers' – non-combatant members of the Maoist party as well as civilians – responsible for transporting food and weapons, carrying away the wounded and providing them with medical treatment.[48]

In Lukum the rebels spent a week preparing for the battle. Division Commander Pasang used a detailed sand-model of Beni and videos to familiarize the brigade commanders with the layout of the town, the routes they would take and the positions from which they would launch their attacks. The troops exercised and practiced battle manoeuvres on the grounds of the local primary school.[49]

Meanwhile, party committees of the western hill districts were busy with other preparations. The entire machinery of the West-Central Command, which had authority over party bodies across half the country, had been mobilized to arrange food, clothing and logistics for the troops. Party committees throughout the western and mid-western regions had organized long caravans of horses and mules, as well as men, women and children to transport food to the Maoist heartland of Rolpa and Rukum. The rebels had bought thousands of buffaloes, cows and goats to feed their combatants. Large quantities of medical supplies had been imported across the Indian border.[50]

The rebel troops, numbering more than 4,000, would be marching for over a week to reach Beni, often through villages where they lacked popular support.[51] In the areas along the route, party committees were tasked with preparing food and shelter for the troops. In the villages around Beni in Myagdi and Baglung districts, the locals were warned not to travel to the district capital after the first week of March; the rebels set up surveillance posts to monitor their movements. Villagers were abducted to cook for the rebels and to work as 'volunteers' during the battle.[52]

On the afternoon of 13 March, the troops gathered on the grounds of the primary school in Lukum. The Pratirodh Cultural Group performed songs and dances. Division Commander Pasang read out letters of congratulation from their top leaders, including one from Maoist Chairman Prachanda. He and Netra Bikram Chand, 'Biplab', the political commissar for the battle, then delivered their speeches.[53]

'Comrades', Pasang announced, 'driven by our intense disgust and anger towards reactionary scoundrels, we have come together to fulfil a historic mission. A *janabadi* state can only be achieved through the efforts of the great People's Liberation Army.'[54] The experience of previous military raids had taught the rebels that 'victory is not possible without sacrifice'. All their victories had been won thanks to their fearless combatants, who had snatched guns from the enemy's hands even amid a hail of enemy fire and kept on fighting even after being wounded. 'If we hate our class enemies strongly enough, then we can take them on even with our bare hands.'[55]

'The essential goal of our action plan,' Pasang continued, 'is to achieve glorious victory at any cost, even at the cost of death, even at the cost of losing our entire division. Each of you must feel personally responsible for bringing the battle to a victorious end.'[56] Those who demonstrated courage in battle would be rewarded, Pasang said. Those who did not would be punished.

After the commanders exchanged garlands and handshakes, the troops of the PLA's Western Division set out on the march to Beni. They walked day after day through fields and forests, up steep hills and across snow. They walked even after it got dark, eating *satu* (powdered cereal) mixed with water to ward off hunger and spending their nights in the most rudimentary shelters. Once in a while, marchers became separated from their formations and lost their way. Some got injured. Many people from the southern plains, unaccustomed to the altitude, fell ill; while some of them were sent back, others carried on with the aid of their comrades.[57]

'What a beautiful procession of warriors!' Dhaneshwar Pokhrel, a Maoist activist from Pyuthan who was taking part in the march, wrote in his diary. 'Is this sight any different from the Long March of the Chinese revolution led by Comrade Mao?'[58] Pokhrel, like many of his comrades, felt a surge of pride when farmers in the fields stopped their work and stared in awe at the sea of Maoists.

Passing through villages and hills in Rukum, Rolpa and Baglung, the Maoist troops arrived in Darbang village in Myagdi, a three-hour walk from Beni, on 19 March. They camped in various settlements across the district where food and shelter had been arranged for them. That evening the rebels received information that a unit of the RNA battalion in Beni was patrolling a nearby hill. Their leaders ordered them to hide inside the houses in the vicinity. A section of the PLA's First Brigade prepared to launch an attack, but the RNA contingent passed on, oblivious that thousands of rebels were hiding close by. This incident worried the Maoist commanders. They had scheduled their attack on Beni for the night of 22 March, but they now decided to shift it forward by two days, fearing that the RNA would come to know of their plan and whereabouts if they waited so long.[59]

The local government offices stood in a row to the south of Beni bazaar, overlooking the Myagdi River. At the farthest ends of the row stood the District Police Office (DPO) and the office of the District Development Committee (DDC), with the chief district officer's residence, the district court and other offices in between. The police office and the DDC office each had twenty army personnel standing guard on the roof. There were, in addition, ninety police personnel in the DPO and around 120 army personnel stationed in a conference hall behind the DDC office. The barracks of Shri Kali Prasad Battalion were around 300 metres distant from these offices.[60] In Pasang's estimate, there were around 450 army personnel in the barracks;[61] the commanding officer of the RNA battalion later claimed there were only 250.[62] Across the river from Beni bazaar stood the district prison, guarded by around twenty policemen.[63]

Shortly before 10 pm on 20 March 2004, the Maoist troops descended the hills around Beni, crept unimpeded into the town, and surrounded the army barracks, the government offices and the district jail.[64] They had already sent armed contingents to block the security forces that might advance from the nearby districts of Baglung and Parbat and an army camp three kilometres north of Beni. Some combatants burst into the houses that stood parallel to the government offices and took position at the windows on the upper storeys.[65] Those assigned to attack the jail discovered that the policemen had fled. The Maoists freed the thirty-three prisoners and burned the building down.

Lieutenant Colonel Raju Nepali, commanding officer of Shri Kali Prasad Battalion, first learned about the attack when mortar shells started raining into the barracks compound around 10:30 pm.[66]

Pasang had commanded his artillery groups to destroy selected points on the perimeter walls with mortars, grenades, rocket launchers and machine guns. Assault groups would then charge ahead, firing continuously, to breach the fortifications and enter the compound. The remaining troops would follow them and take control of the barracks, police office and government offices. If initial attempts to penetrate the compound failed, the assault groups would withdraw and wait for the artillery to bombard the fortifications once more before trying to re-enter. If the rebels encountered major resistance and failed to break through the fortifications even after repeated attempts, they would bombard the walls from close quarters and the troops would move forward as a single unit.[67]

'We must advance at any cost,' Pasang had instructed his troops during the training, 'even if we have to fight all day and all through the night.'[68] Since it would be a lengthy battle, it was necessary to prevent mental and physical exhaustion. The rebel combatants would therefore operate in relay. An assault group of around ten people would fight for a set period before being replaced by another. Also, as the rebels would be transitioning towards positional warfare through this battle, they needed to overcome the 'guerrilla mentality of the defensive war' and be 'mentally prepared to fight in fortification', in close combat and even in broad daylight.[69]

Evidence indicates that the rebels adhered closely to Pasang's instructions. As soon as the battle started, Maoist combatants dragged tables and rice sacks out of houses and shops to use as front-line barricades. A woman in Mangalaghat bazaar, adjacent to the barracks, later recalled that several rebels, including 'many women and children whose guns were touching the ground because of their small height',[70] had entered her shop shortly after 11 pm and used it as a resting place through the night. 'They went to the front line to fight,' she said, 'and then came back here to take a rest and eat. As one came back, another left … They just appeared not to care about their own lives.'[71]

The battle was messier than the Maoists had expected. After fighting for hours, they had captured neither the army barracks nor the government offices. The army fought back, and, as a combatant recalled, the Maoists could barely identify their own combatants among the dead and wounded in the carnage.[72]

Around 5 am, a military helicopter, presumably sent from the RNA garrison in Pokhara, flew over Beni. Mana Rishi Dhital, on-site reporter for the Maoist newspaper *Janastha*, saw the helicopter drop some bombs before flying away. The battle briefly came to a halt, followed by silence in which the firing seemed to have ceased altogether.[73] By then it was daylight.

The rebels then launched a more vigorous attack. 'They entered the compound but withdrew as soon as we struck back,' said Lieutenant Colonel Raju Nepali. 'They came like waves, one after another. I saw a woman Maoist trying to climb a tree even after she had been hit by fifteen or sixteen bullets.'[74]

Finally, shortly before 8 am, the rebels managed to break into the compound of the police and government offices in the south of Beni. The police and military personnel surrendered. The rebels took CDO Sagar Mani Parajuli, DSP Rana Bahadur Gautam (the most senior police officer in Beni), thirty-four other police personnel and two soldiers under their control.[75] They took weapons, ammunition and money from the district police office and other buildings before setting them on fire. Jubilant rebels poured into the streets, singing and dancing. Thinking the battle had almost reached a victorious end, they prepared to march through the town in celebration.[76]

But the rebel forces attacking the army barracks were still trying to enter the compound. Around 9:30 am, they saw RNA helicopters hovering in the sky above. After dropping ammunition for the security forces in the barracks, the helicopters started bombing the town. Meanwhile, the Maoists received news that the contingent that had headed towards Parbat district had been unsuccessful in blocking RNA troops advancing towards Beni.[77] Around 10:30 am, Pasang, who had been directing the battle from a nearby hill, ordered his troops to withdraw.[78]

So on the morning of 21 March, the Maoist troops began retreating from Beni. They followed the same route back, taking the captured CDO, the DSP, and other security personnel with them. Maoist 'volunteers' carried the wounded on stretchers and in *dokos* (large baskets), along with seized weapons and ammunition. The RNA helicopters followed the retreating Maoists and opened fire on them at regular intervals. As a result, six Maoists and one of the captured policemen died on the first day, while many others were wounded. A number of villagers, cows and buffaloes were also killed and some houses destroyed.[79]

Early the next morning, an RNA contingent sent to ambush the retreating Maoists fired at the rebels in a village near Darbang. Seven Maoists were killed here. The main rebel force made a detour through Baglung district to evade the RNA. At least one more clash occurred between the army and the Maoists during the retreat. Because of the RNA's pursuit, the rebels had to abandon their plan to stop and eat in villages in Myagdi. Many of them were seen eating handfuls of uncooked rice during their dogged march.[80] Towards the end of March, the Maoists arrived in Thabang, a village deep within their base area in Rolpa, where they had tremendous popular support. There they received a hearty welcome from the local Maoists, took part in ceremonies held to honour their fallen comrades, and finally got some rest after weeks of strain and hardship.[81] The government officials and police personnel who had been taken prisoner at Beni were also brought to Thabang. On 6 April, they were released in a ceremony held in the presence of representatives of the International Committee of the Red Cross (ICRC), whom the Maoists had invited to fetch the prisoners.

After Beni, the Maoists staged other attacks on RNA fortifications and continued to expand their People's Liberation Army. But the Maoists had never previously concentrated such a large rebel force on a single target. For them, the battle represented a very high peak in the development of their military prowess. As the Maoist activist Dhaneshwar Pokhrel, euphoric after the battle, wrote in his diary, '[Beni] was perhaps the greatest blow struck by the world proletarian class against the imperialist gangsters after the Vietnam War.'[82] This was grand hyperbole. But it is clear that in some ways the Maoists had been successful.

They had mobilized thousands of cadre and civilians for over a month to transport food, logistics and weapons. They had organized civilians to arrange food and shelter at various points during the long march between Rukum and Myagdi. This amply demonstrated the Maoists' success in consolidating power over Nepal's rural populations and mobilizing them for the party. On the other hand, the state security forces, as already mentioned above, were virtually clueless about these massive preparations, even though villagers only a few hours from Beni had been warned weeks beforehand of a major rebel operation in the area. This reflects the intelligence failure of the state army and their poor relations with local populations.

The attack on Beni was also a significant propaganda victory for the Maoists. It may not have led to the 'strategic offensive' phase in which the rebels would be so powerful as to force the state into a defensive mode, but the battle did disprove the government's claim that the RNA had almost entirely crushed the Maoist army. As the rebels said in a statement, 'Two successful military strikes in Bhojpur and Beni within a span of three weeks have given a mortal blow to the royal military dictatorship that was seeking to legitimize its rule.'[83]

As part of the Maoists' Special People's Military Campaign, the attack on Beni was also meant to inspire the population of western Nepal to rise up against the state. Most of the population, however, felt more oppressed than inspired. Villagers in Darbang interpreted the campaign thus: 'Those who have money have to give [the Maoists] cash, those who have food have to give them rice, those who have clothes have to give them clothes, and those who have nothing have to give them one member of their family.'[84] Similarly, the occupants of Beni were terrorized when the rebels invaded it. There was also grief: sixteen civilians were killed during the battle (eight were killed in crossfire, another eight as a result of the aerial bombing).[85] But the attack also aroused awe among the residents of the town. In the days following the attack, there was much excited talk about the rebels' fearlessness during battle, the astonishingly large numbers of female combatants, and the composed manner in which they had retreated under helicopter fire. Many locals were also greatly impressed with how carefully the rebels had organized medical and logistical teams to support the troops, carry away the wounded and treat them. In contrast, many derided the government and the state security forces for what was perceived to be their negligence and incompetence.[86] When Home Minister Kamal Thapa visited Beni on 22 March, the town's residents gave him a cold reception.[87]

But Beni was obviously not an outright victory for the Maoists. While revealing the strength and tenacity of the rebels, the battle of Beni also showed the limits of their military capability.

The Maoists concentrated over 3,000 armed combatants, almost their entire Western Division, to attack a town that held a single RNA battalion. According to best estimates, there were around 400 army personnel and 100 police personnel in the town that night – a minuscule proportion of the total number of state security forces in the country. The lieutenant colonel of Shri Kali Prasad Battalion told a visitor that the Maoists were 'prepared to take 85 per cent casualties'.[88] He said the RNA battalion could not be ordered to defend the police and government offices, because nearly half the force would have been destroyed in the attempt. According to conservative estimates, seventy-eight Maoists (including two vice-brigade commanders, a battalion commander and a battalion vice-commander) were killed during the attack and over 400 were wounded. In contrast, thirty-three army and police personnel lost their lives. These numbers indicate that the Maoists had to pay a high price in the battle.[89]

Despite their large numbers and high degree of commitment, the rebels also failed to take over the army barracks, even after twelve hours of fighting. They never managed to ransack and occupy any district capital for more than a few hours. Nor did they ever gain the capacity to engage in full-scale positional warfare.[90] The attack on Beni thus also illustrates the limit to the military capacity of a rebel group relying primarily on numbers, stealth and high morale to fight a state army heavily supplied with weapons and training from major global powers such as the United States.

CHAPTER 6

# The Fish in the Sea: Vignettes

## A People's Politics

When the writer Govinda Bartaman visited Rolpa during the 2003 ceasefire, he met a Maoist activist who had adopted the alias 'Comrade Saddam' as a tribute to that infamous arch-enemy of American imperialism. 'There's great turmoil during wartime,' said Comrade Saddam, noting how the conflict had brought production and trade to a halt and forced schools and health facilities to remain closed. 'But politics can heal the wounds of war,' he continued. 'That's the role of a people's politics.'[1] For the Maoists, of course, the purpose of politics was not exactly to alleviate the sufferings of the conflict. Their politics aimed to offer a convincing analysis of the contradictions in, and an alternative vision of, the Nepali state and society. By this means they hoped to draw large sections of the population into active support for the party's struggle.

Their early encounter with Marxism had led Maoist leaders to conceptualize their struggle in traditional Marxist–Leninist terms. They identified potential allies and supporters among the population on the basis of their class: the proletariat, the peasantry, the petty-bourgeoisie and the national industrialists.[2] The rebels could undoubtedly attract support from sections of the peasantry and the working classes by appealing to their class background. But on the whole, the class-based categorization of the 'motivating forces' of the revolution was too abstract to exert wide popular appeal. Class was only one among the many lenses through which people identified themselves. Class lines were blurred, and other forms of identity took precedence over class. By the time they launched their rebellion, the Maoists had recognized that ethnicity and caste were stronger forms of identity than class, and hence potent bases for political mobilization.

The Nepali state had been under the control of upper-caste Hindus of Pahadi (hill) ethnicity since the late eighteenth century. They had classified all of Nepal's ethno-linguistic groups into a rigid caste hierarchy that determined their rights and functions.

When King Mahendra established the Panchayat system in 1960, he formally outlawed caste discrimination. For Mahendra, however, modernization meant establishing a nation with a homogenous culture. The culture of the elites that had ruled Nepal for almost two centuries was defined as the national culture. The state sought to impose this culture upon a population that spoke over a hundred languages. Hinduism continued to be the state religion. The language of the ruling castes and a national history glorifying the monarchy was propagated through the education system.[3] The upper castes continued to dominate state institutions. The cultures and histories of other groups were not merely omitted from the official narrative but were actively suppressed.

The Panchayat years saw growing resentment against the state and the ruling castes. But given the restrictions on free speech and organization, individuals from marginalized ethnic groups had few avenues for expressing their grievances. The larger political parties, led by upper-caste men, had no idea of the depth of this resentment. The demands of the ethno-linguistic groups formed no part of their programme during the 1990 uprising. The democratic constitution drafted that year, while recognizing Nepal's 'multi-ethnic' and 'multilingual' character, continued to define it as a Hindu state and privileged the Nepali language over all others. The authors of the constitution feared that granting collective rights to ethnic and caste groups would lead to social discord and violence. So, in contrast to India, they deliberately made no provision for affirmative action in favour of historically marginalized social groups. And they banned political parties formed on the basis of 'religion, community, caste, tribe or region.'[4]

The questions of caste and ethnicity had always posed something of a conundrum to Nepal's communists. They recognized that the state had discriminated against particular communities. But, as Marxists, their emphasis was on class rather than on ethnicity or caste. In the 1990s, the CPN–UML rejected ethnic activists' demand for autonomous governance in their areas and the preservation and promotion of their languages. The party thought that such measures would only promote atavistic and irrelevant forms of identity. In this age of capitalism and the nation-state, they argued, the exchanges taking place between various ethnic groups would inevitably, and desirably, lead to the creation of a homogenous national culture.[5] On this point, then, their views converged somewhat with the official doctrine of the Panchayat.

A number of communists from indigenous groups grew disillusioned with this position and left the mother party to establish or join organizations that campaigned for the rights of their communities. There was an upsurge in ethnic mobilization in the 1990s. In the course of their war, the Maoists sought to woo these activists by presenting their party as a vast umbrella organization that represented the demands of the marginalized castes and ethnicities.

The Maoists developed a theory regarding the place of ethnicity in the national fabric that marked a significant departure from the traditional positions of Nepali communists. They argued that ethnic groups, rather than being primordial remnants, had evolved during the process of Nepal's uneven development. As the state expropriated the resources of the population for the benefit of a tiny elite, oppressed communities developed bonds of solidarity based on their common language, culture, and territory. This was how ethnic groups – which the Maoists referred to as 'nationalities', following Leninist theory – had emerged in Nepal.[6]

Like other communists, the Maoists maintained that the various ethnic groups would eventually merge into the broader Nepali nation as a matter of historical necessity. But unlike other communists, the Maoists held that the oppressed nationalities should, in the interim, be allowed to enjoy rights of self-governance and that their languages and cultures should be protected. As the Nepali state had oppressed people on the basis of ethnicity and caste, any act of political assertion against the state too had to be based on ethnicity and caste. Because a person's class was largely determined by his or her ethnicity and caste, the struggle of ethnic and caste groups had to be considered an integral part of the class struggle.

At the same time, however, the Maoists were wary of the unbridled expression of ethnic claims. Ethnicity and caste overlapped with class but they were not equivalent. An overemphasis on the former could lead to a neglect of the latter. It was necessary to guard against ethnic chauvinism, particularly the tendency of ethnic leaders to treat their groups as fixed and immutable and to incite hatred towards other groups. Ethnic claims had to remain firmly under the control of 'the proletariat'. In other words, the Maoists believed that only their party could effectively manage ethnic demands.

I n September 2001, the Maoists announced the formation of the United Revolutionary People's Council (URPC). This body would stand at the helm of the party's united front, which included the party's local 'people's governments' (*jana sarkar*) and mass organizations that functioned as the party's 'transmission belts' (Lenin's phrase) by disseminating its ideology and policies among the population. The URPC's policies and programmes offered a relatively detailed picture of the kind of state structure the party sought to build once it captured state power. According to this plan, People's Houses of Representatives (HoRs) would be elected on the basis of full adult suffrage in four tiers: the centre, the autonomous regions, the districts and the villages/towns. Unlike the parliaments in bourgeois democracies, which the Maoists claimed were 'merely … toothless debating club[s]',[7] the Houses of Representatives in the new regime would enjoy full executive and legislative rights. These bodies would elect People's Governments at all tiers.

Of the four tiers of governance that the Maoists envisaged, those at the centre, district and village/town levels overlapped with institutions that were already in existence. But the second tier, 'autonomous regions', marked a radical departure from the administrative-territorial demarcation of the Nepali state. The Panchayat state had divided the nation into five development regions that stood vertically parallel to each other, so that each band included part of the mountains of the north, the middle hills and the southern plains. These regions included diverse ethnicities, and members of the same ethnicity were divided between regions. Many ethnic activists thought that this demarcation was aimed at preventing ethnic consolidation and political assertion.[8]

In contrast, the Maoists sought to delineate boundaries between territories that certain ethnic groups – officially classified as Janajatis (indigenous nationalities) by the Nepali state in 2002[9] – considered to be their historical homelands. Six of the nine autonomous regions proposed by the Maoists were defined on this basis.[10] Once the rebels captured state power, the dominant ethnic group in each of these regions

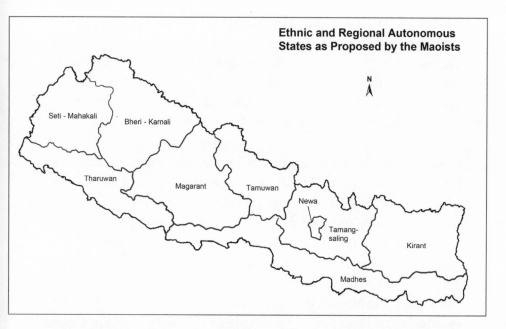

**Ethnic and Regional Autonomous States as Proposed by the Maoists**

N

Seti - Mahakali

Bheri - Karnali

Tharuwan

Magarant

Tamuwan

Newa

Tamang-saling

Kirant

Madhes

would enjoy the rights of self-determination and autonomous governance. All sectors would fall under the jurisdiction of the autonomous
regions, except for matters relating to national defence, foreign relations and international trade that must necessarily be decided by central
government.[11]

There was a major problem, though: all of the autonomous regions
proposed by the Maoists were inhabited by members of diverse ethnic
groups. In some regions, the group with the greatest historical claims
did not even constitute a majority. But the Maoists argued that this was
irrelevant. If certain nationalities no longer formed a majority in their
ancestral homelands, it was because Nepal's dominant groups had come
to live in these areas and displaced their original inhabitants. This too
constituted oppression, and provided all the more reason to give these
nationalities special rights over their neighbours.[12]

The boundaries of the three remaining provinces were not drawn on
the basis of ethnicity. Two of these – Seti-Mahakali and Bheri-Karnali –
corresponded to very poor areas in the western part of the country that
had historically suffered from neglect by Kathmandu. The other, Madhes
in the south-east, was primarily inhabited by people who shared a culture,
language and kinship ties with people across the border in the Indian
states of Uttar Pradesh and Bihar. Madhesis were internally diverse and
had a complex caste system of their own. The Nepali state had always

been suspicious about their commitment to the nation, and discriminated against them.[13] There was to be no autonomous region for Dalits,
those at the bottom of the Hindu caste system and the most oppressed of
Nepal's communities, as they were scattered across the nation. However,
the Maoists stated that 'the state [would] make provision[s] to grant them
special rights until they become equal to others in practical terms.'[14]

It was obvious that for as long as they were at war, the Maoists would not
be able to elect a central House of Representatives or implement autonomous governance for marginalized ethnic groups and regions. These
ideas were largely propaganda aimed at gaining the support of sections
of the population that felt excluded by the Nepali state. Nonetheless, the
'Common Minimum Policy and Programme of the United Revolutionary
People's Council' did include guidelines for the administration of areas
from which the Maoists had driven out state institutions. In lieu of an
elected central House of Representatives, the Maoists set up a 'Central
People's Government', which was led by Baburam Bhattarai and included
thirty-six other top leaders responsible for monitoring and providing
directions to party cadre involved in administration.

Groups of party cadre were tasked with organizing area committees
(overseeing a group of villages) and district committees. Over time, local
inhabitants were to be coaxed or coerced into joining ward, village or
district-level 'people's governments' (*jana sarkars*). After consolidating their hold over the area, the rebels would hold elections to the local
House of Representatives. Elected deputies would include members of
the party and the Maoists' People's Liberation Army (PLA) as well as
civilians representing various sections of the population. The House of
Representatives at the village and town levels would elect members to
the district HoRs, and the district HoRs would elect the HoRs at the level
of the autonomous region.

The purpose of this exercise was, first, to establish firm control over
the population and mobilize people regardless of whether they actively
supported the party. Party committees and *jana sarkars* would monitor
people's activities and collect taxes and levies (schoolteachers, for
example, had to pay a day's salary to the Maoists every month). The *jana
sarkars* would then work to engage people in local governance so as to
give them a greater sense of autonomy and control over their destiny,
and thus sow feelings of gratitude and loyalty towards the party. To that

end the Maoists mobilized people to build roads and other infrastructure, and establish cooperatives and cottage industries.

It was not easy to involve local populations in *jana sarkars* during
the conflict. The Maoists were able to hold elections to their House of
Representatives only in a few areas. The locals often had to be compelled
to vote. In most places, the party committees enjoyed substantially more
power than the *jana sarkars*.[15]

'There will be more democracy in areas where the People's War has
reached a more developed phase and where people's governments are
working in a more open manner,' wrote Baburam Bhattarai. 'There will be
more centralism in areas where they [People's War and people's govern-
ments] are weaker. But centralism will be more crucial than democracy
during the course of the war.'[16]

By placing 'centralism' above 'democracy', Bhattarai was underscor-
ing that the party's needs were paramount and that the primary purpose
of the Maoists' parallel government was to channel the population into
aiding the war effort. It would certainly be desirable if people lent their
support of their own volition. For that, Maoist activists would need to be
as gentle as possible with the population. As Mao had said, 'The guerrillas must move amongst the people as a fish swims in the sea.' But this did
not mean that their bids for goodwill should override the party's needs. If
anyone refused to offer labour, money or shelter for the party, the rebels
would resort to intimidation, even violence, to achieve their ends. The
primary goal was to utilize the resources of the people for the Maoist
cause; the question of whether or not they genuinely supported the party
was secondary.

## Fortress of the Revolution

Naturally, it was in Rolpa and Rukum that the party was most successful in mobilizing the population for its own needs. Here the
rebels gained near total control over a cluster of thirteen VDCs (seven
in eastern Rukum and six in north Rolpa), and could expect unreserved
support from the local population. In April 2002, the Maoists announced
that they had reorganized these thirteen VDCs into a 'special district'
(*bishesh jilla*). Thabang, a village in north Rolpa, was declared the capital
of the 'special district'.

Thabang was a two-day walk from the district headquarters Libang and had approximately 830 households, almost all of them belonging to the Magar ethnic group.[17] It was an obscure, nondescript place where few outsiders ever came. But the Maoist declaration of 2002 lent the village a degree of fame, bringing in a steady stream of travellers including Maoists from other areas, foreigners sympathetic to the insurgency and journalists. Many of them were impressed with the vigorous social and political organization maintained by the rebels. Portraits of Marx, Engels, Lenin, Stalin and Mao painted on the wall of one of Thabang's mud-and-slate houses greeted each traveller entering the village. There was a large portrait of Prachanda on another wall. Red flags hung everywhere. Slogans in support of the party and denouncing the monarchy, the United States and the Royal Nepal Army were emblazoned on the walls of almost every house.[18]

The village had evidently been collectivized. Maoist soldiers in fatigues could be seen chatting over tea or snacks in eateries that were run as cooperatives. They could be seen in party-run grocery stores buying goods that were likely to come from one of the Maoist-run projects, such as the Jaljala cottage industry cooperative that made shawls, caps, bags, handkerchiefs and bags.[19] As dusk fell, the village crier (*katuwal*) could be heard announcing the tasks allocated to residents of a specific locality for the following day, such as tilling a plot of land or gathering firewood. Half of the crop produced collectively was handed over to the party.[20] Locals of Thabang were required to carry messages or goods from one place to another within the special district, organize food and shelter for visiting Maoists from other districts, and build trails connecting Thabang to other VDCs. The party established a commune of families that had lost an important member to the conflict. The commune allowed such families to live together, engage in collective farming and build a support network. In a diary entry from January 2005, a visiting Maoist activist marvelled at how 'every single person in Thabang has been integrated into the party.'[21]

The Maoists glorified Thabang as 'the Maoist capital', 'the Yenan of Nepal', 'the fortress of the revolution' and 'the centre of ideology and belief'. An article in the Maoist newspaper *Janadesh* enthused, 'Everyone here is ready to sacrifice themselves for others. Caste discrimination has been eradicated. There are no inequalities between men and women ... Here you can see the dawn of a new civilization.'[22]

As the rebels gained total political legitimacy in Thabang, Maoist ideology merged with local narratives to explain why that remote village in Nepal's mid-western hills had become more susceptible to radical communist ideology than any other place. The Magars of Thabang were a naturally rebellious people, so the narrative went, unable to countenance any form of oppression or infringement on their autonomy. According to village elders, during an unrecorded period in the distant past, a local raja from Rukum had come to establish dominance over Thabang and its environs. Villagers soon realized that this ruler sought to exploit the Magars and their land and to 'violate the dignity' of their beautiful daughters. So they took a peasant who tilled the raja's lands into their confidence and conspired to fry the raja's grains before they were planted. After his crop failed to grow, the raja went back to where he had come from. The people of Thabang thus regained their freedom.[23]

Barman Budha was a leader who figured prominently in the more recent historical memory of Thabang residents. In the narrative of his Maoist descendants, he embodied the fusion between the broad political vision of the communists and the rebellious character of the people of Thabang. Budha had been at the forefront of various community movements. In 1975, for instance, another local leader, Ram Kumar, tried to establish a monopoly over the sale of alcohol with the support of the local Panchayat administration. Barman Budha and the future Maoist leader Mohan Baidya, who was visiting Thabang at the time, mobilized the village women against the measure.[24] Again, it was under Budha's leadership that the villagers of Thabang voted overwhelmingly against the monarchy in the 1980 referendum and boycotted elections to the Panchayat legislature in 1981. In 1991 Budha contested in the general elections and won a seat in parliament as a member of the SJM, the Maoists' parliamentary front.[25]

The Maoists also claimed that the lifestyle of the people of Thabang (and by extension of all the Kham Magars of Rolpa and Rukum) naturally predisposed them to communism. In contrast to the rigidly maintained hierarchies of the upper castes, the Magars had for centuries cultivated an egalitarian and collectivist culture. Now, under the direction of the Maoist party, they were pooling their resources and working hard in the service of the revolution. In so doing, said the rebels, they not only served the cause of the poor and oppressed across Nepal, but also offered the vision of an emerging proletarian culture to the world. The

Kham Magars, hitherto poor and unknown, now stood at the centre of the world revolution of the twenty-first century.

The people of Thabang were assured that one day the state would inevitably come under the Maoists' control. They would then be free from the rule of the upper castes. Rolpa and Rukum would be included in the Magarat Autonomous Region, where the Magars, the original inhabitants of the region, would exercise complete control over their politics and livelihoods. To reiterate their commitment to the Magar cause, the Maoists held a mass meeting in Thabang on 9 January 2004. In the presence of thousands of spectators (75,000 according to the Maoist media), the party proclaimed the formation of the Magarat Autonomous Region People's Government. Santosh Budha Magar, a long-time Maoist activist from the village, was declared the chairman of this government.[26]

Many Magars of Rolpa and Rukum adopted the Maoist narrative as their own and came to feel a new sense of dignity and empowerment. Their community gained unprecedented recognition as hundreds of young Magar men and women joined the Maoist cause as full-time activists. Locals of Thabang felt honoured by the interest shown in them by visitors. As one man confided to a fellow Maoist activist from another part of the country: 'Many domestic and foreign guests have been visiting Thabang. They hope to find a model from which they might draw lessons for themselves. But it is no easy task to maintain the reputation of Thabang. We worry they may take away a negative impression.'[27] Attention from outsiders had thus reinforced the demands on the locals of Thabang to display commitment and self-sacrifice for the communist cause.

But in Thabang as in other areas in the mid-western hills, the ultimate basis of Maoist rule was state violence and terror. The bonds of solidarity forged in the service of the Maoist cause may have had something to do with the Magars' long-standing culture of resistance and communitarian lifestyle, but a deeper cause lay in the history of oppression in the region. In 2003, when Govinda Bartaman asked a teenage student in Rolpa why the Maoists and the army were fighting, the boy replied: 'A long time ago the police used to rape the women of our village, eat our chickens and loot our homes. That was why the Maoists fought against the police. The police couldn't defeat the Maoists, so the army came in.'[28]

Every person in Thabang had a relative or a neighbour who had been killed by the state security forces. The authorities in the district capital assumed that anyone who lived in a Maoist-ruled village was a rebel. The army continued to make the occasional foray into the villages of Rolpa and Rukum, harassing, torturing and killing villagers. Joining the Maoist movement was the only way the survivors could protect themselves and avenge the loss of their loved ones.

In any case, there was no alternative to supporting the rebels if one wished to continue to live among one's friends and family in a Maoist-controlled village: all those who supported rival political parties had been evicted. Slogans painted on walls threatened potential informers with 'annihilation'. Within a short period after 1996, the rebels had executed four people in Thabang on the charge of spying for the enemy. As Kiyoko Ogura observed during her visit to the village, 'It was clear that people could not live in Thabang without being Maoists and without helping the Maoists.'[29]

The teenage boy who answered Govinda Bartaman with such certainty might at times have felt ambivalent about the Maoist cause. He may have wondered about the rebels' culpability in instigating the conflict when he or his friends were forcibly drafted into the Maoists' local student union, and were interrogated and beaten by the army as a result. There were many occasions on which the villagers of Rolpa and Rukum might have felt resentment towards the party, such as when they were forced to give the party a large proportion of their paltry incomes, or when they had to abandon their farm work in order to construct a public road. They probably begrudged the rebels when they forbade them from travelling to a nearby town, or when they imposed a tax of thousands of rupees on anyone looking to go to India for work. At such moments the populace of Rolpa and Rukum must have feared for their futures and doubted whether the Maoists would ever fulfil their promise for the 'liberation of Magarat'.

The locals did not usually express their fears and doubts to the Maoists.[30] But signs of their frustration can be found in the accounts of the rebels themselves. Uttam Kandel, a Maoist activist, wrote in his diary while he was in Gam, a VDC close to Thabang, in January 2005: 'There is obvious despair among [the old people in the village] … They asked us, "How long will the war go on? How many more of our sons and daughters are yet to get killed?" We tried to reassure them by saying, "Don't panic, we're going to achieve victory soon", but they did not seem convinced.'[31]

Some days later, Kandel saw large numbers of people (thousands, in his estimate) constructing a road. This was to become the famed Martyr's Road, a ninety-one-kilometre stretch connecting the villages of Thabang and Nuwagaon. One of the most ambitious projects carried out under the rebels' direction, the Martyr's Road was often mentioned in Maoist propaganda as proof that the rebels were not engaged in wholesale destruction but that they made genuine efforts to improve the lives of people in the areas they controlled.

Members of the local *jana sarkar* (people's government) who were supervising the road building told Kandel that they had conscripted labour from the surrounding areas. Each conscript had to work eight hours a day for ten days. During that time, they slept in tents by the side of the road. Maoist cultural troupes sang and danced for them in the evenings, and party leaders occasionally lectured them on politics and ideology. This was intended to make them understand that they were donating their labour for a common cause, namely, the struggle against the autocratic king and the establishment of a people's republic. Leaders of the local *jana sarkar* said that many people would initially be upset at having to work for free, but in time they would feel inspired by the rebels' political goals and return home happy to have done their bit for the cause. Many stayed on awhile after the end of the allotted ten-day period. Some of the youth who had come to build the road even enrolled in the Maoist army.[32]

Soon after his conversation with the Maoist foremen, Kandel ran into a group of people who had been brought from the nearby district of Dang to 'provide voluntary labour'. He was surprised at the degree of bitterness they expressed towards the rebels for forcing them into such backbreaking work. Writing in his diary, Kandel sought to justify their coercion by repeating a standard Maoist trope: 'A mother suffers while giving birth to a child. How can she know in advance the joy she will feel after the child is born?'[33]

The construction of the Martyr's Road would have reminded some of the older Maoists of the era in the 1960s when the Chinese came to build roads in Nepal's hills. Back then the Chinese had tried to indoctrinate Nepali workers through their cultural performances. Now the young Maoist activists of Rolpa were using the same methods to win the support of the conscripted workers. Like the Chinese workers during the Cultural Revolution, the rebels were infused with revolutionary fervour.

They felt they were participating not just in the construction of a new road, but in the creation of a new world.

But if they knew anything of Thabang's popular history, the people of Dang who had been dragooned into working on the Martyr's Road would have been reminded of another incident. In 1981, the Rolpa district government decided to construct a mule track between Dang and Libang, the capital of Rolpa district. Although Nepal had come a long way since the pre-1950s days when the rulers could extract resources and forced labour from ordinary people whenever they liked, some of the old habits of the state still persisted. The local government thus decided to conscript the people of Rolpa to build the mule track. The people of Thabang rose up against this decision, asserting that they would provide labour only on condition that the government compensated them, provided funds for the local school, and connected their village to the track. When Barman Budha approached the administration of Libang with these demands, he was jailed for twenty-seven months.[34]

## Class Struggle or Ethnic Autonomy?

Magar activists tried to compete with the Maoists for influence over the locals of Rolpa and Rukum. But the Maoists had penetrated so deeply into these areas that it was difficult to mobilize people solely on the basis of their ethnicity.

However, this was not the case in many other parts of the country. In the eastern hills, the population was predominantly Rai (or Khambu) and Limbu, two closely related ethnic groups within the broader Kirati group.[35] Like the Magars, they are classified among Nepal's indigenous nationalities (Adivasi Janajati). They have a clearly articulated narrative of their own exclusion, which begins with King Prithvi Narayan Shah's conquest of their territories in the eighteenth century. The Maoists had a very limited presence in the eastern hills before they launched their rebellion. Over time the rebels made earnest efforts to engage Rai and Limbu leaders and to convince them that they must participate in the Maoist movement to fulfil their dream of ethnic liberation. In this way, the Maoists gradually gained some support among radical Kirati activists. Their relationship, however, remained fragile and was occasionally marred by tension.

Rajan Mukarung's novel *Hetchhakuppa* sheds light on the experience of humiliation faced by Sangen Kirati, a young Rai man from the eastern hill district of Bhojpur.[36] The men of Sangen's community have for generations sought employment in the security forces of foreign countries, primarily the British and Indian armies, but also the police forces of Singapore, Hong Kong and Brunei. Such jobs are known to guarantee a prosperous life and are much coveted among Rais and Limbus, who have few other alternatives for upward mobility. But the idea of joining a foreign army does not appeal to Sangen. He recoils at the thought of serving under British officers and fighting like a mercenary in foreign wars. So, unlike many of his peers, Sangen completes his SLC exam and goes to Kathmandu for higher education.

Sangen feels alienated in the capital right from the start. He is disconnected from the dominant upper-caste culture that is signified primarily by the Nepali language and the Hindu religion. During a poetry event one day, he goes to the stage and recites a poem he has written. At the end of the programme, Professor Sharma, a well-known novelist and literary critic, rises to offer his closing remarks. His name and his Indo-Aryan features clearly indicate he is a Brahmin. After mispronouncing Sangen's name, the professor voices his surprise that a 'Janajati boy could write such an impressive poem in Nepali'. From the boy's appearance, says the professor (referring to Sangen's Mongoloid traits), 'I thought he was a *lahure* [the colloquial term for men employed in foreign security forces] … His entry into our Nepali literature is a happy event.'[37] Sangen is mortified by his patronizing comment.

After completing his BA degree, Sangen becomes the editor of a small magazine, *Aawaaj* (Voice), which is funded by an organization representing retired British Gurkhas. The job pays him a pitiful salary, and that too rarely on time. He struggles to make ends meet. The irony of his position is not lost on the narrator: 'Destiny is cruel … For a full four years, [Sangen] had to work for retired *lahures,* who represented a system he opposed.'[38]

Still, Sangen feels that working for *Aawaj* is better than working for one of Kathmandu's larger media houses, which are dominated by Brahmins and steeped in a high-caste Hindu cultural ethos. As a member of a marginalized Tibeto-Burman ethnic group, Sangen would feel an outsider in such an environment. He looks different, speaks in a different idiom and sees society from a different vantage point. At least at *Aawaj*, he is among his own kind – Rais, Limbus and members of other ethnic groups that have traditionally served as *lahures*. His job at least allows him to promote his community's struggle for their rights. The magazine's task is limited: to campaign for pay, pensions and privileges for Gurkhas that are commensurate with their British counterparts. But even for this they need broader political support, which is hard to come by, as most politicians belong to the dominant Brahmin and Chhetri castes and are unconcerned with the demands of the *lahures*. A UML politician does once promise to raise their issue in parliament, but nothing comes of it.

Sangen meets other ethnic activists and learns how the Nepali state has historically undermined the culture of his community. Generation after generation, children of his community have had to learn Nepali at the expense of their mother tongue, Nepali being the 'national language' and the medium of instruction at government schools. Since the nineteenth century, Sangen believes, the state had forced Kiratis to abandon their traditional religion (which involves animistic ancestor worship) and practice Hindu rituals and festivals. Markers of their identity have gradually been erased. Sangen's village in Bhojpur, for instance, was originally called Dilungpa or Dilpa, names that have origins in the Bantawa Rai language. But when the Panchayat regime reconfigured Nepal's administrative boundaries, the village was divided into two separate units. One was named Nagi and the other Annapurna – both names from the language of the dominant upper castes. The original names gradually faded into oblivion. The loss of the native name of his village pains Sangen.

Sangen and other ethnic activists see little difference between the absolute monarchs of the past and the current leaders of the parliamentary parties. Janajati communities had responded vigorously to the call of those parties to fight against royal absolutism. Ram Prasad Rai, for instance, was one of the Kirati men who had participated in the Nepali Congress-led armed struggle against the Rana oligarchy in 1950. Ratna Kumar Bantawa had joined the Jhapali communists (who would later form the CPN–UML) and waged class struggle in the eastern hills. But once the Congress and CPN–UML came to power, their high-caste politicians forgot their Kirati counterparts and left them to languish as small-time village leaders.

'The long-nosed ones have long belittled the flat-nosed people as stocky, filthy and dim-witted savages,' says Sangen. 'They have ruled over and exploited them.'[39] Sangen is plainly alluding to a 1952 poem by the Brahmin scholar Rammani Acharya Dixit. Ethnic activists often cite this poem as proof of the upper castes' contempt for the Tibeto-Burman ethnic groups:

> Nepal is a land of savages, idiots, rustics
> Stocky and filthy load carriers
> God, may these people remain this way.
> How will our supremacy survive
> If they become aware and civilized?
> We must appoint only Brahmins and Chhetris
> Of the topmost tier, to the council of ministers
> And allow no Matwalis.[40]

Sangen believes that his community must recover the symbols of their culture in order to regain their dignity. He makes it his mission to excavate such symbols from Kirati mythology. He begins writing a novel loosely based on the life of Hetchhakuppa, a mythical ancestor of the Kirati people. According to legend, Hetchhakuppa was orphaned at a very early age and raised by his two sisters, who left home one day and never returned. Hetchhakuppa had to fend for himself from then on. Sangen wants to retell Hetchhakuppa's story as an allegory for the struggles of the modern Kirati man.

Several of Sangen's childhood friends have joined the Maoists. Their ambition to establish autonomous ethnic provinces resonates with him. One day he hears of a battle between Maoists and RNA forces in his home district of Bhojpur. A rebel from his ethnic group, Shibahang Khambu, has died in the battle. Sangen is instantly reminded of Atal Singh Rai, a member of a Kirati ruling clan from the early nineteenth century. After the forces of the Shah monarchy conquered the regions inhabited by the Kirati people, Atal Singh Rai waged a long guerilla campaign against the new rulers. But the campaign was eventually crushed. The government in Kathmandu arrested Atal Singh and his fellow rebels, sentenced them to death and confiscated their property.

In the preface to the novel, Mukarung describes the protagonist as his literary alter ego. More broadly, the character of Sangen Kirati gives voice to the experiences of many Rai and Limbu men who came of age after the democratic transition of 1990. The novel portrays the historical conditions that sharpened their ethnic consciousness and made them sympathetic towards the Maoist cause. In so doing, it illustrates how class struggle intersected with identity politics in Nepal.

G opal Kirati was one of the Janajati leaders whom the Maoists won over to their side after persistent efforts. He was born into the Khambu community in 1955, in the mountain district of Solukhumbu in eastern Nepal. His memoir offers a familiar leftist narrative of rural oppression and victimhood during the Panchayat regime. Kirati recalls how his family suffered under the *pradhan pancha* (local chief) in his village.[41] He was in his early teens when his father died, and his mother had to sell their family land, livestock, jewellery and their prized radio set to pay off their loans to the *pradhan pancha*. Kirati quit school after seventh grade and worked as a porter for six years, carrying loads for tourists trekking through Nepal's mountains. Despite the hardships, Kirati enjoyed travelling and observing the various peoples and cultures across the country.

Like many others who would later join the Maoists, Gopal Kirati was initiated into the communist movement by a relative. Hari Narayan Thulung, his brother-in-law, was a schoolteacher affiliated with one of the communist factions. In 1983, when the twenty-eight-year-old Kirati was considering joining the British Army, Thulung tried to dissuade him by giving him a copy of *Seema*, a play by the popular leftist poet-musician Rayan. The play depicted the sufferings of Nepalis recruited into the British army. It had a shattering effect on Kirati. He recalled that after reading the play, he said to his brother-in-law: 'We are indeed a wretched lot. I must do something with my life. What should I do if I don't join a foreign army?' Hari Narayan replied, 'We have to launch a revolution in the name of the country and the people.'[42]

However, in succeeding years, Kirati's attraction to communism was superseded by his growing empathy for the ethnic struggle. While staying in Kathmandu during his travels, he became involved with various organizations working to preserve and promote Kirati culture. Kirati made friends with fellow Janajatis who worked as labourers in the tourist and carpet industries. He helped organize celebrations during important Kirati festivals such as Yokwa, Chasok and Sakewa. He told his friends Kirati folk tales that he had heard from his mother as a child, the same stories he used to tell his childhood friends back in the village.

'Looking back,' Gopal wrote years later, 'I feel that it was through telling stories that I started to become a leader.'[43]

Gopal Kirati participated in the 1990 movement for democracy, but refused to support any of the major parties. Along with some friends, he published and distributed pamphlets which, while supporting the cause of democracy, prioritized ethnic claims. 'There should be democracy, not Brahminism (*Bahunbad hoina, prajatantra hunuparchha*),' was their message. 'Ethnic rights should be guaranteed, the state should be made secular.' On 6 April Kirati took part in demonstrations in Durbar Marg, the street in front of the royal palace. He was badly beaten by the police and had to get eight stitches on his head. He was still in hospital when he heard the news that the king had agreed to dismantle the Panchayat system and restore multi-party democracy. The news caused widespread jubilation, but Kirati was unmoved. By now he firmly believed that violent struggle alone could bring about a real social transformation: 'I believed that a new political system could only be established through the sacrifice of thousands of martyrs.'[44]

Like many other ethnic activists, Kirati started his own organization, the Khambuwan National Front (KNF), soon after the establishment of parliamentary democracy. The KNF aimed to forge a more militant ethos than other ethnic organizations. 'The 1990 constitution enabled the oppressed nationalities to rise up,' wrote Kirati, 'but it did not give them their rights.'[45] As the constitution did not allow formation of parties along ethnic lines, the particular grievances of ethnic groups remained unaddressed. This, according to Kirati, was what led him to choose the path of armed struggle.

The Maoists' declaration of People's War in 1996 emboldened Gopal Kirati. He issued a public statement indicating 'qualified support' for the Maoists. On 22 July 1997, the KNF carried out bomb attacks in three locations in Bhojpur and Solukhumbu districts. In each location the target of the attack was a Sanskrit school – a potent symbol of upper-caste culture and tradition. Kirati had launched his struggle for ethnic autonomy.

Kirati's statement came at a time when few people openly supported the Maoists. It attracted the attention of Maoist leaders, even though his organization was relatively obscure. Thinking that an alliance with Kirati could gain them support in the east, the Maoists sent Suresh Ale Magar to meet him. Later, Baburam Bhattarai invited him to Gorakhpur, a town in North India.[46] In April 1998, following negotiations, the two publicly declared that they had formed an alliance.

But the alliance fell apart after seven months. Kirati denounced the Maoists and resumed his armed struggle independently. The Maoists managed to placate him, only to antagonize him again. This became the pattern of their relationship. As both sides were caught in the perils of war against the state and had few allies, each would periodically reach out to the other. Before long, quarrels would erupt and Kirati would announce that he had parted ways with the Maoists.[47]

The friction arose partly because the Maoists sought not only to cultivate Kirati but also to educate him. In a May 1998 piece about the Khambuwan National Front, Bhattarai praised Kirati's writings for expressing rage against ethnic oppression and commitment to armed struggle. The KNF's desire to ally with the Maoists was commendable, he said, but Kirati seemed guided more by passion than reason. 'Revolutionaries need both intellect and emotion,' Bhattarai wrote. 'Although emotions dominate in the early phase, intellect must eventually take precedence over emotions.'[48]

In Bhattarai's view, the KNF's singular focus on ethnicity was misguided. Kirati had not understood that ethnic groups had evolved with the development of productive forces, he wrote. There are no inherent differences between the various ethnic groups. Rather, the characteristics of each ethnic group were determined by their position in the changing relations of production. Because the KNF had not grasped this properly, its members perceived the upper castes of the hills as their sole enemy and main obstacle to their liberation. Their demand for autonomy hearkened back to the tribalism of a bygone era, when the country was divided into many tiny principalities. But a return to the days of self-contained and self-governing ethnic units was no longer possible or desirable. The KNF's struggle should be directed not merely against the upper castes, but rather against the 'feudal thought and behaviour' within all caste and ethnic groups.[49] KNF members should develop class consciousness and ally with the poor and oppressed from all groups.

Although he was not in principle opposed to these Maoist beliefs, Gopal Kirati was deeply suspicious of them. Through the 1970s and 1980s, communist leaders who would later form the UML had preached the doctrine of the primacy of class in the eastern hills. Kirati supporters were told that their traditions were retrogressive, and urged to break from them. But after the UML transformed into a parliamentary party, its predominantly upper-caste leaders had abandoned their Kirati cadre. 'The UML reduced Marxism, which emphasizes the need to fight against all kinds of injustice including ethnic oppression, to the trite slogan of class liberation,' wrote Kirati. 'Today it has degenerated into a party of Brahminical counter-revolutionaries.'[50] Kirati believed that by emphasizing class and undermining the importance of ethnicity, the upper-caste communist leaders had deliberately tried to perpetuate their dominance over the marginalized ethnic groups.

As part of their effort to discipline and educate Gopal Kirati, the Maoists tried to merge the Khambuwan National Front into their own organization. In October 2001, following negotiations, the KNF was officially merged with the Maoist-affiliated Limbuwan Liberation Front to form the Kirat National Front. Kirati proposed that he should lead a separate armed force, but the Maoist leaders rejected the idea. They believed that Khambuwan cadre were undisciplined and needlessly violent in their dealings with the population, and had to be tamed. They also insisted that a centralized military structure was necessary for the success of the armed struggle. They demanded that KNF cadre be merged into the People's Liberation Army. Kirati and his supporters, chafing at what they perceived to be Maoist high-handedness, once again severed ties with the Maoists. On some occasions, the cadres of the two organizations beat up and even killed one another.

Eventually, however, Kirati was won over. On 15 July 2003, his organization permanently merged with the Maoists. It had become clear that he would not be able to wage armed struggle independently. His organization remained small and negligible, while the Maoists had become immensely powerful. They commanded substantial influence even in the eastern hills. Moreover, by now Kirati was convinced that the Maoists were genuinely committed to ethnic demands, even though their top leaders were predominantly upper-caste. On several occasions Maoist chairman Prachanda met Kirati privately to convince him of the Maoists' positive intentions. Kirati was given membership in the Maoist central committee and the United Revolutionary People's Council (URPC), the Maoists' parallel government.

The degree to which Kirati had internalized the Maoist point of view was manifest in a speech he made in Khotang district in January 2004. The occasion was a mass meeting where the Maoists declared the establishment of the Kirat Autonomous Region People's Government and appointed him as its head. In the past, said Gopal Kirati, the struggle of the Kirati people had been of a purely ethnic nature. But as Kiratis had now achieved leadership of the parallel government under Maoist leadership, they should not seek to dominate the members of the other castes and ethnicities who lived in the region. Otherwise they would be no different from the feudal rulers. Rather, class should now take precedence over ethnic claims. The Maoists would work to ensure that the *jana sarkars* represented all the caste and ethnic groups in the region. Those who did not accept this policy would be guilty of ethnic chauvinism.[51]

The character of Sangen Kirati, the protagonist of Rajan Mukarung's novel, evolves along with Nepal's communist and ethnic movements. As a teenager, he is influenced by an older generation of Kirati communists who rejected their traditions and were self-consciously engaged in a modernist nation-building project. In his early twenties, Sangen marries a Brahmin girl, Savitra, despite strong opposition from his mother. Years later, he reflects that he had married outside of his ethnicity partly because of the influence of communists.

But the humiliations he faces in Kathmandu and his growing proximity to ethnic activists disabuse him of the notion that ethnic and caste groups must blend together to end discrimination and establish a strong national culture. His marriage is strained. His wife constantly complains about their lack of money. She is cynical about politics and speaks disparagingly of both the parliamentary politicians and the Maoists. To Sangen's dismay, she remains committed to Hindu rites and rituals. At times he regrets his marriage and wishes he had married a Janajati woman who shares his cultural ethos and sensibility.

And yet Sangen does not entirely reject Marxism. With the rise of the Maoist movement, it has become possible to argue that ethnic claims are compatible with demands for socio-economic transformation. Like the Maoists, Sangen invokes Lenin's idea that nationalities should have the right to self-determination. He advocates Mao's policy of letting 'a hundred flowers bloom'. He rejects accusations that he is an ethnic chauvinist. He stresses that he neither hankers for a pristine, imagined past, nor wishes for his community to dominate others. He only wants an end to discrimination and the peaceful coexistence of the diverse ethnic and caste groups across the country.

But such lofty principles were difficult to translate into action. The Maoists may have upheld the theory that all ethnic groups and castes were equal, but the promise of ethnic liberation and territorial autonomy for one group inevitably made others living in the same area insecure. Besides, it was a time of war, and fear of both the rebels and the army was widespread. Locals in the villages had become suspicious of outsiders. In such an atmosphere, it was not easy to promote harmony and goodwill across caste and ethnic boundaries.

Sangen becomes painfully aware of this when he returns to Bhojpur after many years of absence. A gloomy silence hangs over his village. The local bank, police post and post office have been shut down. The VDC office is locked up. All the parliamentary parties have fled the village; the Maoists are the sole political force. The villagers are afraid to gather in public places. The community fabric has broken down. Members of each ethnic group keep to their own kind. Questions arise in Sangen's mind: 'Marxism never taught that ethnic and caste groups should be divided … How come people forgot that they should stay united, form a front and fight against the primary enemy? Why do they think that ethnic liberation means finishing off other ethnicities?'[52]

The Maoists might have seen this problem as an unintended consequence of the People's War. But in fact the Maoist position on ethnicity had inherent contradictions. Maoist leaders advocated ethnic autonomy and stressed the need to protect cultures and traditions that had suffered as a result of state policy. But the top Maoist leaders did not really value these cultures and traditions. As Marxists, they viewed all tradition as retrograde. Some of them even feared that the emphasis on ethnic rights and autonomy might fragment and weaken the nation.

Many ethnic activists remained suspicious of the Maoists' ambivalence towards ethnic claims. 'I get worried whenever our communist friends go into hiding,' says Bhattachan Sir, a character in *Hetchhakuppa* who is clearly modelled on a prominent Janajati activist in Kathmandu.[53] Many Maoist activists are crafty Brahmins and Chhetris, says Bhattachan Sir, repeating a stereotype about the upper castes. These activists, he continues, seek refuge in Janajati households to evade state security forces. Janajati families, being generous by nature, welcome them with open arms and offer food and shelter. If there are pretty young women in these households, the Maoists might even find partners. But no upper-caste communist ever deigns to marry a poor, unattractive or uneducated Janajati girl.

Bhattachan's comment may sound flippant and indicative of his patriarchal attitude towards the women of his community. But it also stems from a deep anxiety about the Maoist goal of eliminating caste discrimination through inter-ethnic marriage. Gopal Kirati, the Khambuwan activist turned Maoist, shared this anxiety. Even after he joined the Maoist party he vehemently opposed their emphasis on inter-ethnic marriage. Like Bhattachan in the novel, he argued that in most marriages between upper-caste men and Janajati women, the women were among the most educated and capable within their community. Inevitably, the women would assimilate into their husbands' culture. The emphasis on inter-ethnic marriage would thus allow the upper castes to continue encroaching on the 'cultural forms, identity and dignity' of the already marginalized Janajati groups.[54]

## A New Cultural Revolution

In addition to creating a new *janabadi* culture among their rank and file, the Maoists sought to bring about a 'cultural revolution' among the population they controlled.[55] This entailed getting rid of retrograde beliefs and customs. Religious festivals, caste discrimination and socially harmful habits such as alcohol consumption were to be banned.

Such decrees were imposed with varying degrees of severity in areas all across the Nepali countryside. They were often met with resentment and hostility. Knowing it was counterproductive to antagonize the population, the Maoist leadership urged party cadres to exercise a judicious flexibility. In a village in Rolpa, for instance, angry protests forced the party to withdraw its ban on an annual sacrifice to a local deity.[56]

Yet there were occasions on which the cultural revolution helped the party gain supporters, weaken opponents and consolidate its hegemony. This was particularly true in villages plagued by glaring social inequalities. In such areas the Maoists could champion a subjugated group against the more powerful one. The rebels focused much energy on Dalits, those lowest in the Hindu caste hierarchy. 'Dalits, [who are] the most oppressed amongst all oppressed people,' wrote Hisila Yami, 'urgently need the instrument of dictatorship over those reactionary forces that are still practicing archaic medieval oppression.'[57]

The Maoists actively included Dalits in their campaign to upend traditional social norms and punish those who clung to them. Egged on by party cadres, groups of Dalits would forcibly enter the homes of their upper-caste neighbours and touch their sacred objects and cooking utensils. The Maoists would stage events where upper-caste people would be forced to eat food cooked by Dalits. Often styled as elaborate ceremonies, such events reflected both the imagination and cruelty of their organizers. Pustak Ghimire recounts an incident in Khotang district where a Brahmin pandit continued to perform Vedic rituals despite Maoist warnings. The entire village was summoned to observe the pandit perform a traditional Hindu ritual in which the officiant walks around his house seven times. On this occasion, however, the pandit was made to carry that most tainted of animals, a piglet, on his shoulders during his circumambulation. Afterwards, the piglet was let loose into his house. The Maoists and their Dalit supporters then slaughtered the animal, cooked it in the Brahmin's kitchen and ate it.[58]

Such incidents were deeply traumatic for the members of the upper castes, who held ingrained notions about ritual purity and pollution. Many Dalits too initially felt some resistance to the subversion of long-standing societal taboos. But once they overcame their misgivings, many were excited by this licence to transgress caste boundaries, and felt sympathy, if not gratitude, towards the Maoist rebels. As a Dalit from the Kami sub-caste explained, 'I want to eat with Brahmins because by sharing a meal, I become a Brahmin myself, [and] they become Dalit, like me. Only when we are able to sit at the same table under the same roof can we actually call ourselves equal and the same.'[59]

The Maoist-led campaign aimed not only to end caste discrimination but also to transform the culture of the Dalits. Maoist leaders observed that Dalits had internalized the dominant social prejudices, and an invidious hierarchy existed among the various Dalit sub-castes: Dalits from one sub-caste tended to ostracize members of a sub-caste they considered inferior. This made it harder for them to undertake collective political action against their real oppressors. Further, although Dalits provided indispensible services to society through their traditional occupations as cleaners, blacksmiths, tailors and musicians, they were accorded no respect. As a result, they felt little pride in their work and were crushed by inertia and fatalism.

The task for the Maoists, then, was to make all Dalits aware of their common predicament, unify them by erasing sub-caste boundaries and spur them to violent collective action against their oppressors. '[The] People's War,' wrote Hisila Yami, 'has given … Dalits … revolutionary ideology and ammunition.'[60] Those who wished could join the movement and travel across the country, disseminating the revolutionary message of the party or fighting battles with the RNA. Those who did not desire active participation could use their traditional skills to support the party. Blacksmiths could make and repair homemade weapons, tailors could stitch uniforms and bags for the rebels, and musicians could sing revolutionary songs. Using their traditional skills towards revolutionary ends would breed in them a sense of pride and purpose.

Although Maoist decrees against caste discrimination may have barely shaken the prejudices of the more traditional upper castes, many of them, fearful of repercussions, at least refrained from more blatant forms of discrimination. The rhetoric and actions of the Maoists thus appealed to broad swathes of Dalits across Nepal. Along with Magars and Tharus, Dalits were among the firmest backers of the armed rebellion.

But if one outcome of Dalit mobilization in the war was their empowerment, the other was doubtless their greater dispossession. Although the Maoists claimed that the Dalits willingly donated their skills to the cause, more often than not their labour was forcibly expropriated. Dalit blacksmiths in Dang had to make guns, knives and other weapons for the rebels since the earliest days of the conflict. When the state security forces found out, they harassed and threatened the entire community. 'If you don't make the weapons, the Maoists will harass you,' said Bir Man Biswokarma of Purandhara VDC, Dang. 'If you do, the army could kill you.'[61] Many Dalits gave up their traditional livelihoods due to fear. In one village in Purandhara VDC in late 2001, more than 100 out of the 160 blacksmith households stopped producing agricultural implements and household utensils. Some of them migrated to India. Others took up whatever work they could get to make ends meet. Asare Biswokarma's family, for example, started making flower garlands and leaf plates from which they earned fifty to sixty rupees a day.[62]

The journalist Kishore Nepal recounts the story of a porter he met while travelling in the remote mountain district of Mugu. The porter said that he used to be called Dan Singh Kami until a group of young armed Maoists came to his village and ordered the Kami villagers to change their surnames to Bishwokarma.[63] This was no doubt part of the Maoist campaign to forge greater unity among Dalits. While the word

'Kami', which translates as blacksmith, denotes a particular caste among Dalits that traditionally works with metals, 'Bishwokarma' is a more generic surname that encompasses various sub-castes. But it appears that the significance of the Maoist diktat was lost on Dan Singh, and he had simply changed his name in a spirit of fatalistic acquiescence.

What Dan Singh told journalist Kishore Nepal about his clothing showed the extent of destitution among certain Dalits. 'These are the only clothes I have,' he said, pointing to the ragged garments he had on. 'If I wash them, they will get damaged. Until some time ago, I had a little money and managed to stay clean, but I lost my job due to the violence.'[64] A goldsmith by occupation, Dan Singh had been left without clients when those who could afford gold ornaments in his village fled to towns to escape Maoist demands. For some time after that, he eked out a living by making periodic trips to North India as a wage labourer. But once the Maoists imposed a ban on foreign employment, he had to give up that option. At the time journalist Nepal met him, Dan Singh was working as a porter at the airport in the district headquarters of Mugu.

'I don't know whether the Maoists are good or bad,' said Dan Singh. 'They are against caste discrimination and have [helped eliminate] alcoholism and gambling. They are encouraging cooperative farming. But they are also killing people, disrupting schools and extorting money. How would I know what is best when even [important local] leaders … cannot explain what's happening?'[65]

## Retaliation in Dailekh

At one point the Maoists must have thought they could cultivate and exploit the 'rebellious instincts' of the people of Dullu, a relatively remote VDC in the hills of Dailekh district. By 2000, most police stations in the districts had been closed as a result of Maoist attacks. But a large one – manned by around fifty personnel – continued to exist in Dullu's main bazaar. The locals chafed under the curfews and other restrictions imposed by the police. When the anthropologist Marie Lecomte-Tilouine was visiting Dullu in 2000, news broke one morning that a policeman had seduced a local woman, taken her to the district capital on a promise of marriage, and abandoned her. There was public uproar, and that night the villagers burned down the police station (it was empty at the time). The next day a procession of over a hundred people, mostly women, marched through the area, chanting slogans against the police.[66]

Although Dullu was then a Nepali Congress stronghold, its inhabitants harboured little animosity towards the Maoists. The few local Maoists were seen as young dropouts and ne'er-do-wells who had joined the rebels as a last resort.[67]

This was to change in the following years. In 2000, the police abandoned Dullu as the locals continued to protest against them, even refusing to sell them food. In 2001, the Maoists attacked and destroyed a police post in the neighbouring village of Naumule. This was a significant show of strength, given that the police post in Naumule was even larger than the one in Dullu. From then on, Maoist rule over the rural areas of the district became absolute.

The Maoists imposed severe restrictions on religious practices. They shut down all five temples in the area, and when a seventy-two-year-old priest tried to reopen one of them, they broke his legs. Popular festivals and music were banned. The Maoists tried to fill the resulting vacuum with their own revolutionary culture. They made it mandatory for the locals to attend their mass meetings and musical and dance performances. But these do not seem to have stirred their audience. The locals were sullen and withdrawn, restricting their lives to their homes and fields so as to avoid engaging with the Maoists. Even then they were not left in peace. In October 2004 the rebels demanded that each household in Dailekh send a member to work full-time for the party. The alternatives the rebels offered were for the people to flee their homes or to have their limbs broken.[68] Most people thus felt compelled to acquiesce to rebel demands. But the following month, the village witnessed an event that caused latent grievances to burst out into the open, sparking the largest ever grass-roots uprising against the Maoists.

On the morning of 6 November 2004, a platoon of RNA soldiers marched into Dullu. On seeing them, Raju Bajracharya, an erstwhile supporter of the Nepali Congress who had been forced to become a member of a ward-level *jana sarkar*, became nervous and broke into a run. The soldiers fired, killing him on the spot. Before they left, the soldiers warned the locals not to move the corpse as they had attached a bomb to it that would explode when touched.[69]

The villagers gathered around the body. They wanted to take it away for cremation, but were afraid to touch it. Some pointed out that it was the rebels' responsibility to dispose of the body, as the victim was a member of the local *jana sarkar*. The day wore on, but there was no sign of the Maoists. Finally some locals tried to remove the supposed bomb from the body with the help of a long bamboo pole. There was no explosion; the bomb scare was a hoax. The corpse was carried to Raju Bajracharya's house. According to tradition, it should have been cremated that very day. But the Maoists had banned traditional funerary practices and had not issued precise instructions on alternative arrangements. The villagers were confused. In any case, as Raju Bajracharya was a *jana sarkar* member, they expected his fellow party members to accord him respect and make arrangements for an official funeral.

The night passed. No Maoist showed up. The villagers grew restive the next morning and criticized the rebels for neglecting their fellow cadre. They decided to disregard Maoist orders and cremate the body according to traditional rites. A large procession of men, women and children followed the corpse as it was carried to the cremation site. Two Maoists approached them on the way. They insisted that the red communist flag they had with them be draped over the body as a sign of respect for a 'martyr' of their party. The villagers were incensed by the rebels' attempt to claim a body that they had ignored for an entire day. 'Where were you or your party when his body was lying in the dirt for a full day?' they asked. 'Why didn't you come to recover your cadre's body and console his family?'[70] The argument became heated; some of them pushed and shoved the Maoist carrying the flag. The two left, and the villagers proceeded to the cremation ground and cremated the body according to traditional rites.

For many in Dullu, this act of resistance symbolized a rejection of all the claims that the rebels had made on them so far. Their grief, rage and desperation had emboldened them. The next day, 8 November, six *jana sarkar* officials, including the most senior in the locality, came to Dullu to meet the villagers and soothe tensions. The villagers confronted the Maoists with sticks and clubs. The women shouted at the Maoists, 'You kill our husbands, you take our sons away and force them to run away from home. You might as well kill us now.'[71] The Maoists called for order and discipline. But the villagers were in no mood to comply. One local struck a Maoist official on the head with a wooden stick, and this led to an open brawl between the two sides. Outnumbered, the Maoists fled.

Loosely organized networks of women known as 'mothers' groups' led a procession against the Maoists the next day. 'Down with the Maoists! (*Maobadi murdabad!*)' they chanted, 'We don't want murderers!'[72] Encouraged by their audacity, people from neighbouring villages came to join forces with them. Over the following weeks, thousands of villagers took part in the anti-Maoist campaign. They apprehended the Maoists in their own areas, forced them to renounce the party and join the protests. The *jana sarkar* chief of one village surrendered bombs and Rs 1.6 million in cash to the villagers. In some cases, villagers handed over Maoist cadres to the army garrison at the district capital. At least one of them was killed in custody.

The Maoists retaliated viciously. They killed three villagers from Salleri VDC on 16 November, and abducted many others. On another occasion, they lobbed a grenade at a march, killing one person and injuring sixteen others. Around 2000 people from Salleri and Naumule VDCs – the areas that bore the brunt of the Maoist retribution – fled their homes to take refuge in Dullu.

But these measures did not succeed in quelling the revolt or re-establishing Maoist rule. The anti-Maoist uprising attracted the attention of the government in Kathmandu. Realizing its propaganda value, top government officials including some ministers flew to Dullu. At a mass meeting held on 23 November, which was attended by thousands of locals, Home Minister Purna Bahadur Khadka praised the people of the area for their courage in fighting against 'terrorism' and pledged that the government would stand behind them. Soon after, the government provided Rs 30 million for those who had been forced out of their villages by Maoists. An army garrison was established in Dullu. The Maoists' parallel government vanished and their demands upon the population largely ceased. Government agencies – a post office, a bank branch, a health post and an office offering agricultural support – were gradually re-established.

Among the many places under Maoist rule, why did Dailekh alone witness a full-fledged revolt against the Maoists? The contingent cause was of course the death of the *jana sarkar* member Raju Bajracharya. According to Saubhagya Shah, despite their suffering and resentment, the villagers had certain expectations of their new rulers. In this particular case, they expected party officials to take charge of the funerary rites. By ignoring the body for almost two full days, the rebels lost legitimacy among the population. The rage and grief unleashed by the experience then drove the people to acts of defiance that were previously unimaginable.

Thoroughly embarrassed that the people they claimed to represent had turned openly hostile towards them, the Maoists accused their enemies of instigating the uprising. 'The army, informants and leaders of other political parties,' stated a report in the Maoist newspaper *Janadesh*, 'gathered women, children and disinterested peasants of Dullu and the neighbouring [areas], and forced them to protest ... against the Maoist activists and the People's War.'[73] This was obviously a fiction. The revolt had been spontaneous; only after it was already underway had the government moved to take advantage of it.

Even the Maoists could not entirely ignore the fact that there was substantial popular participation in the Dullu uprising. In fact, in a statement issued in the name of the Dailekh District Committee, the party admitted that it had engaged in excesses that had antagonized the population. The document stated that there had been several 'errors and weaknesses' on the Maoists' part. These included their demand that at least one member of every household work full-time for the party and their ban on local traditions and festivals. Similarly, the Maoists said that party cadres had been wrong to murder the journalist Dekendra Raj Thapa in August 2004, on charges of embezzling funds from a local drinking-water project and supporting the monarchy.[74] These excesses, the document implied, were in opposition to party policy. For, while it was necessary to recruit people into the party and eradicate superstition, it was also important for party members to be receptive to popular opinion.

Generally the Maoists tended to be more responsive to popular complaints in areas where local residents with strong social links to the population headed the party committees and *jana sarkars*. In Thabang, for example, the party had been active for decades and formed an integral part of local self-conception and history. This was not the case in Dullu. Most of its inhabitants appear to have remained supporters of the Nepali Congress even after the Maoists established domination over the area. Raju Bajracharya was a Nepali Congress activist who had joined the Maoist *jana sarkar* against his will. The area was inhabited predominantly by Brahmins and Chhetris, whose support the rebels sought to gain on grounds of their economic marginalization. But the Maoist policy of autonomy for oppressed indigenous groups could hardly resonate with these members of the Hindu upper castes. The Maoists in the area did not succeed in kindling a dream of liberation, and they came to be perceived as an unjust and tyrannical force.

## At the Mercy of the People

On the night of 18 March, 2004, Ganga Bahadur Lama came to Chhailung VDC in Lamjung district as political commissar of a group of twenty-two Maoist cadres. In their campaign to mobilize support for the party, the militants had been travelling round the villages, painting slogans and putting up posters, informing locals about the party's policies and ideology and warning them about the consequences of acting against the Maoists.[75]

Lamjung is in the Gandaki region, a hill area just west of the Bagmati region, where Kathmandu lies. The region has historically benefited from its proximity to the capital. There are more roads here, for example, than in the districts further west. It was therefore harder for the Maoists to consolidate their rule here than in a far-flung and neglected district like Rolpa. While they had managed to establish party committees and people's governments across the Gandaki region, they had not been able to totally eliminate the state's presence. It was not always wise for the rebels to travel openly, or to remain for too long in one place.

Before coming to Lamjung, Ganga Bahadur Lama and his team had travelled through the villages of the adjacent district of Gorkha spreading the party's message. As there was a large group of soldiers patrolling one of the villages, the rebels were forced to lie low in a forest cave for five days. Having finished whatever rations they were carrying on the first day, they had to scrounge for food. On one occasion they collected nettles from the jungle, which they boiled and ate; on another they managed to procure some rice and goat meat from a house on the periphery of the village. But most of the time they went without. Ganga Bahadur Lama recalls in his memoir how these young Maoists, maddened by boredom and hunger, 'passed the time by crying one moment and laughing the next, screaming one moment and singing the next.' When the army finally left, the Maoists climbed down to the village and built a gate there, as a 'symbol of victory.'[76]

The rebels had even more reason to be cautious while travelling through Lamjung district. Their comrades in the local party committee had informed them that the Royal Nepal Army could easily get from the district capital to the remotest corners of the district in less than four hours. Moreover, at that time a battalion of the People's Liberation Army that was usually stationed in a village in Lamjung had gone west to participate in the aforementioned attack on Beni. This meant the proselytisers lacked even a military force to protect them.

Nor were the people of Lamjung particularly sympathetic towards the Maoists. The inhabitants of Chhailung were predominantly Gurung, an ethnic group that refer to themselves as the Tamu. In Lama's estimate, there were between fifty and sixty Gurung households in the village. The Maoists had promised that once they took over state power, they would transform the Gandaki Region into the Tamuwan Autonomous Province. For this reason the Maoists assumed that the Tamus would become their primary source of support in the Gandaki region. But while the promise of ethnic autonomy may have resonated among some of Chhailung's inhabitants, most of them were afraid of the Maoists.

In an ethnography of a Tamu village not far from Chhailung, Judith Pettigrew shows how locals resented the Maoists who intruded into their homes in search of food and shelter.[77] They were also keen to avoid Maoist intervention into local matters. Disputes between villagers had traditionally been mediated by VDC officials and, in serious cases, by the police. After the Maoists chased away government officials and police personnel, locals formed ad hoc committees to resolve disputes. These committees lacked authority, and their meetings were chaotic and often unable to find a solution. Pettigrew witnessed one such meeting, convoked to resolve a dispute between two brothers. The inquiry was arbitrary and inconclusive, but all the assembled villagers were unanimous in their opinion that the case should not be taken to the Maoist 'people's court', even though it would pass swift judgment. Some of them seemed anxious that the local Maoist commander might show up. If he did, he would take a decision based on his limited knowledge and his particular conception of justice, which would likely be very different from that of the villagers. As Pettigrew writes, '[I]nevitably the punishment would involve a severe beating followed by humiliation (a garland of shoes placed around the neck and the face smeared with soot).'[78]

A day after Ganga Bahadur and his team arrived in Chhailung, the Maoist activists assembled the villagers, made speeches on the necessity of armed rebellion and performed revolutionary songs and dances.

Maoist fighters, including Barsha Man Pun 'Ananta' (right), salute a fallen comrade.

Police remove the bodies of personnel killed in a Maoist attack in Rukumkot, Rukum district on April 3, 2001.

Pushpa Kamal Dahal 'Prachanda' at the meeting announcing the formation of the PLA in Kureli, Rolpa in September 2001.

Nepali Congress president Girija Prasad Koirala in 2005.

King Birendra Shah (front), Queen Aishwarya and then–Prime Minister Girija Prasad Koirala (back) in 2000.

Sagar Shrestha

King Gyanendra Shah in 2005.

Sagar Shrestha

Sagar Shrestha

Maoists cross a river in Banke district in October 2005.

Janadesh

Commander of the Maoist army's Western Division, Nanda Kishore Pun
'Pasang' addresses troops before the march to Beni on March 13, 2004.

Portraits of Marx, Engels, Lenin, Stalin and Mao painted on a building in Thabang, Rolpa in 2005. The slogan reads: 'The proletariat has nothing to lose but its chains, yet it has the world to win.'

Students at the Martyr's Memorial School in Thabang, Rolpa in 2005. The Maoist-run school was established primarily for the children of rebels who had lost their lives during the war. Its curriculum included instruction in Marxism-Leninism-Maoism.

Bodies of Maoist fighters killed during an attack on Royal Nepal Army barracks at Khara, Rukum on 17 April 2005.

Maoist activist Krishna K.C. is reunited with his family at the Supreme Court in Kathmandu on 22 September 2005. K.C. had been in army detention since September 2003, and was finally brought before the Supreme Court after his wife filed a series of habeas corpus petitions. The court ordered his release, but police personnel re-arrested him as soon as he stepped outside the court premises.

A procession on Kathmandu's Ring Road during the 2006 uprising.

Sagar Shrestha

Prachanda addresses a mass meeting in Kathmandu in 2007.

Sagar Shrestha

Maoist leaders campaigning for elections in Kirtipur, Kathmandu on
23 February 2008. In the front row, from left to right: Ananta, Prachanda,
Baburam Bhattarai and Hisila Yami.

A Maoist cultural troupe performs at a mass meeting in Kathmandu in May
2010. The scene depicts a moment of reconciliation between Maoist rebels and
the Royal Nepal Army in the aftermath of the war.

Ganga Bahadur was pleased with the response of the locals. 'We felt that the entire village was greatly inspired by the songs and music,' he wrote later.[79]

The locals, however, would have felt slightly more ambivalent. A villager in Pettigrew's account recalls how the Maoists invited locals to participate in a song and dance session during the festival of Tihar. Although amused by the sight of the Maoists and the children dancing together, she said she and her friends 'wouldn't allow [our children] out of our houses because we thought [the singing and dancing] was a trick to get them to join the Maoists. We kept them in for three days; only the very small children went out.'[80] These women were understandably worried that their children would develop a fascination for the Maoists. At a time when the war had brought most public activities to a halt, and the village had few exciting possibilities to offer, many young people saw the Maoists as fearless and awe-inspiring adventurers.

The next evening Lama and his comrade Buddhiram climbed a nearby hill and were listening to the news on their radio when they heard gunshots ring out in the distance. They instantly realized that soldiers had entered the village. Thrown into a panic, they took off in what they thought to be the opposite direction from where the noise was coming – only to find they had run directly into the line of fire. Ganga Bahadur quickly changed course and sprinted down a terraced hillside. Soldiers pursued him, firing non-stop. He was shot in the leg, fell to the ground and waited, hearing dogs bark and women and children scream in the distance. The soldiers spent some time looking for him. But it was dark and they could not find him. So they left.

Unable to move, Ganga Bahadur spent the night there, drifting in and out of sleep. He was to spend three more nights and three full days on that terraced hill slope, increasingly debilitated by hunger and thirst. Flies swarmed about his festering wound. A large group of locals gathered around him the afternoon following the night on which he was shot. They were returning from the cremation of a woman who had been killed in the blind firing of the night before. They discussed the wounded rebel as though he was not there. Some sounded sympathetic; others thought he'd got what he deserved. Ganga Bahadur pleaded for help. He begged them to at least inform his comrades of his whereabouts. But the villagers gradually dispersed, apparently without addressing a word to him.

Throughout the time Ganga Bahadur lay helpless, none except the marginal and the eccentric paid him any attention. The first person to approach him was an illiterate shepherd who appeared to be in his late fifties. Ganga Bahadur asked him to bring him some water, but the shepherd refused. He tried to cajole him, even offering 200 rupees for the favour, but the shepherd was firm. Ganga Bahadur lost his temper and told him that he would be in serious trouble if the Maoists came to know that he had refused to help their comrade. The shepherd burst into tears and said he could not bring water, as the army would kill his entire family if he did so.

Perhaps because his conscience overruled his fear of the army, two days later the shepherd brought him a cooked meal of rice and vegetables and locally brewed alcohol. Ganga Bahadur ate, but he had fasted for so long he immediately had diarrhoea. He had no choice but to defecate in the spot where he was lying. The shepherd also informed him that the influential people in the village had held a meeting to discuss what they should do with the wounded rebel. Some of them had suggested raising money and taking him to a hospital for medical treatment. Others had pointed out that the RNA soldiers would harass them if they saw them carrying him to a hospital. So in the end they had concluded that their only option was to ignore him.

Thus the villagers of Chhailung regarded the warring sides with mixed feelings. They feared the army. There had been numerous occasions when villagers had been killed or injured when security forces came looking for Maoists. They resented the rebels for needlessly endangering their lives. However, they were not entirely unsympathetic towards rebels who were suffering. Pettigrew presents many instances where the villagers' hearts went out to the rebels. An old woman described how she felt when she saw the body of a young Maoist, a member of a dance troupe, with his guts spilled out on the road after an ambush by security forces: 'I knew him well and fed him many times. I felt very upset when I saw him. When we feed a dog, it is grateful and wags its tail, and he was like that.'[81] What prevented the locals from helping Lama was more fear of army reprisals than antipathy towards the Maoists.

After he had been lying wounded for two nights and almost two full days, someone finally came to Lama's rescue. It was Buddhiram, who had been with him when they heard the gunshots. He arrived with a jerrycan full of water, some fried noodles and basic medicines for his comrade.

Buddhiram had managed to escape, but had come back to perform the funeral rites for a fallen comrade whose body was lying in the village. He had asked the locals to help him bury the body, but they had refused; the RNA soldiers had threatened to bury them in a mass grave if they helped the Maoists. But they had informed him of Ganga Bahadur's state and whereabouts. After dropping off the supplies he had brought for Lama, Buddhiram went to look for people who might help him carry Lama to a safe place.

Buddhiram left at dusk. Lama waited for him to return; the hours passed but there was no sign of him. Buddhiram had been asking every person he met for help, but each of them turned down his request. There did not seem to be any party members around. Lama fell asleep in the early hours of the morning. When he woke up, he saw an elderly man standing on an upper terrace of the field, aiming a rock at him. According to Lama's account, he told the old man that he was waiting for death, and that if he did throw the rock he should use enough force to kill him. The man dropped the rock and came near him. He asked Lama if he was hungry, thirsty or cold. No one except the shepherd and Buddhiram had shown such concern for Lama since he had been shot. Lama responded in the affirmative: 'I am only human, after all.'

To his great shock, the old man suddenly picked up the jerry-can, poured out all the water over Lama's head and flung the container away. 'Such a healthy fellow,' the man exclaimed to himself as he walked off. 'He could have joined the police or the army. He could have made a living farming the land. He could have gone to work in another country.' Making sure that Lama heard him, he said, 'Because of you, our peaceful and beautiful village is being ravaged by a conflict. Innocent villagers are losing their lives for nothing.'[82]

Lama spent one more night on that terrace. Four of the comrades who had been travelling with him through Gorkha and Lamjung found him the next day. They had managed to flee during the RNA operation, and had returned to the village the previous night. But it was only in the morning that the villagers had told them about their wounded comrade. They were horrified to see their leader in that state. They too sought the villagers' help in carrying him, but to no avail. Tired and dejected, they returned to the place where he was lying. At that point Lama lost patience and ordered his friends to intimidate and threaten the locals. The Maoists went back and told the villagers that if they continued to refuse to help, the Maoist army battalion that was returning victorious from Beni would arrest them or evict them from the village.

The villagers were made to collect ropes, bamboo sticks and cloth to build a stretcher on which the wounded Maoist could be carried away. In his memoir, Lama shows a clear-eyed understanding of the foundations of Maoist rule when he observes that the people finally came around to assisting him due to a combination of factors: their desire to help a fellow human being, along with the rebels' attempts to persuade, assert their authority and impose 'red terror' upon them.[83]

As the stretcher was being prepared, Buddhiram appeared with two other Maoist cadres. The seven comrades carried him off to safety. Over the following weeks, he was passed on from one group of Maoists to another, until he was secretly taken to a hospital in Chitwan district, where, in August, his wounded leg was amputated.

CHAPTER 7

# Blunders and Realignments

## The High Command

Most of the country knew Prachanda only through his statements and some grainy photographs. Some even doubted his existence. Nonetheless, his name evoked fear. Although most Maoist cadres had never met or seen Prachanda, they felt awe and reverence for him. Some worried that they would never meet him. Others remembered the pride and elation they had felt as they shook his hand at a party convention.[1]

From the earliest days of the rebellion, Prachanda had enjoyed uncontested power over the party. His authority only increased over the years. Other senior Maoist leaders in the standing committee and the politburo could certainly challenge him on policy matters, but never once did they consider replacing him. The histories of the Soviet Union and China had convinced them that a leader with charismatic authority was necessary for the success of the revolutionary party.

The party made various efforts to buttress Prachanda's position as supreme leader. In 2001, his title was changed from 'general secretary' to 'chairman', a term that reflected the power concentrated in his person. That same year, the party undertook a comprehensive re-evaluation of its ideology, its strategy and its official view of the history of the communist movement in Nepal. These 'guiding principles of the party' were collectively termed 'Prachandapath'. The doctrine contained specific features such as the strategy of fomenting a popular uprising and demanding elections to a Constituent Assembly.[2] Over time, however, the term lost its specificity and came to represent the Maoist struggle in general. If the

Maoists destroyed an army position, for example, cadres would refer to it as a 'victory of Prachandapath'.

In person, Prachanda exuded restlessness, often manifested in the way he jerked his shoulders while talking. He had boundless enthusiasm for meeting party members of all ranks. He usually convinced those he met that he had complete trust in them. But he constantly probed party members on their colleagues' strengths and weaknesses, and used this information to reassign responsibilities. He was known to keep a close watch over the party's finances.[3]

Prachanda was the party's most effective public speaker. He had an acute sense of political theatre, and could project a variety of emotions depending on the mood of the crowd he was addressing. He would use fiery, even incendiary rhetoric to arouse passionate anger and hatred among the cadre. If necessary he would not hesitate to publicly criticize his own failings, thus dousing the potential resentment of his audience. He was also prone to sentimentality, shedding uninhibited tears if the occasion demanded it, as when addressing the families of party members killed during the conflict or while watching musicals depicting the suffering and martyrdom of Maoist fighters.

Prachanda's power also derived from his role as one of the party's chief military strategists and the supreme commander of the Maoists' People's Liberation Army. Although he never participated in battle, he had studied the strategies and tactics of guerrilla war for decades and had personally trained many of the party's field commanders. He had helped draft battle plans on a number of occasions. He commanded the fierce loyalty of some of the most important Maoist commanders, such as Pasang and Ananta.[4]

In matters of ideology, Prachanda was a pragmatist. He was rarely the one to initiate the long debates on ideology and its relation to strategy during politburo or central committee meetings; instead he would listen carefully to all the views put forward, often for days on end. Sometimes he mediated disputes. His strategic choices were not constrained by a rigid ideology or by precedent. Rather, he would choose one of the available options based on how effectively it might increase the energy and commitment of the rank and file, the rebels' power in relation to the state, and his own control over the party. Once he took a decision, he stuck to it with great confidence and tenacity, winning enthusiastic support and commitment from the entire party. But if circumstances changed, he shifted course without qualms or nostalgia for the older policy.

In 1991, for example, some of the radical Maoists argued that their party, at that time called the Unity Centre, should not compete in elections as that would entrench them in parliamentary politics and inhibit them from starting an armed rebellion. It was Prachanda, along with Baburam Bhattarai and some others, who advocated that the party should field a front organization that would participate in the parliamentary process. Only three years later, however, Prachanda pulled the party out of the parliamentary process and began serious preparations for the rebellion.[5] Similarly, until 2001, the Maoists viewed the parliamentary parties as their chief enemy. After the massacre at the royal palace, they shifted their attack to the monarchy. Although a number of leaders, including Bhattarai, were in favour of this move, others felt misgivings about the new policy. Such a decisive policy shift would not have been possible without Prachanda's firm backing.[6]

When asked to evaluate the nature of his leadership, Prachanda once said, 'I have never been firmly committed to any fixed position.'[7] He obviously considered this a strength. When Baburam Bhattarai was asked about Prachanda, he said something similar: 'He has the ability to make swift decisions for the benefit of the party, even taking risks if necessary.'[8] According to Bhattarai, these were the qualities that enabled Lenin to steer the Russian revolution toward success. Prachanda would have appreciated this assessment. Lenin was, after all, his great personal hero.

But the same characteristics were also deplored within the party. Party members occasionally said that Prachanda showed dangerous signs of 'instability'. This criticism came mostly from Maoist leaders who felt betrayed when Prachanda abandoned a particular line which they themselves were wedded to. It was also a more general criticism of Prachanda's seeming lack of ideological commitment.

Baburam Bhattarai was a different kind of leader. The popular press often referred to him as the Maoists' 'chief ideologue'. The US ambassador Michael Malinowski called him the Maoists' 'most authoritative wordsmith'.[9] It is certainly true that he was one of the most prominent theoreticians in the party. But there were also others who were considered 'experts' in Marxist–Leninist–Maoist doctrine. Bhattarai's particular strength was that his ideology was never abstract, but always linked to political strategy.

While Prachanda wielded two of the 'magic weapons' of Maoist protracted war, namely the party and the army, Baburam Bhattarai stood at the helm of the third – the united front or the United Revolutionary People's Council (URPC). In this role, he formulated policies on how the party should engage with the population. He drafted the guidelines for the formation and operation of *jana sarkars* (people's governments). He was one of the chief theorists of the Maoist conception of ethnicity and caste, which justified the mobilization of ethnic and caste groups as part of the class struggle. And he defined the negotiation agenda that the Maoists presented to the other political forces, including the demands for an interim government, round-table conference and elections to a Constituent Assembly.[10]

Bhattarai was thus indispensible to the party. In other ways, however, his position was not entirely secure. Most members of the core Maoist leadership had worked together since the late 1970s, notably in the Mashal faction. Bhattarai had joined them only in 1991, and so he was viewed as somewhat of an outsider. His possession of a PhD caused many in the party to perceive him as an over-educated bourgeois.[11] In the mid-1990s, when the rebels were preparing to launch an armed rebellion, many of them openly wondered whether Bhattarai would be able to endure the inevitable hardships. The initiative and energy he displayed during the war subdued these criticisms, but some hostility and suspicion remained.[12]

A cerebral man, Bhattarai could not immerse himself wholeheartedly in the kind of collective life that the Maoists valued. His engagement with the party's cadre base was not as deep as Prachanda's, and when he did address mass gatherings or party meetings, he came across as stiff and aloof. A number of rebels in the upper echelons of the party supported him, but, unlike Prachanda, he was not able to command fierce loyalty towards his person.

Ideologically, too, Bhattarai differed significantly from the rest of the Maoist leaders, most of whom were committed to an orthodox form of communist doctrine. They regarded the Chinese Cultural Revolution as a pinnacle of revolutionary achievement. The collapse of the great communist regimes and the global rise of liberal democracy had not really affected their views. They doggedly maintained that the evolution of the

Soviet communist party since Khrushchev and of the Chinese party since Deng marked only a 'degeneration into revisionism'. Bhattarai's struggle, on the other hand, was aimed against 'feudalism' or, more specifically, the monarchy. He envisaged that the Maoists would lay down their arms and participate in a multi-party system once the monarchy was abolished.[13] Unlike his colleagues, he was aware of the weaknesses of the communist regimes of the past. He asked: why had communist movements that had made such huge sacrifices mutated into 'bureaucratic, revisionist and counter-revolutionary parties' after gaining state power? Why had the 'capitalist-imperialist' system succeeded in projecting itself as a true democracy, whereas the systems created by 'true proletarian democrats' were retrospectively denounced as brutal and oppressive dictatorships? How could a socialist party of the twenty-first century avoid the mistakes of previous communist regimes?

Recognizing that a critique of communism from a liberal-democratic perspective would be unacceptable to most of the party leadership, Bhattarai rather ingeniously invoked the authority of Mao to answer these questions. In Mao's well-known formulation, Stalin was 70 per cent right and 30 per cent wrong. His primary error was to concentrate excessively on the communist party. Without any curbs on its power, the communist party in the Soviet Union became a model of extreme 'bureaucratic centralism'. Stalin handled the party in an arbitrary and heavy-handed manner, resorting to violence and persecution that far exceeded the demands of 'class struggle'.[14]

To remain committed and receptive to the people's needs, Bhattarai argued, the socialist party of the twenty-first century would need to modify the structure of the party, the army and the state. Among other things, Nepali Maoists when in power would allow rival political parties to function. Unlike in China, where the smaller parties were more or less controlled by the communist party, the other parties in Nepal would be allowed freedom and autonomy. The communist party would have to compete with them in regular elections.[15]

Although many in the Maoist leadership were very sceptical about these ideas, Bhattarai managed to include them in the 2003 resolution of the party, titled 'The Development of Democracy in the Twenty-First Century'.[16] This was possible partly because they were couched in the language of orthodox Maoism. The resolution stated, for instance, as a concession to the purists in the party, that only 'anti-feudal' and 'anti-imperialist' forces would be allowed to compete under the new political dispensation.

More importantly, it was because Prachanda lent his immense authority to Bhattarai's proposals that they were codified into the official doctrine of the party. It was Prachanda who presented the resolution to the Maoist central committee. Had Bhattarai done so, it is extremely unlikely that it would have been accepted. It appears that Prachanda, despite some initial wavering, was genuinely convinced by Bhattarai's arguments. He also thought they were useful in the current political circumstances. 'The Development of Democracy in the Twenty-First Century' was adopted in June 2003, in the midst of the ceasefire and the negotiation process. At the time, Bhattarai was spending much of his time in Kathmandu trying to negotiate an alliance with the parliamentary parties against the monarchy. It was clear that this strategy could help the Maoists exacerbate rifts between the two, and possibly even weaken the king. The ideological revision that Bhattarai proposed was useful in convincing the broad Maoist base that a negotiation strategy that favoured a movement towards multi-party democracy was not only tactically efficacious but also ideologically sound.

There was one area, however, on which Prachanda could not reconcile his views with Bhattarai's. In his criticism of Stalin, Bhattarai not only suggested that the communist party should revise its stance towards other political forces, but also sought to alter the traditional conception of communist party leadership. In Bhattarai's analysis, the communist parties of Russia and China had erred in entrusting such great power to a single leader. It was the cult of personality that had developed around such leaders that had allowed them to commit their excesses. For this reason it was necessary to place institutional checks on the power of the supreme leader.[17]

In voicing such concerns, Bhattarai ran up against not just Prachanda, but a substantial section of the party leadership, notably Mohan Baidya, alias 'Kiran'. Born in 1946, Kiran was the oldest of the Maoist leaders and had entered underground communist politics some years before Prachanda and Bhattarai. He was revered among the rebels both for his age and his grasp of orthodox Marxist theory. Prachanda himself said, as did many other Maoists, that he had never met anyone with Kiran's depth of knowledge of Marxist philosophy and aesthetics.[18]

Prachanda was once Kiran's protégé. For much of the 1980s, Kiran headed Mashal, but even then he seems to have realized that he lacked the leadership skills required to lead a rebellion. He was a poor orator and without charisma. Organizational work did not come naturally to him. He spent much of his time studying Nepali history and writing poetry and literary criticism from a Marxist perspective. He felt that Prachanda possessed the qualities he lacked, and often sent him to address gatherings of party cadre across the country.

On 1 April 1986, Mashal cadres, under the instructions of their leadership, attacked a number of police posts in Kathmandu. Some were arrested, and forced to reveal the identities of other party members during interrogation. Three years later, the party leadership admitted that the attacks had been a mistake, and asked for a demotion as penance. It was in these circumstances that Kiran renounced his leadership of the party and nominated Prachanda to the top position. After the Maoists finally launched their rebellion, Kiran made it his mission to strengthen Prachanda's position. Kiran emerged as the firmest proponent of the idea of Prachandapath, which he explicated in numerous articles published during the war.[19]

Kiran and other Maoist leaders worked so hard to create an aura around Prachanda partly because they were suspicious of Baburam Bhattarai's ideological leanings, and resented his public profile.  In  the early 1990s, when the rebels were in the Unity Centre, most leaders including Prachanda and Kiran were underground, preparing for the rebellion. Bhattarai was much more visible. As coordinator of the Samyukta Jana Morcha – the front that participated in open politics – he was often protesting on the streets or explaining the party's vision in seminars and through newspapers in Kathmandu. When Kiran was in Dang district once, he was apparently asked whether he was a member of 'Baburam Bhattarai's party'. Kiran, who was older than Bhattarai and had longer experience in the communist movement, felt humiliated, and told Prachanda about the incident.[20] After the armed rebellion began, Bhattarai became responsible for garnering publicity for the party, and the Nepali media tended to treat him as the pre-eminent Maoist leader.

Many top Maoists felt that Bhattarai was getting undue publicity himself. It was necessary to convey, they thought, that the most important Maoist leader was Prachanda, not Baburam. At the fourth expanded plenary meeting in August 1998, the party decided to take measures to 'centralize' the leadership. The Maoists would release a picture of Prachanda to the press, and from then on all party members would have to quote Prachanda in their speeches and writings.[21] The 2001 decision to name the party's strategy and ideology 'Prachandapath' was also intended to raise Prachanda's profile and diminish Bhattarai's.

Bhattarai complained against such measures on repeated occasions. He accepted that Prachanda was the supreme leader of the Maoist party, he said, but objected to the attempt to create a personality cult around him. He also emphasized that naming the party's guiding principles 'Prachandapath' did not imply that Prachanda was the sole authority in the party. Rather, Prachandapath should be understood as the 'centralized expression of collective leadership'.

Bhattarai constantly stressed that his views were based on principle, not self-interest, and that he had no designs on the party's leadership. Acknowledging that he lacked capacity to be the supreme leader, he expressed his continued commitment to playing a secondary, supportive role.[22] Despite these protestations, Prachanda and other Maoist leaders would sometimes interpret Bhattarai's criticism of 'centralized leadership' as an attempt to undermine Prachanda's position.

Although he depended on the party chairman, Baburam Bhattarai in turn had reasons to be wary of Prachanda. After King Gyanendra took over power, Prachanda gave the impression that he fully backed Bhattarai's political line directed towards establishing a democratic republic. But occasionally Bhattarai suspected that the chairman had been giving similar reassurances to party leaders who opposed that line.

At the heart of the matter was the question of how Nepali communists should view the monarchy, the parliamentary parties and the Indian state. This was a long-standing debate. The Maoists had identified two trends in the history of Nepali communism. The first was the 'Pushpa Lal-tendency', named after a leader of Nepal's original communist party, Pushpa Lal Shrestha. In 1960, after King Mahendra dissolved the multi-party system, Pushpa Lal had sided with the Nepali Congress and declared that a parliamentary democracy was preferable to monarchical autocracy. The second was the 'Rayamajhi-tendency', named after another old communist leader, Keshar Jung Rayamajhi, who had joined the Panchayat regime, stating that monarchy was more capable of safeguarding Nepal's sovereignty than a democratic system.[23]

To the Maoists, both these tendencies represented deviations. Pushpa Lal had succumbed to the Nepali Congress, which represented the 'comprador bourgeoisie' and the interests of the Indian state. Rayamajhi, on the other hand, had succumbed entirely to the forces of feudalism. In theory, the Maoists held that it was necessary to resist both tendencies. The monarchy, the parliamentary parties and the Indian government were equally their enemy.

In practice, however, the Maoist leaders were divided in their inclination towards one of the two tendencies. One group, represented by Baburam Bhattarai, preferred the parliamentary parties to the monarchy, a view that inclined more to the 'Pushpa Lal-tendency'.[24] Their primary goal was to destroy the feudal order and create a more egalitarian society. Among the Maoists, this group was said to prioritize 'democracy' over 'nationalism'. Others, including Kiran, seemed closer to the 'Rayamajhi tendency', with their overriding emphasis on 'nationalism'. They sought, above all, to establish a strong and autonomous state that was capable of resisting the machinations of the Indian government and other 'imperialist' powers.

Throughout the course of the war, the Maoists thought it wise to maintain secret diplomatic links with all the important forces in Nepali politics. In 2001, when the government declared a state of emergency and deployed the RNA, the Maoist leaders were living in various towns in North India.[25] They were worried that the Indian government would pursue and harass them. A number of Bhattarai's colleagues from university had gone on to careers in Indian politics, civil service and academia, and so he was tasked with contacting them. In early 2002, Bhattarai managed to contact the Indian Prime Minister's Office through his old acquaintance, S. D. Muni, a scholar of Nepali politics at the Jawaharlal Nehru University who had briefly been ambassador to Laos.

The Indian government asked the Maoists to submit their case in writing. Bhattarai wrote a letter, signed by both him and Prachanda, stating that the Maoists were committed to good relations with India and had no intention of acting against its interests. Later, representatives from the Indian intelligence agencies, the Internal Bureau (IB) and the Research and Analysis Wing (RAW), started meeting Bhattarai and a few other Maoist leaders on a regular basis. The surveillance over the Nepali Maoists was relaxed and Maoist leaders could move and hold meetings on Indian soil with greater ease.[26]

However, the Indian government remained wary of the Nepali rebels and concerned that they might be helping the Indian Maoists. The Maoists knew this, but they also counted on the Indian government's reluctance to eliminate them. Royalists in Kathmandu believed that the Indians were tacitly encouraging the rebellion in the hope of using their leverage over the Maoists to expand their influence in Nepal. The Nepali government often complained that the Indian government was not cooperating in apprehending the rebels and deporting them to Nepal.[27]

While Baburam Bhattarai was responsible for maintaining links with representatives of the parliamentary parties and the Indian state, a number of other Maoist leaders – Rabindra Shrestha and Krishna Bahadur Mahara among them – were in contact with the palace. These leaders were votaries of the 'nationalist' tendency among the Maoists, and Bhattarai and his supporters distrusted them. A dispute had arisen between these two groups in the period following the royal massacre. Shrestha and Badal had not fully accepted the party's decision to focus their attack on the monarchy. Shrestha, in particular, was keen to engage with the palace. Mumaram Khanal, a Bhattarai supporter, opposed them.[28] When the issue was discussed in a politburo meeting held in Faridabad, Haryana, in late 2001, Prachanda, Bhattarai and a number of other leaders found themselves on one side of the dispute. A majority of the politburo, including Shrestha, Badal and Kiran, were on the other.[29]

Although Prachanda continued to support Bhattarai's political line, and the party resolutions continued to uphold it, Prachanda worried that he was alienating too many of his old comrades. In February 2002, during a long conversation in Delhi, Prachanda told Bhattarai that he could not go on antagonizing so many top leaders of the party. Bhattarai was disheartened.[30] He felt that Prachanda was gradually shifting towards a more conciliatory position vis-à-vis King Gyanendra. One night in early 2003, Prachanda told Bhattarai that Gyanendra had sent a message to the rebels: if they accepted the continued existence of the monarchy, the king would allow the Maoists to lead the government, and would also address their demand for a new national army comprising both the RNA and the Maoists' PLA.[31] Although nothing came of this proposal, Bhattarai found it unsettling. These parallel negotiations threatened to undermine his plan to build an alliance with the parliamentary parties against the monarchy.

Baburam Bhattarai's efforts to engage the parliamentary parties were public knowledge, written into party documents and known to all who read the newspapers. By contrast, the substance of negotiations with the king's emissaries was kept highly secret and mostly withheld even from other top Maoist leaders, including Bhattarai.

Even as Prachanda publicly supported Baburam Bhattarai's strategy, he was kept informed by the other Maoist leaders regarding negotiations with King Gyanendra. No doubt he also instructed Rabindra Shrestha and Krishna Bahadur Mahara on what to say to the king's emissaries. Prachanda seemed to be pursuing two strategies for resolving the conflict in favour of the Maoists. One was public and backed with theoretical arguments; the other was private and conspiratorial. And they represented opposing ideological strands.

## Trouble at the Top

After the collapse of the 2003 ceasefire, the RNA almost decimated the Maoist organization in and around the Kathmandu valley. The disagreements between Prachanda and Baburam Bhattarai also became more pronounced. 'The failure to achieve a decisive military victory and the unhealthy struggle within the leadership,' wrote the Maoist activist Anil Sharma, a member of the Ring Bureau responsible for the areas around the Kathmandu valley, 'led to increasing indiscipline, desertions, resentment and factionalism in the lower committees.'[32]

In Bhattarai's view, the frustration that had arisen among the ranks was a result of the class system that had emerged within the party. He claimed that the problem could be mitigated by implementing his proposals for collective leadership and regular rotation of cadres between different positions. But the party continued to be run in the traditional Stalinist manner. The behaviour of some of the top leaders and their families also drew criticism from Bhattarai and others, notably Ram Bahadur Thapa. Prachanda, for example, drank too much and indulged in 'loose talk' about other party leaders. His wife often treated party members in a scornful manner.[33]

Prachanda's supporters retaliated against Bhattarai. At a January 2004 meeting in Delhi, for instance, there was a bitter quarrel between Ananta, who supported Prachanda, and Mani Thapa, who supported Bhattarai.

Mani Thapa violently denounced the concept of Prachandapath; Ananta accused Thapa of 'losing his mind' and belittled his capabilities.[34]

Next, the Indian police started arresting Maoist leaders. Until early 2004, the only top-tier rebel leader in Indian captivity was Chandra Prakash Gajurel. He had been arrested in August 2003 at Chennai (Madras) airport when he was attempting to fly to London with a forged passport. But in February 2004, three more Maoist leaders – Matrika Yadav, Upendra Yadav and Suresh Ale Magar – were arrested from an apartment in Delhi.[35] In March, Mohan Baidya 'Kiran' was arrested at a hospital in Siliguri in West Bengal, where he was recovering from an eye operation. And in June, eleven Maoists including the politburo member Kul Prasad K. C. were arrested at a hotel in Patna, the capital of the state of Bihar.[36]

These arrests caused fresh anxiety. The Maoist leaders had lived and moved on Indian soil for years, but this was the first time they had been pursued in such a planned and systematic way. They were not aware that the arrests were a consequence of greater cooperation between India's IB and the Nepal government, and growing concern within the Indian government that the Nepali Maoists were encouraging Indian Maoists.[37] They thus wondered: had the Indian government changed its policy towards them? And had some Maoists been personally targeted? Mohan Baidya was known to hold pretty hostile views about the Indian government. The rebels arrested in Patna were loyal to him. Matrika Yadav, who was intensely loyal to Prachanda, had been arrested almost immediately after his arrival in Delhi. He, along with Suresh Ale Magar, was deported to Nepal. But Upendra Yadav, arrested with them, had been released. Also, how had the Indian security agencies discovered the whereabouts of the rebels? Could it be that certain members of the party had informed on their comrades?

Maoist leaders hostile to Baburam Bhattarai, such as Rabindra Shrestha and Maheshwar Dahal, tried to convince Prachanda that Bhattarai had colluded with the Indian security agencies to have their comrades arrested. They painted it as an indirect attack on the chairman himself. Anil Sharma, one of those arrested in Patna, was a proponent of this view. He wrote: 'The history of the world communist movement shows that when the inner-party struggle grows acrimonious, the dissatisfied section forms an alliance with the enemy to attack the revolutionary headquarters ... Like other friends, I reached the conclusion that our arrest was not a coincidence but the result of a planned conspiracy.'[38]

Before the arrests took place, the Maoist leaders were already considering moving back to Nepal in order to reduce the growing gap between the leadership and the rank and file. Now, Prachanda was convinced that the Indian government was intent on destroying the Maoist organization in India. He decided that the leadership would relocate to their base area in Rolpa and Rukum.

Most of the top leaders moved to Nepal towards the end of June. Prachanda, Bhattarai and Hisila Yami travelled together. Relations between Prachanda and Bhattarai had grown cold, and they barely spoke to each other during the long and arduous journey to Rolpa. Soon after they arrived, Prachanda accused Bhattarai of coveting the party leadership and setting other Maoist leaders against the chairman. Bhattarai admitted that he had been unhappy with Prachanda's behavior and therefore kept silent when other party leaders criticized the chairman. But he denied participating in any conspiracy, and asked Prachanda to produce evidence for his claim.[39]

In August 2004, ninety-five members of the Maoist central committee convened in the village of Phuntibang in Rolpa. Prachanda told the gathering that he had met Upendra Yadav and Matrika Yadav when they were in Delhi in February. Upendra had said that the Maoists had no alternative but to work closely with Indian officials. Prachanda had immediately become wary; it seemed to him that Upendra was secretly in touch with Indian security officials, whose message he was implicitly conveying. After the meeting, Upendra and Matrika had gone to rest at Suresh Ale Magar's apartment. The next day Prachanda was supposed to meet them in the evening, but he had meetings all day and was quite exhausted. At his wife's suggestion, he decided not to go out. The raid on Ale Magar's apartment occurred at exactly the time when the Maoist chairman was scheduled to visit there. Prachanda had no doubt that Upendra Yadav had informed on him. The raid was a clear indication that the Indian government wished to arrest the Maoists' supreme leader and quash the Nepali revolution. Prachanda recounted this story with great urgency and passion. The central committee members were stunned.[40]

According to the document that Prachanda presented at the meeting, it had always been the party's policy to attack the 'reactionary' group that was in power and directly responsible for suppressing the people. For the first five years of the rebellion, therefore, the Maoists had focused their attack on the parliamentary parties, those 'brokers of Indian expansionism who had betrayed the Nepali people's nationalist ideals by signing various unequal treaties and agreements with the Indian government'.[41] After the palace massacre in 2001, the king had usurped power, and waged war against the Maoists with US backing. The forces of feudalism and American imperialism had then become the rebels' chief enemy, and it was then that the party decided to reach out to representatives of the Indian government. However, after the Maoist attack on Beni, it became clear that the feudal and American strategy to eliminate the Maoists militarily had failed. India too came to realize that the Nepali rebels had become far too powerful and that it was now necessary to weaken them. That was why the Indian security agencies had arrested so many of the Maoist leaders in early 2004.[42]

In these changed political circumstances, said Prachanda, the Maoists needed to change their tactics once again. They needed to ally with all the 'patriotic' forces within the country and launch a nationwide mobilization campaign against the political forces that had historically surrendered to Indian expansionism. As the 'nationalist struggle' of the Nepali people gained momentum, he said, it was likely that the Indian army would prepare to invade Nepal.[43] The PLA had to immediately start digging trenches and tunnels across the country, especially in areas along the border, to resist the potential incursion.

Encouraged by Prachanda, many central committee members including Rabindra Shrestha denounced Baburam Bhattarai as a 'rightist capitulationist'. They said that Bhattarai's plan to ally with the parliamentary parties against the monarchy was not merely a tactic to sow division among enemy forces, but a long-term strategy to lead the Maoists straight into bourgeois democracy.[44]

Bhattarai was not directly blamed for the arrests of senior Maoist leaders. But Devendra Poudel, a politburo member close to Bhattarai, was declared to be under suspicion of providing the information to the Bihar police that led to the arrests in Patna. He was forced to resign from his position, and a formal investigation into his activities was announced.[45]

Prachanda also proclaimed that the rebels were currently engaged in the third and final stage of Maoist protracted war, namely, the strategic offensive, which required great initiative, aggression and a highly centralized party structure. The majority of the central committee members supported a proposal to bring all of the party organs – the party itself, the army and the united front or URPC – under a 'centralized leadership'. Bhattarai saw this as a direct assault on the principle of collective leadership that he had been trying to introduce in the party. He offered to resign from his positions as head of the united front and member of the standing committee.[46]

The resolution passed at the Phuntibang meeting castigated Bhattarai. It stated that certain leaders had a tendency 'to be more concerned about their position and prestige than about the struggle for the collective ideals of the proletariat, to bargain and issue threats if things don't go according to their will ... [and] to consider themselves know-it-alls and treat others as ignorant fools.' The entire party was called upon to 'struggle' against such 'individualistic anarchism'.[47]

It is unclear whether Prachanda really believed that the raid in Delhi had been timed to coincide with his visit to Suresh Ale Magar's apartment. He would later tell his colleagues that he had been mistaken. Upendra Yadav had not informed on his comrades. Rather, the Delhi police had been trailing Ale Magar for some time and had found out where he lived. It was pure coincidence that they raided his apartment at a time when Prachanda was supposed to visit him.[48]

What seems certain, however, is that Prachanda did not anticipate an all-out war with the Indian state. His statement about launching a 'nationalist struggle' against 'Indian expansionism' and digging bunkers and trenches to fight the Indian army was meant to serve a different purpose. The arrest of his close comrade Mohan Baidya had deeply alarmed him. He was also concerned about the resulting anxiety within the party and the murmurs of discontent regarding his leadership. By claiming that he too had been the target of a grave conspiracy and by discrediting Bhattarai, he hoped to rekindle sympathy and loyalty towards himself. By pointing to India as the great enemy of the revolution, he hoped to provoke outrage among party members. And by urging them to launch a struggle against Indian expansionism, he hoped to channel that outrage into energetic activity.

By means of all this, Prachanda wanted to create the conditions for executing a new strategy. Although only a select group of his confidants was aware of his precise intentions, the Phuntibang resolution does signal the direction the chairman wished to take at the time. For instance, the document declared that as part of their 'nationalist struggle', the Maoists would need to ally with all the 'patriotic forces' (that is, the king and his supporters) against the political forces that had historically 'surrendered to Indian expansionism' (that is, the parliamentary parties). The resolution also stated that while the Maoists were open to negotiation, they would only negotiate with the 'master', not the 'servants of the old regime' – terms that clearly referred to the king and the parliamentary parties respectively.[49]

In the period after the Phuntibang meeting, hundreds of Maoist cadres enthusiastically dug bunkers and tunnels to prepare against an Indian invasion. They forcibly recruited villagers and worked to indoctrinate them in anti-Indian sentiment. Meanwhile, Prachanda communicated with King Gyanendra. Rabindra Shrestha was in contact with RNA General Rookmangud Katawal. Krishna Bahadur Mahara was in touch with Gyanendra's son-in-law, Raj Bahadur Singh.[50] Through these emissaries, Prachanda proposed that the Maoists and the monarchy form an alliance to preserve the nation's autonomy and sovereignty. The parliamentary parties had caused grave damage to the Nepali state during their years in power, he said, so they should not be given a role in governance any more.

Prachanda raised the spectre of an Indian invasion to provide ideological justification for a royalist–Maoist alliance among the party's rank and file. He encouraged the vilification of Bhattarai in order to silence those who regarded the monarch as the Maoists' chief enemy. The Maoists also looked to Cambodia for an example where an insurgent communist group had allied with a monarch. In 1975, after the Khmer Rouge captured Phnom Penh and Pol Pot took control of the country, Sihanouk was still retained as a symbolic head of state.[51] The situation in Nepal, of course, was very different. For one, Gyanenda was vastly more powerful than Sihanouk, and it would be almost impossible for the Maoists to reduce him to a figurehead. Nevertheless, the Cambodian example was held up as a precedent to justify the Maoists' proposed alliance with Gyanendra.

Bhattarai did not remain silent. He continued to protest the charges against him. He criticized Prachanda for his 'instability', his tendency to view minor incidents as symptoms of grave conspiracies, and his penchant for spreading malicious rumours. Bhattarai submitted letters of dissent to the party headquarters and circulated them through the rank and file. In them, he restated his arguments against the centralization of leadership and the personality cult that had formed around Prachanda. He criticized the manner in which he had been singled out for vilification. 'The inner-party struggle,' he wrote, 'is being conducted in a very unhealthy, wrong and opportunistic manner.'[52] The attacks on him had been focused on his personality and faction rather than his ideology and politics. Instead of confronting him directly, his rivals had launched a 'clandestine' and 'conspiratorial' smear campaign against him.[53] 'Above all, an environment has been created in which leaders from different ranks denounce anyone who dares to criticize them as "anarchist". The party is characterized by rampant hypocrisy, servility and general anarchy rather than proletarian discipline and "voluntary centralism".'[54]

Bhattarai also argued that the new policy was based on flawed premises. It went against the 'true communist policy' whereby the rebels would 'tactically concentrate their struggle against the force that has seized state power'. The parliamentary parties were neither in power, nor did they have an armed force of their own. And there were no signs that the Indian state was preparing to invade Nepal. On the battlefield, the rebels were still fighting the Royal Nepal Army. As such, 'the principal contradiction is between the revolutionaries and the monarchy that survives on the strength of the royal army and the support of the imperialist and expansionist forces.'[55]

Further, Bhattarai argued, to ally with the monarch against the parliamentary parties was to go against the grain of history. A socialist state could be attained only after progressing through the stages of feudalism and capitalism. The Maoists' first task was to complete the capitalist revolution. To that end Nepal would first need to go through the 'sub-stage' of a 'democratic republic', in which all vestiges of feudalism would have been abolished.[56] An alliance with the monarchy would hence be a historical regression based on the misguided notion that feudalism is more progressive than capitalism.[57]

In mass meetings and during small gatherings, party leaders close to Prachanda attempted to delegitimize Bhattarai's views. In a meeting with members of the party's intellectual organization, Prachanda told this parable: a parent wanting to educate his children took them to a guru. The guru asked whether the children had received any previous education. The parent replied that the younger one had not, but that the older one had studied for three years under another guru, and so only required some additional learning. The guru told the parent that he would teach the younger child for three years, but the older one would need six years, three of which would be devoted to unlearning what he had been taught in the past.[58] The story, of course, was meant to refer to the over-educated leader who had yet to 'unlearn' all his theories.

According to Rabindra Shrestha, in mid-January 2005 King Gyanendra sent a message saying that he was willing to share power with the Maoists and make Prachanda prime minister. Keen to finalize the details of this arrangement, Prachanda invited the king to meet him in Thabang. Gyanendra apparently responded that Dorpatan in Baglung district would be a safer choice. Prachanda accepted. But Gyanendra kept postponing the meeting on one pretext or another.[59]

A meeting of the Maoist politburo was convened in Labang, Rukum, on 25 January 2005. If Shrestha's account is true, Prachanda was then preparing for his much-anticipated meeting with the king. Presumably, then, his primary objective at the time was to convince the party leadership to accept a settlement with Gyanendra. Bhattarai was the only remaining obstacle in the way of this goal. It was necessary to thoroughly discredit him.

At the meeting in Labang, Prachanda presented a charge sheet against Bhattarai. Bhattarai's criticism of the party's decision to 'centralize' leadership, it stated, was motivated by pure self-interest. He 'suffered from vengeful emotions', and had tried to establish a parallel power centre through his leadership of the united front; he had criticized the party from a 'bourgeois class perspective'. In proclaiming himself the 'thinker' of the party and offering everyone unsolicited advice, he demonstrated his 'bourgeois individualist intellectual arrogance'. He was so preoccupied with theoretical knowledge that he implicitly devalued 'revolutionary practice'.[60]

The politburo held daily meetings for over a week. Each day Bhattarai was denounced for various 'crimes', including that of being an agent of Indian expansionism. Bhattarai tried to refute these charges as he had done before.

On 31 January, the Maoist politburo voted on Prachanda's charge sheet against Bhattarai. Ten of its members, including Prachanda, Ram

Bahadur Thapa, Krishna Bahadur Mahara and Rabindra Shrestha, voted in its favour. Four voted against and one abstained.[61] The majority decided to strip Baburam Bhattarai and his supporters Hisila Yami and Dina Nath Sharma of their leadership positions. For the next few months they were detained in a house in Mirul, Rolpa, kept under close surveillance of the PLA, and their communications with the outside world were severely restricted.


## Groping in the Dark

In Kathmandu, Girija Prasad Koirala and his Nepali Congress party had continued to protest against the dissolution of parliament and the king's dismissal of Sher Bahadur Deuba. They demanded that the king revive the democratic process by reinstating the dissolved parliament. The reinstated parliament would then reach out to the Maoists and negotiate a settlement to the conflict. The king would be allowed to remain as a constitutional monarch. But if Gyanendra refused to 'hand back the rights he had snatched away from the people', Koirala said, the votaries of constitutional monarchy (the parliamentary parties) would join the republicans (the Maoists). Together, they would launch a vigorous struggle that would dismantle the institution of the monarchy.[62]

Having realized that Gyanendra would only embrace old Panchayat-era politicians, the UML and the Nepali Congress-Democratic (the breakaway Congress faction led by Sher Bahadur Deuba) joined the Nepali Congress to carry out street protests against 'royalist regression'. In May 2004, however, Prime Minister Surya Bahadur Thapa resigned. Meanwhile, the international community too was putting pressure on the king to reach out to the parliamentary parties and show his support for democracy. So, a month after Thapa resigned, the king appointed Deuba as prime minister, notwithstanding the fact that less than two years before he had sacked Deuba for his 'incompetence'. Deuba was tasked with persuading the other parties to participate in his administration. Lured by the prospect of sharing in the spoils of power, the UML joined the government, claiming that the 'regression had been half corrected'.

The new government, comprising parties that had led the 1990 movement, had a more representative façade than its predecessor. Koirala stuck to his demands, but he was now left with no supporters except for some fringe parties. Sections of the media also turned against him. The *Nepali Times* editorialized: 'What [Koirala] sees as consistency others see as stubbornness, what he perceives as a struggle against regression most Nepalis see as a self-seeking effort to put himself and his coterie back in power.'[63]

And yet, Gyanendra had made no significant concession to the parties. He had appointed the new prime minister in the same undemocratic manner as he had appointed the last two prime ministers: by invoking Article 127 of the constitution, that granted the monarch the 'power to remove difficulties' in the face of constitutional impasse. He had selected Deuba because he considered him the most pliant among the leaders of the parliamentary parties.

Deuba made every effort to ingratiate himself with the king. He included, despite UML's objections, three of Gyanendra's loyalists in his council of ministers, even though they did not belong to any party. He went so far as to appoint a royal nominee – Mohammad Mohsin – as the government's spokesperson. The royal nominees were obviously expected to report to the king on cabinet discussions and ministerial activities. The king also pressed Deuba's council of ministers to increase the budget for the palace and the security forces. In the absence of a parliament, the cabinet sent all bills to the palace. Bills that were amenable to the king's interests were then passed as ordinances. Others, such as bills proposing a Women's Commission or an amendment to the civil code, were withheld indefinitely.[64]

Gyanendra told Deuba to focus on a specific agenda: negotiate with the Maoists, bring the conflict to an end and hold elections by April 2005. To that end Deuba established a Peace Secretariat that would lay the groundwork for negotiations. In September he invited the Maoists for talks. But the Maoists refused to negotiate with the government. 'We want to talk with the person and institution that holds power and the authority to make decisions,' said Maoist spokesperson Krishna Bahadur Mahara.

UML leaders suggested that the government lure the Maoists with some concessions – such as to declare a unilateral ceasefire and tell the Maoists that the government would negotiate without preconditions, as well as consider the Maoist demand for elections to a Constituent Assembly. But in practical terms, the government lacked the power to make such concessions. Whenever the UML ministers brought up these proposals in cabinet meetings, Deuba said that he would have to consult the king and the chief of the army.[65] Needless to say, the palace and army would not endorse such an approach. The RNA claimed that it was engaged in a successful offensive against the Maoists and that a cease-fire would only allow the rebels to expand and consolidate their power. Meanwhile, the king's views were echoed by Deuba, who said that both the monarch's position as head of state and the 1990 constitution were non-negotiable.

The political parties, civil society and the media debated these matters with great urgency. In retrospect, however, they had unwittingly missed the point. At the time Deuba's government was trying to draw the Maoists into negotiations, the Maoist party was torn by internal strife. Baburam Bhattarai was gradually being marginalized and Prachanda had declared the necessity of a tactical alliance with the king against the parties. The rebels were secretly in contact with the king's emissaries. Whereas the details of the government's activities were common knowledge, the government had no inkling of the Maoists' internal issues or their dealings with the palace. Deuba would otherwise have realized that he was in no position to negotiate a settlement to the conflict. Throughout his term as prime minister, his government was groping in the dark.

The Maoists repeatedly turned down the government's call for negotiation. In December, Deuba finally issued an ultimatum: if the Maoists did not agree to negotiations by mid-January, the government would hold general elections. The deadline passed without a response. It was evident to all that no credible elections were possible: the Maoists controlled most of the countryside, and would foreseeably assassinate candidates and prevent people from voting. But the only way Deuba could salvage his image before the king was by going ahead. He insisted on preparing for a poll even as the UML ministers in his government stressed that this wasn't feasible. Sceptical election commissioners were ticked off with the words: 'I am the king's employee, and so are you. You should stick to the mandate given to us.'[66]

In the end, King Gyanendra himself put Deuba out of his misery. On the morning of 1 February 2005, he delivered an address to the nation. 'Nepal's bitter experience over the past few years tends to show that democracy and progress contradict each other,' he said. He stressed the flaws of the political parties and blamed them for failing to tackle the Maoist insurgency and weakening the morale of the army. It had hence become 'imperative' for him to take a step 'in the greater interest of the nation and the people'. Once again invoking the preventive power granted to him by the constitution, he there and then dismissed the government, which, he said, would be replaced by a new council of ministers chaired by the king himself. Accusing the Maoists of spreading terror and destruction, he announced: 'From now on, such crimes will be dealt with firmly in accordance with the law. Our security forces have been mobilized to carry out their responsibilities more effectively to end terrorism and restore peace and security in the interest of the nation and people.'[67]

As Gyanendra delivered his address, phone lines were cut and the internet was shut down. Security personnel sprang into action and placed Girija Prasad Koirala, Sher Bahadur Deuba and Madhav Kumar Nepal under house arrest. Several hundred other political leaders and civil society activists were also detained at their homes or at army and police camps. Army personnel burst into newspaper offices, television and radio stations and imposed editorial control over the media. The palace's press secretariat issued a communiqué declaring a nationwide state of emergency and the suspension of civil liberties. Thus, only a day after the Maoists in Rolpa stripped Baburam Bhattarai of all his positions and placed him under detention, the king in Kathmandu dismissed the government, arrested the leaders of the parliamentary parties and took over total executive power.

## The Battle at Khara

The Maoist leaders were in a politburo meeting in Labang, Rolpa, when they heard the king's address on the radio. The coup came as a shock to Prachanda. Over the past months he had reached out to the king several times, and the king's response had seemed encouraging. But now it was clear that the king had betrayed him. Some Maoist leaders, such as Rabindra Shrestha, said the takeover was actually a positive development, as it would be easier to negotiate with an absolute authority.[68] But Prachanda realized that seeking a settlement with the monarch would now be suicidal. The Maoist goal of forging a power-sharing agreement with the king, and then reducing him to a figurehead, had become unattainable. It was clear that Gyanendra had no intention of relinquishing power, and would accept no settlement that did not subordinate the rebels to his will.

Hours later, Prachanda issued a statement denouncing Gyanendra's proclamation. 'Our party vows ... to fight to ... end feudal autocracy,' it said. 'The fire of the People's War will rage on until the Royal Nepal Army is dissolved and its weapons handed over to the People's Liberation Army.' He urged all the political parties and sections of society to join forces with the rebels to unleash a 'storm of revolt' that would end the monarchy, lead to elections for a Constituent Assembly and establish a 'people's democratic republic'.[69]

Despite his bravado, Prachanda was in a tight spot. In pursuing negotiations with Gyanendra, he had burned his bridges with all potential allies. Having antagonized India by his declaration of a 'nationalist struggle' against the country, he could no longer travel to Indian territory or appeal to individuals in the Indian intelligence agencies and bureaucracy. Nor was it possible at this time to engage leaders of the parliamentary parties. They remained deeply suspicious of the Maoists, especially as the rebels had rejected all their overtures over the past year. Besides, most leaders of the Nepali Congress and the UML were now under house arrest. Baburam Bhattarai, the Maoists' key interlocutor with India, the parliamentary parties and civil society, had just been stripped of his authority and placed under detention. Moreover, Maoist cadres were still hostile towards India, the parliamentary parties and Bhattarai – a mood that the chairman himself had actively fuelled.

Now that negotiations seemed out of the question, Prachanda decided to resort to the military path. Soon after the king's takeover, he asked the PLA deputy commanders Nanda Kishore Pun 'Pasang' and Janardhan Sharma 'Prabhakar' to select the most suitable Royal Nepal Army position for a Maoist attack.[70] They chose the RNA base at Khara, in Rukum district, which held around 250 army personnel.[71]

As Prachanda told his commanders, the attack on Khara was primarily directed against the monarchical-military regime that had seized total control over the state. A successful attack on a major army position would make the army psychologically vulnerable and expose the regime's weaknesses. The other objective of the attack was to 'protect nationalism', meaning that it would symbolize the party's struggle against the Indian state. Lastly, the attack was aimed against 'reformism' within the Maoist party, which obviously referred to the line represented by Bhattarai. Prachanda worried that his failed strategy of joining the king to fight against the parliamentary parties and India would undermine his leadership. A successful attack on a major RNA position would salvage his prestige within the party while allowing the continued marginalization of Bhattarai.[72]

But it should have been clear that Prachanda was on shaky political ground. Many senior Maoists had long ago realized that they could not capture the state through purely military means, and that they required the support of a section of the political class to enter mainstream politics. The dispute between Prachanda and Bhattarai had centred on whether it was wiser to ally with the parliamentary parties or the monarchy. Now, it seemed that Prachanda had discarded all such tactical considerations. The attack on Khara was not just targeted against *both* the king and India (and, by implication, the parliamentary parties), but also against an important leader within the party. Desperate and isolated, Prachanda seemed to have latched onto the idea of destroying his enemies with the support of the Maoist army alone. And so the Khara battle, he told his commanders, was part of a *digvijjaya abhiyan*, 'a campaign of conquest'. Explaining what this meant, a brigade commander said, 'We will launch attack after attack. We will achieve success after success. We will destroy the enemies' forts.'[73] After taking it over, the Maoists planned to make Khara their base from where they would chase away the army from all areas of Rolpa, Rukum and Salyan and then declare the entire region their 'permanent base area'.[74]

However, the Maoists had overestimated their military capacity. The army base at Khara might have looked like an easy target, being located in the midst of Maoist-controlled territory, but the position stood on high ground, and attacking it would mean advancing uphill through minefields and barbed wire obstacles while under enemy fire. The Maoists had already made a failed assault on the base in May 2002, with the loss of over 150 combatant lives. Since then the RNA had further strengthened their fortifications, making a successful attack even more difficult.[75] But that did not deter the Maoists from trying.

They knew it would be a large-scale operation. The party had reorganized their army into three divisions in August 2004. Two of them, the Central Division and the Western Division, led by Nanda Kishore Pun 'Pasang' and Janardhan Sharma 'Prabhakar' respectively, would participate in the battle. This made it the largest military operation launched by the Maoists. During preparations, however, major differences emerged between the two commanders over strategy. Pasang wanted to carry out a swift, single-day operation, and drilled his troops accordingly. Prabhakar, in contrast, formulated a strategy that envisaged up to three days' fighting. These differences, which were not resolved even after the attack was launched, caused considerable resentment between the two commanders and hampered the effectiveness of the attack.[76]

Shortly after 10 pm on the night of 17 April, rebel troops under Pasang's command started moving up the hill at Khara, firing at the army base at the summit. The RNA troops retaliated with machine-gun fire. Sometime later, M-17 helicopters appeared in the sky and fired a hail of bullets on the rebels. In the words of Sam Cowan, 'carnage is probably the most appropriate word to describe what took place, as wave after wave of attackers were mowed down by machine-gun fire amidst the maze of barbed wire and strong fortifications.'[77] The fighting went on all night. The small group of around ten combatants that succeeded in penetrating the camp perimeter were rapidly shot dead. An RNA helicopter with reinforcements landed at the base in the morning. Pasang called off the attack. The Maoists retreated. Around 250 rebels were killed in the battle.[78]

## A Crisis of Legitimacy

In his 1 February address to the nation, King Gyanendra had vowed to restore parliamentary democracy as soon as he had resolved the Maoist crisis and stabilized the country. But his actions in the following months indicated that he was nostalgic for the Panchayat system that his father had established, and aspired to put a similar regime in place.

Gyanendra filled senior government positions with ultra-royalists. In July he appointed Tulsi Giri, an aging Panchayat-era politician, as his deputy in the council of ministers. It was as though history was being repeated: in 1960, after imprisoning the leaders of political parties and seizing absolute control over the state, King Mahendra had appointed Giri chairman of the council of ministers. Since the democratic transition of 1990, Giri had been in political retirement in the Indian city of Bangalore. It was unlikely that he could fully grasp, let alone manage, the political circumstances of 2005. His unstinting devotion to the crown was his sole qualification for the post.

The king replaced many of the remaining democratic institutions with ones that resembled Panchayat-era institutions. He reinstated the positions of commissioners to Nepal's fourteen zones, and they were made to report directly to the palace. He formed committees to monitor the activities of the political parties and the bureaucracy. He banned civil service unions, which had flourished since the 1990s and were known to be sympathetic towards the parliamentary parties.[79] He visited temples, travelled across the country granting audiences to his subjects, and awarded medals to those who pleased him. All over Kathmandu one could see large billboards displaying the king's calls to order, discipline and patriotic duty.

Gyanendra pursued his political rivals in ways that blatantly violated the constitution. He established a new body, the Royal Commission for Corruption Control (RCCC), that usurped the role of the constitutionally mandated Commission for the Investigation of the Abuse of Authority (CIAA). Filled with palace loyalists, the RCCC was granted powers not only to charge individuals with corruption, but also to investigate and prosecute them. Its first targets were Sher Bahadur Deuba and other Nepali Congress leaders. The United States government condemned the RCCC as an 'extrajudicial organization'.[80] Meanwhile, the government was not subject to even the most basic standards of accountability. Members of the new council of ministers included a convicted criminal and an individual accused of corruption.[81] The government issued an ordinance that allowed the king to appropriate state funds at will.

But 2005 was not 1960. The king, ensconced in his palace, listening to only a handful of advisors, had been carried away by hubris. It was one thing to seize state power, quite another to control society. The RNA had assured Gyanendra that they would destroy the Maoist organization provided they were not hobbled by the political parties, media and human rights activists. But even after the king and army gained total control over the administration, the state's writ was limited to Kathmandu and district capitals. The Maoists continued to dominate much of the countryside. They ordered strikes and road blockades that brought the entire capital city to a halt. There was not much the army could do besides escorting a number of heavy vehicles transporting essential goods into the valley.

Gyanendra was mistaken if he thought that the urban population would remain passive as he clamped down on political parties and democratic institutions. Civil society, which had grown increasingly vocal over the past decade, would not countenance such restrictions on democratic space. On the very day of the coup, the Federation of Nepalese Journalists (FNJ) and the Nepal Bar Association (NBA) issued statements denouncing it. A few days later, twenty-five human rights organizations issued a joint statement criticizing the 'illegal military rule headed by the King' and urging the international community to cease all military support to the government.[82] Amid direct threats from the army, the media censored itself for a temporary period but soon began clamouring for the restoration of democracy. Activists and journalists took to the streets in protest. The Maoist proposal for elections to a Constituent Assembly started to attract wider support.

The reaction from foreign powers with influence in Nepal was almost uniformly negative. Besides some minor countries who came out in the king's support, only China declined to oppose the coup, saying that it was Nepal's 'internal affair'.[83] India issued a statement recalling that 'India has consistently supported multi-party democracy and constitutional monarchy enshrined in Nepal's constitution as the two pillars of political stability in Nepal,' and describing the king's coup as a 'serious setback to the cause of democracy'.[84] Soon after, India announced a freeze on military aid to Nepal, as did the United Kingdom and the United States.[85] These countries urged the king to reverse his 1 February move and reconcile with the political parties. Amid such pressure, Gyanendra started releasing political detainees in March. He lifted the state of emergency on 29 April. Through the joint efforts of Nepali civil society, Western governments and international human rights organizations, the government was forced to allow the UN Office for the High Commissioner for Human Rights (OHCHR) to establish a mission in Nepal.[86]

These concessions revealed the weaknesses of the regime and further emboldened activists across the country. But India, unplacated, maintained its arms embargo. Gyanendra then resorted to a strategy his father had used in the past: he sought to cultivate China as a counterweight against India. In August, the Nepali government purchased US$1.2 million worth of ammunition from China. It also agreed to push for China's participation in a summit of the South Asian Association for Regional Cooperation (SAARC). India, ever wary of

Chinese influence in Nepal, only grew more hostile towards the Nepali government.[87]

Gyanendra's diplomatic manoeuvres showed his ignorance of geopolitical reality. He had thought that the US would continue to support his government even if India did not. Among all the countries with influence in Nepal, the US had adopted the hardest line towards the Maoists. Gyanendra, however, failed to realize that the US would not openly support an autocratic regime in a country where it had few strategic interests. After meeting Gyanendra's deputies, the American ambassador noted: 'Both [Tulsi] Giri and [Kirtinidhi] Bista appeared stunned by the Ambassador's reminder that [the Nepali government's] course of action could ultimately result in [its] becoming an isolated, international pariah relying solely on brute force and the backing of a single autocratic state [China] to stay in power.'[88]

Inevitably, the 1 February coup united the parliamentary parties against the monarchy. Girija Prasad Koirala, who alone among the major leaders had consistently stood against the 2002 dissolution of parliament, emerged as their undisputed leader. Sher Bahadur Deuba's Nepali Congress (Democratic) and the CPN–UML, which had only recently participated in a government appointed by the king, had no option but to join the octogenarian Nepali Congress leader. The three parties, along with some smaller groupings, formed the Seven Party Alliance (SPA). On 28 May the alliance announced a common minimum programme and a movement against the monarch. The SPA soon began to stage protests across the country demanding restoration of democracy, reinstatement of parliament, the formation of an all-party government and negotiations with the Maoists.[89] But in the immediate aftermath of the royal takeover, their movement received little public support.

Thus, in the face of the royal coup, the parliamentary parties not only came together but also became more radical in their demands. Decisively isolated from the monarchy and aware that they could not attract mass support on their own, the parties became more open to negotiating with the Maoists.

## Strategic Shift

The debacle at Khara finally convinced Prachanda that a major shift in party policy was necessary. The attempts to negotiate directly with the king and to weaken him through military action had both failed. Now the only alternative was to seek a rapprochement with the parliamentary parties and India. In May, Prachanda quietly released Baburam Bhattarai and his wife Hisila Yami from detention and sent them to Delhi to contact influential Indians and politicians from the Nepali political parties. Relations between the two Maoist leaders were still strained, however, and Bhattarai was still under a cloud of suspicion. Krishna Bahadur Mahara, a senior Maoist leader and steadfast supporter of the chairman, was sent along to keep an eye on Bhattarai's activities. From then onwards, Prachanda also dropped his anti-Indian rhetoric.

Delhi became a hub of Nepali oppositional activity after the coup. Nepali students at Jawaharlal Nehru University protested and issued statements against the royal regime. Several politicians fled to Delhi to escape detention. Many of those who had been arrested eventually flew there after their release, under the flimsy pretext of getting medical treatment. A number of Indian leaders from the Nationalist Congress Party (NCP) and the Communist Party of India-Marxist (CPI-M) formed the Nepal Democracy Solidarity Group to bolster the anti-monarchical movement.[90]

Bhattarai and Mahara began meeting Indian officials, Nepali politicians and civil society activists immediately after arriving in Delhi. Bhattarai's old mentor S. D. Muni introduced him to the influential CPI-M leader Prakash Karat, and soon after the Maoist leader was in regular contact with other Indian politicians from the Nepal Democracy Solidarity Group. Another CPI-M leader, Sitaram Yechury, became the chief conduit between the Maoists and prominent figures in the upper echelons of the Indian government.[91] Never before had the Maoists been able to establish contacts at such high levels of the Indian establishment. Antagonized by Gyanendra's extreme measures and his efforts to cultivate China, the Indian political class, which had hitherto seen the Maoists only as a terrorist group, was growing less reluctant to recognize them as a political force.

Amid these developments, Prachanda too arrived in Delhi towards the end of May. His relations with Bhattarai became warmer. He met with a wide range of political figures, including Girija Prasad Koirala, who arrived from Kathmandu in June. The Maoists' chief goal was to form a united front with the Nepali parliamentary leaders against the monarchy. They knew that their struggle would gain international legitimacy only if it was aligned to a pro-democracy movement headed by the mainstream parties. But neither the SPA leaders nor the Indian establishment was ready to trust the Maoists yet. Prachanda and Bhattarai sought to convince them that they were willing to participate in a liberal democratic system after the king was overthrown, and that they were committed to friendly relations with India. Over the next four months the Maoists held meetings with various Nepali and Indian political actors. Prachanda deployed all his charisma to win their confidence. A number of prominent civil society activists visiting from Kathmandu, such as Devendra Raj Panday, also played a key role in bridging differences between the parties.

On 22 November 2005, the Seven Party Alliance and the Maoists signed the *12-Point Memorandum of Understanding* (MOU), which outlined their joint course of action. The Maoists were forced to make a number of concessions. They notably had to give up their demand for the establishment of a republic, because the parliamentary parties and India did not favour the idea of abolishing the monarchy altogether. As a compromise, the document left the future status of the king ambiguous, stating only that the goal of the SPA–Maoist alliance was to 'establish full democracy by ending autocratic monarchy'.[92]

The term 'full democracy' did not preclude the abolition of the monarchy; it left open the possibility of reviving the demand for a republic. Meanwhile, by signing the twelve-point MOU, the rebels had made a binding commitment to 'democratic norms and values such as competitive multi-party system of governance, civil liberties, human rights [and] the concept of the rule of law'. This meant they had to renounce their goal of capturing the state and establishing one-party rule. The Maoists also agreed to cease violence against rivals and allow their political opponents who had fled during the war to return home and resume their lives in peace.

For their part, the parliamentary parties agreed to the Maoist demand for elections to a Constituent Assembly. But there were some differences over procedure. The parliamentary parties led by Koirala wanted the 2002 parliament to be reinstated before the formation of an all-party government and elections to a Constituent Assembly. The Maoists were not keen to see the parliament revived. But these minor differences were left for future resolution. Similarly, the parliamentary parties accepted, at least in principle, the Maoist claim that the 'problems related to class, caste, gender and region' could only be solved through a 'radical restructuring of the state'. The specifics of this 'restructuring' were not spelled out for the time being.

Although India was not a signatory to the twelve-point agreement, it did influence its content. Various Nepali leaders had long been requesting mediation from international bodies like the UN to resolve the conflict. India did not want any third-party involvement in a country that it considered to be in its sphere of influence. But after discussions with Koirala, Indian officials became less averse to the idea of an international body mediating the postwar settlement and monitoring the troops of both the Maoists and the RNA.

The leaders of the democratic parties returned to Kathmandu. The Maoists leaked the contents of the twelve-point MOU to the press via email. On 19 February, at a press conference held at G. P. Koirala's residence, the Seven Party Alliance formally acknowledged that they had formed an alliance with the Maoists. They called on all Nepalis opposed to the autocratic monarchy to unleash 'a storm of protests' across the country.[93]

# CHAPTER 8

# Uprising

## The Gandak Campaign

On 3 January 2006, Kshitiz Magar, vice-commander of a battalion under the Maoist army's Fifth Division, joined a large contingent of his comrades at Narikot in Pyuthan district. Born on 30 December 1978 in Rolpa's Jelbang VDC, he had, like so many young people of the region, encountered the Maoists while still at school. He had completed his SLC exams in the same year that the Maoist rebellion began and had not so much made a conscious decision to join them as been socialized into their culture. Sixty-eight people from Jelbang's 519 households were killed during the conflict, which made it the village with the highest number of wartime casualties.[1] Like many other Maoists, Kshitiz Magar spent the early days of the rebellion scrambling through jungles and villages under cover of darkness, seeking refuge in people's homes in far-flung settlements where he hid for days on end. Afraid to even step outside, he would excrete into plastic bags and ask the household members to dispose of them. Over time he grew bolder and found his place in large groups that, in his words, 'broke the legs of scoundrels and eliminated informers'.[2] He went on to participate in many attacks on the police and army, including the one on Beni. Now, along with fighters from the Fifth, Sixth and Seventh divisions of the Maoist People's Liberation Army, he was marching eastwards on the Gandak campaign.

The Gandak Campaign was part of the Maoists' latest military strategy. In September 2005, at a meeting of the party's central committee in Rukum's Chunbang, the leadership had reiterated that they were engaged in the 'strategic offensive' phase and reorganized their army into seven divisions. The twelve-point agreement stated that the Maoists and the Seven Party Alliance would 'launch attacks upon the autocratic monarchy from their respective positions'. The Maoists interpreted this to mean that while the parliamentary parties would organize protests in urban areas, the rebel army, moving out from villages, would attack the state security forces. According to Mao's military doctrine, rebel forces, having brought the villages under their control, must concentrate their forces for the final attack on the capital. Prachanda termed the new strategy 'Climb on the back and strike at the head'. The 'head' referred to Kathmandu and other district capitals that formed the nerve centre of the regime. The 'back' referred to those areas that surrounded 'the head' – the regions around Kathmandu and the highways that connected to urban centres.[3]

The Maoists envisaged that their army would move towards Kathmandu from both the west and the east; the march eastwards from Rolpa was termed the Gandak Campaign. The three assigned PLA divisions were to spread across the Gandaki, Lumbini and Dhaulagiri zones. These areas, with a relatively strong state presence, lay adjacent to the Bagmati zone, at the heart of which stood Kathmandu. Their task, as understood by Kshitiz Magar, was to 'destroy the remnants' of the state, engage the RNA's active forces in combat and rouse the local populations to launch a mass uprising against the regime.[4]

At the time, Gyanendra was preparing to hold elections to municipal authorities. While the king claimed this was a first step towards re-establishing democratic institutions, the political parties perceived it as merely a ruse. If they participated in the elections, it would allow the king to claim he was doing his best to accommodate them. But they would still be excluded from the all-powerful central government. In addition, if the municipal elections came off successfully, Gyanendra might claim to have achieved what previous governments had failed to do, and thus gain legitimacy. Desperate to foil the king's plan, the major parliamentary parties declared that they would not participate in the polls and appealed to the electorate to boycott them.[5] G. P. Koirala and other political leaders tacitly agreed that the Maoists, through acts of violence, should create an atmosphere of fear that would prevent local politicians from registering their candidacies and intimidate people into staying at home on election day. This was the more immediate goal of the Gandak Campaign.

During the three-month campaign, Kshitiz Magar crossed the hills of Arghakhanchi, Palpa and Nawalparasi districts on foot. He marched with his comrades in formation and hid when army helicopters flew overhead. He stayed at houses where the local party committees had arranged food and lodging. Being new to these areas, he kept a diary recording his impressions. In Dewalchaur, Arghakhanchi, he was surprised by the high-quality rice the rebels were served. 'Apparently this kind of rice is widely available here,' he noted on 9 January. 'Only officials and the rich get to eat such good rice in Rolpa.' He recalled the coarse, thick grain people had to eat in his home village, which he blamed on unscrupulous traders: 'The people are badly cheated by the traders. Shame on traders who are willing to do anything for money.'[6]

Through the radio, Kshitiz Magar received news of the unrest that was spreading across the country. Each day brought reports of skirmishes between Maoists and the RNA, of mass meetings and rallies organized by the parliamentary parties, of the government's attempts to foil these gatherings by imposing curfews and deploying the police. He was jubilant when he heard that the rebels had killed state security forces and captured weapons, whereas news of the death of comrades ignited a 'fire in my heart' and filled him with the desire for revenge.[7] But even in grief and anger, he remained philosophical: 'It is necessary for us to accept that the dialectical rule of war includes both victory and defeat.'[8]

On the night of 31 January, four of the seven Maoist army divisions, led by deputy commander Janardhan Sharma 'Prabhakar', attacked Tansen, the headquarters of Palpa district. To the consternation of the town's inhabitants, they burned down the century-old palace in the town centre that housed government offices. Kshitiz Magar was among the attackers. The next day was the first anniversary of the royal takeover. In his address to the nation, King Gyanendra boasted that security conditions in the country had improved over the past year. '[In Kathmandu, the king claimed that] the Maoists are losing,' Kshitiz wrote in his diary. 'Here in Tansen smoke is rising. How hollow are the king's words. In reality, his head must be spinning over what has happened in Tansen. Even the Election Commission must be trembling.'[9]

The elections were scheduled for 8 February 2006. As the day approached, the national mood grew increasingly hostile towards the regime. People also feared an outbreak of violence. Only parties with an insignificant support base had registered for elections. On 22 January,

Maoists assassinated Bijay Lal Das, a leader from a royalist party who had planned to run for mayor of the southern town of Janakpur.[10] Many other candidates subsequently withdrew from the race. In the streets of Pokhara and Kathmandu, protestors paraded dogs and oxen with 'Vote for me' signs on their backs. The night before the elections, the Maoists burned down government offices in the eastern town of Dhankuta and set off bombs in a number of other towns. Voting day was quieter. Thousands of security personnel were deployed at polling centres across the country. There were reports that RNA and police personnel had themselves stamped ballots and stuffed them into ballot boxes. Even according to official figures, only 20 per cent of the electorate voted. Kunda Dixit, editor of the *Nepali Times*, told Reuters: 'These municipal elections were a referendum on the king's takeover a year ago. The message to the king is that 80 per cent of the people don't support him.'[11] India, the US and the UK all issued statements doubting the elections' credibility. The king's gambit to legitimize his rule had failed.

K shitiz Magar's diary entries mainly dwelt on political and military matters. But in quieter moments, he also reflected on literature and wrote poems of his own.

> I am an atheist who doesn't believe in your Vedas
> I am an outlaw who doesn't believe in your laws
> There is no need to believe in the Vedic sutras and laws
> That discriminate between people
> That destroy the soul of humanity
> So I turned against you and picked up a gun
> I became a spark that ignites the gunpowder
> I became a Maoist[12]

Immediately before setting out on the Gandak Campaign, Magar and his friend Jitman Pun, vice-commander of the Mangalsen Smriti brigade, had published some of their poems in a collection titled *The Wall of Belief* (*Aasthako Parkhal*). On 16 January 2006 he met Mana Rishi Dhital, the Maoist journalist who was following the campaign. Though Magar had met him before, and even given him some of his poems for publication, it seemed Dhital remembered neither him nor his work. Still, he willingly read Magar's new poems and offered him feedback. Dhital judged that the poems possessed an authentic quality rooted in battlefield experience. Formal education may help one express oneself better, he said, yet 'pure content arises from personal experience.'[13] He encouraged Magar to write regularly and hone his skill.

Kshitiz Magar appreciated the encouragement, but remained sceptical. He had asked several writers to look at his poems in the past. 'They pretend to look [at my writing] … and wrinkle their noses as though it stinks.' He found such responses disheartening. 'I want to ask them: How would you feel if a rich man called your child a poor, ill-clad urchin? That's how I feel.'[14]

Insecure about his lack of formal education, Kshitiz Magar felt resentment not only towards the colleagues to whom he showed his poems, but also towards the arbiters of culture in 'bourgeois society', who 'do not even deign to look at the writings that come from within the war.'[15] In his diaries, he railed against the 'dishonesty and intolerance' of 'civilized society'. 'The reactionaries always say that education has to remain apolitical,' he wrote, referring to the mainstream press, which accused the Maoists of disrupting education and spoiling the future prospects of an entire generation. He subscribed to the common Maoist view that bourgeois education only equips students for the use of specific instruments of production. It keeps them ignorant of social reality and the ways in which the 'superstructure is inextricably linked to the base'. It is a system devised by 'reactionaries' to sustain the status quo. It produces citizens who only care about their own interests.[16]

'I write poems, but I am not a poet,' Kshitiz Magar wrote in his diary. 'I write of my experiences but I am not a writer. I sing because I want to, yet I am not a singer.' His task, he consoled himself, was far more important:

> The party has given me the responsibility to carry a gun. This is a historical necessity. I strongly believe that 'a state that rests on guns can only be toppled by guns.' Comrade Mao taught this a long time ago. What guns can accomplish is far superior to what is accomplished by refined literature written in lavish mansions … Yes, we have created literature with our guns. We have created ideology with guns. And with guns we have transformed this decadent society.[17]

However, diary entries from the final days of the war also reflected his nascent doubts: 'This principle may not hold forever. We may need to take other tactical routes according to the changing circumstances.'[18]

## The Testimony of Bise Nagarchi

Kshitiz Magar's poetry may not have found an audience outside a small circle of Maoist cadres. But that did not mean there was no demand for literature that might help people make sense of those turbulent times. During the Gandak Campaign, Shrawan Mukarung's 'Testimony of Bise Nagarchi' was perhaps the most popular poem in the country.[19]

Bise Nagarchi was a minor figure in Nepali history. He was a tailor who worked for King Prithvi Narayan Shah, the ambitious ruler of Gorkha whose expansionist campaigns in the mid-eighteenth century led to the unification of Nepal. As late as the early 2000s, Bise Nagarchi's descendants were still living near Prithvi Narayan's palace in Gorkha. But they were evicted from their homes when the government decided to extend the perimeter of the palace compound. Mukarung witnessed their eviction and expressed his outrage in this poem, voiced by a Bise Nagarchi who serves as an allegory for all the historically marginalized communities of Nepal.

> Master!
> After two hundred and fifty years in the Gorkha kingdom
> I have gone mad
> My head is spinning
> The world is turning
> Upside down
> Where are my feet resting?
> Where is Bise Nagarchi?
> Master! I have gone mad

In August 2005, Mukarung recited the poem to a packed hall at Gurukul Theatre in Kathmandu. The work was then widely circulated through magazines and the Internet, for it evidently encapsulated the generalized mood of frustration and despair. Around the same time, a number of prominent Kathmandu-based individuals formed what they called the Citizens' Movement for Democracy and Peace (CMDP). One of the founding members was Devendra Raj Panday, a former government official and vocal champion of human rights and democracy. He had served as finance secretary during the Panchayat era and as finance minister for the Nepali Congress-led interim government in 1990. In recent years he had become increasingly radicalized, and exasperated by the fecklessness and timidity of the parliamentary parties. Recognizing the need for an independent movement against the regime, he founded CMDP.[20] In July and August 2005, CMDP organized mass rallies in Kathmandu that were attended by thousands of people. These were the largest demonstrations the nation had witnessed since the royal takeover. Even the urban classes, often reluctant to join protests called by the political parties, seemed willing to accept CMDP's leadership.[21] Panday, along with other CMDP leaders such as Krishna Pahadi, forcefully articulated the demands and aspirations of the broader public. Their voices were complemented by the resounding testimony of Bise Nagarchi.

> I should have been serving you, Maharaj
> To protect history
> I should be touching Gorakhkali's feet
> To repay my debts
> But what has happened to me now
> After two hundred and fifty years?
> An omen has struck this Bise, master!
> I have gone mad
>
> It was only my wretched wife who was killed
> It was only my wretched daughter who was raped
> It was only this Bise's wretched hut that was burnt down ...
>
> My hands are broken
> Now I cannot sew clothes
> For your courtiers
> I cannot play the *narsinga* or the *sanai*
> Or sing about the seasons or your glory[22]

Bise Nagarchi, who has endured centuries of oppression, has stood up to his oppressor. To his own astonishment, he has begun to question history.

Questioning history in a slightly different vein, Devendra Raj Panday wrote, 'The fifty-five years since 1950 have gone to waste and the nation is in a humanitarian, political and economic crisis.'[23] He recalled how the kings of Nepal had repeatedly broken their agreements with the people. In 1960, King Mahendra had dissolved the parliamentary system and established the autocratic Panchayat regime. Since 2002, his son Gyanendra had acted in the same manner, riding roughshod over the

1990 constitution that forbade the monarch to engage in direct politics. 'That is why the state system must be created, not through agreement between vested interests, but through the decision of the sovereign people,' wrote Panday.[24]

In Nepali, the variations of the word 'democracy' have significant political implications. During the 1990 movement, the demand was for *prajatantra* – the word for democracy that more literally translates as 'rule by subjects'. This term was shorthand for parliamentary democracy with a constitutional monarch, corresponding to the system Nepal had during the 1990s. The demand in 2005 and early 2006, however, was for *loktantra* – 'rule by the people'. The word denies the king any role in the country's political system.

> Yes –
> I may have ignored your Divine Counsel
> In my drunken state
> I may have said I too can lay claim to this country
> I may have said
> My needle is worth as much as
> Bard Bhanubhakta's[25] song ...
> I may have thought that the country woven from my threads
> Is greater than the country won by the sword[26]

Bise Nagarchi belongs to the Dalit community that occupies the lowest rung in the Hindu caste hierarchy. His traditional occupation – making clothes and music – is considered lowly by those who use his services. For two and a half centuries he has been denied both dignity and rights. He has been systematically excluded by the state since its formation. His testimony thus symbolizes the radical change in the consciousness of Nepal's marginalized people.

Addressing the historical exclusion of various caste and ethnic groups was one of the primary goals of *loktantra*. '*Loktantra* includes all those who feel they have been excluded by the 1990 constitution – Janajatis, Dalits, Madhesis and women,' wrote Devendra Raj Panday.[27] Unlike the *prajatantra* of the 1990s that only underwrote civil and political liber-ties, *loktantra* would aim to fortify the representation of historically marginalized groups in all state structures. CMDP's call was taken up by the organizations representing historically excluded groups. According to a member of the National Dalit Federation, 'We mobilized people by telling them that the liberation of Dalits and the institution of monarchy are antithetical to each other – that Dalits cannot be liberated unless the monarchy which derives its legitimacy from the Hindu caste system is dismantled.'[28]

> I have been serving you for two hundred and fifty years
> Master!
> How can I be a terrorist?[29]

Gyanendra had cited the Maoist terrorist threat to justify the state's emergency measures and the army's counter-insurgency campaign. Shrawan Mukarung's poem does not refer directly to the rebels. However, the above lines are significant in light of the fact that marginalized groups, including Dalits, made up a sizeable proportion of the Maoist rank and file.

The poem's silence regarding the Maoist movement and its refusal to glorify armed struggle were among the reasons for its widespread popularity. Most of Mukarung's audience was deeply ambivalent about the rebellion. They sought to distance their movement of peaceful civil resistance from that of the Maoists. Kathmandu civil society held the Maoists equally responsible for the violence and bloodshed. The goal of the civil society movement was not only to topple the regime, but also to compel the rebels to lay down their arms and join the mainstream political process. 'We see *loktantra* and peace as complementing each other,' said Devendra Raj Panday. 'The Maoists have an important role in establishing permanent democracy and peace.'[30]

However, there were also substantial disagreements within civil society with regards to recent Nepali history. Some CMDP members, including Panday, rejected the means employed by the Maoists but felt they represented genuine grievances and demands. These activists wholeheartedly endorsed the Maoist call for elections to a Constituent Assembly and the establishment of *loktantrik ganatantra* – a democratic republic. For Panday, it was necessary to channel the 'political energy'[31] of the Maoist movement into peaceful politics, and reform the state in such a way that 'no one will have to take the violent route to fight for their rights.'[32] Panday was also critical of the parliamentary parties. He believed that their tendency towards intra-party factionalism and failure to represent popular aspirations were partly responsible for pushing the country into such a grave crisis.

Other activists, however, rejected this interpretation. The prominent journalist Kanak Mani Dixit, for instance, largely exonerated the democratic system established in 1990 and the parties that participated in it; in his view, the Maoist rebellion had derailed the political process and created conditions for the monarch's usurpation of power. He castigated Panday and other CMDP activists for sympathizing with the Maoists. In his view, the demand for a republic (*ganatantra*) veered dangerously close to the Maoist position. The institution of monarchy was not necessarily detrimental to democracy so long as the monarch was denied an active role in public life. The priority was to protect the values of liberal democracy – human rights, an end to impunity, and pluralism. Recalling this period some years later, Dixit said: 'I did not think it necessary to advocate *ganatantra* … I felt that the demands for *ganatantra* threatened to undermine the agenda of democracy and peaceful politics.'[33]

These disputes were sometimes bitter. Panday lambasted 'the small group of knowledgeable individuals' who were willing to accept 'ceremonial monarchy' as long as there was democracy.[34] For the time being, however, the opposing camps were united in their opposition to the regime.

## Fear of the Tiger

The American ambassador, James Moriarty, was the most outspoken and colourful figure in Kathmandu's diplomatic circles. 'I try to give my friends in the press plenty to do even while away on vacation,' he joked.[35] But his attempt to reconcile the king with the parliamentary parties had failed, and he was perturbed at the latter's growing proximity to the Maoists. After the parties and the Maoists signed the twelve-point agreement, Moriarty sought to scupper the new alliance. 'Absolutely nothing justified such measures,' he said, referring to the Maoists' assassination of municipal election candidates, 'and all supporters of a just and peaceful Nepal should condemn them.'[36] According to him, the leaders of the democratic parties were wrong to ask, 'How can we use the Maoists to advance our immediate political position?' Rather, they and the king should both be asking: 'How can we work together to return democracy to Nepal, and defeat the Maoist threat to our country and its people?'[37]

Moriarty reminded the democratic parties that the Maoists were armed, while they were not. If the regime was toppled and the Royal Nepal Army neutralized, the Maoists could well exploit the chaos to forcibly seize state power. 'There is certainly no way for the parties or the king to successfully ride the Maoist tiger for their own advantage. One could easily fall off ... and tigers get hungry.'[38]

Similar thoughts preoccupied some influential members of civil society. The journalist Yuvaraj Ghimire, for instance, interpreted the slogan 'climb on the back and strike at the head' to mean that the Maoists planned to exploit the leverage gained through a temporary alliance with the parliamentary parties to 'physically annihilate [all] political rivals and non-supporters.'[39] Baburam Bhattarai denied these allegations.[40] But fears persisted. On 14 January 2006, the rebels attacked police posts in Thankot and Dadhikot, both on the edge of the Kathmandu valley. Bhattarai claimed that these were a 'clear message to the royal fascist elements that they were not secure even within Kathmandu, and that the people's morale had increased a hundredfold.'[41] But the attacks mainly served to increase anxiety levels among Kathmandu's inhabitants. The regime exploited public fear and uncertainty to thwart the parties' attempts at mobilizing the population. On 16 January, Home Minister Kamal Thapa announced nightly curfews and a ban on political gatherings, supposedly to prevent the rebels from infiltrating into the capital.

These events shook the resolve of the parliamentary parties. They feared that their legitimacy would be compromised – both at home and abroad – if they were perceived to be abetting Maoist violence. They also worried that continued attacks by the rebels and restrictions imposed by the regime might intimidate the population into staying at home instead of coming out on the streets.

Various Nepali Congress and UML leaders raised these concerns with the Maoist leaders and asked them to suspend their violent campaign. The leaders were resistant at first: 'It is troubling,' said Bhattarai, 'that some international forces, political leaders and intellectuals think autocracy can be defeated by peaceful means alone.'[42] He was certain that the regime would send out the RNA to suppress the imminent uprising, and then the PLA would be compelled to respond with force.

But the rebels were vulnerable to pressure. Only an alliance with the democratic parties would give them the legitimacy they sought. They also recognized that only these parties were capable of leading a popular uprising against the monarch on the streets of Kathmandu.

In March, top leaders from the parliamentary parties met Bhattarai and Prachanda in Delhi. Some disagreements persisted, but an accord signed on 19 March stated that all sides remained committed to the twelve-point MOU. The Seven Party Alliance called a nationwide general strike between 6 and 9 April. The Maoists announced that they would support the strike. Although they were not willing to cease armed activity altogether, they agreed to withdraw blockades and *bandas* (general strikes) to 'forestall potential disturbances to the peaceful programmes of the mass movement.'[43] Soon after, Chairman Prachanda announced that the Maoists would halt all military operations in and around the Kathmandu valley.

The new agreement marked a significant compromise on the part of the rebels. The twelve-point memorandum had stated that its signatories would 'attack the autocratic monarchy from their respective positions'. This indicated parity between the Maoists and the parliamentary parties, and, by implication, between the armed and the unarmed struggle. The Maoists' new commitment to cease some of their military activity and support the strike called by the parties relegated the rebels to a subordinate role.

## Prison Struggle

Soldiers in plain clothes had arrested Krishna K. C., a leader of the Maoist student union, on 13 September 2003. For the next two years he remained in Kathmandu in army custody, first at the barracks of the Bhairavnath battalion in Maharajgunj and later with the Ranger Mahavir battalion in Chhauni. He was severely tortured during interrogation. Much of the time he lay on the floor blindfolded and with his hands tied behind his back. With the help of human rights lawyers, his wife Durga filed two habeas corpus petitions at the Supreme Court, which required the RNA to produce him before a court. The army repeatedly denied that he was in their custody, until news of his whereabouts leaked out to the press, and the army came under pressure. On 22 September 2005, Krishna K. C. was produced before the Supreme Court and the bench that heard his case ordered his release. But police personnel rearrested him even before he left the court. They presented him before the appellate tribunal in Lalitpur, which remanded him for his alleged involvement in a murder (which he denied) and in an armed insurgent attack.[44]

On 12 October, Krishna K. C. was taken to Nakkhu prison, in the southern part of Lalitpur district, on the outskirts of Kathmandu. Soon after, a number of other prominent rebel leaders in army custody – including Matrika Yadav and Suresh Ale Magar, who had both been arrested in Delhi[45] – were also brought there. The new inmates were free to converse and hold meetings with the more than sixty other Maoists at Nakkhu. After spending almost two years in harsh and solitary detention in army barracks, Krishna K. C. thus finally regained a community. His wife and children regularly came to see him. 'It has been sixty-five days since I was brought to Nakkhu,' he wrote in his diary on 14 January 2006. 'Each day seemed like a year in army custody, but these sixty-five days went by swiftly. I am still not well; my entire body is swollen [from torture]. Even so, my life has gained new energy.'[46]

Once in Nakkhu, Krishna K. C., Matrika Yadav and Suresh Ale Magar started organizing the Maoist inmates. On 20 December 2003, while at the Bhairavnath barracks, K. C. had witnessed over forty detainees woken up at night by soldiers and taken away on trucks. They never returned to Bhairavnath, nor had they been released. It was widely believed that the soldiers had taken them to the forested Shivapuri hills in the north of Kathmandu and executed them. The rebels in Nakkhu jail decided that their immediate task now was to campaign for an investigation into these disappearances. A letter was sent to Ian Martin, head of the Office of the UN High Commissioner for Human Rights (OHCHR) in Nepal: 'The Maoist prisoners of conscience at Nakkhu jail [demand an investigation into cases of disappearances and torture at the] human slaughterhouses of the Royal Nepal Army.' The results of the investigation, said the letter, should be publicly divulged and 'the war criminals' should be tried at the International Criminal Court.[47] Krishna K. C. and Matrika Yadav went on hunger strike to draw attention to their demands.

The campaign of the militants in Nakkhu prison received widespread publicity. Journalists flocked to see them, and their interviews were published in newspapers. Civil society activists visited them and formed their own investigation committee. OHCHR officials collected their testimonies about torture and disappearances at the barracks of the Bhairavnath battalion. The campaign was also of acute interest for many others whose family members had been disappeared by the army. They had spent frantic months visiting human rights activists, courts and army barracks to find out the whereabouts of their loved ones. They now came to Nakkhu to find out if Krishna K. C., Matrika Yadav or any of the other Maoist inmates had seen their relatives while in army custody.

The Maoists in Nakkhu urged the families of the disappeared to campaign against the state. They gave them advice on how to organize. The Maoists had formed an organization of the families of disappeared cadres as early as 1999. But it had been only sporadically active, and dormant since the royal takeover. Now, the campaign of these families gained new momentum. They submitted habeas corpus petitions to the Supreme Court, organized demonstrations and locked up the offices of the National Human Rights Commission (NHRC), in protest at NHRC's servility to the regime. They attended party rallies and launched a signature campaign demanding that the whereabouts of their detained kin be made public.

Krishna K. C's wife was initially frustrated and depressed by her inability to organize the families of the disappeared. But the campaign gradually inspired and motivated her. K. C. marvelled at her transformation in his diary:

> Durga did not understand politics or know how to speak [in public] ... She knew very little about how to build an organization, ensure inclusion and launch a struggle. But now she has ... learned to fight and become skilled at organizing ... I am glad to see her energy and commitment ... I am happy that my wife, who was confined to the household, has learned to be free and independent.[48]

The Maoist inmates were enthused by the growing scale and intensity of the anti-monarchy protests in Kathmandu in late 2005 and early 2006. The attacks at Thankot and Dadhikot raised hopes that the rebels would soon attack Nakkhu and liberate its inmates. 'The other inmates congratulated us prisoners of conscience and asked when it would be Nakkhu's turn,' wrote Krishna K. C. 'They said they should probably sleep with their shoes on.'[49] Together with Matrika Yadav and Suresh Ale Magar, he wrote to the Maoist chairman, urging him to organize a raid on the prison and providing information about the prison layout, security personnel and possible escape routes.[50]

The immediate goal of the demonstrations staged by the Maoist inmates was to improve prison conditions – an end to harassment of visitors; provision of healthcare; and access to the telephone, sports equipment and newspapers. In addition, they conceptualized their movement as being dialectically related to the broader Maoist struggle. Prison, they said, was one of the many fronts of the war, and the inmates' struggle too was a contribution to the movement for establishing a democratic republic. But it was difficult for the Maoists in detention to rise up on their own; they needed the support of individuals and organizations that had greater freedom of movement, knowledge of political events and the ability to influence public opinion. 'To mobilize the prison front more effectively,' wrote Krishna K. C., 'we must unite the struggle inside the prison with the popular revolt and the People's War.' In fact, these considerations also played a part in the decision to mobilize the families of inmates and the disappeared: 'the families of inmates can work as a bridge [between us and the outside world].'[51]

The Maoist inmates had not received the help they had expected from the party. No one from the party had contacted K. C.'s wife during his two-year detention at army barracks, leaving her alone in her struggle to get him released. After he arrived at Nakkhu prison, he felt that the local party leadership, instead of aiding their movement, seemed intent on crushing it. When Matrika Yadav and Krishna K. C. announced they were going on hunger strike, the party committee in Kathmandu wrote asking them not to do so. And once they started mobilizing the families of inmates and the disappeared, they entered into direct conflict with the party committee. The inmates and the committee disagreed on who should lead the organization of the families of the disappeared. The committee appointed a chairperson without informing the inmates. There were now two factions within the organization, one loyal to the inmates and the other to the party committee. The local leadership accused the prisoners of establishing a parallel organization that undermined the legitimate one.

K. C. and other inmates wrote to the party's top leaders for help in resolving the dispute. But the leaders were consumed by the complex politics of the moment; all they could do was urge the factions to reconcile. In any case, the leadership had no incentive to side with the inmates, who had long been out of touch with the recent political developments and the wider struggle. Also, party members tended to view captured

Maoists with suspicion, as if they might have gone over to the enemy, or lost their faith in the cause and informed on their comrades. As Matrika Yadav wrote some years later, '[The party] seemed to think that anyone captured by the enemy had committed a crime. Instead of receiving support, the families of inmates were humiliated, ignored and psychologically tortured.'[52]

Another reason for the party's reservations towards the inmates' campaign was ambivalence about the rhetoric of human rights. The Nakkhu prisoners and the families they mobilized accepted the help of human rights activists, and adopted their language in their campaign against the state. This was not the first time that Nepali Maoists had tactically used the language of universal human rights. In order to convince the international community that they were not a murderous band of outlaws but a legitimate political force, the Maoists had promised to abide by international law and the Geneva Convention. To demonstrate their commitment to humanitarian norms, they had freed prisoners in ceremonies attended by representatives of the International Committee of the Red Cross. And to discredit the regime for its use of disproportionate violence against Maoists and civilians, they demanded, as they had during the 2003 ceasefire, 'impartial investigation of the abuse of human rights in the course of the civil war.'[53] Ideologically, however, the Maoists rejected the notion of universal civil and political rights. They saw it as a liberal hoax designed to perpetuate the structural violence inherent in society – a concealed, insidious violence that could only be eliminated through overt violence. That was how they justified armed struggle, the assassination of political rivals, the extortion of civilians and the use of forced labour.

It seems that members of the Kathmandu Valley committee were also riled by the Nakkhu inmates' close association with civil society and human rights organizations. The Maoists regarded international aid agencies and the domestic NGOs they funded as instruments of imperialism. Human rights organizations – both domestic and foreign – fell into this category. To blacken the inmates' movement, the committee members accused them of taking money from international NGOs. The Maoists' distrust of foreign-funded NGOs was not entirely groundless. There was, in fact, a distinct antipathy towards NGOs and their foreign donors throughout Nepali society. But in this particular case the leaders of the Kathmandu party committee were acting no different from the regime, which claimed that all human rights and civil society organizations rallying against it were guided by external elements.[54]

Although isolated from their party, the Maoists at Nakkhu agitated in the prison and helped the families of the disappeared to mount demonstrations. The growing movement against the king emboldened them. Various groups of people were taking to the streets at the time: journalists protesting against censorship, lawyers demanding an independent judiciary, peace activists calling for an end to the conflict. Their overarching demand was the establishment of *loktantra*, and they sought to unite a broad spectrum of individuals and organizations for this cause. They regarded OHCHR as one of their allies, since the UN agency had been exposing human rights violations by the state security forces. Their solidarity was also extended to the Maoists at Nakkhu. The goals of the Maoists and civil society organizations had converged after the signing of the twelve-point agreement. Activists visited the rebels in jail and spoke at events organized by families of the disappeared. The parliamentary parties became more receptive to the Maoist inmates' human rights concerns and demand for an end to inhumane treatment in captivity. As the rebels grew more confident, their captors began to lose their assurance. When Krishna K. C. first came to Nakkhu, he would hear the wardens chanting royalist slogans during their daily rounds. But as the popular mood turned against the monarch, they could be heard chanting praises to the Hindu god Pashupatinath instead.[55]

## The Regime Overthrown

The parliamentary parties counted on all streams of opposition coming together during the nationwide general strike starting 6 April 2006. They hoped the strike would turn into a mass civil disobedience movement that would topple the regime. The movement for *loktantra* unfolded as they had expected. Political party cadres, students and civil society activists were the first to come out into the streets. The police arrested and detained many of them for violating the government-imposed curfew. Young men vandalized the vehicles that ignored the strike call. When the police used tear gas, demonstrators retaliated by hurling stones and bricks. Large numbers of protesters were rounded up and taken away in police vans. Some were chased down and beaten up. Enraged by the display of police brutality, many locals joined the swelling mass of marchers.

Protests intensified over the following days. Civil associations with normally specialized concerns – the Nepal Poultry Entrepreneur's Forum or the Airline Operators Association, for example – expressed solidarity through paid advertorials in the press.[56] The more apolitical sections of the Kathmandu bourgeoisie, such as employees of international NGOs and banks, held demonstrations. Employees at the Nepal Electricity Authority, the Nepal Water Supply Corporation and other public sector organizations wore black armbands to work as a sign of dissent.[57]

The general strike was scheduled to end on 9 April, but the Seven Party Alliance (SPA), emboldened by the success of the movement, called for it to be extended until the king capitulated. The movement quickly spread into the heart of the regime. On 17 and 18 April, employees at the ministries at Singha Darbar – including the ministry of home affairs, which controlled the police – organized gatherings where they chanted slogans against 'autocracy'.[58]

Unlike the 1990 movement, which was largely concentrated in Kathmandu and a few other cities, the 2006 uprising turned out to be a nationwide phenomenon. Demonstrations were held in almost every district capital, and outside major urban areas as well. In Kathmandu, protesters swarmed down the twenty-eight-kilometre-long Ring Road around the main city. This was largely because of curfews within the Ring Road perimeter. But the location of the protests was also indicative of a major demographic change affecting Kathmandu since 1990. Hundreds of thousands of people had migrated to the capital in the intervening years and taken up residence on the fringes of the city. Large numbers of working-class immigrants lived in suburbs off the Ring Road such as Kalanki and Gongabu, where the most intense demonstrations took place. Further, thousands of people from villages in surrounding districts, many of them at the Maoists' instruction, came to join the movement in Kathmandu. Ananta, who was coordinating the rebels' operations from nearby Kavre district, later estimated that they had sent over 91,000 people to the capital.[59] They had to pass through a section of the Ring Road to enter the city, and joined the enormous crowds of demonstrators they encountered on the way. It was evident that a huge section of the population had been radicalized since the 1990 movement achieved the restoration of parliamentary democracy.

The government, however, denied the popular character of the movement. Minister of State for Information Shrish Shamsher Rana blamed the Maoist 'terrorists' for the occasional outbreak of violence on the streets and for intimidating villagers into going to the cities to demonstrate.[60] The parliamentary parties, in turn, alleged that the government was sponsoring vigilantes and that plainclothes provocateurs were infiltrating crowds and attacking civilians. In Nepalgunj, a UN human rights team saw RNA soldiers infiltrate a demonstration; at least one of them was carrying a grenade.[61] Such incidents lent credence to the parties' claims.

Although the parliamentary parties denied it, the crowds of protesters did in fact include Maoists. In many areas outside Kathmandu, relatively well-known rebel leaders addressed mass meetings and led rallies. But they had to operate more discreetly in the capital. Maoist cadres carrying Nepali Congress and UML flags managed crowds and headed demonstrations. Many of them carried leafy branches to signal their identity to their comrades. Although they were undercover, Maoist activists were known to be responsible for the more organized and militant actions. They had, for instance, been at the forefront of the laborious task of hauling boulders and logs onto the streets to blockade police and army vehicles.[62]

The Maoists at Nakkhu prison, who had eagerly anticipated the uprising, could feel the infectious energy on the streets. They heard the clamour outside. They banged their pots and plates and shouted slogans in support of the movement. They collected funds for the treatment of injured protesters. When the political parties called for a nationwide blackout, the inmates turned off all the prison lights at the appointed hour. The guards tried in vain to break up the protests. Nearly all the inmates, including those detained for non-political reasons, were united against them.

Krishna K. C., one of the organizers of the prison protests, was overcome with awe and exhilaration at what was happening beyond the walls: 'A prison diary simply cannot capture the scale of the ongoing political events,' he wrote on 11 April.[63] The political parties had called for a massive turnout on the Ring Road on 21 April. Scattered demonstrations across the city had merged into a few mammoth rallies like rivulets into raging rivers. In some areas, such as Baneshwar, they broke through cordons set up by demoralized security personnel and stormed into the main thoroughfares that had been declared 'no-protest zones'. After watching footage of the crowds on television, K. C. wrote, 'Watching the sea of humanity on the streets fills me with elation. But I also feel disheartened that I am confined in prison and cannot physically take part in the uprising.'[64]

A similar mood had overcome Kshitiz Magar, the versifying battalion vice-commander out on the Gandak Campaign. He was still in Palpa when the general strike began and watched with excitement the swirling tide of protest. On 14 April, however, his superiors informed him that his detachment would be returning to Rolpa. The mass movement had gained such momentum that the Maoist army in the western region had no need to continue their military campaign for the time being. Kshitiz Magar was devastated. 'I found it difficult to understand [why we were being sent back],' he wrote in his diary. 'We had come to climb on the back [and strike on the head]. None of us thought we'd have to return so soon. We haven't even fought a proper battle yet ... How strange! Were we really to return? This thought made me feel like I was burning inside.'[65]

Maoist cadres who participated in the uprising may not have felt the same pang of exclusion, but many still had misgivings about the Maoists' subordinate position in the movement. The SPA was the acknowledged leader of the movement. It would fall to Girija Prasad Koirala and other Nepali Congress and UML leaders to negotiate the settlement with King Gyanendra. The rebels feared that the parliamentary parties would call off the movement and accept whatever paltry concession the king offered. In the Maoist view of history, after all, the bourgeois parties (the Nepali Congress in particular) had repeatedly succumbed to pressure from the monarchy and the Indian government at decisive moments. In 1990 they had accepted a constitution that granted significant powers to the king. As Krishna K. C. wrote in his diary on 13 April, 'Everyone is worried that the seven parties will once again betray the people by giving in to the palace, and lose the historical opportunity to be liberated from feudal slavery.'[66]

Under immense pressure from the streets and growing international condemnation, Gyanendra had been consulting a number of political leaders, diplomats and an emissary sent by the Indian state, Karan Singh. They had all advised him to offer concessions. On the night of 21 April, Gyanendra spoke: 'We, through this Proclamation, affirm that the Executive Power of the Kingdom of Nepal, which was in our safe-keeping, shall, from this day, be returned to the people and be exercised in accordance with Article 35 of the Constitution of the Kingdom of Nepal – 1990.'[67] He asked the Seven Party Alliance to nominate a candidate for the post of prime minister, adding that the current council of ministers would continue to hold executive power until that appointment had been made.

The royal proclamation made no reference to the demands for the reinstatement of parliament, or elections to a Constituent Assembly. It merely implied that the king would let the parties choose the prime minister while retaining his position as the supreme authority of the state. The Maoists worried that the parties, lured by the promise of power, would accept the offer, abandon the twelve-point agreement and turn against the rebels. They denounced the proclamation and warned the SPA not to compromise with the king.

In fact, there was little cause for worry. It was true that major external powers including India, the European Union and the United States issued statements welcoming the proclamation, and calling on the SPA to reconcile with the king. But the parliamentary parties remained suspicious: the king had not mentioned the reinstatement of parliament. Even if the parties formed a government, there would still be no legislature, without which they would remain subservient to the king. Besides, they were under enormous popular pressure. Large crowds continued to demonstrate on the streets, chanting slogans against the proclamation: 'The royal proclamation is a betrayal. It is not a concession but a trap!' ('*Shahi ghoshana dhoka ho, naso hoina paso ho!*') They warned the parties not to let down the masses that were demanding immediate abolition of the monarchy. The SPA released a statement to allay people's doubts: 'The king's proclamation has not addressed the agenda and goals of the people's movement and has devalued the sentiments of the people … Sovereignty, state authority and the right to rule must be handed over to the people. The peaceful movement will continue until we achieve these objectives.'[68]

Demonstrations carried on. According to plans, around two million people would be marching down the Ring Road on 25 April. The chief of the army informed the king that there was nothing the RNA could do to bring the crowds under control and that the existence of the monarchy would come under threat if the king did not give in to the popular demands.[69] Abandoned by the army, the king made another proclamation on 24 April: 'We, through this Proclamation, reinstate the House of Representatives which was dissolved on 22 May 2002 on the advice of the then Prime Minister in accordance with the Constitution of the Kingdom of Nepal – 1990.' He said that the current government would be dissolved, and asked the SPA to form a new one. The SPA was jubilant, and called a halt to the movement.

The Maoists were still sceptical: the parliamentary parties had not consulted them when they agreed to the king's terms. No allusion had been made to the Maoist demands for elections to a Constituent Assembly and ultimately a republic. Prachanda issued a statement calling for continued blockades and strikes. But the parties assured the rebels that they remained committed to the twelve-point agreement. The Maoists also realized that the public was in a euphoric mood and that it would be difficult for them to unilaterally continue the struggle. They called off their planned protests and accepted the terms on offer.

Girija Prasad Koirala was appointed prime minister, and formed a government consisting of leaders from the seven parliamentary parties. The first meeting of the reinstated parliament was convened on April 28. Subsequently both the rebels and the government announced a ceasefire. Political prisoners were freed. The parliament promptly passed a resolution to hold elections to a Constituent Assembly. Nepal, hitherto defined as a 'Hindu kingdom', was declared a secular state. The king was stripped of all powers and privileges, including control of the army. His ultimate fate would be decided by the Constituent Assembly, and until then he would remain as a ceremonial monarch. Prachanda, Bhattarai and other top Maoist leaders came to Kathmandu and began what was to be a prolonged and painful process of peace negotiations with the parliamentary parties. The 1990 constitution was abrogated and replaced with an Interim Constitution, designed to guide the political process until the elected Constituent Assembly agreed on a permanent constitution for the nation. On 15 January 2007, the Maoists were inducted into parliament according to the terms of the provisional constitution. Four months later, they joined the interim government under Koirala's leadership.

Reckoning

The people's movement of 2006 redeemed Girija Prasad Koirala's political career. As the first elected prime minister after 1990, he was widely held responsible for much of the mismanagement and corruption of those early years of parliamentary democracy. Later, after parliament was dissolved and King Gyanendra took the reins, he became the lone voice demanding revival of the legislature. His critics thought he was driven primarily by hunger for power. By opposing the regime, he was also seen to be hampering its ability to tackle the Maoist threat. His repeated warnings that the king harboured a 'grand design' to dismantle Nepal's democratic institutions were taken as a sign of his paranoia. But when the king grabbed absolute power on 1 February 2005, it appeared that the old man had been right after all. His unswerving claim that the absence of a legislative chamber would jeopardize democracy had turned out to be accurate. In hindsight, his willingness to allow political rivals such as Sher Bahadur Deuba to join the anti-king alliance seemed an act of magnanimity. Koirala received much of the credit for negotiating with the Maoists, ushering them into mainstream politics and thus restoring peace across the country. It was an indication of Koirala's newfound stature that the parliamentary parties, notorious for their fractiousness, had unanimously nominated him for prime minister when the monarchical regime fell.

Maoist Chairman Prachanda could also take a share of the credit for the success of the alliance with the parliamentary parties. He deployed all his charisma and rhetorical powers to convince the Nepali political parties and the Indian establishment of the Maoists' commitment to multi-party democracy. Through 2004 and early 2005, the Maoists' official attitude towards the parliamentary parties and India had been one of wholesale enmity. But in September 2005, at the party's central committee meeting in Chunbang, Rukum, Prachanda had artfully persuaded the party body to change course, direct their hostility against the king and accept entry into a multi-party system. At the same meeting, he had staged an emotionally charged reconciliation with Bhattarai, thus firmly reuniting a party that was plagued by factionalism and on the verge of a split.

But if there was a single Maoist leader who had been vindicated by the latest events, it was surely Baburam Bhattarai. He had argued for years that the parliamentary parties should join forces with the rebels to overthrow the monarchy and establish a democratic republic. In 2004, the party had denounced him and removed him from positions of authority. Prachanda and others, demoralized by the arrest of high-level Maoist leaders in India, were so desperate for a political solution that they tried to work out a settlement with the king. They were confident that once such a settlement had been reached, they would be able to manipulate political circumstances and eventually reduce the king to a mere figurehead. But it should have been clear that even had they managed to reach such an agreement, the Maoists would not have achieved their goals. If a monarchical–military regime was unacceptable to important external powers like India and the United States, a royalist–Maoist one would have been downright anathema. It would probably have turned Nepal into a pariah state. Given the country's heavy dependence on Indian largesse and Western aid, such a regime would not have survived for long.

In any case, the idea of a royalist–Maoist alliance fell through. Gyanendra outwitted the rebels, at least in the short term. He led them on, only to suddenly assume absolute authority and declare an all-out assault against them. Prachanda found himself with no choice but to rehabilitate Bhattarai and adopt his line.

Who made a greater contribution to the downfall of the monarchy: the Maoists or the parliamentary parties? This question was hotly debated within Nepal's political and intellectual circles in the aftermath of the 2006 uprising. Some sections of public opinion that were implacably hostile to the rebels strove to give all the credit to the parliamentary parties. They maintained that the nineteen days of peaceful uprising accomplished what the Maoists had not been able to do over a decade of armed struggle.

It was true that the SPA, rather than the Maoists, led the movement in urban areas. The middle classes, whose participation in the rising was critical, did not support the rebels. It was also true that the civil disobedience movement, not the armed struggle, was decisive in the regime's overthrow. By the time the movement began, the rebels had formally agreed to give up armed struggle and participate in a multi-party system. Partly for this reason, commentators such as Kanak Mani Dixit could claim that the 2006 movement opposed not just monarchical autocracy but also Maoist violence, and as such represented a defeat for the rebels.[70] Dixit was known for his view that the Maoists had wrecked what he thought were the halcyon days of democracy in the early 1990s. After the 2006 movement, he devoted his political energies to vilifying and trying to undermine the Maoists.

However, it cannot be denied that the Maoists had considerable impact on the uprising. The parliamentary parties only began gaining mass support after they signed the twelve-point agreement with the rebels. As journalist Sudheer Sharma observed, 'The decade-long People's War was the foundation [of the people's movement] … And the Maoists were at the forefront in heating up the movement on the streets.'[71] The vast scale of the movement revealed a rising groundswell of discontent among the population – not just the middle classes, but also peasants, labourers and marginalized ethnic groups. The widespread political ferment was to a great extent a consequence of the brutalization of ordinary people by state security forces during the war. The Maoists had played an important role in politicizing these sections of the population. As Baburam Bhattarai said, 'The decade-long People's War cut the roots of feudalism in the villages, and that is why rural peasants and women participated in such unprecedented numbers in the movement staged in urban areas.'[72]

Another undeniable fact is that the Maoists shaped the key agenda of the movement. A long labour of preparation was necessary before people came out on the streets shouting slogans for elections to a Constituent Assembly and the establishment of a republic. Baburam Bhattarai and Prachanda had begun these preparations as early as 2001. On various occasions, like during the 2003 ceasefire, they had met politicians and civil society activists and tried to convince them that the Maoists were willing to abandon violence if their demand for a Constituent Assembly was fulfilled. Over time, influential sections of Kathmandu civil society had accepted the social and political programme proposed by the Maoists. Apart from the election of a Constituent Assembly and the abolition of the monarchy, this agenda included radical restructuring of the Nepali state to ensure greater representation of previously marginalized social groups. By the time of the 2006 movement, such demands had been thoroughly assimilated into mainstream discourse; they no longer appeared as the partisan demands of an extremist rebel group.

CHAPTER 9

# The Aftermath of People's War

## Rebels in the Capital

Chairman Prachanda lost a good deal of his mysterious aura once he arrived in Kathmandu. The rebel leader who had spent so much of his adult life in hiding was suddenly transformed into a public figure and media darling. Thousands gathered to watch his first public address in Kathmandu. 'In the New Nepal,' he declared in a fiery speech, 'the exploited and suffering masses will impose a dictatorship on those who have ruled for the past two hundred and fifty years.'[1] His oratorical skills and charisma were much in evidence, and even those who dubbed him a populist demagogue became fascinated by his personality.

On 21 November 2006, Prachanda and Prime Minister Girija Prasad Koirala signed the Comprehensive Peace Agreement (CPA). The CPA required the rebels to give up many of their key sources of power. The People's Liberation Army would be confined to seven cantonments (with three satellite camps at each location) across the country, and monitored by a United Nations political mission. Some of the combatants were to be eventually integrated into the Nepal Army (the prefix 'Royal' was removed by a decision of parliament), and the rest discharged into civilian life. The agreement also stated that the Maoists would dissolve their parallel regime structures and allow the re-establishment of government offices, police posts and branches of the parliamentary parties in areas they had controlled during the war.

In exchange, the parliamentary parties agreed to incorporate many provisions proposed by the Maoists for the transformation of Nepali state and society. The CPA promised to transform the 'existing centralized and unitary state system' into 'an inclusive, democratic and progressive' state responsive to the demands of marginalized social groups. It committed to 'end all forms of feudalism' by formulating 'policies for scientific land reform'. The Nepal Army was to be 'democratized'. This meant reducing the size of the army, which had been bloated during the years of the war; recruiting marginalized social groups into its ranks to dilute the hegemony of Chhetris and Thakuris, caste groups close to the monarchy; and training army personnel in 'democratic principles and human rights values' to ensure that the army remained loyal to elected governments and refrained from committing excesses against civilians, as they had during the war.[2]

The Maoists retained their wartime fervour during those early days of peace. They saw themselves as the primary agents of social transformation, and feared that traditional parliamentary parties and powerful social groups would conspire to thwart their agenda. Months before the uprising, at a central committee meeting in September 2005, they had discussed the regime that would replace the monarchy. In their conception, this new regime should be neither 'bourgeois' nor 'New Democratic', but rather a 'transitional' one that lay somewhere between the two. They were worried that the mainstream parties would try to re-establish a purely bourgeois system, seeking to entrap the rebels in traditional parliamentary politics, and thus to defang them of their progressive agenda. Meanwhile the Maoists vowed to continue their efforts to transform the state into a 'New Democracy'.[3] In this way Maoist leaders had reassured the rank and file that although they had abandoned war, they had by no means abandoned their struggle; that their commitment to the peace agreement would not lessen their power, and that they would push the agreement's boundaries in ways that would give the rebels an advantage over the other parties.

Hence Prachanda and other Maoist leaders continued to make demands of the government even after the peace agreements were signed. They may not have achieved an outright military victory, but they believed they had gained a political victory through the uprising. They insisted on the equal status of the state army and the rebel army, and demanded that the two be merged to create a new national army.

The question regarding the fate of the monarchy was yet to be resolved. The parties had decided that the Constituent Assembly to be formed after the election would settle the matter. A number of Nepali Congress leaders were in favour of retaining the institution, albeit in a ceremonial role; the Maoists wanted the monarchy abolished at once. Further, all elections in Nepali history had been held according to the first-past-the-post system. The Maoists demanded that the Constituent Assembly elections be held in accordance with the proportional system, which would benefit smaller parties and marginalized groups. In December 2007, following months of debate, the parties finally agreed that the decision to abolish the monarchy would be finalized through a vote of Constituent Assembly members at the first meeting of the Assembly. They also agreed that the proportional system would be used to elect 335 out of the 575 elected seats (58 per cent) in the Assembly. An additional twenty-six members were to be nominated, bringing the total number of members to 601.

The Maoists had had to forsake their old power bases, but they soon gained new ones.[4] They may have loosened their grip on the countryside, but they now had open access to cities and towns. Maoist trade unions penetrated industries and businesses. Their militant campaigning on behalf of workers earned them tremendous support. They caused disruptions and compelled owners to negotiate. For instance, all of Kathmandu's casinos started paying the Maoist trade union significant cuts of their profits in return for protection.

The Young Communist League (YCL) emerged as the most important of the party's affiliate organizations. It was formed in December 2006, a month after the CPA was signed. Now that the PLA was cantoned, the YCL took over responsibility for expanding the party organization and propagating its ideology. According to a senior YCL leader, Kul Prasad K. C. 'Sonam', 'The main force of the PLA was put in the cantonments, but the secondary force, [i.e.,] the village and local defense teams, became the YCL.'[5] The party leadership transferred a number of PLA commanders and commissars to the YCL. For instance, YCL head Ganesh Man Pun had been a PLA division commander before the end of the war.

The YCL quickly drew a lot of public attention. YCL leaders claimed that their chief purpose was to serve the people. During 2007 and 2008, YCL cadres were a common sight on the streets of Kathmandu. Wearing red bandanas and waving party flags, they could be found collecting garbage, demolishing illegal makeshift constructions and even building roads. However, they rarely completed these projects, most of which were publicity stunts aimed at improving the YCL's image.

Public relations campaign notwithstanding, the YCL's primary tactics were intimidation and coercion. Taking advantage of the state's poor capacity to enforce the rule of law, the YCL established itself as a parallel law enforcement body. Its cadres regularly abducted or abused individuals accused of corrupt or criminal activities, and often handed them over to the police. Many victims of crime or injustice who had failed to obtain redress from the state's legal system applied to the YCL for help, as did others who simply wanted to intimidate their enemies.[6] The YCL was also involved in lucrative deals. For instance, it reportedly brokered property transactions and took a share of the profits, as well as used intimidation 'to obtain development contracts for beneficiaries', taking a percentage cut for its 'mediation services'.[7]

In essence, the Maoists penetrated areas where there were breaches of the contract between the state and its citizens. They offered the security that the state failed to provide and charged fees for their services. They took advantage of the rampant corruption in government contracting to install themselves as dominant players in the game. Thanks to the demoralized police force and lack of law enforcement, they could step forward and provide quasi-governmental services, thus raising revenue for the party and strengthening their hold over large sections of the populace.

After several delays, the parties finally decided to hold elections to the Constituent Assembly in April 2008. The Maoists launched their electoral campaign with unmatched zeal and vigour. Having reorganized their party and campaign machinery to maximize their range, they made their presence felt in remote villages where other parties rarely appeared. They trekked to areas beyond the reach of the Election Commission's voter education programmes, educated people about the electoral system and taught them how to fill out ballots. In contrast to other major parties, they fielded youthful candidates from marginalized socio-economic groups who were native to their constituencies. They also engaged in a series of abuses, beating and temporarily abducting members of rival political parties, disrupting their campaigns and intimidating voters. When other political parties finally began campaigning outside district capitals, they had difficulty competing with the established Maoist presence.[8]

The conventional wisdom among the parliamentary parties, the media and diplomatic circles was that people had had enough of Maoist coercion and violence during the conflict, and that the revolutionaries stood little chance of performing well in the election. To the shock and dismay of the Nepali Congress and the UML, the former rebels emerged as the largest party in the Constituent Assembly, winning an astonishing 220 of 575 elected seats (the Nepali Congress, which came second, won only 110 and the UML won 103).[9] The rebels' aggressive campaigning had paid off. They had successfully projected themselves as a force of social transformation, especially before historically marginalized communities. The other parties seemed old and tired in comparison, with nothing to offer but the worn-out politics of the 1990s that had already caused deep disenchantment among the public.

## Backlash

Prachanda became prime minister and Baburam Bhattarai finance minister in August 2009. As the Maoists did not have an outright majority in the Constituent Assembly, they ruled at the helm of a coalition. The Nepali Congress refused to join, after the Maoists refused to accept Girija Prasad Koirala as president. Although this was a mostly symbolic position, the Maoists argued that a leader as powerful as Koirala would use it to encroach upon executive power. This difference soured relations between the two parties. The UML and the Madhesi Janadhikar Forum (MJF), the party with the fourth largest number of seats, on the other hand, agreed to become the Maoists' partners in government. But despite being in coalition, the former rebels proceeded as though they had a firm mandate, taking aggressive decisions that soon antagonized many powerful groups.

For instance, the Maoists tried to shake up the civil service. There was a widespread perception that civil servants sympathetic to the Maoists were being offered coveted ministry posts. The party also alienated much of the bureaucracy when it decided to retire all civil servants over the age of fifty or with more than twenty years of service; to disallow civil servants from moonlighting to supplement their incomes (a common practice, given the dismal government salaries), and to make it compulsory for their children to study in government-owned schools (notoriously inferior to the country's private schools).[10]

Similarly, the Maoist government riled the judiciary when it tried to force a member of the judicial council to resign.[11] It also turned the entire private school industry against it by announcing that all educational institutions would in due course be nationalized, and until then private schools would have to pay heavy taxes to subsidize the government-run education system.

The Nepali Congress and the UML, disconcerted by the former rebels' electoral success, were further perturbed by their expanding power. The leaders of the older parliamentary parties complained bitterly that the Maoists had only won so many seats through intimidation and electoral fraud. The older parties had expected to maintain their pole position after the fall of the monarchy. Their objective was to tame the former rebels by dissolving their military apparatus and socializing them into parliamentary politics. While they knew the process would be difficult, they had not imagined that the rebels would so quickly seize the levers of power, relegating the other parliamentary parties to a secondary role. At public events and in newspaper columns, Nepali Congress and UML leaders claimed that the former rebels were just waiting for the right moment to stage an armed revolt and capture total state power. They recalled that the Maoists had not formally renounced violence or accepted the values of democracy and pluralism. They also pressured Prachanda to disband the YCL and to expedite the return of property that the Maoists had seized during the war.

Having led the government for much of the 1990s, the Nepali Congress knew all too well how the party in power could use state resources to strengthen the party organization. It made them uneasy to see the Maoist party distributing patronage to its supporters. For instance, the health minister in the Maoist-led government, Giriraj Mani Pokharel, granted Rs 10 million (approximately US$140,000) to the Maoist-owned Janamaitri Hospital,[12] in violation of the rule that forbids state funding of private healthcare institutions. Finance Minister Baburam Bhattarai earned much public respect for his success in raising revenue. But it turned out that the bodies assigned to collect taxes and investigate tax evasion would largely consist of Maoist cadres, potentially allowing the party to control government revenues. Nepali Congress leaders claimed that funds allocated to the finance ministry's self-employment programme flowed primarily into the hands of YCL and other Maoist cadres.[13]

India too remained wary of the Maoists. Indian politicians and bureaucrats had facilitated the twelve-point agreement between the

Maoists and the parliamentary parties, and they had become something like the unofficial guarantor of the peace process. In 2007, for instance, when the disagreements between parties had threatened to derail the peace process, Indian diplomats had stepped in and pushed all sides to hold elections. They were deeply enmeshed in the political culture of Kathmandu, where a few actors played an endless game of shifting alliances and solicited support from powerful interest groups. Indian embassy officials wielded influence over various political leaders by offering them financial and other forms of support, and manipulated the divisions among leaders and parties. They were familiar with these leaders' susceptibility and adept at exploiting their personal ambitions.

Their goal was to see the Maoists transform into another Nepali Congress or UML: demilitarized, socialized into the old political culture and responsive to the same incentives. The Maoist agenda of state reform was considered secondary. Like a number of parliamentary party leaders, Indian diplomats thought the Maoists' agenda hindered their transformation into a mainstream political party that operated according to the familiar rules of the parliamentary game.[14]

India thus had little interest in the implementation of most of the CPA's provisions (such as the establishment of a Truth and Reconciliation Commission (TRC), a commission to investigate disappearances, and land reform). Indian officials were staunchly opposed to provisions that would revamp the political structure and potentially increase the Maoists' power over the state military. They were thus opposed both to the Maoists' idea of 'merging' the two armies on equal terms and to more substantive security-sector reform, including the CPA provisions mandating 'right-sizing' and 'democratization' of the Nepal Army. India saw the army as the ultimate bulwark against a potential Maoist military takeover, and sought to prevent any action that could undermine the morale and institutional coherence of the army.

The Indian government initially tried to be accommodating to the Maoist-led government, but was soon irked by its decisions. Right after becoming prime minister, Prachanda attended the closing ceremony of the Olympic Games in Beijing, inadvertently violating the time-honoured tradition whereby Nepali heads of government paid a courtesy visit to New Delhi before travelling to any other country. Prachanda affirmed his commitment to strong India–Nepal ties, but added that Nepal should have a 'relationship of equidistance' with its two neighbours. He spoke of revising the 1950 Indo–Nepal Treaty of Peace and Friendship, which allows residents of both countries free movement and the right to work across the border; the Maoists wanted to impose tighter border controls. At the same time, they cultivated Chinese politicians and diplomats and mulled over a treaty to allow freer movement across Nepal's northern border. New Delhi grew concerned that the Maoists were trying to extricate Nepal from India's sphere of influence.

Then, in a fit of nationalist fervour, the government tried to replace the South Indian priests at Pashupatinath, Nepal's most important temple, with local ones. There were reports that YCL cadres had manhandled and forcibly tried to evict the Indian priests from the temple premises. Hindu groups in both Nepal and India were outraged by the godless regime's tampering with sacred tradition. The government revoked the decision, but by then the Maoists had antagonized influential sections of Indian public opinion.

Finally, when tensions erupted between the Maoists and the Nepal Army, the other parliamentary parties, India and most of Kathmandu's media decisively united against the government.

The Nepal Army had silently accepted the severing of its relations with the crown. It also abided by the provisions in the CPA that confined it to barracks. But it chafed at these restrictions and remained hostile to the Maoists. In private, senior officers rejected the claim that the rebels had fought the Nepal Army to a stalemate. They insisted that they had been on the verge of defeating the Maoist army, and only certain political mistakes committed by the regime – the king's takeover in February 2005, for instance – prevented them from doing so. Most of the army's top brass opposed the CPA provisions regarding the 'democratization' of the institution, viewing this as politicians' interference in matters they knew nothing about. They also defended the army's wartime conduct, insisting that any human rights violations were unfortunate but unavoidable.

General Rookmangud Katawal, a key intermediary between the Maoists and the king in 2004 and 2005, had become chief of army staff in September 2006. A committed royalist, he was known for his distaste for democracy. In 2002 he had published a number of articles arguing for the king's 'enlightened despotism'. His office wall displayed a portrait of Prithvi Narayan Shah, the first king of modern Nepal, even after all government buildings had been stripped of symbols of the monarchy. As army chief he became a highly visible figure, frequently making public appearances and speaking to the media.

Katawal's goal was to preserve the autonomy and privileges of the army. He was particularly exercised by the Maoist claim that the rebel army enjoyed equal stature to the state army in the changed political scenario. 'State is state', Katawal often said, meaning that state institutions had a legitimacy that a rebel army could never aspire to.[15] He publicly opposed the CPA provision for a merger of the two forces. In his view, allowing the rebels into the state army would undermine the integrity of the institution. He also resisted a proposal by the government to recruit Madhesis into the army so as to make the institution more inclusive. Neither was he reconciled to other recent political changes. Under his leadership, the army submitted some proposals they wanted included in the interim constitution. Among the recommendations was that major decisions regarding the future of the state – such as the decision to make the Nepali state secular, or to restructure it to allow greater representation of marginalized groups – should not be taken by the elected Constituent Assembly, but rather put to a referendum.

When the government refused to extend the tenures of eight brigadier generals on the verge of retirement, Katawal told them to disregard the decision and to continue in office. The army also started recruiting soldiers, in violation of peace agreements. The government ordered it to stop, but this directive too was ignored. On 18 April 2009, Defence Minister Ram Bahadur Thapa, a Maoist, wrote to Katawal demanding an explanation for his acts of insubordination. Instead of responding, Katawal began lobbying with the other parties and diplomatic missions against the Maoists.

Under pressure from other Maoist leaders, Prachanda prepared to dismiss Katawal. There was a huge outcry. The older parliamentary parties and most of the media seemed to have forgotten how the government's inability to control the army had repeatedly undermined democracy in the past. Judging that the Maoists posed the more serious threat, they flew to Katawal's defence. General Kul Bahadur Khadka, the Maoists' choice for Katawal's replacement, had allegedly promised the rebels to facilitate the integration of large numbers of Maoist combatants into the army, including at officer level. Through this step, the opposition chorused, the Maoists intended to establish control over the army, seize state power and establish a communist dictatorship.

In a cabinet meeting on 3 May, the Maoists decided to proceed with Katawal's dismissal. The UML instantly walked out of the meeting and withdrew its support to the government. Eighteen parties, including the Congress and the UML, sent a letter to President Ram Baran Yadav (a former Congress politician whom parliament had elected head of state, a largely symbolic position, after the abolition of the monarchy) asking him to overturn the Maoists' decision. Yadav called Katawal and told him to ignore the government's letter. The next day, stating that 'regressive … elements had hatched a conspiracy against the fledgling republic', Prachanda announced his resignation and the Maoists pulled out of the government.

'I would also like to draw the attention of all patriotic Nepali brothers and sisters towards the visible and invisible role of some international power centres regarding the Army chief issue,' Prachanda had said in his resignation speech. 'We are not willing to bow our heads in front of foreign masters and ignore the blood sacrifice of tens of thousands of patriotic individuals.' The reference to India was implicit but unmistakable. India had indeed played a crucial role in the fall of the government. Embassy officials had aggressively lobbied the Maoists' allies to withdraw from the coalition. Indian Ambassador Rakesh Sood and Foreign Minister Pranab Mukherjee had assured the president of their support for revoking the government's decision.[16] This was important, for the president's intervention rested on shaky legal ground: the Interim Constitution did not allow the head of state to make an executive decision. After the fall of the Maoist-led government, Indian diplomats in Kathmandu helped cobble together a new governing alliance under the leadership of the UML's Madhav Nepal, who had lost the 2008 election from two constituencies. This was no easy task: the Congress and the UML together had only 213 out of 601 seats in the legislature. Twenty other parties had to be herded together to form a majority.

As part of their campaign to weaken the Maoists, the Madhav Nepal government pressured the United Nations Mission in Nepal (UNMIN) to stop monitoring the Nepal Army camps while continuing to monitor the PLA. The government, the army and India felt that UNMIN's presence in the country unnecessarily granted legitimacy to the Maoists, creating the perception that the PLA was equivalent to the army. UNMIN, however, refused to violate the terms of the armed monitoring agreement as demanded by the government. Influential politicians and journalists accused the UN mission of pro-Maoist bias. UNMIN withdrew from Nepal in early 2011 after the government refused to extend its term.

New Delhi and the traditional parliamentary parties hoped that the Maoists, having been forced out of power, would undertake what Indian diplomats called a 'course correction'.[17] They calculated that stripping the party's access to state resources would diminish its scope for patronage and that the rank and file would become disaffected with the leadership. Furthermore, in May 2009, the Indian government, in alliance with the mainstream parliamentary parties, hardened its stance on key Maoist demands, most importantly on the integration of Maoist combatants into the army. They thought these actions would make the Maoist leaders look incapable of delivering on their promises, thereby sapping their authority.

The wager was that fomenting discontent among the Maoist rank and file would cause cracks within the party, forcing its leadership to kowtow to New Delhi and renegotiate the terms and conditions for returning to power. If these negotiations succeeded, a suitably chastened and compliant Maoist party could once again enjoy the perks of power. If not, internal tensions would keep increasing and the party would gradually become open to influence from Delhi, thus losing its cohesion. The Indian state was familiar with such games. They had, after all, been played before, often successfully, in dealing with hostile groups in Kashmir and Northeast India.

## The Trouble with Government

At its first sitting on 28 May 2008, the Constituent Assembly had voted to abolish the monarchy and establish a republic. The major parties showed rare unanimity: 560 of the 564 assembled delegates voted in favour of the resolution. The dethroned King Gyanendra vacated the Narayanhiti palace, which was then turned into a museum. But the unanimity between parties did not last beyond this. The Constituent Assembly was meant to be the historic platform where people's representatives would draft the law of the land on their own terms. But the assembly was also an arena of ideological battle between the rebels and the incumbents (the older parliamentary parties), with their radically divergent views on the future of the Nepali polity. One of the most intractable disputes concerned the form of government that the country should adopt.

The Maoists had officially abandoned their dream of a one-party state and accepted the core democratic principles: regular elections, freedom of expression and freedom of association. But they still desired a strong and effective state that could achieve rapid structural transformation of Nepali society. They believed that only a government with concentrated executive power and few constraints could overcome resistance from vested interests, eliminate the vestiges of feudalism and render the state impervious to external manipulation.[18]

For years the Maoists had derided parliament as a 'toothless debating club'. They now argued that parliamentary democracy was directly responsible for protracted political instability. For most of Nepal's recent history, no single party had commanded a majority in parliament. Governments collapsed soon after they were formed due to changes in political alignments. As a result, no government was able to undertake far-reaching reforms. Knowing their tenure was likely to be short, those in government focused instead on enriching themselves and distributing patronage to their supporters. Further, in most parliamentary democracies, the provision for separate heads of government and state led to competition between the two. In Nepal's case, the monarch – as the head of state – had exploited ambiguous provisions in the constitution and grasped powers that rightfully belonged to the prime minister.

For these reasons, the Maoists argued, the parliamentary form of governance was unsuited to the country's needs and had to be replaced by a presidential system. Unlike a prime minister, who was elected by parliament, a president would be directly elected by the population. Thus liberated from the legislature's control, each government would be able to remain in office for a significant period of time and enjoy greater authority than in the past. In order to avoid problems arising from dual authority, the president would be head of both government and state.[19]

The Maoists wanted to remove institutional barriers from other organs of the state as well. They proposed, for instance, replacing the bicameral legislature of parliamentary democracy with a unicameral one. In many democracies the primary object of an upper house is to moderate the more extreme urges of the lower. This, in the Maoist view, prevented the lower house from passing legislation aimed at bringing radical structural transformation. They believed it was necessary to take decisions through consensus in order to avoid the partisan conflict that had plagued Nepali democracy. There should hence be no provision for an opposition in the legislature. Rather, all parties should be represented in government in proportion to the number of seats they occupied.[20]

What was thus envisioned was a strongly majoritarian regime. Sovereignty was to be concentrated in the figure of the directly elected president who would represent the general will of the people. Meanwhile the legislature, disencumbered of the upper house, would be able to make unanimous decisions on behalf of the population. As liberals argue, however, the general will is a revolutionary abstraction, and attempts to realize it can undermine the checks and balances that are integral to a liberal democracy. In the Maoist model of state, the dominant party would be able to carry out swift and far-reaching reform at the cost of smothering the concerns of minority groups.

Although some Congress and UML leaders agreed on the necessity of institutional measures to prevent the rapid turnover of governments, most of them were strongly opposed to the Maoists' demand for a strong executive. The older parliamentary parties feared the idea of radical social transformation directed by the state. They interpreted the Maoist proposals for a strong and effective state as yet another attempt by the party to establish authoritarian control. They were unwilling to accept the adoption of institutions that differed too greatly from those in a traditional parliamentary democracy.

## Balancing Territorial Claims

The debate over federalism was even more fraught than the one over the form of government. In the Maoist view, a federal state structure would fulfil their wartime promise of autonomy to various ethnic groups. But it was not only the Maoists who wanted federalism. Marginalized ethnic groups, in particular Madhesis, had strongly been voicing their demand for federalism since the 2006 uprising. After the Nepali Congress and UML refused to provide a clear commitment to federalism in the interim constitution, the Maoists had for the time being accepted a vague reference to 'the progressive restructuring of the state'.[21] However, political parties representing Madhesi interests, excluded from the negotiations, had rejected their decision and burned copies of the interim constitution on the streets. In January 2007, the Tarai, or southern plains of Nepal, witnessed weeks of angry protests and riots that came to be known as the Madhesh *andolan* (movement). There were violent clashes between agitating Madhesis and the police in which over forty people died. Finally, on 7 February, Prime Minister G. P. Koirala declared in a speech that federalism would be enshrined in the constitution. On 12 April, the Interim Constitution was amended to include a provision that guaranteed a 'democratic, federal system'.

During that time, the agenda of federalism, which the Maoists had claimed as their own, seemed to have escaped their grasp. Madhesi leaders asserted that the constitutional guarantee of federalism was the result of *their* struggle. The Maoists had given in too easily during negotiations over the interim constitution, they said, and this reflected the party's weak commitment to the issues of marginalized ethnic groups. A number of Maoists quit to form parties representing the interests of their own communities in the aftermath of the People's War. Upendra Yadav, who was at the forefront of the Madhesh movement, had been affiliated with the Maoists in the later years of the war. Laxman Tharu, a prominent Tharu leader of the rebellion, also left the party. 'Prachanda and Baburam never paid any attention to the Tharus,' he said, 'even though over 2,000 of us sacrificed our lives for the war. The Maoists may say they are going to form ethnicity-based federal provinces, but that's only a tactical slogan to get popular support.'[22] Laxman Tharu and others like him were resentful that the party that claimed to represent the marginalized was dominated by the hill upper castes. To them, the 'dictatorship of the proletariat' appeared to be the dictatorship of Brahminism.

Having failed to encompass ethnic claims within the party, the Maoists now sought to form alliances with the newly assertive ethno-linguistic parties. The Madhesis in particular had emerged as a formidable force after the 2008 elections. The three largest Madhesi parties – the Madhesi Janadhikar Forum, the Tarai-Madhes Loktantrik Party and the Sadbhavana Party (Anandidevi) – held a total of eighty-four seats in the Constituent Assembly. If the Maoists were to act as champions of the marginalized, they had to wrest back some control over the federalism agenda. And in order to push that agenda in the Constituent Assembly, they needed the support of the Madhesi parties.

The Maoists claimed that a federal state structure would represent the culmination of the ethnic policy they had pursued during the war. But in reality there were substantial differences between the two. Previously, the rebels had envisaged subordinating the 'liberated provinces' to the centralized control of the party. As Marxists, they emphasized class struggle over ethnic struggle. Their programme included ethnic autonomy and affirmative action, but its focus was redistribution. All elites, regardless of their ethnic identity, fell into the category of 'class enemy'.

After joining mainstream politics, the Maoists found it difficult to gain support for class struggle. The leaders of the Madhesi and Janajati groups were mostly concerned with gaining rights and recognition for their identities. They had little interest in, and were even opposed to, the radical redistributive agenda that the Maoists proposed. As participants in an open, democratic framework, the former rebels could not coerce others into accepting their policies. In negotiations within the Constituent Assembly, they had to form alliances with the more powerful ethno-linguistic parties. Even among the marginalized groups, the Maoists were more attentive to the demands of the more influential groups. As a consequence, leaders of marginalized communities that lacked political clout and organizational strength felt excluded. This was particularly true for Dalits. Although they rank lowest in the caste hierarchy, Dalits speak the same language and share cultural roots with upper-caste Hindus. As a group that has been oppressed on the basis of their caste, they could not claim rights based on ethnicity. Being scattered across the country, they could not claim a separate province of their own. They were hence ambivalent about the idea of federalism.[23]

The issue was further complicated by the conflicting territorial claims of different ethnic groups. While the Madhesis wanted to demarcate the entire swathe of the southern plains as a single Madhesh province, Tharus claimed the eastern part of this region to be their historic homeland and rejected the idea of being subsumed under a Madhesi province. The Limbus for their part claimed a vertical slice of the eastern territory, parts of which overlapped with areas claimed by Madhesis. And these were only some of the larger ethno-linguistic groups. Nepal was home to over 100 ethnic groups, some comprising only a few thousand members. How were they to be included? Between 2008 and 2012, leaders of the different ethnic groups held several rounds of negotiations, with the Maoists sometimes serving as mediators. They constantly revised the maps of their territorial claims. The Maoists, who had proposed nine provinces during the conflict, proposed thirteen provinces in their 2008 election manifesto.[24] Once they entered the Constituent Assembly, they proposed fourteen provinces, and then later, in the State Restructuring Commission, they recommended ten. In addition, they also proposed a complex system of sub-autonomous regions within provinces for smaller ethnic groups.

Despite their differences, the Maoists, Madhesis and Janajatis were united during negotiations with the Nepali Congress and the UML. These older parliamentary parties did not reject federalism outright. After all, the prime minister who had promised it following the Madhesh movement was from the Nepali Congress. Many minorities felt only a federal state structure would provide them access to state resources and the right to self-government. Demands for inclusion and collective rights had gained unprecedented momentum in the post-2006 period. To completely reject federalism in such a situation would be downright reactionary. It would mean upholding the unitary state structure of the ancien régime that was based on exclusion.

Nonetheless, the Nepali Congress and the UML were not entirely comfortable with the idea of federalism. Their ambivalence was shared by influential sections of the population such as the hill upper castes, the royalists and most of Kathmandu's bourgeoisie. Federalism would dilute the hegemony of Brahmins and Chhetris, who had controlled the Nepali state for centuries. If states were carved along ethnic lines, the hill upper castes would remain dominant only in the remote areas of far-west Nepal. Moreover, these groups were emotionally attached to the culture of the unitary Hindu state that had developed over the past three centuries. They were grateful to the Shah kings who had expended great effort in forging the nation-state amid extremely unfavourable geopolitical circumstances. In their view, federalism threatened to unravel the nation. It would disperse authority and lead Nepal towards disintegration, or harden ethnic identities and cause strife and bloodshed.

Thus, although the Nepali Congress and UML accepted federalism in principle, they sought to dilute ethnic demands. They argued that provinces should not be demarcated on the basis of identity. Rather, the focus should be on the provinces' capacity to function as self-governing units. It was necessary to create a federal structure where all provinces enjoyed adequate and roughly equivalent shares of natural resources, revenue streams and administrative infrastructure. They stressed that the models proposed by the Maoists lacked such balance: some provinces included millions of people and a relatively developed economy, while others had a small population and not even a decent motorable road. Also, as a peripheral and impoverished country, Nepal would find it hard to administer numerous provinces. Their numbers had to be kept as small as possible. In their federal model, therefore, the Congress and the UML proposed only six provinces.

Although it made a few concessions to Madhesi demands, their proposed model was not significantly different from the existing structure that was established during the Panchayat era. It did not reflect the aspirations of the agitating minorities; it offered mere administrative decentralization and devolution of power, rather than the right to self-government.

In negotiations, the Maoists, Madhesis and Janajatis gave up some of their initial claims. For instance, they had demanded that the dominant ethnic group in each province be given 'prior rights' (*agradhikar*). This included preferential rights to natural resources and to political power. The Congress and UML insisted that this would be unfair and would cause resentment among the other ethnic groups residing in the area. The proponents of ethnic-based federalism then agreed to withdraw this demand. But they still insisted that each province be named after the dominant ethnic group in the area and demarcated in such a way that the group had a demographic advantage. The Nepali Congress and the UML refused even this. Negotiations thus dragged on, in a seemingly interminable impasse.

## Parliamentary Quicksand

The Maoists carried out a series of protests after their government fell. They asserted that the army, with support from the president, other political parties and India, had violated the principle of 'civilian supremacy'. They denounced the new UML-led government as India's 'puppet'. They claimed that their party alone had the right to lead government, as they occupied the highest number of seats in the legislature and were the only party to represent progressive aspirations. Their protests reached a climax in the first week of May 2010, when they staged a general strike in Kathmandu in an attempt to force the government to resign.

Tens of thousands of hardened Maoist cadres were bussed into the city, where they held hundreds of mass meetings and rallies. They halted traffic and forced shops and offices to shut down. Their leaders hoped to trigger a popular movement against the regime similar to the one in 2006. But the inhabitants of Kathmandu were not impressed. Many of them resented the disruption of their daily routines and the sudden presence of the rural, unwashed hordes in their midst. They saw the general strike as an open declaration of class war. It didn't help that the Maoist leader Ram Bahadur Thapa threatened to 'dig graves for compradors and feudals' at a huge mass meeting on 1 May.[25] Far from supporting the Maoist strike, many members of the urban bourgeoisie flocked to a 'peace rally' convoked by such organizations as the Federation of Nepalese Chambers of Commerce and Industry. The primary object of the rally was to oppose the Maoist strike. There were a number of violent clashes between Maoist cadres and their opponents. The parties in government stood firm and the Indian government made it known that it continued to support them. Prachanda denounced the 'well-fed and well-dressed' (*sukila-mukila*) for opposing the Maoists, but was eventually forced to lift the strike.

The general strike of May 2010 represented the first major mass mobilization by the Maoists since the end of the war. It was also the last. The strike showed the Maoists the limits of street action. From then onwards, the Maoist leadership followed the paths of negotiation and parliamentary manipulation. Prachanda and Bhattarai threatened the other parties that unless the government stepped down, the Maoists would not cooperate on the two major tasks of the peace process: the drafting of the new constitution and the integration of former Maoist combatants into the Nepal Army. After intense pressure, Madhav Nepal finally resigned as prime minister on 30 June. However, this did not mean the Maoists could easily regain control of the government. They still needed to gain a majority in the legislature, which was a challenge, as India remained hostile to them and very few of the other parties were willing to support them. Having fielded Prachanda as their prime-ministerial candidate, the Maoists set to work trying to garner support. They appealed to the smaller parties representing Madhesis and other ethnic groups on the basis of their shared commitment to federalism. Apparently they also offered them other kinds of enticements, as suggested by an audio tape leaked by Kathmandu-based Indian intelligence operatives in September.

The tape contained phone conversations, held in faulty English, between a Nepali man, allegedly Prachanda's loyal aide Krishna Bahadur Mahara, and an unidentified man with a Chinese accent.[26]

> UNIDENTIFIED PERSON WITH CHINESE ACCENT: Mr Mahara, how is the situation right now in Nepal? I know that the next election [voting by members of the Constituent Assembly for a new prime minister] coming up. Do you think there will be a result?
>
> NEPALI MAN: It is very near, but right now it is also not clear.
>
> UNIDENTIFIED PERSON: Do you think Maoists can get enough seats?
>
> NEPALI MAN: No chance. We are trying but it is so difficult.
>
> UNIDENTIFIED PERSON: What causing the problem to not have enough seats?
>
> NEPALI MAN: We have maybe ten to fifteen seats already but [we need] maybe around fifty.
>
> UNIDENTIFIED PERSON: You need additional fifty? And Mr Mahara what kind of help could help you to get the fifty seats?
>
> NEPALI MAN (laughs): You know. That is most difficult task, because the south center they are guided, controlled to them [meaning: India controls the other parties]. So the first thing, it is necessary to neutralize south [meaning: to wean the other parties away from Indian influence]. Second thing some of the money also needed.
>
> UNIDENTIFIED PERSON: What the amount you are talking about? ...
>
> NEPALI MAN: ... I have discussed with my chairman [Prachanda]. And he says because the election is now only four days left – from outside [i.e., other parties], [we need a] minimum fifty members. For fifty members, if we cost them then they need minimum 10 million Nepalese rupees per person ...
>
> UNIDENTIFIED PERSON: Alright. Actually, the friend that I have mentioned he might be ... but I don't want to mention his name over the phone for his own protection. Mr Mahara, he can come up with some kind of help; he wants to talk to you first because he needs to know detail due to his ... if you will be able to pay a visit in Hong Kong.[27]

Mahara initially claimed the recordings had been fabricated. Later, he said that it did not matter whether or not they were genuine; more important was that 'the phone-tapping incident has highlighted the extent of direct interference by foreign powers in our national security issues.'[28] The voice of the Nepali man in the recording did, however, sound like Mahara's. India, the other parties and large sections of public opinion took the recording as clear evidence that the Maoists had solicited finan-cial support from a certain section of the Chinese state in order to come to power. In the past the Chinese had lent their unwavering support to the monarchy, even when the latter became dictatorial and alienated the United States and India. Now, it seemed the Chinese were eager to cultivate the Maoists.

In the end, the Maoists failed to get the necessary support in the leg-islature. So they backed Jhalanath Khanal, a UML politician who was perceived to be more amenable to the Maoists. Khanal became prime minister in February 2011. But his government did not last long. Six months later, the Maoists, with the help of a number of Madhesi parties, were finally able to muster a majority in the legislature. Baburam Bhattarai became prime minister on 28 August. But unlike in 2008, when the Maoists formed a government for the first time, this time there was no jubilation. It had been almost five years since the rebels aban-doned People's War. They had made little headway in their agenda for socio-economic transformation. The tasks of resolving the problem of the two armies and drafting a new constitution too remained woefully incomplete.

The Maoists had entered mainstream politics with the hope of carry-ing out swift and widespread reform. But in the meantime they seemed bogged down in what Nepali leftists disparagingly termed 'parliamentary quicksand' (*samsadiya bhas*). As the Mahara tape indicated, the former rebels who had for years denounced the 'buying and selling of parlia-mentarians' were now themselves embroiled in the kinds of shady deals that had done so much to discredit parliamentary democracy during the 1990s. Each government formed after the collapse of the first Maoist-led government followed a similar pattern. The parties would spend months trying to put together a governing coalition. And once the government was in place, the leading party would be hobbled by the demands of its coalition partners. The aggrieved parties in opposition would refuse to cooperate, fearing that successful delivery of services to the population would increase the government's popularity. For instance, they would disrupt parliamentary proceedings to prevent the government from passing the annual budget. They would then accuse the government of incompetence, demand that it step down and do all they could to over-throw it. Politics was reduced to closed-door negotiations between small coteries of influential leaders.

By the time the Maoists returned to power in 2011, Prachanda and Baburam Bhattarai – the two party leaders most deeply involved in the high politics of the period – had scaled down their ambitions. Their priority was no longer to expand power and achieve rapid socio-economic transformation, but to complete the tasks of the peace process. The parties' failure to agree on a new constitution had deepened public disillusionment. Former Maoist combatants were becoming restive: they had languished in makeshift cantonments for five years and the parties had still not reached consensus on their future. The Maoists recognized that these issues could not be resolved without cooperation from the other political parties. Hence they chose a less confrontational approach. Prachanda let another aspect of his character supersede his fiery persona: that of the patient politician and negotiator. Instead of giving incendiary speeches, he now tried to narrow down differences between seemingly irreconcilable positions.

The Nepali Congress and the UML insisted that they would not participate in negotiations over the new constitution until the Maoist army was disbanded. The first major task for the Bhattarai government, then, was to reach an agreement on the integration of former Maoist combatants into the Nepal Army. By this time the Maoist leaders had abandoned all hopes of reforming the institution. All they sought was a 'respectable' face-saving deal – one that would not appear to be total capitulation on their part and which would ensure a secure future for Maoist combatants. An agreement signed in November stated that out of the 19,602 combatants who were still in cantonments, a maximum of 6,500 were to be recruited into a newly formed directorate of the Nepal Army. The Maoists compromised on their original position and agreed that potential recruits would have to fulfill the 'standard norms' of the army with regards to education, age and marital status. It was clear that most combatants would not meet these criteria, in particular the education requirements. As a result, only 1,451 former combatants were recruited in the end. Those who were ineligible or did not wish to join were offered alternatives such as further education and vocational training. But almost all of them regarded this offer as an insult, and opted for the cash packages ranging from Rs 500,000 to Rs 800,000 before leaving cantonments to re-enter civilian life.

During this period, the Maoist leadership also tried to repair relations with India and the Nepal Army. Prachanda ceased fulminating against the Indian government in speeches and interviews. In August 2011, Jayant Prasad replaced the virulently anti-Maoist Rakesh Sood as the Indian ambassador in Kathmandu. As prime minister, Baburam Bhattarai established a relationship of consultation and cooperation with him. Similarly, the Maoists' relations with the Nepal Army thawed after General Chhatraman Gurung replaced the belligerent Rookmangud Katawal as army chief. Since the peace process began, Prachanda had repeatedly condemned the army for refusing to endorse the political changes of 2006. Now, asked why he had accepted the integration of Maoist combatants into an army against which the Maoists had waged war, he replied: 'The war was against the Royal Nepalese Army. Integration is taking place with the Nepal Army. That was a royalist army; this is a republican army. That is a qualitative difference ... We are now leading the government, and the way we view the NA and the PLA has changed accordingly.'[29]

Although the Maoists' attempt to cultivate the army was largely tactical, there was at least one area where the interests of the two converged: their desire to prevent prosecutions for human rights violations committed during the conflict. The Nepali Congress and UML too were not much concerned with the matter. They agreed with the Maoists that the general approach to dealing with wartime abuses should be to offer amnesty to perpetrators and cash compensations to victims and their families.

In the later years of the war, the Maoists had treated OHCHR and other human rights organizations as allies in the campaign to delegitimize the regime. After the fall of the monarchy, however, activists demanded the prosecution of both Maoists and Nepal Army personnel guilty of killing and wounding civilians. But impunity persisted. As two prominent human rights defenders pointed out: 'Although the army and the Maoists responded in slightly different ways to calls for their personnel to be held accountable, the end result was the same – a refusal to cooperate with investigations and inquiries that had any chance of resulting in criminal liability.'[30] The Maoists now felt that human rights defenders were allying with conservative groups in an attempt to delegitimize their rebellion and the political changes of recent years. They argued that opening old wounds could only cause political chaos, and that it was best to forgive and forget. They became openly hostile towards OHCHR. Baburam Bhattarai's government refused to renew its mandate and the organization was forced to leave the country.

In October 2012, Bhattarai agreed, at the request of the Nepal Army, to promote Colonel Raju Basnet to the position of brigadier general. Basnet had commanded the Bhairavnath battalion in 2003, when forces under his command had carried out some of the most extreme cases of torture and disappearance that occurred during the war. It will be remembered that in late 2005, Krishna K. C. and other Maoist inmates of Nakkhu prison had demanded that the officers of the Bhairavnath battalion be prosecuted at the International Criminal Court.[31] Now the Maoist leaders were willing to forget the atrocities committed by the army, in return for its political goodwill. They were even willing to shield army personnel who had violated international human rights law from prosecution. This offered perhaps the clearest indication that the Maoists were well on their way to becoming an establishment party.

## Disillusionment and Rage

From early on, the Maoists were divided into two broad camps with regards to their approach to the peace process. When the twelve-point memorandum was signed, senior leaders like Mohan Baidya 'Kiran' and C. P. Gajurel were in prison in India. After they were released and returned to Nepal, they made it known that they were sceptical about the decision to enter mainstream politics. Within the party, Baidya represented the section that was dubbed 'hard-line' by the popular press. He argued that the rebels should not be too eager to implement the commitments made in the peace agreements; rather, they should maintain a tactical approach to the entire peace process. In his view, the game of peaceful multi-party politics would gradually corrupt the Maoists and rob them of their revolutionary edge. A long-term alliance between the Maoists and the older parliamentary parties was impossible, given their irreconcilable ideologies. The other parties would in no circumstances agree to promulgate a constitution that was acceptable to the Maoists. Now that the monarchy had been abolished, the party had to focus their struggle against the parliamentary parties. Rather than abandon their army, the Maoists had to strengthen it, so that they could launch an armed urban insurrection and seize state power.[32]

Baburam Bhattarai represented the other line within the party. He had long advocated an alliance with the parliamentary parties against the monarchy. He believed that once the Maoists gained control over the state, they had to allow greater political freedom than had existed in the communist regimes of the twentieth century. Now, Bhattarai argued that the peace process should not be viewed merely from a tactical angle. Rather than breaking the peace agreement at the first opportunity, the Maoists should recognize the remarkable political changes brought about by the People's War and the 2006 People's Movement. The monarchy had been overthrown and the country declared a secular state, shaking the very foundations of Hindu chauvinism, upper-caste hegemony and feudalism. The Constituent Assembly was engaged in negotiations over how best to emancipate Nepal's oppressed castes and ethnic groups. It was necessary to draft a constitution that would safeguard and institutionalize these gains for the long term. The remnants of feudalism would gradually be eroded through land reform and other measures. Nepal would see steady economic growth and eventually become liberated from the chains of dependency. But the nation would only move in this direction if the Maoists continued to work within the democratic framework and abide by the peace agreements.

Baidya and Bhattarai both appealed to Prachanda to uphold their respective positions as the party's official line. The chairman agreed with Bhattarai that the Maoists could not immediately launch an insurrection and capture state power. The state institutions in Kathmandu remained too powerful for them to take over by force, the party lacked the mass support required for an urban insurrection, and major foreign powers would not accept a one-party Maoist state. At the same time, Prachanda could not afford to alienate Baidya and his supporters. After all, they had been loyal to him since the days before Bhattarai had even joined the party. Moreover, during his stint as finance minister, Bhattarai had gained a reputation as a competent and reliable politician and become popular even among the bourgeois classes that were otherwise ill-disposed towards the Maoists. Bhattarai was also trying hard to establish his own loyalist faction within the party. The chairman felt it was necessary to retain Baidya's support to ensure that Bhattarai did not gain too much power.

Prachanda's chief strategy was to try and convince Baidya and his supporters that the party was still on a revolutionary path. He argued that a long period of preparatory work was necessary before the Maoists could seize state power. The great Lenin himself was able to lead a successful insurrection only after twenty-five years of peaceful struggle. Addressing PLA commanders in 2008, Prachanda said: 'Yesterday, war meant holding a machine gun and killing or being killed by our enemies. Today war means sitting with our enemies at the same table and chatting over cups of tea. Although the war looks different now, its essence is the same.'[33] On occasion, the chairman even argued that a violent insurrection might not be necessary after all; the Maoists could gain total control over the state if they won a substantial majority in subsequent elections.

Prachanda's reasoning did not fully convince the radical faction and the rank and file. But in the initial years of the peace process, he managed to keep the party united under his command. For instance, after the Maoist-led government fell in 2009, Prachanda gained much support from the radical faction when he railed against Indian interference and called upon 'nationalists' who had previously supported the monarchy to join hands with the Maoists. In fact, even as late as May 2010, Maoist cadres had strong faith in their revolutionary mission. Most of the Maoist cadres who came to Kathmandu to participate in the general strike genuinely believed that they were going to topple the government and capture state power.[34]

In reality, Prachanda recognized the necessity of completing the peace process and drafting a constitution. As he became increasingly involved in negotiations with the other parliamentary parties, it became difficult to maintain the fiction that he was committed to the path of revolution. The Maoist rank and file watched their leaders in Kathmandu from a distance. It seemed to them that the party was irrevocably sinking into parliamentarism. The cadres now had little work to do. They did not have to scour far-flung villages and convince people to join their cause as they had done during the war. Their leadership was no longer concerned with expanding the party's organization or staging strikes and demonstrations.

Samjhana Gharti Magar, an activist from Rolpa, resembled many others who had sacrificed the best years of their lives to the rebellion. She had joined the Maoists when she was sixteen, and spent her youth amid great danger and adversity. On the run from the police and army, she had been forced to leave her daughter in the care of relatives. Her husband and two of her brothers, all Maoist militants, were killed during the war. In late 2011, Samjhana was living in a single-storey, two-roomed house in Ghorahi, a town in Dang district a few hours' drive south of Rolpa. She had built the house with the cash compensation provided by the government for the loss of her husband. Her daughter, now nine years old, was living with her. This was the most comfortable her life had ever been. And yet she was restless. She was still a Maoist and responsible for overseeing a few villages in Rolpa, but the party organization there had become largely moribund. 'After spending a few days in Ghorahi,' she said, 'I always feel like going back to Rolpa to work on the organization. But when I go to Rolpa, I see there is not much to do. So I again feel like returning to my daughter in Ghorahi.'[35]

A small collection of communist literature translated into Nepali sat on a shelf in the space that served as both bedroom and living room. While the classics that included Mao's selected writings and Engels's *The Origin of the Family, Private Property and the State* were covered in dust, a copy of a Maoist party journal seemed to have been recently perused. The journal contained an article by the young and radical Maoist leader Netra Bikram Chand 'Biplab'. Samjhana had carefully read the article and underlined certain passages:

> The Nepali people have ... had to bear the brunt of the counter-revolution led by parties and their leaders. [At one point in history], the Congress led a revolution and the people supported the Congress. But later, Congress leaders lost faith in revolution and the party surrendered to the old ruling class and the Indian ruling class ... The people who had supported the Congress ... were thus betrayed. Similarly, between 2028 and 2032 v.s. [1971/72–1975/76], the UML also tried to lead a revolution ..., but later the UML also surrendered to the ruling class, and became counter-revolutionary. The people were betrayed again ... Today, once again, counter-revolution stalks the Maoist party and its leaders and is pressuring them to deviate from revolution.[36]

To many Maoists, the biggest betrayal was when Prachanda and Bhattarai agreed to disband the Maoist army by integrating a small number of combatants into the Nepal Army and sending the rest to join the civilian population. After all, Prachanda himself had often repeated Mao's dictum, 'Without a people's army, the people have nothing.' In September 2011, in a symbolic gesture marking their transition from a rebel group into a democratic party, the Maoists handed over the keys of their weapon containers to the government. 'I cried for hours that night,' recalled Samjhana Magar. Her daughter too cried with her and asked, 'Mother, does this mean that the Maoist party is now finished?'[37]

The agreement on integration and rehabilitation of Maoist combatants caused much discontent within party ranks. According to the stringent terms on offer, most combatants would not be eligible to join the Nepal Army. Only a few Maoists were to be given officer-level positions. Many of them thought that the compensation packages they were due to receive were insufficient. They also accused their commanders and political leaders of embezzling funds that the state had allocated for their upkeep. On the night of 10 April 2012, fights broke out between aggrieved combatants and commanders who remained loyal to Prachanda. At the Maoist chairman's behest, the government sent in the Nepal Army to the cantonments to prevent further violence. For many former rebels, this was the ultimate betrayal: their own chairman had ordered the army that had until recently been their enemy to contain the Maoists' internal disputes.

By this time, the culture of collectivism and self-sacrifice that the Maoists had fostered during the war had largely crumbled away. Many Maoist cadres felt that their leadership had used them to come to power and was now abandoning them. Combatants regularly complained that they had sacrificed their youth for the Maoist cause but had received nothing in return. They had believed their leaders when they urged them to leave schools that provided useless 'bourgeois education'. Now, left without a cause to fight for, and forced to return to normal life, their lack of education placed them at a big disadvantage. According to Shyam Kumar Budha Magar, who had joined the Maoists at the age of twelve,[38] 'Earlier, the PLA was united by emotion, ideology and organization. But none of that exists any longer. Thankfully, they have not raised arms [against their leaders] so far.'[39]

For Mohan Baidya and other senior Maoists still committed to revolution, the disbandment of the PLA was only one in a series of betrayals by Prachanda and Baburam Bhattarai. They also accused the duo of surrendering to Indian expansionism. In their view, the trade agreement that Bhattarai signed with the Indian government when he was prime minister was yet another 'unequal treaty' that compromised Nepal's interests. They were ambivalent about the party's support for ethnic movements. In its pursuit of federalism, they argued, the party had succumbed to 'imperial and expansionist' pressures and come to privilege identity claims over class struggle. The dominant section of the party had grown too attached to the spoils of government and had exploited their new-found power to benefit themselves and their cronies. In short, Prachanda and Bhattarai were 'ideological opportunists, rightist-revisionist liquidationists and national and class traitors'.[40]

Despite repeated attempts, Baidya and his supporters were unable to make the dominant party leadership change course. So they began cultivating a parallel faction within the party. They urged former combatants to reject Prachanda's call to sign up for recruitment into the Nepal Army and join a new 'People's Volunteer's Bureau' instead. On 19 June 2012, after months of deliberation, the Baidya faction formally split into a separate party. They named it the Communist Party of Nepal–Maoist (CPN–M), the name of the original party during the years of the conflict. (The original party had been renamed the Unified Communist Party of Nepal–Maoist (UCPN–M) in January 2009, following unification with Unity Centre–Masal, a small left party consisting of leaders who had split from the Maoists in 1994 after the party decided to launch People's War.[41])

It was not just in their name that the new party expressed nostalgia for the past. At their first meeting, the CPN–M passed a resolution highlighting what they thought were the key achievements of the war, namely, the establishment of parallel government and judicial mechanisms, a standing army and militias. They also set out to analyse how their parent party had squandered those gains. As the meeting record stated, the original sin had been committed at the 2001 Second National Conference when they decided to negotiate with the state for a Constituent Assembly. While the decision was tactically correct, it had allowed certain leaders to push the party onto the 'opportunist' path. The Maoists had made another blunder when they ratified the 2003 resolution 'The Development of Democracy in the Twenty-First Century', a document that was largely drafted by Bhattarai and approved by Baidya and the other Maoist purists only at Prachanda's request. The 2003 resolution stated that the revolutionary party of the twenty-first century must accept multi-party competition. Baidya and his supporters now claimed that the resolution violated basic Marxist–Leninist–Maoist principles and had sunk the party into the 'quicksand of rightist-revisionism'.[42]

The leaders of the new Maoist party further claimed that it had been a mistake to place so much faith in Prachanda and adopt the doctrine of 'Prachandapath' as the party's guiding principles. 'The Prachanda faction used all forms of diplomatic scheming and skullduggery to trick us,' they wrote in their document. 'They emptied the party of content and agenda and led it to surrender.'[43] This realization must have vexed Mohan Baidya the most. No other Maoist leader had done as much to promote Prachanda. In 1989, he had stepped down from his position as party chief so that Prachanda could take his place. He had relentlessly championed Prachanda as the supreme and ultimate leader of the party. He had been Prachanda's staunchest defender against Baburam Bhattarai.[44] Now, after decades of close comradeship, the chairman had turned his back on him and what he stood for.

The composition of the new Maoist party was not insignificant. It drew in many wartime cadres who felt abandoned by the parent party, and enjoyed huge support in Rolpa and other districts that had been rebel strongholds during the war. The party comprised 30 per cent of the parent party's central committee members and around one third of the Maoist members of the Constituent Assembly.[45]

Yet, from its very inception, the CPN–M was hamstrung by the lack of a clear strategy. They defined themselves in opposition to the parent party, but did not know exactly what they stood for. They claimed their goal was to launch a 'people's revolt' and complete the New Democratic revolution, but they also recognized that a revolt was not possible in the existing conditions.[46] They lacked public support – very few people were willing to come out on the streets to protest on their behalf. As embittered as they were, the former Maoist combatants were too exhausted by the ten years of conflict to plunge back into war. Moreover, their leaders were now well-known public figures; they could not simply go underground and operate incognito as they had done in the mid-1990s.

Thus the splinter Maoist party had no choice but to continue working in the existing system. Within this political framework, however, they were isolated and marginal players. They were not invited to any of the negotiations between the major political parties. They refused to even compete for positions in government. They did try to form a tactical alliance with the Nepali Congress and UML to bring down the Baburam Bhattarai government, but these parliamentary parties knew Baidya's eventual intention and did not trust him. The radical Maoists even appealed to former royalists, on the basis of their common 'nationalist' sentiments. But right-wing monarchists had pretty well lost their political relevance, and in any case, the social gulf between them and the Maoists was too wide to create any meaningful alliance. Baidya also tried to cultivate Madhesi and Janajati groups. But their leaders rejected any notion that class should take precedence over identity claims, and they preferred working with Prachanda and Bhattarai.

The new Maoist party tried to organize former Maoist combatants into a militant wing. But they lacked the resources needed for its upkeep; the party had refused to participate in government and strike lucrative deals with powerful business interests. Besides, the distant promise of a 'people's revolt' was not enough to sustain organized forces. In an effort to gain relevance and attention, they vandalized private schools with foreign-sounding names and forced cinemas to halt screenings of Hindi films for a few days. But this only earned them the wrath of Kathmandu's middle class.

Prachanda regarded the radical faction with open contempt. In his words, they were 'ideological dogmatists with a mechanical [and] narrow interpretation of objective reality; leftist liquidationists … with petty-bourgeois impatience.'[47] Privately, however, he tried to woo Baidya into returning to the original party. The split had left Prachanda at a disadvantage. He had lost some of his staunchest defenders in the internecine struggles against Bhattarai. He was also worried that division would damage his party's future electoral prospects.

Still, in the broader picture Prachanda was in a good position in 2012. He had moved from his modest lodgings into a large house in the wealthy area of Lazimpat, close to the residences of the prime minister and president, the Indian embassy and the royal palace-turned-museum. He rewarded his supporters with power and opportunity. For example, Barsha Man Pun 'Ananta', the PLA commander who had led numerous attacks beginning with the Holeri action in 1996, was made finance minister in the Bhattarai-led government. There were even rumours that Prachanda had invested in the country's largest private telecom company and in a number of newspapers. His cronies were known to be raking in huge profits from real-estate deals in Kathmandu and other towns.

Whether one admired or despised Prachanda, one could not avoid seeking his support for any significant political initiative. Nepali Congress leaders needed his help in resolving the frequent political impasses. Madhesi and Janajati leaders requested him to push for their demands amid opposition from the other parties. There was no doubt that Prachanda had become the central figure in Nepal's turbulent politics.

## The Death of the Assembly

As the Constituent Assembly failed to meet the initial deadline for writing the new constitution, its tenure was extended for two more years. In November 2011, the Supreme Court ruled that there could be no more extensions. If the constitution was not drafted by 27 May, the parties would be left with two options: either a referendum on outstanding constitutional matters, or fresh elections to another Constituent Assembly.

The parties knew that their legitimacy would be severely compromised if they failed to promulgate the constitution by the new deadline. By then they had reached an agreement on the form of government. The Maoists, backtracking somewhat, had agreed to a bicameral legislature. It would be neither a purely parliamentary government, as demanded by the Nepali Congress, nor a purely presidential one, as demanded by the Maoists. Instead, a directly elected president would share executive power with a prime minister elected through the legislature.

In April, the parties began serious negotiations over federalism. The top Maoist leaders tried to find a federal model that would be acceptable to both the Nepali Congress and the UML on the one hand, and Madhesi and Janajati groups on the other. On 15 May, the parties agreed on a model that included eleven provinces. They did not specify the names and boundaries of the provinces, as these were to be decided by a commission in the future.

The agreement instantly angered large numbers of Madhesis and Janajatis, who had been demanding a constitution with a complete federal model. They feared that postponing crucial discussions on federalism would mean that they would never be addressed. Janajati leaders insisted that each province should be named after the dominant ethnic group in the region. Madhesis felt aggrieved that the eleven-province model divided the Tarai – the southern plains that they consider their homeland – into five provinces. Three hundred and twenty Madhesi and Janajati members of the Constituent Assembly, mostly from the UML and the Maoist party, signed a petition opposing the agreement. The Nepal Federation of Indigenous Nationalities called a three-day strike that brought life in the capital and other urban areas to a standstill.

Maoist leaders who had long advocated ethnic rights and autonomy could not afford to alienate the Janajati and Madhesi groups. They withdrew their support from the agreement. Along with their Madhesi allies, they declared that they would accept one of the two federal models they had supported earlier. The first had been developed by the state restructuring committee under the Constituent Assembly, and included fourteen states. The second, developed by the State Restructuring Commission, included ten. In each model, the Tarai was divided into just two states. The Nepali Congress opposed both models, even rebuffing the demand that the states be named for the ethnic groups with historic claims over those areas. Negotiations continued but no agreement was in sight. At midnight on 27 May, the Constituent Assembly expired without having produced a constitution.

The dissolution of the Constituent Assembly led to a fresh political and constitutional crisis. The parties had failed to institutionalize a new political order. The country was now devoid not just of a body that would draft a new constitution, but also of its legislature. On the night of 27 May, Prime Minister Baburam Bhattarai announced fresh elections to a new Constituent Assembly. But the opposition parties refused to participate unless the government stepped down. Months passed in bitter wrangling. Finally, in March 2013, the parties agreed that the chief justice of the Supreme Court would lead a new interim government that would hold elections the following June or November.

# Postscript

Politics catapults people from the streets into mansions. It ejects them from mansions onto the streets.

– An RNA soldier[1]

Election to a new Constituent Assembly was held on 19 November 2013. The Mohan Baidya–led faction of the Maoist party and its few allies boycotted it. Days before the election they announced a transport blockade and vandalized vehicles to intimidate people into staying home. One person died and several were injured in these attacks. Right before polls, Baidya's cadres planted a few improvised explosive devices across the country. A child in Kathmandu was maimed when one of these went off on the morning of election day. However, on the whole violence was limited and failed to dampen people's enthusiasm. Voter turnout was over 75 per cent – the highest ever in Nepali history.

The Prachanda-led Maoist party was in a buoyant mood before the election. Despite being somewhat aware of its waning popularity, the party believed that large sections of the population supported its agenda of federalism. As results emerged, however, it became clear that the Maoists were trailing far behind their rivals. The final standings marked a major reversal from the 2008 election. This time the Congress won 196 seats and the UML 175. The Maoists gained a mere 80 seats.

On the morning of 21 November, when the vote count was still underway, the Prachanda-led party called an emergency press conference. Ashen-faced Maoist leaders sat beside their chairman and listened as he accused the army, election officials and the other parties of conspiring against the Maoists. Prachanda alleged that ballot boxes had been replaced while being transported from polling booths to counting stations. He called for a halt to the counting process and an investigation into irregularities. If these demands were not met, he said, 'We will not participate in the Constituent Assembly.'

Maoist activists in the room cheered at their leader's defiance. But the evidence of electoral fraud that the party provided was weak, and they had no option but to continue participating in the political process. In December, the Maoists formally agreed to participate in the Constituent Assembly. In exchange, the Congress and the UML pledged that they would remain committed to secularism, republicanism and federalism, and that the Maoists would continue to have an important role in constitutional negotiations. They also acceded that a parliamentary committee would investigate election irregularities, a promise that was quickly forgotten.

In private the Maoists admitted that election fraud had not been as widespread as they had claimed and the real causes of their defeat lay elsewhere. They conceded that people's disillusionment with the party had been far greater than they had realized. It was not just that their novelty had worn off. Many of their well-wishers were bitterly disappointed that they had failed to take many immediate steps towards fulfilling their promises. The Maoists seemed overly focused on grand plans such as state restructuring rather than on concrete programs and policies for improving people's lives.

Granted, the Maoists were never in a position to fully meet people's expectations. Although they had won the highest number of seats in the 2008 election, they were never comfortably established in power. Until the dissolution of the first Constituent Assembly, they had led government for only eighteen months (August 2008–May 2009 and August 2011–May 2012). However, many voters thought of the Maoists as the incumbent party. A common refrain across the country went: 'I voted for them once, but they did nothing for me. Why should I vote for them again?'

Moreover, the growing wealth of Maoist leaders had invited much public derision. When the Maoists first came to Kathmandu, they lived in conditions that were not drastically different from the poor they claimed to represent. Over the years, many of them displayed a taste for luxury that seemed unbefitting of proletarian leaders. Prachanda's new house, his new car, and even his new bed and his expensive new watch became the subject of media attention. Although Bhattarai was generally seen as principled and upright, there were reports that his wife Hisila Yami was involved in widespread corruption during his stint as prime minister. Across the country, local Maoist leaders had used their newfound influence to broker deals and capture government contracts.

These developments had caused a rising tide of resentment within the party. The increasing wealth of some of the more established leaders had been a major factor behind the party's split. During the election, members of the Kiran faction actively campaigned against their former comrades. Many of them reportedly urged their supporters to vote for the Nepali Congress and the UML.

Even those who remained in the Prachanda faction had lost their zeal and initiative. A Maoist student leader who went to Rupandehi to campaign for Baburam Bhattarai was shocked to see the nearly moribund party organization and the lackadaisical attitude of cadres in the district. Bhattarai lost the Rupandehi constituency, though he did win in Gorkha-1. Similarly, Prachanda lost his constituency in Kathmandu, but won with a narrow margin in Siraha.[2]

The Maoists' opponents claimed that the election results indicated a wholesale rejection of a federal structure that would recognize the identities of historically marginalized groups. Those who had long felt threatened by the demands of Madhesis, Janajatis and Dalits found much cause for triumphalism. The outcome of the election did reflect people's aversion for the manner in which the federalism debate had polarized society. Some feared that federalism would aggravate tensions and instigate conflicts between communities. Others thought that federalism would make movement difficult, as people would have to pay a tax to transport goods or enter another province. These fears were compounded by misinformation and misunderstanding. Having failed to gauge public sentiments, the Maoists had made little effort to dispel such misconceptions. They had not adequately clarified that federalism would neither allow some groups to dominate others, nor restrict free movement between provinces.

In a way the 2013 election marked the Maoists' total transformation into an establishment party, one that went through regular cycles of electoral victory and defeat. The odds against which they had fought and risen seemed like a distant memory. Yet not too long ago, they had been rebels who controlled vast sections of the countryside. Only seven years had elapsed since they entered the capital and five since they won the elections to become the nation's strongest political force. This was a rare achievement, considering that few guerrilla movements of recent times have been able to break through the urban barrier. What had enabled this?

There were fortuitous causes behind the Maoists' rise to power. The palace massacre of 2001, for example, severely weakened the monarchy. The new king, Gyanendra, made the grave mistake of usurping executive power. This robbed the monarchy of the last vestige of legitimacy and compelled the political parties to rally against his regime.

There were millenarian aspects to the Maoist movement. Many of its members were driven by the vision of an impossible utopia. In retrospect, however, it is clear that the Maoists were not solely driven by ideological fervour. Their leaders were also pragmatists who had made sound strategic calculations. They were fully aware that the geopolitical situation was not favourable for a communist rebellion. The guerrilla group they had learned the most from in the 1980s, Peru's Shining Path, had been crushed and its chairman Abimael Guzmán jailed. But on the domestic front, circumstances were ripe. As Prachanda wrote, 'The multi-party system provides more opportunities to intensify class struggle than the Panchayat regime.'[3] There was now a free press, which the Maoists could utilize to disseminate their political message. The political sphere had become open and chaotic, which meant that the Maoists could establish secret fronts and find allies to protest against state excesses. None of this would have been possible in the repressive atmosphere of the Panchayat era.

Further, the Maoists knew that the 1990 political settlement was an uneasy compromise and that they could exploit the contradictions within the parliamentary system. Prachanda had scoffed at those who drew parallels between Nepal's constitutional monarchy and the European bourgeois republics of the nineteenth century. In his view, Nepal's parliamentary democracy was an 'unnatural' alliance between bourgeois and feudal forces.[4] The palace still controlled the army and retained substantial power. For this reason the Maoists scrupulously avoided antagonizing the palace and the army in the early years of the rebellion, directing their attack only towards the parliamentary parties and the police. Whenever the occasion arose, the Maoists would fan the tension between the palace and the parties to their advantage.

The Maoist leaders were also keenly aware of their weaknesses relative to the state. They knew they could not rely solely on military force to expand their power. Prachanda often reminded the rank and file that the Maoist rebellion in Peru and in other countries had collapsed due to the rebels' excessive reliance on military force, ideological dogmatism and failure to understand the importance of negotiation.[5]

The Maoists recognized from the outset that it was not enough to eliminate the state presence in the countryside and establish base areas. If they were to become a powerful political party, they had to engage seriously with all the political forces in the country. They had to be alert to groups – no matter how small or negligible – with whom they could forge tactical alliances. It was also important for them to gain publicity by regularly intervening in the ongoing political debates. They had to appear amenable to negotiation and propose feasible political solutions to which the government would be forced to respond. As this book makes clear, a scrupulous adherence to such principles enabled the Maoists' rise to power.

Had the Maoists' ultimate goal been only to gain state power, one might say the rebellion achieved a measure of success. But the Maoists had envisaged nothing less than a total transformation of Nepali state and society. Attracted by their professed goals, thousands of Nepalis had joined the rebels. Almost 18,000 people were killed during the war and around 1,500 were disappeared. Approximately 100,000 people were displaced from their homes. The Maoists thought of these as regrettable but necessary sacrifices. But one might ask: what did those sacrifices amount to? To what extent were the Maoists able to fulfill their promises?

One of the Maoists' chief goals was to destroy iniquitous social structures. When they murdered landlords or evicted them from villages, they created an atmosphere of terror. But there were also many instances when indigenous and lower-caste groups genuinely felt a sense of liberation. The rebels earned gratitude and support when they punished those who perpetuated discriminatory customs.[6] Such measures were discontinued after the Maoists came to the capital. Old norms re-emerged in areas that had formerly been under rebel control. The Maoists' claim that they had completely uprooted feudalism from the countryside was thus an exaggeration. Nonetheless, the social fabric of the villages transformed significantly through the ten years of the Maoist rebellion. The image of the exploitative moneylender-landowner, for example, which appeared in almost every popular representation of Nepali rural life until the 1990s, had almost vanished from public consciousness by the time the Maoist war ended.

There were, of course, other reasons besides Maoist intervention behind this change. Labour migration was one. Hundreds of thousands of Nepalis, many of them poor and lower-caste, were now working in the Gulf or Southeast Asia and sending money home. Their families used the money to buy land and build houses. These remittances transformed the class structure of villages and helped reduce caste discrimination. Further, the efforts of development NGOs and civil society organizations campaigning for the rights of the marginalized also contributed to the erosion of old social hierarchies.

But this does not diminish the importance of the Maoists' contribution. Many Maoist activists interviewed for this book said that a major outcome of the rebellion had been to 'make people aware of their rights'. Villagers across the country corroborated this claim. Even the Maoists' political rivals grudgingly conceded this. No one could deny that the Maoists had taught large sections of the population to organize and agitate in the face of injustice, instead of quietly accepting their position in the social hierarchy.

After they entered peaceful politics, the Maoists focused their energy on making the state more representative of historically marginalized groups. Nepal was declared a secular state and the monarchy was abolished. The Hindu religion and the monarchy had for decades been symbols and props of Nepali nationalism, and the dismantling of these symbols altered the character of the nation. Several restrictions imposed during the Panchayat era and the 1990s were lifted. Citizens were no longer banned from forming political parties that represented specific ethnic groups, and new parties emerged accordingly, bringing long-neglected ethnic grievances and demands to the fore of public consciousness. The Maoists aided the process in a significant way. It was the rupture caused by the rebellion and the 2006 uprising that enabled these changes. As the political analyst C. K. Lal wrote, 'There should be no hesitation in giving credit where it is due: the Maoists changed the way nationality had been defined for centuries in Nepal.'[7] Nonetheless, there were also setbacks to this process of transformation. The Maoists' demand for a 'radical restructuring of the state' may have stood at the heart of the Constituent Assembly debates. But the assembly's demise in May 2012 represented a failure to institutionalize this demand. The Maoists' electoral defeat in 2013 further pushed back the agenda.

The Maoists' other major goal was the establishment of a strong and autonomous state – something that was clearly not achieved in the post-revolutionary years. Their entry into Kathmandu disrupted the political process in a profound way, but they still could not impose their will on the other parties. The struggle for power continued to dominate Nepali politics. Frequent changes of government virtually paralysed the state. Key Maoist demands that had found their way into the Comprehensive Peace Agreement, such as land reform, remained unimplemented. While they were fighting the state, the Maoists had derided the parliamentary regime for its inefficiency. But chaos and instability persisted even after they came on the scene.

The Maoists' emphasis on national autonomy was largely expressed as opposition to Indian interventions in Nepal. But the various governments formed after the 2008 elections were too weak to resist Indian influence. Constantly hobbled by the parties in opposition, each government's hold on power was tenuous. The Indian establishment, through its Kathmandu-based diplomatic and intelligence officials, remained well able to exploit the deep divisions between the parties. Moreover, Nepali political leaders actively solicited Indian support to outdo their rivals or to mediate agreements. Even the Maoists, who had vociferously opposed India's meddling, realized upon entering mainstream politics that they could not afford to antagonize the powerful neighbour. Like other political forces throughout the history of modern Nepal, the Maoists too sought to cultivate the Indian establishment in order to strengthen their position within the domestic sphere.

In any case, Nepali communists had always tended to denounce India with exaggerated fervour. Politicians regularly exploited anti-India sentiment to rouse anger and gain public sympathy. Faced with the imminent fall of his government in 2009, Prachanda himself had tried to rally public sympathy by denouncing 'Indian expansionism' at mass gatherings. In 2004, when the civil war was still going on, he had raised the spectre of Indian invasion to gain support for a potential alliance with the king.

The Maoists' excessive focus on India distracted from other aspects of Nepal's dependency, most evidently the dependence on foreign aid. In the fiscal year 2009–10, foreign aid comprised 19.16 per cent of the government's total expenditure and 55.15 per cent of development expenditure. This dependence had political and social costs. Donor priorities substantially influenced the policies of all government ministries. Much of the country's educated class coveted employment in aid organizations, which provided more lucrative jobs and more opportunities for upward mobility than the government bureaucracy. Many critics therefore argued that foreign aid further weakened the Nepali state.

Greater still was Nepal's dependence on remittances. The economy, which had come to a standstill during the war, continued to stagnate when the war ended. Chronic political instability and lack of employment forced hundreds of thousands of Nepalis to leave the country each year. Remittances comprised 23 per cent, or nearly one-fourth, of Nepal's GDP in 2010. It was the marginalized poor labouring in harsh conditions in the Gulf countries or Southeast Asia who sent these funds. The affluent migrants chose other destinations, mainly the United States or Europe, and rarely transferred substantial amounts of money to Nepal.

The two dreams of the Maoists – establishing a more equal and just society, and achieving national autonomy – seemed increasingly incompatible. If the militant assertion of historically marginalized groups initiated a process of building a more just society, it was also true that the proliferation of parties increased the competition for state power and contributed to its paralysis.

The new government was not formed until three months after the 2013 election. Following protracted power-sharing negotiations, the Nepali Congress and the UML finally formed a governing coalition in February 2014. Congress leader Sushil Koirala became prime minister. A former aide and a relative of Girija Prasad, he had become party president after the latter's death on 20 March 2010. Sushil Koirala repeatedly expressed his commitment to draft a new constitution 'within a year'. But this seemed challenging amid the long-standing disputes that had yet to be resolved.

The Maoists had become such familiar fixtures in Kathmandu's political circuit that it was easy to forget their insurgent past. Yet the consequences of the Maoist rebellion were evident everywhere. Significant numbers of wartime cadres, now members of the breakaway Maoist party led by Mohan Baidya, remained committed to the idea of revolutionary Maoism. For the time being, they were a marginal political force. They did not have the wherewithal to launch another rebellion and capture the state. But their frustration ran deep, and they remained capable of violence and disruption.

Besides hardened Maoist cadres, it was the family members of those killed or disappeared who were most tormented by the memories of war. They continued to demand justice. Although the Comprehensive Peace Agreement had guaranteed a Truth and Reconciliation Commission and a commission to investigate disappearances, these had not yet been established, partly owing to disputes over their mandates. While the army and the political parties (including the Maoists) desired amnesties for crimes committed during the war, human rights organizations and Western governments pushed for prosecution. In early 2014, these questions continued to shape Nepal's political debate. The intractable nature of this dispute illustrated the challenge of coming to terms with the history of armed conflict.

# Acknowledgements

Prashant Jha, friend and comrade; his intelligence, tenacity and warmth have shaped and inspired me over the years.

Bhaskar Gautam and Anagha Neelakantan for their friendship, astute advice and unstinting support. James Sharrock for reading my work-in-progress, providing valuable feedback and helping me choose a title. Manjushree Thapa, Ian Martin, Sam Cowan, David Gellner and A. Peter Burleigh for taking time out of their busy schedules to read my manuscript and offering sharp and insightful comments.

Akhilesh Upadhyay has been a friend and encouraged me since my early days as a columnist for *The Kathmandu Post*. Yohn Vivanco-Medina, Sarah Levit-Shore, Suman Pradhan, Subel Bhandari and John Bevan have broadened my perspective on critical issues in Nepal and elsewhere. Michael Hutt gave me helpful advice and pointed me toward critical sources.

Devendra Raj Panday, Khagendra Sangroula and C. K. Lal have been models of integrity and moral courage, and a constant source of inspiration. Pratyoush Onta, Seira Tamang and other friends at Martin Chautari have offered a much-needed sense of intellectual community.

Conversations with Anubhav Ajeet, Bimal Aryal, Vijay Kant Karna, Yug Pathak, Gyanu Adhikari, Daulat Jha, Rakesh Mishra, Thomas Bell and Deependra Jha have deepened my understanding of Nepali politics and society. Post Bahadur Basnet and Feyzi Ismail put me in touch with sources that were crucial for my project. Kiyoko Ogura generously shared her deep knowledge about the Maoist movement. Amish Mulmi for his advice and encouragement. Thomas Matthew and Laurie Vassily for their hospitality and conversation. Ashok Gurung has provided important platforms for Nepalis including myself to engage scholars and learners from other parts of the world.

Niraj Gorkhali created the maps for the book. Sagar Shrestha, Mana Rishi Dhital, Subel and Kashish Das Shrestha provided photographs from their remarkable collections.

Sebastian Budgen, Mark Martin and Lorna Scott Fox at Verso Books for their thoughtful advice and editorial support and for helping my book come to fruition. Ravi Singh for showing interest in the book and for initiating the process of bringing out an Indian edition for readers in South Asia.

Akshaya Adhikari read the manuscript in its initial stages and spurred me on. Nisha Biswas helped shape my political consciousness. My parents, Neelam and Ramesh Adhikari, and sister, Nidhi, who made everything possible. Shradha Ghale for her essential role in shaping the book into its present form and for our shared pursuits and life.

# Notes

## Preface

1 'Ahuti' (Bishwa Bhakta Dulal), *Tapaswika Geetharu* (*Songs of an Ascetic*), Kathmandu: Pragati Pustak Sadan, 1992 (2049 v.s.), p. 16. Here and through-out, 'v.s.' is an abbreviation for vikram samvat, the official Nepali calendar.

## Chapter 1: The Sun in the Hearts of the People

1 Dhruba Kumar, 'An Interlude in Nepal–China Relations during the Cultural Revolution', *Nepalese Journal of Political Science* 2, no. 2 (May 1980), p. 31.
2 Ibid., p. 39.
3 Ibid., p. 27.
4 Ibid., p. 28.
5 Ibid.
6 Ibid., p. 29.
7 Bhuwan Lal Joshi and Leo Rose, *Democratic Innovations in Nepal: A Case Study of Political Acculturation*, Kathmandu: Mandala Publications, 2004 (University of California Press, 1966), p. 296.
8 Leo Rose, 'Communism under High Atmospheric Conditions: The Party in Nepal', pp. 363–80 in Robert A. Scalapino, ed., *The Communist Revolution in Asia: Tactics, Goals and Achievements*, New Jersey: Prentice Hall, 1969, pp. 374–5.
9 Ibid., p. 381.
10 Yam Chaulagain and Rashmi Kandel, *Janayuddhaka Nayakharu* (*Leaders of the People's War*), Kathmandu: Jayakali Prakashan, 2008 (2065 v.s.), p. 98.
11 Ibid., p. 42.
12 Ibid., p. 16.
13 Ibid., pp. 13–21.

14  Anirban Roy, *Prachanda: The Unknown Revolutionary*, Kathmandu: Mandala Book Point, 2008, p. 14.

15  Ibid., p. 7.

16  Chaulagain and Kandel, *Janayuddhaka Nayakharu*, p. 115.

17  Ibid., p. 69, p. 102

18  According to the 2001 census, ninety-three different languages are spoken in Nepal. The state historically privileged the Nepali language, placing those who did not speak it as a mother tongue at a disadvantage.

19  For more on the circulation of communist literature and its reception during the 1960s and 1970s, see David N. Gellner and Mrigendra Bahadur Karki, 'The Sociology of Activism in Nepal: Some Preliminary Considerations', pp. 361–93 in H. Ishii, D. Gellner and K. Nawa, eds, *Political and Social Transformation in North India and Nepal: Social Dynamics in Northern South Asia*, New Delhi: Manohar Books, 2007, pp 383–8.

20  See Benoît Cailmail, 'Mohan Bikram Singh and the History of Nepalese Maoism', pp. 11–38 in *European Bulletin of Himalayan Research* 33/34 (Autumn 2008–Spring 2009), p. 23.

21  Purna Basnet, 'Maobadi Sena: Udbhav, Bikas ra Bistar (The Maoist Army: Beginning, Development and Expansion)', pp. 164–5 in Sudheer Sharma, ed., *Nepali Sena: Nagarik Niyantranka Chunauti (The Nepali Army: Challenges to Civilian Control)*, Kathmandu: Martin Chautari 2010 (2067 v.s.), p. 165.

22  For accounts of the 1990 movement see Martin Hoftun and William Raeper, *Spring Awakening: An Account of the 1990 Revolution in* Nepal, New Delhi: Penguin Books India, 1992, and Kiyoko Ogura, *Kathmandu Spring: The People's Movement of 1990*, Kathmandu: Himal Books, 2001.

23  Louise T. Brown, *The Challenge to Democracy in Nepal*, London: Routledge, 1996, p. 100.

24  Mahesh Maskey, 'Maobichar (Mao-thought)', pp. 239–80 in *Studies in Nepali History and Society* 7, no. 2 (December 2002), p. 274.

25  'Prachanda' (Pushpa Kamal Dahal), 'Purvi Yuropka Ghatanabare Ek Tippani' (A Comment on the Events in Eastern Europe), in *Prachandaka Chhaiyeka Rachanaharu: Khanda 1 (Prachanda's Selected Writings: Volume 1)*, Kathmandu: Janadisha Prakashan, 2007 (2063 v.s.), pp. 56–7.

26  The SLC is a standardized exam that students in Nepal are required to take at the end of their tenth-grade education. Held simultaneously nationwide, the SLC is something of a national event. The names of the top ten SLC candidates were until recently displayed prominently in the newspapers. Schools are still judged by the proportion of their pupils gaining high marks in the SLC.

27  For a short overview of Baburam Bhattarai's life see Chaulagain and Kandel, *Janayuddhaka Nayakharu*, pp. 125–33.

28 The analysis in this paragraph is based on conversations with a number of Maoist leaders, including Bhattarai himself.

29 Interview with senior Maoist leaders, August 2010. Also see CPN(M), 'Samyukta Rastriya Janaandolanka Das Sutriya Tatkalin Magharu (The Ten-Point Demands of the United National People's Movement)', in CPN(M), *Maobadi Mag ra Manyataharu* (*The Maoists' Demands and Positions*), Kathmandu: Pairavi Prakashan, Kathmandu, 2006 (2063 v.s.), pp. 1–2.

30 Rose, 'Communism under High Atmospheric Conditions', pp. 367–8.

31 Joshi and Rose, *Democratic Innovations in Nepal*, p. 175.

32 Ibid., p. 281.

33 The issue of the Constituent Assembly was raised once again within Nepal's Communist movement after King Mahendra took over power in 1960. At a meeting of the central committee held in Darbhanga, India, in March 1961, Mohan Bikram Singh demanded elections to a Constituent Assembly and the eventual establishment of a republic. See Rose, 'Communism under High Atmospheric Conditions', pp. 374–5.

34 For details, see Michael Hutt, 'Drafting the 1990 Constitution', pp. 29–36 in Michael Hutt, ed., *Nepal in the Nineties*, New Delhi: Oxford University Press, 1994.

35 Ibid., pp. 42–6.


## Chapter 2: Democracy and Its Discontents

1 Other parties that won seats included: Rastriya Prajatantra Party (Chand) – one seat; Rastriya Prajatantra Party (Thapa) – one seat; Nepal Sadbhavana Party – six seats; Nepal Worker's and Peasant's Party – two seats; Communist Party of Nepal (Democratic) – two seats. For more on the election see Martin Hoftun, William Raeper and John Whelpton, *People, Politics and Ideology: Democracy and Social Change in Nepal*, Kathmandu: Mandala Book Point, 1999, p 183.

2 For details on the liberalization measures of the 1990s, see Ram Sharan Mahat, *In Defence of Democracy: Dynamics and Faultlines of Nepal's Political Economy*, New Delhi: Adroit Publishers, 2005. The writer, a Nepali Congress leader, was finance minister for much of the 1990s and responsible for the adoption of many liberalization policies. As is evident from its title, the book is largely a defence of these policies and the period of the 1990s in general.

3 A critical view of the liberalization policies can be found in Jagannath Adhikari, *Changing Livelihoods: Essays on Nepal's Development since 1990*, Kathmandu: Martin Chautari, 2008. A wide-ranging and damning account

of the political and economic system of the 1990s can be found in Devendra Raj Panday, *Nepal's Failed Development: Reflections on the Mission and the Maladies*, Kathmandu: Nepal South Asia Centre, 1999.

4  Khagendra Sangraula, *Junkiriko Sangeet* (*The Music of Fireflies*), Kathmandu: Bhudipuran Prakhashan, 1990 (2056 v.s.).

5  Personal communication with Khagendra Sangraula, March 2011.

6  Ibid.

7  Baburam Bhattarai, *The Nature of Underdevelopment and Regional Structure of Nepal: A Marxist Analysis*, New Delhi: Adroit Publishers, 2003.

8  Baburam Bhattarai, 'The Political Economy of People's War', in Arjun Karki and David Seddon, eds, *The People's War in Nepal: Left Perspectives*, New Delhi: Adroit Publishers, 2003, pp. 117–64.

9  Ibid., p. 132.

10  Ibid., p. 137.

11  Ibid., p. 138.

12  In Bhattarai's expressive Marxist terms: 'Since the 1950s, many efforts have been made to introduce reforms in Nepali agriculture without destroying the basic class relations – specifically to develop the productive forces while preserving the existing production relations. After the Second World War and especially after the end of Rana rule, attempts were made to implement limited "land reforms" with a view to bringing about agrarian change without destroying the old feudal structure and to facilitate the penetration of imperialist financial capital … But just as the demon cannot act as the exorcist, it proved impossible for programmes designed and directed by imperialists and implemented by feudals and bureaucratic capitalists to transform a rural economy dominated by feudalism and imperialism.' Ibid., pp. 139–40.

13  *Sanatan dharma* is a commonly used synonym for Hinduism. It can be translated as 'eternal religion'.

14  Sangroula, *Junkiriko Sangeet*, p. 30.

15  Khagendra Sangraula, *Jana-Andolanka Chharraharu* (*Fragments of the People's Movement*), Kathmandu: Bhudipuran Prakashan, 2006 (2063 v.s.), p. 40.

16  Sangroula, *Junkiriko Sangeet*, p. 121.

17  Liz Alden Wily, with Devendra Chapagain and Shiva Sharma, *Land Reform in Nepal: Where Is It Coming From and Where Is It Going?* Kathmandu: Department for International Development (DFID), 2009, pp. 115–24.

18  Ibid., p. 123.

19  Ibid., p. 44.

20  Ibid., p. 46.

21  'Chaitanya' (Mohan Baidya's literarary alias), 'Junkiriko Sangeetma Lamkhutteko Swar ra Shabdaharu (The Voices and Words of Mosquitoes in

*The Music of Fireflies)',* in Chaitanya, *Kranti ra Saundarya (Revolution and Aesthetics),* Kathmandu: Pragatishil Adhyayan Kendra, 2007 (2064 v.s.), p. 213.

22 Dipak Gyawali and Ajaya Dixit, 'Mahakali Impasse: A Futile Paradigm's Bequested Travails', pp. 236–305 in Dhruba Kumar, ed., *Domestic Conflict and Crisis of Governance in Nepal,* Kathmandu: Centre for Nepal and Asian Studies, 2000, pp. 240–1.

23 Ibid., p. 244; Sanjay Upadhya, *The Raj Lives: India in Nepal,* New Delhi: Vitasta Publishing, 2008, p. 100.

24 See article 126 of the 1990 constitution.

25 Upadhya, *The Raj Lives,* pp. 101–3.

26 Gyawali and Dixit, 'Mahakali Impasse', pp. 246–8.

27 Hoftun, Raeper and Whelpton, *People, Politics and Ideology,* pp. 203–13.

28 Ibid., p. 214.

29 Gyawali and Dixit, 'Mahakali Impasse', pp. 249–50.

30 Officially titled 'Treaty Concerning the Integrated Development of the Mahakali River Including Sarada Barrage, Tanakpur Barrage and Pancheswar Project'.

31 Surendra K. C., *Nepalma Kamyunist Andolanko Itihas: Bhag 3 (2050–64) (History of the Communist Movement in Nepal: Volume 3),* Kathmandu: Bidyarthi Pustak Bhandar, 2008 (2065 v.s.), pp. 69–70.

32 Gyawali and Dixit, 'Mahakali Impasse', pp. 254–8.

33 K. C., *Nepalma Kamyunist Andolanko Itihas,* pp. 73–4.

34 Upadhya, *The Raj Lives,* p. 117.

35 'Jaba Rashtrabhanda Kursi Pyaro Banchha (When the Chair Becomes Dearer than the Nation)', *Mulyankan* (October–November 1996) (Kartik-Mangsir 2053 v.s.), p. 4.

36 Baburam Bhattarai, *Nepali Krantika Aadharharu (Foundations of the Nepali Revolution),* Kathmandu: Janadhwani Prakashan, 2006 (2063 v.s.), p. 101.

37 Baburam Bhattarai, 'The Phobia of Guerrilla War Is Hounding the Reactionaries', *The Independent,* Kathmandu, 5, no. 41 (13–19 December 1995). Republished in Deepak Thapa, ed., *Understanding the Maoist Movement in Nepal,* Kathmandu: Martin Chautari, 2003, pp. 45–6.

38 Gyawali and Dixit, 'Mahakali Impasse', p. 277.

39 INSEC Human Rights Yearbook 1996; Shyam Kumar Budha Magar, *Ti Aandhimaya Dinharu: Ek Janamukti Yoddhaka Samsmaranharu (Those Turbulent Days: The Memoirs of a People's Liberation Fighter),* Kathmandu: Bhimkumari Bantha, 2007 (2064 v.s.), pp. 19–20.

40 VDCs are administrative units adopted in the 1990s that include a cluster of villages. There are 3,913 VDCs in Nepal.

41 Magar, *Ti Aandhimaya Dinharu,* pp. 19–20.

42  Anne de Sales, 'The Kham Magar Country, Nepal: Between Ethnic Claims and Maoism', *European Bulletin of Himalayan Research* 19 (Autumn 2000); David Seddon and Prabin Manandhar, *In Hope and in Fear: Living through the People's War in Nepal*, New Delhi: Adroit Publishers, 2010.

43  *Tagadhari*: thread-wearing. Hindu men from the upper castes wear a thread around their torsos.

44  András Höfer, *The Caste Hierarchy and the State in Nepal: A Study of the Muluki Ain of 1854*, Kathmandu: Himal Books, 2004.

45  Anne de Sales, 'Biography of a Magar Communist', in David N. Gellner, ed., *Varieties of Activist Experience: Civil Society in South Asia*, New Delhi: Sage Publications, 2010, p. 29.

46  Kiyoko Ogura, 'Maoists, People, and the State as seen from Rolpa and Rukum', pp. 459–502 in H. Ishi, D. Gellner and K. Nawa, eds, *Political and Social Transformation in North India and Nepal: Social Dynamics in Northern South Asia*, New Delhi: Manohar Books, 2007, p. 490.

47  Magar, *Ti Aandhimaya Dinharu*, pp. 9–10.

48  Ibid., p. 15.

49  Pancha: a common term for those occupying positions of authority in the Panchayat regime.

50  Magar, *Ti Aandhimaya Dinharu*, p. 15.

51  De Sales, 'Biography of a Magar Communist', p. 36.

52  Ogura, 'Maoists, People, and the State', p. 494.

53  INSEC Human Rights Yearbooks 1992, 1993, 1994.

54  Magar, *Ti Aandhimaya Dinharu*, p. 15.

55  CPN(M), 'Political Line of CPN (Unity Centre)', pp. 1–6 in *Some Important Documents of Communist Party of Nepal (Maoist)*, Kathmandu: Janadisha Publications, 2004, p. 6.

56  'Prachanda' (Pushpa Kamal Dahal), 'Aajako Nepali Rajnitiko Mul Pravritti ra Dhruvikaranko Prashna (The Main Tendencies in Nepali Politics Today and the Question of Polarization)', in *Prachandaka Chhaniyeka Rachanaharu: Khanda 1*, p. 98.

57  CPN(M), 'Strategy and Tactics of Armed Struggle in Nepal (Document adopted by the Third Expanded Meeting of the Central Committee of the CPN [Maoist] in March 1995)', pp. 7–23 in *Some Important Documents of Communist Party of Nepal (Maoist)*, p. 11.

58  Ogura, 'Maoists, People, and the State', p. 492.

59  INSEC Human Rights Yearbook 1995, p. 378.

60  Magar, *Ti Aandhimaya Dinharu*, p. 31.

61  Cited in Seddon and Manandhar, *In Hope and in Fear*, p. 37.

62  INSEC Human Rights Yearbook 1995, p. 12.

63  See de Sales, 'The Kham Magar Country'.

64  Li Onesto, *Dispatches from the People's War in Nepal*, London: Pluto Press, London, 2005, p. 88.


## Chapter 3: Blinding the Elephant

1  Basnet, 'Maobadi Sena: Udbhav, Bikas ra Bistar', p. 165.

2  'Pasang' (Nanda Kishore Pun), *Itihaska Raktim Paila: Janayuddhaka Mahatwapurna Fauji Karbahiharu* (*The Red Strides of History: Historic Military Actions of the People's War*), Kathmandu: Samvad Prakashan Abhiyan, 2007 (2064 v.s.), p. 19.

3  Magar, *Ti Aandimaya Dinharu*, p. 36.

4  Ibid., p. 37.

5  Ganga Shrestha, *Gadhi Darbardekhi Singha Darbarsamma* (*From Gadhi Darbar to Singha Darbar*), Kathmandu: UCPN-Maoist, Kochila State Committee Publication Department, 2010 (2067 v.s.), p. 5.

6  'Prachanda' (Pushpa Kamal Dahal), 'Janayuddhako Pahilo Gauravshali Barsha (The Great First Year of the People's War)', pp. 314–68 in *Prachandaka Chhaiyeka Sainya Rachanaharu* (*Prachanda's Selected Military Writings*), Kathmandu: Janadisha Prakashan, 2007 (2063 v.s.), p. 328.

7  Ibid., p. 329.

8  Ibid.

9  A compilation of these plans can be found in Prachanda, *Prachandaka Chhaniyeka Rachanaharu: Khanda 2* (*Prachanda's Selected Writings, Volume 2*), Kathmandu: Janadisha Prakashan, 2007 (2064 v.s.), and CPN(M), *Nepal Kamyunist Party-Maobadi ka Aitihasik Dastavejharu* (Historic Documents of the Nepal Communist Party-Maoist), Kathmandu: Prasavi Prakashan, 2006 (2063 v.s.).

10  See 'Dipak' (Udaya Bahadur Chalaune), *Janayuddha ra Janamukti Sena: Saidhantik Aadhar ra Karyaniti* (*The People's War and the People's Liberation Army: Theoretical Basis and Tactics*), Kathmandu: The People's Liberation Army, Nepal, Sixth Division, 2009 (2066 v.s.).

11  Prachanda, 'Janayuddhako Aitihasik Pahalsambandhi Simhavalocan tatha Partiko Aagami Rananiti (Review of the Historic Initiation of the People's War and the Party's Forthcoming Strategy)', in *Prachandaka Chhaniyeka Rachanaharu: Khanda 2*, p. 71.

12  Dipak, *Janayuddha ra Janamukti Sena*, p. 47.

13  Onesto, *Dispatches from the People's War in Nepal*, p. 38.

14  Dipak, *Janayuddha ra Janamukti Sena*, p. 47.

15  Amnesty International, 'Nepal: Human Rights at a Turning Point?' 1999, p. 5.

16  Amnesty International, 'Human Rights Violations in the Context of a Maoist "People's War"', 1997, p. 7.

17  INSEC Human Rights Yearbook 1996, p. 120.

18  Amnesty International, 'Human Rights Violations', p. 7.

19  Deepak Thapa, Kiyoko Ogura and Judith Pettigrew, 'The Social Fabric of the Jelbang Killings, Nepal', *Dialectical Anthropology* 33 (2009), p. 475.

20  Amnesty International, 'Nepal: A Spiraling Human Rights Crisis', 2002, p. 29.

21  Prachanda, 'Janayuddhako Pahilo Gauravshali Barsha (The First Great Year of the People's War)', pp. 314–68 in *Prachandaka Chhaiyeka Sainya Rachanaharu*, p. 332.

22  Seddon and Manandhar, *In Hope and in Fear*, p. 51.

23  'Ajayashakti' (Surul Pun Magar), *Aandhisanga Khelda* (*Playing with the Storm*), Kathmandu: People's Liberation Army, Fifth Division, 2009 (2066 v.s.), p. 13.

24  Ogura, 'Maoists, People, and the State', page 439.

25  INSEC Human Rights Yearbook 1996, p. 100.

26  Dipak, *Janayuddha ra Janamukti Sena*, p. 170.

27  Prachanda, 'Janayuddhako Aitihasik Pahal Sambandhi Simhavalocan ra Aagami Rananitiko Purak Prastav', in *Prachandaka Chhaniyeka Rachanaharu: Khanda 2*, p. 91.

28  Prachanda, 'Aadharilaka Nirmanko Charanma Praveshko Dosro Yojanako Samagra Dastavej (The Complete Document of the Second Plan After Entering the Phase of the Formation of Base Areas)', in *Prachandaka Chhaniyeka Rachanaharu: Khanda 2*, p. 201.

29  Kashish Das Shrestha, 'The Heartland – Journal from Rolpa', *Wave* magazine 80 (August 2002).

30  Amnesty International, 'Nepal: A Spiraling Human Rights Crisis', p. 39.

31  Prachanda, *Prachandaka Chhaniyeka Rachanaharu: Khanda 1*, pp. 30–1.

32  Ganga Bahadur Lama, *Dasbarse Janayuddha: Smritika Dobharu* (*The Ten-Year-Long People's War: The Marks of Memory*), Kathmandu: Jagaran Book House, 2009 (2065 v.s.), pp. 19–20.

33  CPN(M), 'Janayuddhako Aitihasik Pahal Sambandhi Simhavalocan ra Aagami Rananitiko Purak Prastav', p. 86.

34  Mary Des Chene, '"Black Laws" and the "Limited Rights" of the People in Post-Andolan Nepal: The Campaign against the Proposed Anti-Terrorist Act of 2054 v.s.', *Himalayan Research Bulletin* 18, no. 2 (1998), p. 41.

35  For the full text of the proposed Act, see ibid., pp. 58–62.

36  Ibid., p. 49.

37  Ibid., p. 66–7.

38  K. C., *Nepalma Kamyunist Andolanko Itihas*, pp. 79–80.

39  Lama, *Dasbarse Janayuddha*, p. 25.

40  Ibid., p. 23.

41  K. C., *Nepalma Kamyunist Andolanko Itihas*, pp. 75–88.

42  'Nau Bam ra Sarkarbichko Sahamati Kasto Lagyo? (What Did You Think of the Agreement Between the Nine-Left and the Government?)' *Mulyankan* (August–September 1998) (Bhadra 2055 v.s.), p. 5.

43  Prachanda, 'Aadharilaka Nirmanko Mahan Charanma Praveshko Pahilo Yojanako Samagra Dastavej (Complete Document of the First Plan After Entering the Great Phase of Establishing Base Areas)', in *Prachandaka Chhaniyeka Rachanaharu: Khanda 2*, p. 161.

44  This section is mostly based on the account in Pasang, *Itihaska Raktim Paila*, pp. 54–62. It has been supplemented with one other memoir and interviews conducted in Rolpa and Dang in September 2011.

45  Ibid., p. 55.

46  Interview with PLA brigade vice-commander, 29 September 2011.

47  Magar, *Ti Aandimaya Dinharu*, p. 55.

48  Amnesty International, 'Nepal: A Spiraling Human Rights Crisis', pp. 17–18.

49  Sudheer Sharma, 'Four Districts in Maoist Hands', *Nepali Times*, 26 July–1 August 2000.

50  Ibid.

51  Source: INSEC, in Bhaskar Gautam, Purna Basnet and Chiran Manandhar, eds., *Maobadi Bidroha: Sashastra Sangharshako Avadhi* (*The Maoist Rebellion: The Period of Armed Struggle*), Kathmandu: Martin Chautari, 2008 (2064 v.s.), p. 594.

52  For a complete list of the UML's demands, see K. C., *Nepalma Kamyunist Andolanko Itihas*, pp. 91–5.

53  INSEC Human Rights Yearbook 1999, p. 129.

54  *Nepali Times*, 'Who's in Charge?' 27 September–3 October 2000.

55  Ibid.

56  Pasang, *Itihaska Raktim Paila*, pp. 85–100.

57  *Nepali Times*, 'Who's in Charge?'

58  Vivek Shah, *Maile Dekheko Darbar: Sainik Sachibko Samsmaran* (*The Palace I Knew: Memories of a Military Secretary*), Kathmandu: Shangrila Books, 2010 (2067 v.s.), pp. 156–7.

59  *Nepali Times*, 'Joshi Hits Army', 4–10 October 2000.

60  Pasang, *Itihaska Raktim Paila*, p. 86.

61  Binod Bhattarai, 'Mao the Designer Revolution', *Nepali Times*, 30 August–5 September 2000.

62  Keshar Bahadur Bhandari, 'Saidhantik Prishthabhumima Nagarik–Sainya Sambandha (Civilian-Army Relations in Theoretical Context)', in Sharma, ed., *Nepali Sena*, pp. 92–3.

63  I am grateful to Sam Cowan for bringing this to my attention.

64  Prakash Nepali and Phanindra Subba, 'Civil-Military Relations and the Maoist Insurgency in Nepal', *Small Wars and Insurgencies* 16, 1 (March 2005).

65  Deepak Prakash Bhatta, 'Loktantrik Niyantranma Mukhya Chunauti (The Chief Challenges to Democratic Control)', in Sharma, ed., *Nepali Sena*, p. 72.

66  HMG–N (His Majesty's Government–Nepal), Nepal Adhirajyako Sambidhan 2047 v.s. (Constitution of the Kingdom of Nepal 1990), Art. 118.

67  Ibid., Art. 119.

68  Vivek Shah, 'Sarkar, Sena ra Tatkalin Rajtantra (The Government, The Army and the Then Monarchy)', in Sharma, ed., *Nepali Sena*, p. 137.

69  The law is titled 'Act on the Right, Duty, Function and Terms of the Service of Commander-in-Chief'.

70  Nepali and Subba, 'Civil-Military Relations and the Maoist Insurgency'.

71  See Shah, *Maile Dekheko Darbar*; Bhandari, 'Saidhantik Prishthabhumima Nagarik-Sainya Sambandha'.

72  Bhandari, 'Saidhantik Prishthabhumima Nagarik-Sainya Sambandha', p. 93.

73  Narahari Acharya, 'The Nepalese Army', in Bishnu Sapkota, ed., *The Nepali Security Sector: An Almanac*, Pecs: Geneva Centre for the Democratic Control of Armed Forces, Geneva and European Studies Centre, Faculty of Humanities, University of Pecs, Hungary, 2009, p. 124.

74  See Surendra Pandey, 'The Role of the National Security Council: An Analysis', in Sapkota, ed., *The Nepali Security Sector*, p. 82.

75  Bishweshwar Prasad Koirala, 'Sena Bhitrako Sena (The Army within the Army)', in Sharma, ed., *Nepali Sena*, p. 120.

76  Bishweshwar Prasad Koirala, *Jail Journal*, Kathmandu: Jagadamba Prakashan, 1997, p. 156.

77  Nepali and Subba, 'Civil-Military Relations and the Maoist Insurgency'.

78  Personal communication with Nepali Congress politician, July 2011.

79  Binod Bhattarai, 'Whose Army?' *Nepali Times*, 27 April–3 May 2001.

80  Shah, 'Sarkar, Sena ra Tatkalin Rajtantra', p. 133.

81  *Nepali Times*, 'What the Chief Sa'ab Said', 27 April–3 May 2001.

82  Shah, *Maile Dekheko Darbar*, pp. 197–8.

83  See Rita Manchanda, 'Fresh political challenge', *Frontline* 18, no. 16 (4–17 August 2001); Binod Bhattarai, 'Still Quiet on the Western Front', *Nepali Times*, 20–26 July 2001.

84  Bhattarai, 'Still Quiet on the Western Front'.

85  Shah, *Maile Dekheko Darbar*, p. 213.

86  Pasang, *Itihaska Raktim Paila*, pp. 117–18.

87  Chaulagain and Kandel, *Janayuddhaka Nayakharu*, p. 186.

88  Pasang, *Itihaska Raktim Paila*, p. 118.

89  Manchanda, 'Fresh political challenge'.

90  Ameet Dhakal, 'Trust yet to be nurtured', *Kathmandu Post*, 23 August 2006.

91 Prachanda, 'Janayuddhako Aitihasik Pahal Sambandhi Simhavalocan ra Aagami Rananitiko Purak Prastav', in *Prachandaka Chhaniyeka Rachanaharu: Khanda 2*, p. 91.

92 Utpal Parashar, 'Prachanda Blames India for Nepal's Palace Massacre', *Hindustan Times*, 10 January 2010.

93 Sudheer Sharma, *Prayogshala: Nepali Sankramanma Dilli, Darbar ra Maobadi* (*Laboratory: Delhi, the Palace and the Maoists in Nepal's Transition*), Kathmandu: Fineprint, 2013 (2070 v.s.), pp. 65–67.

## Chapter 4: The State at War

1 For details of the report and an account of public reactions to the palace massacre, see Manjushree Thapa, *Forget Kathmandu: An Elegy for Democracy*, New Delhi: Penguin Books India, 2005, Chapter 1.

2 The writer Khagendra Sangroula published a series of columns after the massacre questioning the official version of events. Written with his characteristic wit and irony, these columns became hugely popular. They are collected in Sangroula, Khagendra, *Itihasma Kalo Potiyeko Anuhar* (Black Stained Faced in History), Kathmandu: Antarkriya Prakashan, 2001 (2058 v.s.).

3 Binod Bhattarai, 'King G's 100 Days', *Nepali Times*, 31 August–6 September 2001.

4 Parts of the diary have also been quoted in Chapter 3.

5 Shah, *Maile Dekheko Darbar*, p. 145.

6 Ibid., p. 227.

7 Ibid., p. 217.

8 Ibid., p. 218.

9 Quoted in Deepak Thapa and Bandita Sijapati, *A Kingdom Under Siege: Nepal's Maoist Insurgency, 1996 to 2004*, Kathmandu: The Printhouse, 2004, p. 121.

10 Ibid., p. 122.

11 Kunda Dixit, 'Let's Get This Over With', *Nepali Times*, 30 November–6 December 2001.

12 Shah, *Maile Dekheko Darbar*, p. 277.

13 Ibid., pp. 306–7.

14 Article 127 of the 1990 Constitution reads: 'If any difficulty arises in connection with the implementation of this Constitution, His Majesty may issue necessary Orders to remove such difficulty and such Orders shall be laid before Parliament.'

15 The freedoms of expression and opinion, assembly and movement were enshrined in Article 12 (2) of the 1990 Constitution. The rights against

censorship and to information were granted in Articles 13 and 16, respectively; the rights to property and privacy in Articles 17 and 22. All of these were suspended by the emergency declaration, as were the rights against preventive custody (Article 15) and to constitutional remedy (Article 23).

16  Dhruba Kumar, 'Impact of Conflict on Security and the Future: The Case of Nepal', *Journal of Security Sector Management* (March 2005), p. 16.

17  *Nepali Times*, 'Amnesty International's Concerns', 7–13 December 2001.

18  Dhruba Kumar and Hari Sharma, *Security Sector Reform in Nepal: Challenges and Opportunities*, Kathmandu: Friends for Peace, 2005, pp. 92–3.

19  Hari Roka, 'Militarization and Democratic Rule in Nepal', *Himal Southasian* (November 2003).

20  Prajwalla S. J. B. Rana, 'Who Brought the Nation to Its Present Condition?' *Nepali Times*, 29 March–4 April 2002.

21  Binod Bhattarai, 'Emergency Exit', *Nepali Times*, 21–27 December 2001.

22  Rana, 'Who Brought the Nation to Its Present Condition?'

23  International Crisis Group, 'Nepal Backgrounder: Ceasefire – Soft Landing or Strategic Pause?' 10 April 2003, p. 22.

24  Kumar, 'Impact of Conflict on Security and the Future'.

25  Ibid., p. 12.

26  Roka, 'Militarization and Democratic Rule in Nepal'.

27  Kumar, 'Impact of Conflict on Security and the Future', p. 12.

28  Ajay P. Nath, 'Democracy: Is It Just for Voting Right?' *Rising Nepal*, 5 September 2002.

29  Quoted in Kumar and Sharma, *Security Sector Reform in Nepal*, p. 46.

30  CPN(M), *Some Important Documents of Communist Party of Nepal (Maoist)*, p. 63.

31  The political document of the Second National Conference states: 'The party needs to move forward in a planned manner in order to organize a national-level conference of all political parties and people's organizations, hold elections for an interim government through the conference and guarantee the drafting of a constitution by the people under the leadership of this elected interim government.' Ibid., p. 118.

32  Baburam Bhattarai, *Monarchy vs. Democracy: The Epic Fight in Nepal*, New Delhi: Samakaleen Teesari Duniya, 2005, p. 21.

33  Baburam Bhattarai, *Yuddha ra Barta (War and Negotiation)*, Kathmandu: Janadhwani Prakashan, 2006 (2063 v.s.), p. 13.

34  The preamble of the 1990 constitution states: '... keeping in view the desire of the people that the State authority and sovereign powers shall, after the commencement of this Constitution, be exercised in accordance with the provisions of this Constitution, I, KING BIRENDRA BIR BIKRAM SHAH DEVA, by virtue of the State authority as exercised by Us, do hereby

promulgate and enforce this CONSTITUTION OF THE KINGDOM OF NEPAL on the recommendation and advice, and with the consent of the Council of Ministers.'

35  Bhattarai, *Yuddha ra Barta*, pp. 12–18.

36  Ibid.

37  CPN(M), 'Bartama NeKaPa (Maobadi) ko Tarfabata Prastut Prastavko Sarsamchep (Summary of the Proposal Presented by the CPN [Maoist] in Negotiations)', in Surendra K. C., *Maobadi Janayuddha: Vibhinna Aayog ra Varta (The Maoist People's War: Various Commissions and Negotiations)*, Kathmandu: Makalu Prakashan Griha, 2007 (2064 v.s), p. 497.

38  Ibid., pp. 497–8.

39  For more detail on conflicts within the top Maoist leadership, see Chapter 7.

40  Interviews with senior Maoist leaders, April 2011 and January 2013.

41  CPN(M), *Some Important Documents of Communist Party of Nepal (Maoist)*, p. 71.

42  Ibid., p. 142.

43  International Crisis Group, 'Nepal Backgrounder', pp. 6–7.

44  See Bhattarai, *Yuddha ra Barta*, pp. 53–7.

45  *Nepali Times*, 'Empty Vessels', 28 February–6 March 2003.

46  Bhattarai, *Yuddha ra Barta*, p. 19.

47  Shah, *Maile Dekheko Darbar*, p. 431.

48  Ibid., p. 392.

49  US Embassy, Kathmandu, 'Nepal: Maoists on Media Overkill; Government Keeping Own Counsel', WikiLeaks, 10 April 2003.

50  International Crisis Group, 'Nepal: Back to the Gun', 22 October 2003, p. 2.

51  Bhattarai, *Yuddha ra Barta*, p. 68. Singha Darbar, an old palace in the heart of Kathmandu, is the official seat of government in Nepal and houses various ministries and government offices. Khula Manch is a public space where most political parties hold mass meetings.

52  Shah, *Maile Dekheko Darbar*, p. 418.

53  Ibid., p. 427.

54  International Crisis Group, 'Nepal: Obstacles to Peace', 17 June 2003, p. 7.

55  Shah, *Maile Dekheko Darbar*, pp. 439–41.

56  Ibid., p. 432.

57  International Crisis Group, 'Back to the Gun', p. 4.

58  HMG–N, 'Government's agenda of reforms presented at the third round of talks with the CPN (Maoist) in response to the Maoist proposal of April 27', reproduced in Thapa, *A Kingdom under Siege*, p. 231.

59  Ibid., p. 236.

60  US Embassy, Kathmandu, 'Nepal: Maoists see "Imperialist Design" in Negotiation Process', WikiLeaks, 21 August 2003.

61  International Crisis Group, 'Back to the Gun', p. 6.

62  CPN(M), *Some Important Documents of Communist Party of Nepal (Maoist)*, p. 137.

63  Ibid.

64  National Human Rights Commission, 'Doramba Incident, Ramechhap', Kathmandu, 2003; Manjushree Thapa, *The Lives We Have Lost: Essays and Opinions on Nepal*, New Delhi: Penguin Books India, 2011, pp. 51–60.

65  International Crisis Group, 'Nepal: Dealing with a Human Rights Crisis', March 2005, p. 12.

66  Anne de Sales, 'From Ancestral Conflicts to Local Empowerment: Two Narratives from a Nepalese Community,' *Dialectical Anthropology* 33 (2009), pp. 370–1.

67  Judith Pettigrew and Kamal Adhikari, 'Fear and everyday life in rural Nepal', ibid., p. 409.

68  Human Rights Watch, 'Between a Rock and a Hard Place: Civilians Struggle to Survive in Nepal's Civil War', October 2004, vol. 16, no. 12(C), p. 36.

69  Interview with Maoist politburo member, November 2009.

70  Interviews with Maoist and Nepali Congress activists, Libang, Rolpa, September 2011.

71  Interview with PLA division vice–commander, Ghorahi, Dang, September 2011.

72  Pettigrew and Adhikari, 'Fear and everyday life in rural Nepal', p. 409.

73  Cf. Sam Cowan, 'Nepal's Two Wars', *Himal Southasian* (March 2006).

74  United Nations Office of the High Commissioner for Human Rights, 'Conflict-Related Disappearances in Bardiya District', December 2008.

75  See Arjun Guneratne, *Many Tongues, One People: The Making of Tharu Identity in Nepal*, New York: Cornell University Press, 2002, pp. 91–8.

76  UNOHCHR, 'Conflict-Related Disappearances in Bardiya District', p. 22.

77  Ibid., pp. 47–8.

78  Ibid., p. 52.

79  Ibid., pp. 59–60.

80  Ibid., p. 57.

81  Ibid., p. 24.

82  Ibid., p. 25.

83  See Stathis N. Kalyvas, *The Logic of Violence in Civil Wars*, New York: Cambridge University Press, 2006.

84  Interviews with Tharu activists in Dang, September–October 2011.

85  Interviews with Tharu activists in Dang. Also see Govinda Bartaman, *Sorha Sanjhaharu: Yuddhaka Asarharubich Yatra (Sixteen Evenings: Travels through the Effects of War)*, Kathmandu: The Printhouse, 2005 (2061 v.s.), p. 118. In the book, the writer recounts a conversation in Kailali, another

district with a large Tharu presence. An NGO worker he meets tells him that many Tharus initially joined the Maoists after the Maoists seized land from landowners and redistributed it. Those who did not join were eventually forced to do so after the local government harrassed them for being Maoists.

86  Personal communication, Nepal Army general, October 2011.

87  Pettigrew and Adhikari, 'Fear and everyday life in rural Nepal', p. 410.

88  Interview with shopkeeper in Dolakha, December 2004.

89  Personal communication, retired Nepal Army officer, October 2011.

90  US Embassy, Kathmandu, 'Nepali Army's Evolving Approach to Human Rights', WikiLeaks, 27 September 2002.

91  Ibid.

92  US Embassy, Kathmandu, 'Nepal: Human Rights in the Context of the Insurgency', WikiLeaks, 19 March 2004.

93  It was only in 2005, during the final months of the war, that the army became more cautious about detaining people without legal recourse. This was in large part due to the presence of the UN Office for the High Commissioner for Human Rights (OHCHR) in the country. See Chapter 8.

94  UNOHCHR, 'Report of investigation into arbitrary detention, torture and disappearances at Maharajgunj RNA barracks, Kathmandu, in 2003–2004', May 2006, p. 5.

95  In his account of his detention in army barracks in Kathmandu, for example, the Maoist activist Krishna K. C. reveals that soldiers who tortured him were as keen for information regarding human rights activists and journalists as they were for information about Maoist leaders. Krishna K. C., *Manav Badhshalako Yatra* (*Journey to a Human Slaughterhouse*), Kathmandu: self-published, 2006 (2063 v.s.).

96  A retired Indian General provides a list of the weaknesses of the RNA's counterinsurgency effort, much of which corresponds with those identified in this section, in his monograph Mehta, Ashok, *The Royal Nepal Army: Meeting the Maoist Challenge*, New Delhi: Rupa and Co., 2005.


## Chapter 5: Among the Believers

1  Kishore Nepal, *Under the Shadow of Violence*, Kathmandu: Centre for Professional Journalism Studies, 2005, p. 96.

2  Ibid., 109.

3  Ibid., p. 36.

4  Sushil Sharma, *Napurine Ghauharu* (*Wounds that Cannot be Healed*), Surkhet: Manavadhikar Janautthan Kendra Nepal, 2008 (2065 v.s.), p. 45.

5  See Human Rights Watch, 'Children in the Ranks: The Maoists' Use of Child Soldiers in Nepal', vol. 19, no. 2(C), February 2007.

6  'Rabindra', Devi Prasad Dhakal, *Ujyalo: Gajuri Byarek Breksammako Atmabrittanta* (*Light: My Story up to the Gajuri Barrack Break*), Kathmandu: Jhilko Prakashan, 2011 (2068 v.s.).

7  During a visit to Jumla district during 2005, the journalist Sushil Sharma met a group of schoolchildren who had been attracted by Maoist propaganda and joined the party. Unable to bear the hardships, they had soon returned home. But the local Maoists threatened the school authorities with consequences if they allowed the children to re-enroll, and urged them to rejoin the party. Sharma, *Napurine Ghauharu*, pp. 56–63.

8  Mohit Shrestha, *Jyudo Sapana* (*Living Dreams*), Kathmandu: Akhil Nepal Janasanskritik Mahasangh, Kendriya Samiti, 2009 (2065 v.s.), p. 120.

9  Lekhnath Neupane, *Chitthima Janayuddha* (*The People's War in Letters*), Kathmandu: Vivek Sirjanshil Prakashan, 2008 (2065 v.s.), p. 55.

10  Li Xintian, *Chamkilo Rato Tara* (*Bright Red Star*) [1974], translated by Sitaram Tamang, Kathmandu: Pragati Pustak Sadan, 2003 (2060 v.s.). In her study on youth participation in the Maoist rebellion, Ina V. Zharkevich notes how the majority of her informants mentioned this novel as their favourite book. She further writes that newcomers to the Maoist military camps in Kathmandu were each given a copy of the novel, which, along with an English–Nepali dictionary and Sun Tzu's *The Art of War*, was considered essential reading for PLA fighters. Ina Zharkevich, 'A New Way of Being Young in Nepal: The Idea of Maoist Youth and Dreams of a New Man', *Studies in Nepali History of Society* 14, No.1 (2009), p. 86.

11  Li, *Chamkilo Rato Tara*, p. 59. The translation is from the Nepali.

12  Khil Bahadur Bhandari, *Kalamharu Jungle Pasepachhi* (*When the Pens Enter the Jungle*), Kathmandu: self-published, 2006 (2063 v.s.), p. 23.

13  'Anugra' (Manju Bam), *Sangharshako Goreto* (*The Path of Struggle*), Kathmandu: UCPN-Maoist Seti-Mahakali State Committee, 2010 (2067 v.s.).

14  Hisila Yami, *People's War and Women's Liberation in Nepal*, Kathmandu: Janadhwani Publications, Kathmandu, 2007, pp. 6 and 43.

15  Anugra, *Sangharshako Goreto*, p. 32.

16  Ibid., p. 50.

17  Ibid., p. 66.

18  Mao Zedong, 'Problems of Strategy in China's Revolutionary War', in *Selected Military Writings of Mao Tse-Tung*, Peking: Foreign Languages Press, 1967, p. 81.

19  Anugra, *Sangharshako Goreto*, p. 66.

20  Ibid., p. 67.

21  Ibid.

22 Based on conversations with Maoist activists. Also see Netra Panthi, *Janayuddhama Prem ra Yaun* (*Love and Sex in the People's War*), Kathmandu: self-published, 2009 (2066 v.s.).

23 Quoted in Panthi, *Janayuddhama Prem ra Yaun*, p. 129.

24 Quoted in ibid., p. 134

25 See CPN(M), 'Naya Paristhitika Naya Karyabharharubare (The New Tasks of the New Situation)', in *Nepal Kamyunist Parti (Maobadi) ka Aitihasik Dastavejharu*, pp. 147–9.

26 Neupane, *Chitthima Janayuddha*, p. 89.

27 Lekhnath Neupane, *Bidyarthi Andolanma Bais Barsha* (*Twenty-Two Years in the Student Movement*), Kathmandu: ANNFSU–R (All Nepal National Free Students' Union–Revolutionary) Central Committee, 2011 (2067 v.s.), pp. 61–2.

28 Panthi, *Janayuddhama Prem ra Yaun*, p. 117.

29 Anugra, *Sangharshako Goreto*, p. 81.

30 Satya Shrestha-Schipper, 'Women's Participation in the People's War in Jumla', pp. 105–22 in *European Bulletin of Himalayan Research* 34–5 (Autumn 2008–Spring 2009), pp. 118–19.

31 Magar, Shyam Kumar Budha, *Ti Aandimaya Dinharu*, pp. 95–6.

32 'Dipak' (Udaya Bahadur Chalaune), *Janayuddha ra Janamukti Sena*, p. 17.

33 Ibid., p. 21.

34 Ibid., p. 104.

35 In an interview from September 2003, Prachanda said: 'All the military strategies and tactics are based on the goal of preparing for going into strategic offensive from the present stage of strategic equilibrium. From the tactical point of view, at present the people's army is going ahead with primary and decentralized resistance so as to feel the pulse of the enemy, tire them out and to prepare ground for the centralized offensive.' Quoted in Kiyoko Ogura, 'Realities and Images of Nepal's Maoists after the Attack on Beni', *European Bulletin of Himalayan Research* 27 (August 2004), p. 74.

36 Ibid., pp. 73–74.

37 Dipak, *Janayuddha ra Janamukti Sena*, p. 104.

38 'Pasang' (Nanda Kishore Pun), *Itihaska Raktim Paila: Janayuddhaka Mahatwapurna Fauji Karbahiharu*, p. 202.

39 Ibid., p. 203.

40 Ogura, 'Realities and Images of Nepal's Maoists after the Attack on Beni', pp. 74–5.

41 Ibid., p. 76.

42 Ogura, 'Realities and Images of Nepal's Maoists after the Attack on Beni' (n/p, revised version, unpublished).

43  Mao, 'On Protracted War'.

44  Ibid.

45  Dhaneshwar Pokhrel, *Beni Morchako Smriti: Shabdachitra* (*Memories of the Beni Front*), Kathmandu: Akhil Nepal Lekhak Sangh, 2010 (2067 v.s.), p. 3.

46  Ogura, 'Realities and Images of Nepal's Maoists after the Attack on Beni', p. 123.

47  Pasang, *Itihaska Raktim Paila*, p. 203.

48  Ibid., pp. 198–9.

49  Magar, *Ti Aandimaya Dinharu*, p. 72.

50  Ibid.; Pokhrel, *Beni Morchako Smriti: Shabdachitra*, pp. 4–5.

51  Magar, *Ti Aandimaya Dinharu*, p. 71.

52  Ogura, 'Realities and Images of Nepal's Maoists after the Attack on Beni', pp. 78–80.

53  Pokhrel, *Beni Morchako Smriti*, p. 16.

54  Pasang, *Itihaska Raktim Paila*, p. 202.

55  Ibid., p. 212.

56  Ibid., pp. 203–4.

57  Magar, *Ti Aandimaya Dinharu*, p. 73.

58  Pokhrel, *Beni Morchako Smriti*, p. 17.

59  Ibid., pp. 34–9.

60  Ogura, 'Realities and Images of Nepal's Maoists after the Attack on Beni', pp. 89, 98.

61  Pasang, *Itihaska Raktim Paila*, p. 198.

62  John Bevan, UN Human Rights Advisor, Notes on field visit to Beni, Myagdi, unpublished, March 2004.

63  Ogura, 'Realities and Images of Nepal's Maoists after the Attack on Beni', p. 92.

64  Pokhrel, *Beni Morchako Smriti*, p. 39.

65  Ogura, 'Realities and Images of Nepal's Maoists after the Attack on Beni', pp. 90–1.

66  Bevan, Notes on field visit to Beni, Myagdi.

67  Pasang, *Itihaska Raktim Paila*, pp. 208–9.

68  Ibid., p. 209.

69  Ibid., pp. 205–6.

70  Ogura, 'Realities and Images of Nepal's Maoists after the Attack on Beni', p. 109.

71  Ibid.

72  Magar, *Ti Aandimaya Dinharu*, p. 74.

73  Mana Rishi Dhital, 'Tyo Rat Aafaile Dekheko Beni Akraman (The Beni Attack that I Myself Saw that Night)' in Bhaskar Gautam, Purna Basnet and Chiran Manandhar, eds, *Maobadi Bidroha: Sashastra Sangharshako Avadhi*

(*The Maoist Rebellion: The Period of Armed Struggle*), Kathmandu: Martin Chautari, 2008 (2064 v.s.), p. 367.

74  Ogura, 'Realities and Images of Nepal's Maoists after the Attack on Beni', p. 102.

75  Dhital, 'Tyo Rat Aafaile Dekheko Beni Akraman', pp. 368–9.

76  Pokhrel, *Beni Morchako Smriti*, p. 50.

77  Ibid.

78  Dhital, 'Tyo Rat Aafaile Dekheko Beni Akraman', pp. 368–70.

79  Ibid., p. 371.

80  Ibid., p. 372.

81  Pokhrel, *Beni Morchako Smriti*, pp. 89–90.

82  Ibid., p. 77.

83  Quoted in Ogura, 'Realities and Images of Nepal's Maoists after the Attack on Beni', p. 123.

84  Ibid.

85  Three children died some days later, when mines that the rebels had left behind exploded. Ibid.

86  Interviews with Beni residents, August 2012.

87  Bevan, Notes on field visit to Beni, Myagdi.

88  Ibid.

89  Ogura, 'Realities and Images of Nepal's Maoists after the Attack on Beni', p. 114–15.

90  Even after Beni, the Maoists launched a number of battles that were meant to serve as transition from mobile to positional warfare. See, for example, the account of the April 2005 battle of Khara in Sam Cowan, 'Inside the People's Liberation Army: A Military Perspective', *European Bulletin of Himalayan Research* 37 (Autumn–Winter 2010), pp. 93–4.

## Chapter 6: The Fish in the Sea

1  Bartaman, *Sorha Sanjhharu*.

2  CPN(M), 'Strategy and Tactics of Armed Struggle in Nepal (Document adopted by the Third Expanded Meeting of the Central Committee of the CPN (Maoist) in March 1995.)' in *Some Important Documents of Communist Party of Nepal (Maoist)*, p. 16.

3  See C. K. Lal, *To Be a Nepalese*, Kathmandu: Martin Chautari, 2012.

4  Mara Malagodi, *Constitutional Nationalism and Legal Exclusion in Nepal: Equality, Identity Politics and Democracy in Nepal*, New Delhi: Oxford University Press, 2013, pp. 130–1.

5  Mukta S. Tamang, 'Caste, Culture and Ethnicity in the Maoist Movement',

pp. 271–301 in *Studies in Nepali History and Society* 11, no. 2 (December 2006).

6  For Maoist discussions on ethnicity and caste, see Baburam Bhattarai, *Rajnaitik Arthashastrako Aankhijhyalbata* (*From the Perspective of Political Economy*), Kathmandu: Janadhwani Prakashan, 2006 (2063 v.s.); Bhattarai, *Nepali Krantika Aadharharu*.

7  CPN(M), 'Common Minimum Policy and Programme of United Revolutionary People's Council, Nepal (URPC)', in *Some Important Documents of Communist Party of Nepal (Maoist)*, p. 162.

8  Author interviews with Janajati and Madhesi politicians, November–December 2010.

9  See Pratyoush Onta, 'The Growth of the *Adivasi Janajati* Movement in Nepal After 1990: The Non-Political Institutional Agents', pp. 303–54 in *Studies in Nepali History and Society* 11, no. 2 (December 2006).

10  These included the Tharuwan Autonomous Region for Tharus, Magarant for Magars, Tamuwan for Tamus, Tamsaling for Tamangs, Newa for Newars and Kirat for Rais and Limbus.

11  CPN(M), 'Common Minimum Policy and Programme of United Revolutionary People's Council, Nepal (URPC)', p. 172.

12  Dev Gurung, 'Pradeshik Swayatta Janasattako Ghoshanapachi Utheka Prashnaharu (Questions that Have Arisen after the Declaration of Provincial Autonomous People's Governments)', in Gautam, Basnet and Manandhar, eds, *Maobadi Bidroha: Sashastra Sangharshako Avadhi*, p. 189.

13  For an analysis of the discrimination suffered by Madhesis, see International Crisis Group, 'Nepal's Troubled Tarai Region', Asia Report no. 136, July 2007, and Gaige, Frederick H., *Regionalism and National Unity in Nepal*, Kathmandu: Himal Books, 2009.

14  CPN(M), 'Common Minimum Policy and Programme of United Revolutionary People's Council, Nepal (URPC)', pp. 173–4.

15  Cf. Kiyoko Ogura, 'Maoist People's Governments, 2001–05: The Power in Wartime', pp. 175–231 in David Gellner and Krishna Hachhethu, eds, *Local Democracy in South Asia: Microprocesses of Democratization in Nepal and its Neighbours*, New Delhi: Sage Publications, New Delhi, 2008; Marie Lecomte-Tilouine, 'Political Change and Cultural Revolution in a Maoist Model Village, Mid-western Nepal', pp. 115–32 in Mahendra Lawoti and Anup K. Pahari, eds, *The Maoist Insurgency in Nepal: Revolution in the Twenty-First Century*, London: Routledge, 2010.

16  Bhattarai, *Nepali Krantika Aadharharu*, p. 218.

17  Purna Bahadur Roka Magar, *Krantikari Itihas Bokeko Thabang* (*The Revolutionary History of Thabang*), Kathmandu: self-published, 2011 (2068 v.s.), p. 1.

18  Khil Bahadur Bhandari, *Krantiko Killa Thabang* (*The Revolution's Fortress: Thabang*), Kathmandu: Bhijan Media, 2007 (2063 v.s.), p. 56.

19  Ibid., p. 52.

20  Ibid., pp. 56–8.

21  Uttam Kandel, *Jokhimka Paila* (*Strides of Risk*), Dhading: Shahid Smriti Sanchar Sahakari Sanstha, 2009 (2066 v.s), p. 61.

22  Bhandari, *Krantiko Killa Thabang*, p. 51.

23  Ibid., p. 12.

24  Magar, *Krantikari Itihas Bokeko Thabang*, pp. 8–9.

25  See Chapter 2.

26  Ogura, 'Maoists, People, and the State as Seen from Rolpa and Rukum', p. 480.

27  Kandel, *Jokhimka Paila*, p. 63.

28  Bartaman, *Sorha Sanjhharu*, p. 85.

29  Ogura, 'Maoists, People, and the State as Seen from Rolpa and Rukum', p. 478.

30  Though, of course, they sometimes expressed them to outsiders. Cf. Marie Lecomte-Tilouine, 'Political Change and Cultural Revolution in a Maoist Model Village, Mid-western Nepal'.

31  Kandel, *Jokhimka Paila*, p. 53.

32  Ibid., pp. 104–5.

33  Ibid., pp. 106–7.

34  Bhandari, *Krantiko Killa Thabang*, p. 18.

35  Ethnic activists also hail from other smaller groups such as the Yakkha, Sunuwar and Dhimal within the broader Kirati family.

36  Rajan Mukarung, *Hetchhakuppa*, Kathmandu: Phoenix Books, 2008 (2065 v.s.).

37  Ibid., p. xiii.

38  Ibid., p. 100.

39  Ibid., p. 16.

40  Quoted in Gopal Kirati, *Sarvahara Netritwako Saval: Kirati Drishtikon* (*The Question of Proletarian Leadership: The Kirati Perspective*), Kathmandu: Koshi Bicharpradhan Masik, 2008, p. 131.

41  Ibid., pp. 277–94.

42  Ibid., pp. 283–4.

43  Ibid., p. 284.

44  Ibid., p. 288.

45  Ibid., p. 117.

46  Interview with senior Maoist leader, January 2013.

47  For details see Dambar Krishna Shrestha, 'Ethnic Autonomy in the East', in *People in the 'People's War'*, Kathmandu: Himal Books, 2004, pp. 17–40.

48  Bhattarai, 'Khambu Sangharshako Rooprekhabare Kehi Tippani (Some

Comments on the Form of the Khambu Struggle)', pp. 202–6 in *Nepali Krantika Aadharharu*, p. 202.

49  Ibid., p. 205.

50  Kirati, *Sarvahara Netritvako Saval*, p. 128.

51  Ibid., p. 170.

52  Mukarung, *Hetchhakuppa*, p. 142.

53  Ibid., p. 106.

54  Ibid., p. 136

55  Bhattarai, *Nepali Krantika Aadharharu*, p. 169.

56  De Sales, 'From Ancestral Conflicts to Local Empowerment', p. 375.

57  Yami, *People's War and Women's Liberation in Nepal*, p. 146.

58  Pustak Ghimire, 'Maoism, Violence and Religious Upheaval in a Village in Eastern Nepal', pp. 123–41 in *European Bulletin of Himalayan Research* 33–34 (Autumn 2008–Spring 2009), p. 130.

59  Ibid., p. 133. The translation has been somewhat modified.

60  Yami, *People's War and Women's Liberation in Nepal*, p. 150.

61  Baburam Biswokarma, 'Dalits and the Conflict', pp. 1–10 in *People in the 'People's War'*, Kathmandu: Himal Books, 2004, p. 3.

62  Ibid. p. 4.

63  Nepal, *Under the Shadow of Violence*, p. 102.

64  Ibid., p. 103. The quote has been slightly restructured.

65  Ibid., p. 106.

66  Marie Lecomte-Tilouine, 'What "Really" Happened in Dullu?' pp. 143–70 in *European Bulletin of Himalayan Research* 33–34, (Autumn 2008–Spring 2009), p. 145.

67  Ibid.

68  Kishore Nepal, 'Janabidrohako Jwalama Dailekhka Maobadi Ghatana, Karan ra Parinam (Dailekh's Maoist Incident in the Fire of People's Revolt, Causes and Consequences)', pp. 491–9, in Gautam, Basnet and Manandhar, eds, *Maobadi Bidroha: Sashastra Sangharshako Avadhi*, p. 492.

69  The following account is mostly based on Saubhagya Shah, 'Revolution and Reaction in the Himalayas: Cultural Resistance and the Maoist "New Regime" in Western Nepal', *American Ethnologist* 35, no. 3 (2008), pp. 481–99.

70  Ibid., p. 484.

71  Ibid.

72  Ibid., p. 485.

73  Quoted in Lecomte-Tilouine, 'What "Really" Happened in Dullu?' p. 150.

74  Ibid.

75  The following account is drawn from Lama, *Dasbarse Janayuddha*, pp. 57–75.

76  Ibid., p. 58.

77 Pettigrew, Judith, *Maoists at the Hearth: Everyday Life in Nepal's Civil War*, Philadelphia: University of Pennsylvania Press, 2013.

78 Ibid, p. 135–6.

79 Lama, *Dasbarse Janayuddha*, p. 60.

80 Pettigrew, *Maoists at the Hearth*, p. 111.

81 Ibid., pp. 118–9.

82 Lama, *Dasbarse Janayuddha*, p. 72.

83 Ibid., p. 75.

## Chapter 7: Blunders and Realignments

1 Interviews with Maoist activists in Kathmandu and Rolpa, April and September 2011.

2 CPN(M), 'The Great Leap Forward: An Inevitable Need of History (Political document adopted by the Second National Conference)', in *Some Important Documents of Communist Party of Nepal (Maoist)*, pp. 46–119.

3 Interviews with Maoist leaders, November–December 2011.

4 Interviews, November–December 2011.

5 Cf. Rajendra Maharjan, *Janayuddhaka Nayak* (*The Leader of the People's War*), Kathmandu: Mulyankan Prakashan, 2007 (2063 v.s.), p. 60.

6 Interviews.

7 Maharjan, *Janayuddhaka Nayak*, p. 60.

8 Ibid., p. 144.

9 See John Narayan Parajuli, 'US embassy saw Bhattarai as party's "most authoritative wordsmith" in 2003', *Kathmandu Post*, 30 August 2011.

10 Interviews with Maoist leaders.

11 Ibid.

12 Cf. Maharjan, *Janayuddhaka Nayak*, p. 61.

13 A number of articles on these themes are collected in Bhattarai, *Monarchy vs. Democracy: The Epic Fight in Nepal*.

14 Cf. CPN(M), 'The Great Leap Forward: An Inevitable Need of History', p. 55.

15 Cf. Baburam Bhattarai, 'Naya Dhangako Party Nirmanko Prashna (The Question of Establishing a New Kind of Party)', in *Nepali Krantika Aadharharu*, pp. 168–86.

16 CPN(M), 'Present Situation and Our Historical Task', in *Some Important Documents of Communist Party of Nepal (Maoist)*, pp. 46–119.

17 Cf. Bhattarai, 'Naya Dhangako Party Nirmanko Prashna'.

18 Maharjan, *Janayuddhaka Nayak*, p. 44.

19 See, for example, 'Kiran' (Mohan Baidya), 'Prachandapathko Darshanik Manyata (The Philosophical Position of Prachandapath)', pp. 207–30 in

Kiran, *Sangharshako Darshan* (*The Philosophy of Struggle*), Kathmandu: Janadisha Prakashan, 2002 (2060 v.s.).

20  Maharjan, *Janayuddhaka Nayak*, p. 61.

21  Shubhashankar Kandel, *Maobadi Bidroha: Bibad ra Rupantaran* (*The Maoist Rebellion: Debate and Transformation*), Kathmandu: Pairavi Prakashan, 2010 (2067 v.s.), p. 90.

22  Ibid., p. 94.

23  See Chapter 1.

24  As an admirer of Pushpa Lal, Bhattarai sought to rehabilitate his reputation within the party. The rehabilitation was formalized during the Second National Conference. Kiran and others were not comfortable with this move.

25  Interview with senior Maoist leaders, May 2011.

26  Sukh Deo Muni, 'Bringing the Maoists Down from the Hills: India's Role', pp. 313–31 in Sebastian von Einsiedel, David M. Malone and Suman Pradhan, eds, *Nepal in Transition: From People's War to Fragile Peace*, New York: Cambridge University Press, 2012, pp. 320–1.

27  For a well-articulated right-wing nationalist argument that India was seeking to expand influence over Nepal through the Maoists, see Saubhagya Shah, 'A Himalayan Red Herring? Maoist Revolution in the Shadow of the Legacy Raj', pp. 192–224 in Michael Hutt, ed., *Himalayan People's War: Nepal's Maoist Rebellion,* London: Hurst and Co., 2004.

28  Interviews with Maoist leaders.

29  Baburam Bhattarai, 'NeKaPa (Maobadi) Bhitra Antarsangharsha: Prishthabhumi ra Bartaman Sthiti (Inner Party Struggle within the CPN [Maoist]: Background and Current Situation)', pp. 13–34 in *Maobadibhitra Baicharik-Rajnitik Sangharsha: Kam. Da. Baburam Bhattarailagayat Kamredharudwara Prastut Farak Mat ra Dastavejharu* (*Ideological-Political Struggle among the Maoists: Notes of Dissent and Documents Presented by Comrade Dr Baburam Bhattarai and Others*), Kathmandu: Jhilko Publications, 2010 (2068 v.s.), p. 22.

30  Ibid.

31  Ibid., p. 23.

32  Anil Sharma, *Samjhanama Bharatiya Jail* (*An Indian Prison in Memory*), Kathmandu: Bhijan Publications, 2008 (2065 v.s.), p. 15.

33  Bhattarai, 'NeKaPa (Maobadi) Bhitra Antarsangharsha: Prishthabhumi ra Bartaman Sthiti', p. 25.

34  Ibid.

35  Cf. Amnesty International, 'Fear for Safety/Possible "Disappearance"', 23 February 2005.

36  Sharma, *Samjhanama Bharatiya Jail*, p. 31.

37  Sharma, *Prayogshala*, pp. 145–156.

38  Sharma, *Samjhanama Bharatiya Jail*, p. 39.

39  Bhattarai, 'NeKaPa (Maobadi) Bhitra Antarsangharsha: Prishthabhumi ra Bartaman Sthiti', p. 27.

40  Interviews with Maoist central committee members.

41  See CPN(M), 'Krantikari Rupantaranko Prakriyalai Naya Uchaima Uthaudai Rananaitik Pratyakramanko Charanma Pravesh Garaun: Kendria Samitima Prastut Rajnaitik evam Sanghatanatmak Prastav (Let Us Enter the Phase of the Strategic Offensive While Raising the Process of Revolutionary Transformation to New Heights: Political and Organizational Proposal Presented to the Central Committee)', pp. 252–69 in *Nepal Kamyunist Parti (Maobadi) ka Aitihasik Dastavejharu*, p. 255.

42  Ibid., pp. 255–6.

43  Ibid.

44  Interviews.

45  Kandel, *Maobadi Bidroha, Bibad ra Rupantaran*, p. 106.

46  Ibid., p. 108.

47  CPN(M), 'Krantikari Rupantaranko Prakriyalai Naya Uchaima Uthaudai Rananaitik Pratyakramanko Charanma Pravesh Garaun', p. 265.

48  Maharjan, *Janayuddhaka Nayak*, pp. 116–17.

49  CPN(M), 'Krantikari Rupantaranko Prakriyalai Naya Uchaima Uthaudai Rananaitik Pratyakramanko Charanma Pravesh Garaun', p. 256.

50  Interviews with top Maoist leaders, April 2011 and January 2012.

51  Interviews.

52  Baburam Bhattarai, 'Basic Questions for Inner–Party Discussions', pp. 122–32 in R. K. Vishwakarma, ed., *People's Power in Nepal*, New Delhi: Manak Publications, 2006, p. 131.

53  Ibid.

54  Ibid., p. 129.

55  Ibid., pp. 127–8.

56  Ibid.

57  Ibid., p. 131.

58  Kandel, *Jokhimka Paila*, p. 97.

59  Rabindra Shrestha, 'Prachanda ra Darbarbichka Gopya Sambandhaharu (The Secret Relations between Prachanda and the Palace)', *Samaya* magazine, 19 January 2007 (Falgun 3, 2063 v.s.), pp. 36–7.

60  CPN(M), 'Rajnaitik Prativedan (Political Document)', pp. 279–89 in *Nepal Kamyunist Parti (Maobadi) ka Aitihasik Dastavejharu*, pp. 283–9.

61  Baburam Bhattarai, his wife Hisila Yami, Dina Nath Sharma and Top Bahadur Rayamajhi voted against Prachanda's proposal. Sheetal Kumar abstained.

62  Ramprasad Upadhyay, Anil Krishna Prasai, Sheetal Koirala and Ishwar

'Chandra' Singh, *Aitihasik Byaktitwa: Girijaprasad Koirala* (A Historical Personality: Girija Prasad Koirala), Kathmandu: Oxford International Publications, n.d., p. 118.

63  *Nepali Times*, 'Out of This Maze', 11–17 June 2004.

64  Ishwar Pokhrel, *Magh 19 (1 February)*, Kathmandu: Jagadamba Press, 2006 (2063 v.s.), p. 197.

65  Ibid., p. 178.

66  John Narayan Parajuli, 'Election Engineering', *Nation Weekly*, 6 February 2005.

67  A translation of the address is available at: nepalconflictreport.ohchr.org.

68  Interviews with Maoist leaders.

69  Subhas Devkota, *Shantibarta: Antarkatha (Peace Talks: The Inside Story)*, Kathmandu: Yugantar Prakashan, 2007 (2064 v.s), pp. 115–16.

70  Personal communication with Kiyoko Ogura.

71  Interviews with former PLA commanders, Rolpa, October 2011.

72  Interview with former Maoist central committee member, April 2012.

73  Cowan, 'Inside the People's Liberation Army', p. 94.

74  Sharma, *Prayogshala*, pg. 179.

75  Cowan, 'Inside the People's Liberation Army', p. 91.

76  Bhojraj Bhat, 'Jasle Badalyo Maobadilai (That Which Changed the Maoists)', *Nepal Magazine*, 13 February 2011 (Falgun 1, 2067 v.s).

77  Sam Cowan, 'The Lost Battles of Khara and Pili', *Himal Southasian* (September 2008).

78  Ibid.

79  International Crisis Group, 'Nepal: Beyond Royal Rule, Policy Briefing 41', 15 September 2005, p. 3.

80  Ibid.

81  Ibid.

82  Chudamani Basnet, *From Civil Society to Citizen Society*, Athens, GA: PhD dissertation, University of Georgia, 2010, p. 226.

83  *Times of India*, 'Emergency: Nepal's Internal Affair', 1 February 2005.

84  Muni, 'Bringing the Maoists Down from the Hills', p. 322.

85  International Crisis Group, 'Nepal: Responding to the Royal Coup, Policy Briefing', 24 February 2005, p. 6.

86  Basnet, *From Civil Society to Citizen Society*, p. 231–2.

87  Muni, 'Bringing the Maoists Down from the Hills', p. 324.

88  US Embassy, Kathmandu, 'Review of State of Relationship with Vice-Chairmen Giri and Bista', WikiLeaks, 26 October 2005.

89  Devkota, *Shantibarta: Antarkatha*, p. 81.

90  Muni, 'Bringing the Maoists Down from the Hills', p. 326.

91  Ibid., p. 327.

92  *12 Point Memorandum.*

93  Ibid.


## Chapter 8: Uprising

1  Thapa, Ogura and Pettigrew, 'The Social Fabric of the Jelbang Killings', p. 461.

2  Kshitiz Magar, *Gandak Abhiyan* (*The Gandak Campaign*), Kathmandu: Mangalsen Smriti Brigade, Fifth Division, The People's Liberation Army, Nepal, 2011 (2068 v.s.), p. 94.

3  Mana Rishi Dhital, *The Final Days of the People's War*, Kathmandu: Janadesh Weekly, 2010, p. 10.

4  Magar, *Gandak Abhiyan*, p. vi.

5  Devkota, *Shantibarta: Antarkatha*, p. 6.

6  Magar, *Gandak Abhiyan*, p. 17.

7  Ibid., p. 90.

8  Ibid., p. 35.

9  Ibid., p. 79.

10  Devkota, *Shantibarta: Antarkatha*, p. 13.

11  Gopal Sharma and Terry Friel, 'Anger rising after Nepal's "referendum" on king', Reuters, 9 February 2006.

12  Magar, *Gandak Abhiyan*, p. 5.

13  Ibid., p. 41.

14  Ibid., p. 42.

15  Ibid., p. 18.

16  Ibid., p. 33.

17  Ibid., p. 42.

18  Ibid.

19  Shrawan Mukarung, *Bise Nagarchiko Bayan* (*The Testimony of Bise Nagarchi*), Kathmandu: Shangrila Books, 2010 (2067 v.s.), pp. 3–5.

20  Personal communication with Devendra Raj Panday, May 2010.

21  Basnet, *From Civil Society to Citizen Society*, pp. 248–58.

22  Mukarung, *Bise Nagarchiko Bayan*, pp. 3–4.

23  Devendra Raj Panday, '2062: Samprabhu Janatako Barsha (2005/6: The Year of the Sovereign People)', pp. 19–24 in *Nagarik Andolan ra Ganatantrik Chetana* (*The Citizens' Movement and Republican Consciousness*), Kathmandu: Fineprint, 2007 (2064 v.s.), p. 20.

24  Ibid., p. 22.

25  Bhanubhakta Acharya (1814–68), a Brahmin poet from Tanahun district, was recognized as 'the first [national] poet' (*adi kavi*) by the Nepali state. For

an analysis of how the figure of Bhanubhakta was constructed as an emblem of Nepal's national culture see Pratyoush Onta, 'The Career of Bhanubhakta as a History of Nepali National Culture, 1940–1999', *Studies in Nepali History and Society* 4, no. 1 (1999).

26  Mukarung, *Bise Nagarchiko Bayan*, p. 5.

27  Devendra Raj Panday, 'Loktantrako Pakshyama Nagarik Andolan: Uddeshya ra Upalabdhi (The Citizens' Movement for Loktantra: Goals and Accomplishments)', pp. 33–41 in *Nagarik Andolan ra Ganatantrik Chetana*, p. 36.

28  Bandita Sijapati, 'People's Participation in Conflict Transformation: A Case Study of *Jana Andolan II* in Nepal', Occasional Paper, Kathmandu: Social Science Baha, 2009, p. 24.

29  Mukarung, *Bise Nagarchiko Bayan*, p. 4.

30  Panday, 'Loktantrako Pakshyama Nagarik Andolan', p. 39.

31  Panday, '2062: Samprabhu Janatako Barsha', p. 22.

32  Panday, 'Loktantrako Pakshyama Nagarik Andolan', p. 33.

33  Kanak Mani Dixit, *Dekheko Muluk (The Nation I Saw)*, Kathmandu: Jagadamba Prakashan, 2009 (2066 v.s.), p. 206.

34  Devendra Raj Panday, 'Yaskaran Nagarik Andolan (A Citizens' Movement for This Reason)', pp. 50–2 in *Nagarik Andolan ra Ganatantrik Chetana*, p. 51.

35  US Embassy, Nepal, 'Transcript of Don Camp's Press Meet, June 28, 2005', nepal.usembassy.gov.

36  James F. Moriarty, 'Speech to the Ganesh Man Singh Academy, Kathmandu, Nepal, February 15, 2006', 2001–2009.state.gov.

37  Ibid.

38  Ibid.

39  Yuvaraj Ghimire, 'Shunya Samaya (Zero Hour)', *Samaya* magazine, 5 January 2006 (Poush 21, 2062 v.s.).

40  Baburam Bhattarai, 'Fauji ra Gair-Fauji Sangharshako Samyojanko Prashna (The Question of Integrating Military and Non-Military Struggle)', pp. 11–4 in *Rashtriyata ra Ganatantra (Nationality and the Republic)*, Kathmandu: *Janadesh Weekly*, 2010 (2066 v.s.), p. 14.

41  Bhattarai, 'Bijaya ya Mrityu Rojne Bela Aaundainchha (The Time to Choose Victory or Death is Coming)', pp. 15–9 in *Rashtriyata ra Ganatantra*, p. 17.

42  Bhattarai, 'Fauji ra Gair-Fauji Sangharshako Samyojanko Prashna', p. 11.

43  SPA press release.

44  Amnesty International, 'Further Information on UA 267/03 (ASA 31/033/2003, 17 September 2003) and follow-up (ASA 31/064/2005, 3 August 2005) – Torture and ill-treatment / incommunicado detention / fear for safety / medical concern', 19 October 2005.

45  See Chapter 7.

46  Krishna K. C., *Krantikarika Aastha ra Gathaharu: Bhag 2 (The Beliefs and Travails of a Revolutionary)*, Kathmandu: Oxford International Publications, 2008 (2065 v.s.), p. 2.

47  Ibid., p. 224.

48  K. C., *Krantikarika Aastha ra Gathaharu*, p. 95.

49  Ibid., p. 4.

50  Ibid., p. 218.

51  Ibid., p. 13.

52  Ibid., Foreword.

53  Mandira Sharma and Frederick Rawski, 'A Comprehensive Peace? Lessons from Human Rights Monitoring in Nepal', pp. 175–200 in von Einsiedel, Malone and Pradhan, eds, *Nepal in Transition*, p. 177.

54  Devendra Raj Panday and other members of the Citizens' Movement for Democracy and Peace (CMDP) were also accused of accepting foreign aid. But they could refute this charge with a wholly good conscience. Knowing that all foreign aid came with strings attached, CMDP accepted only voluntary contributions from individuals to meet their costs. See Panday, 'Chunab Hunuparchha tara Sambidhansabhako (There Should Be Elections but for a Constituent Assembly)', pp. 116–22 in *Nagarik Andolan ra Ganatantrik Chetana*.

55  K. C., *Krantikarika Aastha ra Gathaharu*, p. 124.

56  Saubhagya Shah, *Civil Society in Uncivil Places: Soft State and Regime Change in Nepal*, Washington, DC: East–West Center, 2008, pp. 22–3.

57  For a detailed account of the general strike, see Nisthuri, Bishnu, *Unnais Din: Jana Andolan Diary (Nineteen Days: Diary of the People's Movement)*, Kathmandu: Modern Books, 2006 (2063 v.s.).

58  Nisthuri, *Unnais Din*, pp. 130, 143.

59  Sharma, *Prayogshala*, p. 231.

60  Nisthuri, *Unnais Din*, p. 101.

61  See *United We Blog!*, 'State Plays Dirty Game', blog.com.np.

62  Interviews with Maoist leaders and journalists, May 2012.

63  K. C., *Krantikarika Aastha ra Gathaharu*, p. 142.

64  Ibid., p. 156.

65  Magar, *Gandak Abhiyan*, p. 201.

66  K. C., *Krantikarika Aastha ra Gathaharu*, p. 146.

67  Nisthuri, *Unnais Din*, p. 181.

68  Ibid., p. 198.

69  Sharma, *Prayogshala*, pg. 235.

70  Dixit, *Dekheko Muluk*, p. 208.

71  Sudheer Sharma, 'Raja Kina Jhuke? (Why Did the King Step Down?)', pp. 31–8 in Bhaskar Gautam and Chiran Manandhar, eds, *Maobadi Sangharsha:*

*Shantipurna Rupantaran* (*The Maoist Struggle: Peaceful Transformation*), Kathmandu: Martin Chautari, 2008 (2065 v.s.), p. 35.

72  Baburam Bhattarai, 'Naya Itihas Nirmanko Ghadi (The Moment of Creating a New History)', pp. 45–7 in *Rashtriyata ra Ganatantra*, p. 46.

## Chapter 9: The Aftermath of People's War

1  Ujir Magar, 'Maobadi Dwara Brihat Sabha (The Maoists Hold a Mass Meeting)', *Kantipur* daily, 14 February 2007.

2  Text of the Comprehensive Peace Agreement. Available at satp.org.

3  CPN(M), 'Rajnaitik Evam Sangathanatmak Prastav (Chunbang Baithakko Dastavej) (Political and Organizational Proposal [Document of the Chunbang Meeting])', pp. 292–311 in *Nepal Kamyunist Parti (Maobadi) ka Aitihasik Dastavejharu*, p. 297.

4  The following paragraphs have been adapted from my article, Aditya Adhikari, 'Revolution by Other Means: The Transformation of Nepal's Maoists in a Time of Peace', pp. 265–83 in von Einsiedel, Malone and Pradhan, eds, *Nepal in Transition*.

5  World People's Resistance Movement (Britain), 'Interview with Comrade Sonam', 13 September 2009, wprmbritain.org.

6  See UNOHCHR, 'Allegations of Human Rights Abuses by the Young Communist League (YCL)', June 2007.

7  Carter Center, Nepal, 'First Interim Report', 26 August 2009.

8  Numerous election observation groups published reports on the Constituent Assembly elections. While all of them mentioned Maoist abuses, they deemed the results to be broadly credible. See, for example, the Carter Center, Nepal, 'Final Report on Observing Nepal's 2008 Constituent Assembly Election', 10 November 2008; National Election Observation Committee (NEOC), 'Constituent Assembly Election Observation Report – 2008'; European Union, 'Election Observation Mission, Nepal 2008'. For a detailed political analysis of the elections, see International Crisis Group, 'Nepal's Election: A Peaceful Revolution?' Asia Report no. 155, 3 July 2008.

9  Twenty-five out of a total of fifty-five parties that competed in the elections won seats to the Constituent Assembly. For a breakdown of results, see the Carter Center, Nepal, 'Final Report on Observing Nepal's 2008 Constituent Assembly Election', p. 45.

10  Ram Bahadur Rawal, 'Misan Maobadi (Mission Maoist)', *Nepal Weekly*, 10 May 2009.

11  In December 2008, the Maoist minister of law and justice, Dev Gurung, demanded the resignation of judicial council member Moti Kaji Sthapit on

grounds that he was a political appointee of the previous Nepali Congress government, and that it was the government's prerogative to replace him with someone more favourable to the Maoists. Sthapit pointed out that according to the interim constitution, the term of his appointment was for four years and the government could not seek his resignation. The media and other political parties severely criticized the Maoists for this move, interpreting it as an attempt by the executive to infringe on the independence of the judiciary.

12  Rawal, 'Misan Maobadi'.

13  Ibid.

14  Interview with Indian diplomat in Kathmandu, April 2009.

15  Quoted in International Crisis Group, 'Nepal's Future: In Whose Hands?' Asia Report no. 173, 13 August 2009, p. 15.

16  See Prashant Jha, 'A Nepali Perspective on International Involvement in Nepal', pp. 332–58 in von Einsiedel, Malone and Pradhan, eds, *Nepal in Transition*.

17  Interview with Indian diplomat, Kathmandu, May 2009.

18  This section is adapted from my article, Aditya Adhikari, 'The Ideological Evolution of the Nepali Maoists', *Studies in Nepali History and Society* 15, no. 2 (December 2010).

19  See Articles 72, 73, 74 and 82 of the Maoist draft constitution, UCPN(M) (Unified Communist Party of Nepal–Maoist), *Janatako Sanghiya Ganatantra Nepalko Samvidhan 2067* (*Constitution of the People's Federal Republic of Nepal 2067*), 2011.

20  See ibid., Articles 112, 113 and 82.

21  Nepal Government, 'The Interim Constitution of Nepal 2007 (2063 v.s.)', Preamble.

22  Interview with Laxman Tharu, September 2009.

23  Interviews with Dalit activists, Kathmandu and Pokhara, August–September 2010.

24  CPN(M), *Samvidhansabha Nirvachanka Lagi Nepal Communist Party (Maobadi)ko Pratibaddhata–Patra* (*Manifesto of the Nepal Communist Party [Maoist] for the Constituent Assembly Election*), Kathmandu: CPN(M) Kendriya Samiti Kendriya Prachar Prasar Samiti, 2008.

25  Eyewitness account.

26  Personal communication with newspaper editors, September 2010.

27  *República* daily, 'Controversial tape claims Mahara sought Rs 500 m from China to buy lawmakers', 4 September 2010.

28  *República* daily, 'Audiotape could be genuine: UCPN–Maoist', 13 September 2010.

29  Prachanda, 'Interview with *The Hindu*', *The Hindu*, 16 April 2012.

30  Sharma and Rawski, 'A Comprehensive Peace? Lessons from Human Rights Monitoring in Nepal', p. 188.

31  See Chapter 8.

32  See 'Kiran' (Mohan Baidya), 'Bartaman Sandarvama Party ra Krantiko Karyabhar (The Tasks of the Party and Revolution in the Present Context)', Dishabodh, November 2008 (Mangsir 1–15 2065 v.s); Kiran, 'Bartaman Paristhiti ra Hamro Karyabhar (The Present Situation and Our Tasks)', report presented to the Maoist central committee preceding the Palungtar plenary meeting of November 2010.

33  A video recording of Prachanda's speech was leaked in May 2009. It caused great controversy in Kathmandu, as he claimed that the Maoists still planned to stage a revolt to capture state power and that they had tricked the other parties by sending thousands of people into the cantonments who had not been members of the PLA.

34  Interviews with Maoist cadres, May 2010.

35  Interview, September 2011.

36  'Biplab' (Netra Bikram Chand), 'Pratikrantiko Chunauti (The Challenge of Counter-Revolution)', Young Communist, vol. 1, July–August 2010 (Saun 2067 v.s.), p. 53.

37  Interview.

38  See Chapter 2.

39  Kiran Pun, 'Why the cantonments imploded', República daily, 11 April 2012.

40  Press release by Mohan Baidya and Ram Bahadur Thapa, 4 April 2012. Quoted in International Crisis Group, 'Nepal's Constitution (II): The Expanding Political Matrix', Asia Report no. 234, 27 August 2012, p. 4.

41  See Chapter 2.

42  CPN(M) (Mohan Baidya faction), 'Navasamshodhanbad Biruddha Bichardharatmak Sangharsha Chalaundai Krantilai Naya Dhangale Agadi Badhaaun (Let Us Take the Revolution Ahead in a New Manner While Waging Ideological Struggle Against Neo-Revisionism)', June 2012.

43  Ibid.

44  See Chapter 7.

45  ICG, 'Nepal's Constitution (II)', pp. 3–4.

46  CPN(M) (Mohan Baidya faction), 'Navasamshodanbad Biruddha Bichardharatmak Sangharsha Chalaundai Krantilai Naya Dhangale Agadi Badhaaun'.

47  Prachanda, 'Partyko tatkalin karyayojana ra karyakrambare prastav (Proposal Regarding the Party's Tasks and Programmes)', 29 March 2012, quoted in ICG, 'Nepal's Constitution (II)', p. 4.

## Postscript

1 Quoted in Tara Rai, *Chhapamar Yuvatiko Dayari* (*Diary of a Guerrilla Girl*), Kathmandu: Ratna Pustak Bhandar, 2010 (2067 v.s.), p. 68.

2 In Nepal's election system, politicians are allowed to compete from two constituencies. Many senior politicians compete from two places as a way of hedging their bet. They have to give up one of the constituencies in the case that they win at both. Reelection is then held at the abandoned constituency.

3 Prachanda, 'Samsadbad–Murdabad! Naya Janabad–Jindabad!! (Down with Parliamentarism! Victory to New Democracy!!)', in *Prachandaka Chhaniyeka Rachanaharu: Khanda 1*, p. 164.

4 Ibid.

5 Prachanda's speeches on these themes are collected in Netra Panthi, *Maobadibhitra Antarsangharsha (Ekta Mahadhiveshandekhi Party Bibhajansammaka Dastavejsahit)* (*Struggle Among the Maoists [Including Documents from the Unity Convention up to the Party Split]*), Kathmandu: Vishwanepali Publications, 2011 (2069 v.s.), and Arun Baral, *Maobadibhitra Bhukampa* (*Earthquake Within the Maoists*), Kathmandu: Aastha Prakashan, 2005 (2062 v.s.).

6 For accounts of an indigenous community's response to the murder of an upper-caste landowner, see Sara Shneiderman, 'The Formation of Political Consciousness in Rural Nepal', *Dialectical Anthropology* 33 (2009), and Sara Shneiderman and Mark Turin, 'The Path to Jan Sarkar in Dolakha District: Towards an Ethnography of the Maoist Movement', in Michael Hutt, ed., *Himalayan 'People's War': Nepal's Maoist Rebellion*, London: Hurst and Co., 2004, pp. 79–111.

7 Lal, *To Be a Nepalese*, p. 33.

# Bibliography

Acharya, Narahari. 'The Nepalese Army', in Bishnu Sapkota, ed., *The Nepali Security Sector: An Almanac*, Pecs: Geneva Centre for the Democratic Control of Armed Forces, Geneva and European Studies Center, Faculty of Humanities, University of Pecs, Hungary, 2009.

Adhikari, Aditya. 'Revolution by Other Means: The Transformation of Nepal's Maoists in a Time of Peace', in Sebastian von Einsiedel, David M. Malone and Suman Pradhan, eds, *Nepal in Transition: From People's War to Fragile Peace*, New York: Cambridge University Press, 2012.

———. 'The Ideological Evolution of the Nepali Maoists', *Studies in Nepali History and Society* 15, no. 2 (December 2010).

Adhikari, Jagannath. *Changing Livelihoods: Essays on Nepal's Development since 1990*, Kathmandu: Martin Chautari, 2008.

'Ahuti', Bishwa Bhakta Dulal. *Tapaswika Geetharu (Songs of an Ascetic)*, Kathmandu: Pragati Pustak Sadan, 1992 (2049 v.s.).

'Ajayashakti', Surul Pun Magar. *Aandhisanga Khelda (Playing with the Storm)*, Kathmandu: People's Liberation Army, Fifth Division, 2009 (2066 v.s.).

Amnesty International. 'Fear for Safety / Possible 'Disappearance', 23 February 2005.

———. 'Further Information on UA 267/03 (ASA 31/033/2003, 17 September 2003) and follow-up (ASA 31/064/2005, 3 August 2005) – Torture and ill-treatment / incommunicado detention / fear for safety / medical concern', 19 October 2005.

———. 'Human Rights Violations in the Context of a Maoist 'People's War'', 1997.

———. 'Nepal: A Spiraling Human Rights Crisis', 2002.

———. 'Nepal: Human Rights at a Turning Point?' 1999.

'Anugra', Manju Bam. *Sangharshako Goreto (The Path of Struggle)*, Kathmandu: UCPN–Maoist Seti-Mahakali State Committee, 2010 (2067 v.s.).

Baral, Arun. *Maobadibhitra Bhukampa* (*Earthquake within the Maoists*), Kathmandu: Aastha Prakashan, 2005 (2062 v.s.).

Bartaman, Govinda. *Sorha Sanjhaharu: Yuddhaka Asarharubich Yatra* (*Sixteen Evenings: Travels through the Effects of War*), Kathmandu: The Printhouse, 2005 (2061 v.s.).

Basnet, Chudamani. *From Civil Society to Citizen Society*, Athens, GA: PhD dissertation, University of Georgia, 2010.

Basnet, Purna. 'Maobadi Sena: Udbhav, Bikas ra Bistar (The Maoist Army: Beginning, Development and Expansion)', in Sudheer Sharma, ed., *Nepali Sena: Nagarik Niyantranka Chunauti* (*The Nepali Army: Challenges to Civilian Control*), Kathmandu: Martin Chautari, 2010 (2067 v.s.).

Bhandari, Keshar Bahadur. 'Saidhantik Prishthabhumima Nagarik–Sainya Sambandha (Civilian-Army Relations in Theoretical Context)', in Sudheer Sharma, ed., *Nepali Sena: Nagarik Niyantranka Chunauti.*

Bhandari, Khil Bahadur. *Kalamharu Jungle Pasepachhi* (*After the Pens Entered the Jungle*), Kathmandu: self-published, 2006 (2063 v.s.).

———. *Krantiko Killa Thabang* (*The Revolution's Fortress: Thabang*), Kathmandu: Bhijan Media, 2007 (2063 v.s.).

Bhat, Bhojraj. 'Jasle Badalyo Maobadilai (That Which Changed the Maoists)', *Nepal Magazine*, 13 February 2011 (Falgun 1, 2067 v.s.).

Bhattarai, Baburam. 'Basic Questions for Inner-Party Discussions', in R. K. Vishwakarma, *People's Power in Nepal*, New Delhi: Manak Publications, 2006.

———. *Maobadibhitra Baicharik-Rajnitik Sangharsha: Kam. Da. Baburam Bhattarailagayat Kamredharudwara Prastut Farak Mat ra Dastavejharu* (*Ideological-Political Struggle among the Maoists: Notes of Dissent and Documents Presented by Comrade Dr Baburam Bhattarai and Others*), Kathmandu: Jhilko Publications, 2010 (2068 v.s.).

———. *Monarchy vs. Democracy: The Epic Fight in Nepal*, New Delhi: Samakaleen Teesari Duniya, 2005.

———. *Nepali Krantika Aadharharu* (*Foundations of the Nepali Revolution*), Kathmandu: Janadhwani Prakashan, 2006 (2063 v.s.).

———. *Rashtriyata ra Ganatantra* (*Nationality and the Republic*), Kathmandu: Janadesh Weekly, 2010 (2066 v.s.).

———. *Rajnaitik Arthashastrako Aankhijhyalbata* (*From the Perspective of Political Economy*), Kathmandu: Janadhwani Prakashan, 2006 (2063 v.s.).

———. *The Nature of Underdevelopment and Regional Structure of Nepal: A Marxist Analysis*. New Delhi: Adroit Publishers, 2003.

———. 'The Phobia of Guerrilla War Is Hounding the Reactionaries', *The Independent*, Kathmandu, vol. 5, no. 41, 13–19 December 1995. Republished in Deepak Thapa, ed., *Understanding the Maoist Movement in Nepal*, Kathmandu: Martin Chautari, 2003.

————. 'The Political Economy of People's War', in Arjun Karki and David Seddon, eds, *The People's War in Nepal: Left Perspectives*, New Delhi: Adroit Publishers, 2003.

————. *Yuddha ra Barta (War and Negotiation)*, Kathmandu: Janadhwani Prakashan, 2006 (2063 v.s.).

Bhattarai, Binod. 'King G's 100 Days', *Nepali Times*, 31 August–6 September 2001.

————. 'Mao the Designer Revolution', *Nepali Times*, 30 August–5 September 2000.

————. 'Still Quiet on the Western Front', *Nepali Times*, 20–26 July 2001.

————. 'Whose Army?' *Nepali Times*, 27 April–3 May 2001.

'Biplab', Netra Bikram Chand. 'Pratikrantiko Chunauti (The Challenge of Counter-Revolution)', *Young Communist* 1 (July–August 2010) (Saun 2067 v.s.).

Biswokarma, Baburam. 'Dalits and the Conflict', in *People in the 'People's War'*, Kathmandu: Himal Books, 2004.

Brown, T. Louise. *The Challenge to Democracy in Nepal*, London: Routledge, 1996.

Cailmail, Benoît. 'Mohan Bikram Singh and the History of Nepalese Maoism', *European Bulletin of Himalayan Research* 33–34 (Autumn 2008–Spring 2009).

Carter Center, Nepal. 'Final Report on Observing Nepal's 2008 Constituent Assembly Election', 10 November 2008.

————. 'First Interim Report', 26 August 2009.

'Chaitanya', Mohan Baidya. *Kranti ra Saundarya (Revolution and Aesthetics)*, Kathmandu: Pragatishil Adhyayan Kendra, 2007 (2064 v.s.).

Chaulagain, Yam and Rashmi Kandel. *Janayuddhaka Nayakharu* (The Leaders of the People's War), Kathmandu: Jayakali Prakashan, 2008 (2065 v.s.).

Cowan, Sam. 'Inside the People's Liberation Army: A Military Perspective', *European Bulletin of Himalayan Research* 37 (Autumn–Winter 2010).

————. 'Nepal's Two Wars', *Himal Southasian* (March 2006).

————. 'The Lost Battles of Khara and Pili', *Himal Southasian* (September 2008).

CPN(M) (Communist Party of Nepal–Maoist). 'Bartama NeKaPa (Maobadi)ko Tarfabata Prastut Prastavko Sarsamchep (Summary of the Proposal Presented by the CPN (Maoist) in Negotiations)', in Surendra K. C., ed., *Maobadi Janayuddha: Vibhinna Aayog ra Varta (The Maoist People's War: Various Commissions and Negotiations)*, Kathmandu: Makalu Prakashan Griha, 2007 (2064 v.s).

————. *Maobadi Mag ra Manyataharu (The Maoists' Demands and Positions)*, Kathmandu: Pairavi Prakashan, 2006 (2063 v.s.).

————. *Nepal Kamyunist Party–Maobadi ka Aitihasik Dastavejharu* (Historic Documents of the Nepal Communist Party–Maoist), Kathmandu: Prasavi Prakashan, 2006 (2063 v.s.).

————. *Samvidhansabha Nirvachanka Lagi Nepal Communist Party (Maobadi) ko Pratibaddhata-Patra* (*Manifesto of the Nepal Communist Party (Maoist) for the Constituent Assembly Election*), Kathmandu: CPN(M) Kendriya Samiti Kendriya Prachar Prasar Samiti, 2008.

————. *Some Important Documents of Communist Party of Nepal (Maoist).* Kathmandu: Janadisha Publications, 2004.

CPN(M) (Mohan Baidya faction). 'Navasamshodhanbad Biruddha Bichardharatmak Sangharsha Chalaundai Krantilai Naya Dhangale Agadi Badhaaun (Let Us Take the Revolution Ahead in a New Manner while Waging Ideological Struggle Against Neo-Revisionism)', June 2012.

de Sales, Anne. 'Biography of a Magar Communist', in David N. Gellner, ed., *Varieties of Activist Experience: Civil Society in South Asia*, New Delhi: Sage Publications, 2010.

————. 'From Ancestral Conflicts to Local Empowerment: Two Narratives from a Nepalese Community', *Dialectical Anthropology* 33 (2009).

————. 'The Kham Magar Country, Nepal: Between Ethnic Claims and Maoism', *European Bulletin of Himalayan Research* 19 (Autumn 2000).

Des Chene, Mary. '"Black Laws" and the "Limited Rights" of the People in Post-Andolan Nepal: The Campaign against the Proposed Anti-Terrorist Act of 2054 v.s', *Himalayan Research Bulletin* 18, no. 2 (1998).

Devkota, Subhas. *Shantibarta: Antarkatha* (*Peace Talks: The Inside Story*), Kathmandu: Yugantar Prakashan, 2007 (2064 v.s).

Dhakal, Ameet. 'Trust yet to be nurtured', *Kathmandu Post*, 23 August 2006.

Dhital, Mana Rishi. *The Final Days of the People's War*, Kathmandu: *Janadesh Weekly*, 2010.

————. 'Tyo Rat Aafaile Dekheko Beni Akraman (The Beni Attack That I Myself Saw That Night)', in Bhaskar Gautam, Purna Basnet and Chiran Manandhar, eds, *Maobadi Bidroha: Sashastra Sangharshako Avadhi* (*The Maoist Rebellion: The Period of Armed Struggle*), Kathmandu: Martin Chautari, 2008 (2064 v.s.).

'Dipak', Udaya Bahadur Chalaune. *Janayuddha ra Janamukti Sena: Saidhantik Aadhar ra Karyaniti* (*The People's War and the People's Liberation Army: Theoretical Basis and Tactics*), Kathmandu: People's Liberation Army, Nepal, Sixth Division, 2009 (2066 v.s.).

Dixit, Kanak Mani. *Dekheko Muluk* (*The Nation I Saw*), Kathmandu: Jagadamba Prakashan, 2009 (2066 v.s.).

Dixit, Kunda. 'Let's Get This Over With', *Nepali Times*, 30 November–6 December 2001.

European Union. 'Election Observation Mission, Nepal 2008'.

Gaige, Frederick H. *Regionalism and National Unity in Nepal*, Kathmandu: Himal Books, 2009.

Gellner, David N. and Mrigendra Bahadur Karki. 'The Sociology of Activism in

Nepal: Some Preliminary Considerations', pp. 361–93 in H. Ishi, D. Gellner and K. Nawa, eds, *Political and Social Transformation in North India and Nepal: Social Dynamics in Northern South Asia*, New Delhi: Manohar Books, 2007.

Ghimire, Pustak. 'Maoism, Violence and Religious Upheaval in a Village in Eastern Nepal', *European Bulletin of Himalayan Research* 33–4 (Autumn 2008–Spring 2009).

Ghimire, Yuvaraj. 'Shunya Samaya (Zero Hour)', *Samaya* magazine, 5 January 2006 (Poush 21, 2062 v.s.).

Guneratne, Arjun. *Many Tongues, One People: The Making of Tharu Identity in Nepal*, New York: Cornell University Press, 2002.

Gurung, Dev. 'Pradeshik Swayatta Janasattako Ghoshanapachi Utheka Prashnaharu (Questions That Have Arisen after the Declaration of Provincial Autonomous People's Governments)', in Bhaskar Gautam, Purna Basnet and Chiran Manandhar, eds, *Maobadi Bidroha: Sashastra Sangharshako Avadhi (The Maoist Rebellion: The Period of Armed Struggle)*, Kathmandu: Martin Chautari, 2008 (2064 v.s.).

Gyawali, Dipak and Ajaya Dixit. 'Mahakali Impasse: A Futile Paradigm's Bequested Travails', in Dhruba Kumar, ed., *Domestic Conflict and Crisis of Governance in Nepal*, Kathmandu: Centre for Nepal and Asian Studies, 2000.

Höfer, András. *The Caste Hierarchy and the State in Nepal: A Study of the Muluki Ain of 1854*, Kathmandu: Himal Books, 2004.

Hoftun, Martin and William Raeper. *Spring Awakening: An Account of the 1990 Revolution in Nepal*, New Delhi: Penguin Books India, 1992.

Hoftun, Martin, William Raeper and John Whelpton. *People, Politics and Ideology: Democracy and Social Change in Nepal*, Kathmandu: Mandala Book Point, 1999.

HMG-N (His Majesty's Government-Nepal). 'Nepal Adhirajyako Sambidhan 2047 v.s. (Constitution of the Kingdom of Nepal, 1990)'.

Human Rights Watch. 'Between a Rock and a Hard Place: Civilians Struggle to Survive in Nepal's Civil War', October 2004, vol. 16, no. 12(C).

———. 'Children in the Ranks: The Maoists' Use of Child Soldiers in Nepal', February 2007, vol. 19, no. 2(C).

Hutt, Michael. 'Drafting the 1990 Constitution', in Michael Hutt, ed., *Nepal in the Nineties*, New Delhi: Oxford University Press, 1994.

INSEC (Informal Sector Services). Human Rights Yearbooks 1994, 1995, 1996, 1997, 1998, 1999.

International Crisis Group. 'Nepal Backgrounder: Ceasefire – Soft Landing or Strategic Pause?' 10 April 2003.

———. 'Nepal: Obstacles to Peace', 17 June 2003.

———. 'Nepal: Back to the Gun', 22 October 2003.

———. 'Nepal: Responding to the Royal Coup, Policy Briefing', 24 February 2005.

————. 'Nepal: Dealing with a Human Rights Crisis', March 2005.

————. 'Nepal: Beyond Royal Rule, Policy Briefing 41', 15 September 2005.

————. 'Nepal's Troubled Tarai Region', July 2007.

————. 'Nepal's Election: A Peaceful Revolution?' Asia Report no. 155, 3 July 2008.

————. Nepal's Constitution (II): The Expanding Political Matrix', Asia Report no. 234, 27 August 2012.

Jha, Prashant. 'A Nepali Perspective on International Involvement in Nepal', in Sebastian von Einsiedel, David M. Malone and Suman Pradhan, eds, *Nepal in Transition: From People's War to Fragile Peace*, New York: Cambridge University Press, 2012.

Joshi, Bhuwan Lal and Leo Rose. *Democratic Innovations in Nepal: A Case Study of Political Acculturation*, Kathmandu: Mandala Publications, 2004 (University of California Press, 1966).

Kalyvas, Stathis N. *The Logic of Violence in Civil Wars*, New York: Cambridge University Press, 2006.

Kandel, Shubhashankar. *Maobadi Bidroha, Bibad ra Rupantaran (The Maoist Rebellion, Debates and Transformation)*, Kathmandu: Pairavi Prakashan, 2010 (2067 v.s.).

Kandel, Uttam. *Jokhimka Paila (Strides of Risk)*, Dhading: Shahid Smriti Sanchar Sahakari Sanstha, 2009 (2066 v.s).

K. C., Krishna. *Krantikarika Aastha ra Gathaharu: Bhag 2 (The Beliefs and Travails of a Revolutionary: Volume 2)*, Kathmandu: Oxford International Publications, 2008 (2065 v.s.).

————. *Manav Badhshalako Yatra (Journey to a Human Slaughterhouse)*, Kathmandu, self-published, 2006 (2063 v.s.).

K. C., Surendra. *Nepalma Kamyunist Andolanko Itihas: Bhag 3 (History of the Communist Movement in Nepal: Volume 3)*, Kathmandu: Bidyarthi Pustak Bhandar, 2008 (2065 v.s.).

'Kiran', Mohan Baidya. 'Bartaman Paristhiti ra Hamro Karyabhar (The Present Situation and Our Tasks)', report presented to the Maoist central committee preceding the Palungtar plenary meeting of November 2010.

————. 'Bartaman Sandarvama Party ra Krantiko Karyabhar (The Tasks of the Party and Revolution in the Present Context)', *Dishabodh*, November 2008 (Mangsir 1–15 2065 v.s).

————. 'Prachandapathko Darshanik Manyata (The Philosophical Position of Prachandapath)', in *Sangharshako Darshan (The Philosophy of Struggle)*, Kathmandu: Janadisha Prakashan, 2002 (2060 v.s.).

Kirati, Gopal. *Sarvahara Netritwako Saval: Kirati Drishtikon (The Question of Proletarian Leadership: The Kirati Perspective)*, Kathmandu: Koshi Bicharpradhan Masik, 2008.

Koirala, Bishweshwar Prasad. 'Sena Bhitrako Sena (*The Army within the Army*)', in Sudheer Sharma, ed., *Nepali Sena: Nagarik Niyantranka Chunauti* (*The Nepali Army: Challenges to Civilian Control*), Kathmandu: Martin Chautari, 2010 (2067 v.s.).

———. *Jail Journal*, Kathmandu: Jagadamba Prakashan, 1997.

Kumar, Dhruba. 'An Interlude in Nepal-China Relations during the Cultural Revolution', *Nepalese Journal of Political Science* 2, no. 2 (May 1980).

———. 'Impact of Conflict on Security and the Future: The Case of Nepal', *Journal of Security Sector Management* (March 2005).

———. and Hari Sharma. *Security Sector Reform in Nepal: Challenges and Opportunities*, Kathmandu: Friends for Peace, June 2005.

Lama, Ganga Bahadur. *Dasbarse Janayuddha: Smritika Dobharu* (*The Ten-Year-Long People's War: The Marks of Memory*), Kathmandu: Jagaran Book House, 2009 (2065 v.s.).

Lecomte-Tilouine, Marie. 'Political Change and Cultural Revolution in a Maoist Model Village, Mid-Western Nepal', in Mahendra Lawoti and Anup K. Pahari, eds, *The Maoist Insurgency in Nepal: Revolution in the Twenty-First Century*, London: Routledge, 2010.

———. 'What "Really" Happened in Dullu?' *European Bulletin of Himalayan Research* 33–4 (Autumn 2008–Spring 2009).

Li Xintian. *Chamkilo Rato Tara* (*Bright Red Star*), translated by Sitaram Tamang, Kathmandu: Pragati Pustak Sadan, 2003 (2060 v.s.).

Magar, Kshitiz. *Gandak Abhiyan* (*The Gandak Campaign*), Kathmandu: Mangalsen Smriti Brigade, Fifth Division, The People's Liberation Army Nepal, 2011 (2068 v.s.).

Magar, Purna Bahadur Roka. *Krantikari Itihas Bokeko Thabang* (*The Revolutionary History of Thabang*), Kathmandu: self-published, 2011 (2068 v.s.).

Magar, Shyam Kumar Budha. *Ti Aandhimaya Dinharu: Ek Janamukti Yoddhaka Samsmaranharu* (*Those Turbulent Days: The Memoirs of a People's Liberation Fighter*), Kathmandu: Bhimkumari Bantha, 2007 (2064 v.s.).

Magar, Ujir. 'Maobadi Dwara Brihat Sabha (The Maoists Hold a Mass Meeting)', *Kantipur* daily, 14 February 2007.

Maharjan, Rajendra. *Janayuddhaka Nayak* (*The Leader of the People's War*), Kathmandu: Mulyankan Prakashan, 2007 (2063 v.s.).

Mahat, Ram Sharan. *In Defence of Democracy: Dynamics and Faultlines of Nepal's Political Economy*, New Delhi: Adroit Publishers, 2005.

Malagodi, Mara. *Constitutional Nationalism and Legal Exclusion: Equality, Identity Politics and Democracy in Nepal*, New Delhi: Oxford University Press, 2013.

Manchanda, Rita. 'Fresh political challenge', *Frontline* 18, no. 16 (4–17 August 2001).

Mao Zedong. 'On Protracted War', marxists.org.

———. 'Problems of Strategy in China's Revolutionary War', in *Selected Military Writings of Mao Tse-Tung*, Peking: Foreign Languages Press, 1967.

Maskey, Mahesh. 'Maobichar (Mao-thought)', *Studies in Nepali History and Society* 7, no. 2 (December 2002).

Mehta, Ashok. *The Royal Nepal Army: Meeting the Maoist Challenge*, New Delhi: Rupa and Co., 2005.

Moriarty, James F. 'Speech to the Ganesh Man Singh Academy, Kathmandu, Nepal', 15 February 2006.

Mukarung, Rajan. *Hetchhakuppa*, Kathmandu: Phoenix Books, 2008 (2065 v.s.).

Mukarung, Shrawan. *Bise Nagarchiko Bayan* (*The Testimony of Bise Nagarchi*), Kathmandu: Shangrila Books, 2010 (2067 v.s.).

*Mulyankan*. 'Jaba Rashtrabhanda Kursi Pyaro Banchha (When the Chair Becomes Dearer than the Nation)', *Mulyankan* (October–November 1996) (Kartik-Mangsir 2053 v.s.).

———. 'Nau Bam ra Sarkarbichko Sahamati Kasto Lagyo? (What Did You Think of the Agreement Between the Nine-Left and the Government?)', *Mulyankan* (August–September 1999) (Bhadra 2055 v.s).

Muni, Sukh Deo. 'Bringing the Maoists Down from the Hills: India's Role', in Sebastian von Einsiedel, David M. Malone and Suman Pradhan, eds, *Nepal in Transition: From People's War to Fragile Peace*, New York: Cambridge University Press, 2012.

Nath, Ajay P. 'Democracy: Is It Just for Voting Right?' *Rising Nepal*, 5 September 2002.

National Election Observation Committee. 'Constituent Assembly Election Observation Report, 2008', Kathmandu: 2008.

National Human Rights Commission. 'Doramba Incident, Ramechhap', Kathmandu: 2003.

Nepal, Kishore. 'Janabidrohako Jwalama Dailekhka Maobadi Ghatana, Karan ra Parinam (Dailekh's Maoist Incident in the Fire of People's Revolt, Causes and Consequences)', in Bhaskar Gautam, Purna Basnet and Chiran Manandhar, eds, *Maobadi Bidroha: Sashastra Sangharshako Avadhi* (*The Maoist Rebellion: The Period of Armed Struggle*), Kathmandu: Martin Chautari, 2008 (2064 v.s.).

Nepal Government. 'The Interim Constitution of Nepal 2063 v.s.', 2007.

Nepal, Kishore. *Under the Shadow of Violence*, Kathmandu: Centre for Professional Journalism Studies, 2005.

Nepali, Prakash and Phanindra Subba. 'Civil–Military Relations and the Maoist Insurgency in Nepal', *Small Wars and Insurgencies* 16, no. 1 (March 2005).

*Nepali Times*. 'Who's in Charge?' 27 September–3 October 2000.

———. 'Joshi Hits Army', 4–10 October 2000.

———. 'What the Chief Sa'ab Said', 27 April–3 May 2001.

――――. 'Amnesty International's Concerns', 7–13 December 2001.

――――. 'Empty Vessels', 28 February–6 March 2003.

――――. 'Out of This Maze', 11–17 June 2004.

Neupane, Lekhnath. *Bidyarthi Andolanma Bais Barsha* (*Twenty-Two Years in the Student Movement*), Kathmandu: ANNFSU–Revolutionary, Central Committee, 2011 (2067 v.s.).

――――. *Chitthima Janayuddha* (*The People's War in Letters*), Kathmandu: Vivek Sirjanshil Prakashan, 2008 (2065 v.s.).

Nisthuri, Bishnu. *Unnais Din: Jana Andolan Diary* (*Nineteen Days: Diary of the People's Movement*), Kathmandu: Modern Books, 2006 (2063 v.s.).

Ogura, Kiyoko. *Kathmandu Spring: The People's Movement of 1990*, Kathmandu: Himal Books, 2001.

――――. 'Maoist People's Governments, 2001–05: The Power in Wartime', in David Gellner and Krishna Hachhethu, eds, *Local Democracy in South Asia: Microprocesses of Democratization in Nepal and Its Neighbours*, New Delhi: Sage Publications, 2008.

――――. 'Maoists, People, and the State as seen from Rolpa and Rukum', in H. Ishi, David Gellner, and K. Nawa, eds, *Political and Social Transformation in North India and Nepal: Social Dynamics in Northern South Asia*, New Delhi: Manohar Books, 2007.

――――. 'Realities and Images of Nepal's Maoists after the Attack on Beni', *European Bulletin of Himalayan Research* 27 (August 2004).

Onesto, Li. *Dispatches from the People's War in Nepal*, London: Pluto Press, 2005.

Onta, Pratyoush. 'The Career of Bhanubhakta as a History of Nepali National Culture, 1940–1999', *Studies in Nepali History and Society* 4, no. 1 (June 1999).

――――. 'The Growth of the *Adivasi Janajati* Movement in Nepal After 1990: The Non-Political Institutional Agents', *Studies in Nepali History and Society* 11, no. 2 (December 2006).

Panday, Devendra Raj. *Nagarik Andolan ra Ganatantrik Chetana* (*The Citizen's Movement and Republican Consciousness*), Kathmandu: Fineprint, 2007 (2064 v.s.).

――――. *Nepal's Failed Development: Reflections on the Mission and the Maladies*, Kathmandu: Nepal South Asia Centre, 1999.

Pandey, Surendra. 'The Role of the National Security Council: An Analysis', in Bishnu Sapkota, ed., *The Nepali Security Sector: An Almanac*, Pecs: Geneva Centre for the Democratic Control of Armed Forces, Geneva and European Studies Center, Faculty of Humanities, University of Pecs, Hungary, 2009.

Panthi, Netra. *Janayuddhama Prem ra Yaun* (*Love and Sex in the People's War*), Kathmandu: self-published, 2009 (2066 v.s.).

――――. *Maobadibhitra Antarsangharsha* (*Ekta Mahadhiveshandekhi Party*

*Bibhajansammaka Dastavejsahit)* (*Struggle among the Maoists [Including Documents from the Unity Convention up to the Party Split]*), Kathmandu: Vishwanepali Publications, 2011 (2069 v.s.).

Parajuli, John Narayan. 'Election Engineering', *Nation Weekly*, 6 February 2005.

————. 'US Embassy Saw Bhattarai as Party's "Most Authoritative Wordsmith" in 2003', *Kathmandu Post*, 30 August 2011.

Parashar, Utpal. 'Prachanda Blames India for Nepal's Palace Massacre', *Hindustan Times*, 10 January 2010.

'Pasang', Nanda Kishore Pun. *Itihaska Raktim Paila: Janayuddhaka Mahatwapurna Fauji Karbahiharu* (*The Red Strides of History: Historic Military Actions of the People's War*), Kathmandu: Samvad Prakashan Abhiyan, 2007 (2064 v.s).

Pettigrew, Judith and Kamal Adhikari. 'Fear and Everyday Life in Rural Nepal', *Dialectical Anthropology* 33 (2009).

Pettigrew, Judith. *Maoists at the Hearth: Everyday Life in Nepal's Civil War*, Philadelphia: University of Pennsylvania Press, 2013.

Pokhrel, Dhaneshwar. *Beni Morchako Smriti: Shabdachitra* (*Memories of the Beni Front*), Kathmandu: Akhil Nepal Lekhak Sangh, 2010 (2067 v.s.).

Pokhrel, Ishwar. *Magh Unnais* (*February 1*), Kathmandu: Jagadamba Press, 2006 (2063 v.s.).

'Prachanda', Pushpa Kamal Dahal. 'Interview with *The Hindu*', *The Hindu*, 16 April 2012.

————. *Prachandaka Chhaniyeka Rachanaharu: Khanda 1* (*Prachanda's Selected Writings: Volume 1*), Kathmandu: Janadisha Prakashan, 2007 (2063 v.s.).

————. *Prachandaka Chhaniyeka Rachanaharu: Khanda 2* (*Prachanda's Selected Writings: Volume 2*), Kathmandu: Janadisha Prakashan, 2008 (2064 v.s.).

————. *Prachandaka Chhaiyeka Sainya Rachanaharu* (*Prachanda's Selected Military Writings*), Kathmandu: Janadisha Prakashan, 2007 (2063 v.s.).

Pun, Kiran. 'Why the Cantonments Imploded', *República* daily, 11 April 2012.

'Rabindra', Devi Prasad Dhakal. *Ujyalo: Gajuri Byarek Breksammako Atmabrittanta* (*Light: My Story up to the Gajuri Barrack Break*), Kathmandu: Jhilko Prakashan, 2011 (2068 v.s.).

Rai, Tara. *Chhapamar Yuvatiko Dayari* (*Diary of a Guerrilla Girl*), Kathmandu: Ratna Pustak Bhandar, 2010 (2067 v.s.).

Rana, Prajwalla S. J. B. 'Who Brought the Nation to Its Present Condition?' *Nepali Times*, 29 March–4 April 2002.

Rawal, Ram Bahadur. 'Misan Maobadi (Mission Maoist)', *Nepal Weekly*, 10 May 2009.

*República* daily. 'Controversial Tape Claims Mahara Sought Rs 500 m from China to Buy Lawmakers', 4 September 2010.

————. 'Audiotape could be genuine: UCPN–Maoist', 13 September 2010.

Roka, Hari. 'Militarization and Democratic Rule in Nepal', *Himal Southasian* (November 2003).

Rose, Leo. 'Communism under High Atmospheric Conditions: The Party in Nepal', in Robert A. Scalapino, ed., *The Communist Revolution in Asia: Tactics, Goals and Achievements*, New Jersey: Prentice Hall, 1969.

Roy, Anirban. *Prachanda: The Unknown Revolutionary*, Kathmandu: Mandala Book Point, 2008.

Sangroula, Khagendra. *Itihasma Kalo Potiyeko Anuhar (Black Stained Faces in History)*, Kathmandu: Antarkriya Prakashan, 2001 (2058 v.s.).

———. *Jana-Andolanka Chharraharu (Fragments of the People's Movement)*, Kathmandu: Bhudipuran Prakashan, 2006 (2063 v.s.).

———. *Junkiriko Sangeet (The Music of Fireflies)*, Kathmandu: Bhudipuran Prakhashan, 1990 (2056 v.s.).

Shneiderman, Sara Beth. 'The Formation of Political Consciousness in Rural Nepal', *Dialectical Anthropology* 33 (2009).

———. and Mark Turin. 'The Path to Jan Sarkar in Dolakha District: Towards an Ethnography of the Maoist Movement', in Michael Hutt, ed., *Himalayan 'People's War': Nepal's Maoist Rebellion*, London: Hurst and Co., 2004.

Seddon, David and Prabin Manandhar. *In Hope and in Fear: Living through the People's War in Nepal*, New Delhi: Adroit Publishers, 2010.

Shah, Saubhagya. 'A Himalayan Red Herring? Maoist Revolution in the Shadow of the Legacy Raj', in Michael Hutt, ed., *Himalayan People's War: Nepal's Maoist Rebellion*, London: Hurst and Co., 2004.

———. *Civil Society in Uncivil Places: Soft State and Regime Change in Nepal*, Washington, DC: East-West Center, 2008.

———. 'Revolution and Reaction in the Himalayas: Cultural Resistance and the Maoist "New Regime" in Western Nepal', *American Ethnologist* 35, no. 3 (2008).

Shah, Vivek. *Maile Dekheko Darbar: Sainik Sachibko Samsmaran (The Palace I Knew: Memoirs of a Military Secretary)*, Kathmandu: Shangrila Books, 2010 (2067 v.s.).

———. 'Sarkar, Sena ra Tatkalin Rajtantra (The Government, the Army and the Then Monarchy)', in Sudheer Sharma, ed., *Nepali Sena: Nagarik Niyantranka Chunauti (The Nepali Army: Challenges to Civilian Control)*, Kathmandu: Martin Chautari, 2010 (2067 v.s.).

Sharma, Anil. *Samjhanama Bharatiya Jail (An Indian Prison in Memory)*, Kathmandu: Bhijan Publications, 2008 (2065 v.s.).

Sharma, Gopal and Terry Friel. 'Anger Rising after Nepal's "Referendum" on King', Reuters, 9 February 2006.

Sharma, Mandira and Frederick Rawski. 'A Comprehensive Peace? Lessons from Human Rights Monitoring in Nepal', in Sebastian von Einsiedel, David M.

Malone and Suman Pradhan, eds, *Nepal in Transition: From People's War to Fragile Peace*, New York: Cambridge University Press, 2012.

Sharma, Sudheer. 'Four Districts in Maoist Hands', *Nepali Times*, 26 July–1 August 2000.

———. *Prayogshala: Nepali Sankramanma Dilli, Darbar ra Maobadi* (*Laboratory: Delhi, the Palace and the Maoists in Nepal's Transition*), Kathmandu: Fineprint, 2013 (2070 v.s.).

———. 'Raja Kina Jhuke? (Why Did the King Step Down?)', in Bhaskar Gautam and Chiran Manandhar, eds, *Maobadi Sangharsha: Shantipurna Rupantaran* (*The Maoist Struggle: Peaceful Transformation*), Kathmandu: Martin Chautari, 2008 (2065 v.s.).

Sharma, Sushil. *Napurine Ghauharu* (*Wounds That Cannot Be Healed*), Surkhet: Manavadhikar Janautthan Kendra Nepal, 2008 (2065 v.s.).

Shrestha, Dambar Krishna. 'Ethnic Autonomy in the East', in *People in the 'People's War'*, Kathmandu: Himal Books, 2004.

Shrestha, Ganga. *Gadhi Darbardekhi Singha Darbarsamma* (*From Gadhi Darbar to Singha Darbar*), Kathmandu: UCPN–Maoist, Kochila State Committee Publication Department, 2010 (2067 v.s.).

Shrestha, Kashish Das. 'The Heartland – Journal from Rolpa', *Wave* magazine 80 (August 2002).

Shrestha, Mohit. *Jyudo Sapana* (*Living Dreams*), Kathmandu: Akhil Nepal Janasanskritik Mahasangh, Kendriya Samiti, 2009 (2065 v.s.).

Shrestha, Rabindra. 'Prachanda ra Darbarbichka Gopya Sambandhaharu (The Secret Relations between Prachanda and the Palace)', *Samaya* magazine, 19 January 2007 (Falgun 3, 2063 v.s.).

Shrestha-Schipper, Satya. 'Women's Participation in the People's War in Jumla', *European Bulletin of Himalayan Research* 34–5 (Autumn 2008–Spring 2009).

Sijapati, Bandita. 'People's Participation in Conflict Transformation: A Case Study of *Jana Andolan II* in Nepal', Occasional Paper, Social Science Baha, Kathmandu, 2009.

Tamang, Mukta S. 'Caste, Culture and Ethnicity in the Maoist Movement', *Studies in Nepali History and Society* 11, no. 2 (December 2006).

Thapa, Deepak and Bandita Sijapati. *A Kingdom under Siege: Nepal's Maoist Insurgency, 1996 to 2004*, Kathmandu: The Printhouse, 2004.

———. Kiyoko Ogura and Judith Pettigrew. 'The Social Fabric of the Jelbang Killings, Nepal', *Dialectical Anthropology* 33 (2009).

Thapa, Manjushree. *Forget Kathmandu: An Elegy for Democracy*, New Delhi: Penguin Books India, 2005.

———. *The Lives We Have Lost: Essays and Opinions on Nepal*, New Delhi: Penguin Books India, 2011.

*Times of India*, 'Emergency: Nepal's Internal Affair', 1 February 2005.

UCPN(M) (Unified Communist Party of Nepal–Maoist). 'Janatako Sanghiya Ganatantra Nepalko Samvidhan 2067 (Constitution of the People's Federal Republic of Nepal 2067)', 2011.

United Nations Office of the High Commissioner for Human Rights. 'Allegations of Human Rights Abuses by the Young Communist League (YCL)', June 2007.

————. 'Conflict-Related Disappearances in Bardiya District', December 2008.

————. 'Report of Investigation into Arbitrary Detention, Torture and Disappearances at Maharajgunj RNA barracks, Kathmandu, in 2003–04', May 2006.

US Embassy, Kathmandu. 'Nepal: Human Rights in the Context of the Insurgency', WikiLeaks, 19 March 2004.

————. 'Nepal: Maoists on Media Overkill; Government Keeping Own Counsel', WikiLeaks, 10 April 2003.

————. 'Nepal: Maoists See "Imperialist Design" in Negotiation Process', WikiLeaks, 21 August 2003.

————. 'Nepali Army's Evolving Approach to Human Rights', Wikileaks, 27 September 2002.

————. 'Review of State of Relationship with Vice-Chairmen Giri and Bista', WikiLeaks, 26 October 2005.

————. 'Transcript of Don Camp's Press Meet, June 28, 2005', nepal.usembassy. gov.

Upadhya, Sanjay. *The Raj Lives: India in Nepal*, New Delhi: Vitasta Publishing, 2008.

Upadhyay, Ramprasad, Anil Krishna Prasai, Sheetal Koirala and Ishwar 'Chandra' Singh. *Aitihasik Byaktitwa: Girijaprasad Koirala (A Historical Personality: Girija Prasad Koirala)*, Kathmandu: Oxford International Publications, n.d.

Yami, Hisila. *People's War and Women's Liberation in Nepal*, Kathmandu: Janadhwani Publications, 2007.

Wily, Liz Alden with Devendra Chapagain and Shiva Sharma. *Land Reform in Nepal: Where Is It Coming From and Where Is It Going?* Kathmandu: Department for International Development (DFID), 2009.

World People's Resistance Movement (Britain). 'Interview with Comrade Sonam', 13 September 2009, wprmbritain.org.

Zharkevich, Ina. 'A New Way of Being Young in Nepal: The Idea of Maoist Youth and Dreams of a New Man', *Studies in Nepali History of Society* 14, No.1 (2009).

# Index